Ghosts of Jim Crow

Ghosts of Jim Crow

Ending Racism in Post-Racial America

F. Michael Higginbotham

NEW YORK UNIVERSITY PRESS *New York and London*

NEW YORK UNIVERSITY PRESS
New York and London
www.nyupress.org

References to Internet websites (URLs) were accurate at the time of writing.
Neither the author nor New York University Press is responsible for URLs that
may have expired or changed since the manuscript was prepared.

Library of Congress Cataloging-in-Publication Data
Higginbotham, F. Michael.
Ghosts of Jim Crow : ending racism in post-racial America / F. Michael Higginbotham.
pages cm   Includes bibliographical references and index.
ISBN 978-0-8147-3747-7 (cl : alk. paper) — ISBN 978-0-8147-2446-0 (e-book) —
ISBN 978-0-8147-6090-1 (e-book)
1. African Americans—Civil rights—History. 2. African Americans—Segregation—
History. 3. United States—Race relations. 4. Racism—United States—History. I. Title.
E185.61.H58   2013
305.896'073—dc23   2012038383

New York University Press books are printed on acid-free paper, and their binding materials
are chosen for strength and durability. We strive to use environmentally responsible suppliers
and materials to the greatest extent possible in publishing our books.

Manufactured in the United States of America

10 9 8 7 6 5 4 3 2 1

To Mom and Dad, with gratitude for all the wonderful memories

Contents

Acknowledgments

IT IS OFTEN said, "A camel is a horse built by committee." This book is my camel, and there are many committee members to whom I am indebted.

The idea for *Ghosts of Jim Crow* began with the many celebrations of the fiftieth anniversary of *Brown v. Board of Education*. I started thinking about the progress, or lack thereof, that blacks have made since 1954.

The publishing process can be long and arduous. Thankfully, Derrick Bell, Chris Gowen, Tony Kronman, Alan Nierob, Robert Shepard, Wendy Strothman, and Charles Tiefer provided guidance to help me navigate through it.

The University of Baltimore School of Law and the Wilson H. Elkins Professorship of the University of Maryland System provided indispensable research grants to facilitate this project. The support provided by Dean Gilbert Holmes and Dean Phil Closius was invaluable to the completion of this book.

I have been most fortunate to have had many outstanding student research assistants and editors. I thank Anastasia Albright, Phyllis Book, Tyler Buck, Allison Busby, Sam Draper, Ranya Ghuma, Spencer Hall, Patrick Heffron, Alex Hughs, Terri Ann Jones, David Krum, Steve Leroux, Andrew Linberg, Donald "Doc" Lumpkins, Alexis Martin, Andrew Moss, Elaine Nietmann, John Rochester, Malcolm Ruff, G. Adam Ruther, Susan Senkeeto, Jonathan Singer, Jeff Solof, Bjorn Thorstensen, Alana Williams, Matt Williamson, Jeremy Wilson, Kate Winston, and Kate Wolfson.

Deep appreciation goes to the relatives, friends, and colleagues who reviewed draft chapters—their insights helped me to find my way through racial minefields. I thank José Anderson, Kathy Bergin, Taylor Branch, Kevin Brown, Paula Wright Coleman, Eric Easton, Garrett Epps, Leigh Goodmark, Desiree Gordy, John Hagen, Evelyn Brooks Higginbotham, Robert Higginbotham II, Donald Jones, Robert Kaczorowski, Jeff Lifson, Rhonda Overby, Dominic Ozanne, Bob Pool, Arnie Rochvarg, Ernest Rubenstein, and Mike Suter.

To my secretaries, Shavaun O'Brien, Barbara Coyle, and Martha Kahlert, thanks for your dedication and patience. I could not have completed this book without you.

I am grateful to New York University Press, especially my editor, Debbie Gershenowitz, and her assistants, Gabrielle Begue and Constance Grady, for believing in me, the value of the book, and for their patience in giving me time to finish the manuscript.

A special debt of gratitude is owed to those who went above and beyond expectations. I thank Mike Meyerson for protecting my blind side. Without Mike's help and guidance, this book would have remained just an idea. I thank Paul Chandler for adding clarity and style to my vision. I thank Karla Gordy Bristol for her support and encouragement.

Preface

"Spirit," said Scrooge in a broken voice, "remove me from this place."

"I told you these were shadows of the things that have been," said the Ghost. "That they are what they are, do not blame me!"

—Charles Dickens, 1843[1]

I HAVE WRITTEN law textbooks used in colleges, universities, and law schools across the globe. I have been recognized as one of the top professors in the state of Maryland with the award of an endowed professorship, the oldest and most prestigious offered by the University of Maryland system. I have served as interim dean and am a tenured law faculty member at the University of Baltimore, the youngest to be tenured in the school's history. I serve as an advisor to Maryland's senior senator and have chaired commissions by appointment of Maryland's governor and attorney general, in addition to having advised dignitaries internationally in matters of human and civil rights.[2]

I spent most of my childhood and teenage years in some of the most exclusive communities in the country, Beverly Hills, California, and Shaker Heights, Ohio. I attended excellent public and private elementary and secondary schools, some of the top schools in the country. I went on to attend college and law school in the Ivy League, after which I spent two years studying at Cambridge University in England. In all candor, my life has been, and continues to be, pretty darned good.

Given these advantages, some may wonder why I decided to spend decades working to reduce racial inequality. Others may question the timing of this book since America has elected its first black president. Nonetheless, it is more important now than ever to truly reach equality.

In the classic book *A Christmas Carol*, the fictional character Scrooge looked back at his past and saw images that disturbed him.[3] I too look back on events in my life and am disturbed by certain images of race in America, even though, unlike Scrooge's visions, the ones I see seemed beyond my control. I am black, by the way.

From my earliest memories as a child growing up in western Beaver County, Pennsylvania, my parents had always stressed that racial prejudice was wrong, no exceptions. On one side of my house was a white neighbor of Italian descent and on the other side of the street was a white neighbor of Serbian descent. I played with the children of both families without racial incident.

Both my mom's and dad's families had long histories of living in racially diverse communities in Rochester and Sewickley, Pennsylvania, where many whites were considered close, personal, and lifelong friends. My maternal grandfather, born in 1902, was a successful businessman and civil servant, owning a barbershop and serving as the director of the County Housing Authority. Both my grandfather's first home, purchased in 1922, and his barbershop, purchased in 1924, were secured through personal loans from his two closest friends, Cap Moles and Max Barnett, white men who had been his friends since childhood. My grandfather always said, on the basis of this experience, that "friendship, not color, was the currency of life."

My father, Robert Higginbotham, volunteered for military service in the Army Air Corps during World War II, following his older brother, Mitchell Higginbotham, who served as a pilot in the 477th Bombardment Group, part of the famous "Tuskegee Airmen," who were also known as the "Red Tails."[4] After serving in the military, my dad attended the University of Pittsburgh School of Medicine, where he was the only black in his class. After graduating, he began practicing as a general physician in Midland, Pennsylvania, where most of his patients were white. In 1963, my dad became an orthopedic surgery resident at Case Western Reserve University in Cleveland, Ohio. Just a few months earlier, another black former serviceman, civil rights leader Medgar Evers, had been assassinated in Jackson, Mississippi, in response to his efforts to register black voters in the state.[5]

In 1964, when my family moved to Shaker Heights, Ohio, a wealthy suburb of Cleveland, known for excellent public schools, I experienced the betrayal of "white flight." I was excited to move from Western Pennsylvania to the Cleveland area, mostly due to my love of playing football. The city's professional football team, the Cleveland Browns, had just won the National Football League Championship,[6] and its star player was a confident, young, black running back named Jim Brown. Brown was one of my childhood heroes, and as he campaigned, in 1966, for Carl Stokes to be-come the first black mayor of a major city in the United States, I proudly wore my "Stokes for Mayor" button.[7] I wore it because Jim Brown was for Stokes, even though I had no appreciation for the historical significance of the election. I was nine years old and attended Lomond Elementary School, a good school in an excellent school district.[8] At the time, only fif-teen of the 550 students were black.[9] My best friend was a white student, and it surprised me when his family abruptly moved two suburbs away in 1969. Five years after I began school at Lomond Elementary there were 164 black students, roughly a tenfold increase,[10] and a rapid decrease in white students.

My friend's family was one of many white families that moved to far-flung suburbs in the late 1960s and '70s, fleeing the growing black popula-tion of America's cities.[11] While racially isolated schools in suburban Cleve-land, and elsewhere, had good facilities and teachers, they did not match Lomond's recognition or accolades. This suggests that many white families relocated not to seek educational excellence for their children but because they felt a need to isolate themselves from a racially diverse community. Black enrollment at Lomond has increased from 1% in 1964 to over 60% today due to massive white flight and reluctance by many whites to reside in neighborhoods where significant numbers of blacks reside.[12]

In 1967, one of my other childhood heroes, Muhammad Ali, had his world heavyweight boxing title revoked due to his refusal to serve in the military at the height of the Vietnam War. As a member of the Nation of Islam Church and one of its ministers, Ali refused on religious grounds. Responding to a reporter's inquiry regarding his refusal to serve in the military and fight the enemy, Ali responded that "no Vietcong ever called me nigger."[13] Two years later, in the fall of 1969, I felt the pain inflicted from racial slurs when I enrolled at University School in Shaker Heights, an ex-clusive private school requiring entrance by examination. There were only a few black students at the school, and during my first week, one of my classmates referred to me as a "nigger."

I never expected to have to confront Ali's reality at my new school, where all the students were smart and accomplished. I thought racism was something that only ignorant and uneducated people espoused. My par-ents had always discouraged fighting in school, but they had told me not to accept or tolerate racial slurs, especially the word "nigger."

As a result, my parents were not shocked when school officials notified them of the ensuing fight. What did surprise them was the commitment by the white athletic director, who issued a zero tolerance policy for racial epithets. Racial slurs were not permitted at any time or under any circumstances. This was well beyond the antidiscrimination standards at any of my previous schools and clearly had a positive effect on race relations with my classmates. No more incidents occurred during the year. This was when I first began to realize that whites needed to stand up against racism in order for it to cease. When they do, particularly whites with political or economic power, white racism, or at least the negative effects on blacks from such racism, can be reduced.

As a thirteen-year-old in 1970, ten years before acclaimed lawyer and deputy district attorney Johnnie Cochran was stopped and pulled from his car at gunpoint in front of his two children by Beverly Hills police officers because he was black and driving a Rolls Royce,[14] I endured the degradation of racial profiling when my family moved to Beverly Hills, the wealthy California community known for "swimming pools, movie stars,"[15] and excellent public schools, but where few black families resided.[16] I was happy to move to Beverly Hills, as Jim Brown had recently left Cleveland and moved to the area to become a movie star,[17] and my favorite television show at the time was the *Beverly Hillbillies*, a show about a white family who relocates from the South to Beverly Hills.[18] As with the previous move to Shaker Heights, one reason my parents chose Beverly Hills, even though the housing costs were astronomically high, was that it had the reputation of having the best public schools in the area. One evening soon after the move, I began exploring my new surroundings by bicycle. Two white police officers stopped me for questioning, without cause, assuming that because I was black, I did not reside in the area. They asked where I lived and what I was doing in that neighborhood. It took a while to convince them that I was not an "unwelcome outside intruder." Before the officers finally let me go, they warned that there was a curfew for children in the jurisdiction and said they had better not see me out again at night without adult supervision. Not long after this unwarranted stop, I was at a pool party, the only black among white children who had lived in Beverly Hills for years. As darkness arrived, I announced that I had to be going. "Why?" my new friends wanted to know. "Because of the curfew," I replied. "What curfew?" they asked. Their candid question exposed the real motive behind the police officers' "warning." A year later, and after numerous unwarranted stops by Beverly Hills police, my parents asked me if I would prefer to remain in Beverly Hills or move to "a predominantly black area." I chose the latter, without hesitation, partly due to the frustration of constantly being subjected to racial profiling in Beverly Hills.[19] While my Beverly Hills neighborhood was plush and full of exciting venues to visit, I suffered from "integration fatigue" brought on by frequent frustrating racial profiling incidents.

That same year, I experienced the low expectations of black students not being tracked for elite college admission when my mom and I walked into Horace Mann Elementary School, in Beverly Hills, to register me for the eighth grade school year. We had my transcript from a previous school, proof of Beverly Hills residence, and all other necessary paperwork. After graduating from Lomond, I had attended one of the top private schools in the state, University School, and had maintained an "A" average. The Beverly Hills school official reviewed my application and registered me. Over the next four weeks, I completed several tests on which I had perfect scores in math and science. My math teacher approached me and said, "You don't belong in this section. You belong in another section where you might be more comfortable." I told my teacher I would rather stay in my current section because I had made several new friends.

It was not until the end of the school year that I found out what my teacher had meant when he said I belonged in a "different section." He meant that instead of being placed in the intermediate section of the eighth grade, where I would have to make an "A" in my English class in order to be placed into the ninth grade honors English class, I should have been placed in the accelerated section of the eighth grade, where an "A," a "B," or a "C" in my English class would earn me a spot in honors English.[20] My white math teacher questioned the erroneous judgment of the registration official that led to my misplacement. He deserved credit for his caring and objective decision making. Yet, it is deeply troubling that I was placed in the intermediate track rather than the accelerated one. Perhaps it was a failure by the registration official to carefully read my transcript, a lack of understanding of how good my previous schools were, or a failure to pass my transcript along to a guidance counselor with more knowledge about proper placement. But there is also another possibility, given the widespread tracking throughout the country since the 1970s and the low numbers of black students selected for accelerated courses[21]—perhaps the school administrator, who was white, could not imagine that a black child belonged in the accelerated section. I was one of only three black students in the eighth grade at my school. None of us was in the accelerated section, and none of us was informed by school officials of its existence until after I was excluded from the high school honors section.[22]

Later, in 1970, five years after protests against racism and poverty sparked the Watts Riots that left thirty-four people dead in South Central Los Angeles,[23] I experienced the intra-race and -class bias of other blacks when my cousin, who was also thirteen, was visiting from Pittsburgh. We went to visit one of my uncles who lived in an all-black neighborhood near South Central Los Angeles, and walked to a nearby playground where a pick-up basketball game was about to begin. All of the players were black. I asked if my cousin and I could get in the game. One of the guys responded with a question: "Are you any good?" Before I could answer, another asked what school I attended. I said Horace Mann. A third guy said, "Yeah I know that school; it is over near Eighth Street." I specified, "Not that one, the one in Beverly Hills." One of the players then responded, "Rich blacks can't play no ball."[24] When my cousin and I won the game that day, it was particularly sweet. Our abilities on the court had nothing to do with where we lived or our financial resources; our skills came from practice and hard work. I felt those players had judged me negatively because of economic prejudice. I wondered how many black school-age children, like myself, had been prejudged by the police, by their teachers, by their competitors, by their neighbors, and even by their black friends.

Two years later, I feared that I would be the victim of police brutality while riding home from school with a friend's father. My parents had warned me about police brutality after a series of allegations by blacks against law enforcement officers in Southern California. Six years prior, Leonard Deadwyler, a black man, driving his pregnant wife to a local hospital, was shot and killed by Los Angeles police officers during a traffic stop.[25] My friend's father had pulled into a closed gas station, in the Hollywood section of Los Angeles, needing to pick up something from the station office. He knew the owner, who lived nearby, and said he would walk to get him. He told us to wait in the car, which was parked in front of the gasoline pumps.

Shortly after he left, a Los Angeles police car pulled into the station. Two white officers got out of the car, with guns drawn, and asked my friend, who was also black, and me to get out of the car with our hands up. After they searched us and checked the license plate of the car and our identification, my friend told the officers why we were there. The officers then searched the car. Upon finding nothing suspicious, the officers told us to continue standing while they went back to their police vehicle to verify our story. I nudged my friend and joked to him that "they think we are robbing the station." Several seconds later one officer returned, said our story appeared to check out, and asked me what I was smiling about. He then proceeded to take out his billy club, and after slapping it into his hand several times, asked, "How would you like me to take you behind the station and knock that smile off your face?" Before I could answer, the other officer came out of the police car and said, "Let's go; we have another call." In that brief moment, I saw the reality of the tense dynamic between black detainees and white police officers—whether "walking while black," "driving while black," or, as in my case, "smiling while black"—frequently experienced by blacks all over the country.

In the summer of 1974, twelve years before a white mob attacked four blacks who had accidentally ventured into an all-white neighborhood in Queens, New York, when their car broke down,[26] I witnessed the injustice of black mob violence first-hand. While visiting relatives in Western Pennsylvania that summer, I attended a dance at Rochester High School. Rochester was an integrated school with approximately 5% black enrollment.[27] At the dance, a black female student complained to some of her black male friends that a white male student, known to have a hostility toward blacks, had bumped into her on the dance floor and when asked to apologize had responded with profanity and a "racial slur." When the dance ended, attendees exited to the parking lot where ten black males surrounded the alleged perpetrator and, once again, requested an apology. When it was not forthcoming, the black males proceeded to punch and kick the alleged perpetrator until he was bloodied and begging for mercy.

I felt sympathetic. If the facts, as alleged, were true, certainly this white student had been rude and had acted in a racist manner. Yet, I could not stop feeling that what was done to him in retaliation was also very wrong. Ten black guys jumping on one white seemed numerically unfair, but even more troublesome was the thought that these black guys had acted so similarly to the many white mobs during the Jim Crow period when a black had been accused of crossing some invisible racial line. On that day, I saw, for the first time, the reality of black mob violence and how it can be just as vicious and precipitous as white mob violence.

In August of 1972, four years after black Olympic athletes Tommie Smith and John Carlos had their medals rescinded as punishment for raising their fists at the medal ceremony in protest against racism in the United States and in South Africa,[28] I learned about the personal risks of challenging racism. At the end of my freshman year in high school, during which I received Most Valuable Player (MVP) awards for freshman football and baseball,[29] I had earned the right to be elevated and compete at the varsity level in my sophomore year as previous award recipients who were white had been. Yet, while white players, whom I had outperformed only months earlier, were promoted to the varsity level, I was not. In response to this apparent oversight, my parents met with the school district's superintendent. Concerned that I had not been treated fairly by two members of the Beverly Hills High School Athletic Department staff, they questioned whether racism was involved.

While the superintendent appeared sympathetic, he indicated that the athletic director had primary responsibility for making sure athletes were treated fairly. The superintendent arranged a meeting between my parents and the athletic director. At this meeting, the athletic director appeared angry, apparently due to the racism allegation. Rather than question his own conduct, or the conduct of any member of his coaching staff, he instead spent the entire meeting denigrating my performance, ability, and character. Even though we had team members who were earning low grades in academic courses, skipping classes, being placed on detention, drinking alcohol excessively, smoking, and abusing illegal drugs, I was labeled as the "problem" player with all sorts of negative connotations such as lazy, selfish, and uncommitted, all adding up to an easily alleged but hard-to-define character flaw: a "bad attitude." How could the two-sport MVP be "the demon of the team" the athletic director portrayed?

An invaluable lesson was learned that day: do not raise the possibility of racism, especially when it turns out to be true, unless you are prepared to make personal sacrifices to your status and opportunities. Otherwise, you may wrongly be labeled as "uppity" or a "troublemaker" or, in my case, having a "bad attitude." Although neither my life nor my parents' livelihoods was threatened due to the allegations of racism—as had happened to many blacks like Tommie Smith and John Carlos—athletic opportunities for me quickly diminished. From that incident, I learned first-hand some of the risks of challenging racism post Jim Crow.

If I was truly a player with a "bad attitude," I should have been removed from the teams or, at the very least, demoted from the captain's position. Instead, my parents' allegation of racism led to a series of attempts by the athletic director to manipulate me into quitting the teams. Despite being verbally abused and placed in embarrassing situations, I refused to quit. The number of other black athletes at my school who were treated unfairly and encouraged to quit reminded me of my father's and uncle's experiences during World War II, and the stories they shared about the many black pilot trainees, like my father, who were unjustifiably "washed out" by racist white officers determined to prevent black success.[30] Their racist actions subsequently resulted in a black failure rate at 50%, twice that of white pilot trainees.[31] A similar rate of attrition existed at my school for black athletes.

What I found unconscionable, however, was that my athletic director never responded to inquiries about my abilities from college coaches. Early in my senior year, I applied for admission to three Ivy League colleges: Harvard, Yale, and Brown. Although I had a solid application (high GPA and SAT score), in order to be competitive I needed extracurricular activities to set me apart from other qualified applicants. I hoped football success might make the difference. Despite objections by the athletic director, in my junior year I achieved a starting position and was selected as one of the best players in the entire league. During my senior year, as captain of the team and a returning all-conference player,[32] I thought the support of my school's athletic department would be automatic. Yet, inquiries regarding me remained unanswered.

After receiving a letter from Yale's head football coach[33] expressing interest in my career, requesting game film of my performance, and informing me that his two previous requests to my high school athletic department had not been answered, I became very angry. I started to have serious doubts about the sincerity of whites. I distanced myself from my white friends, stopped participating in school activities, and became unduly suspicious of the motives of all whites. My emotional reaction to the racist incidents I endured was anger toward all whites. This blanket anger was not a new concept to me. I had talked with many blacks from my parents' generation who had endured racism under Jim Crow[34] and were adamant that no whites, not even liberal ones, could be trusted. These blacks talked about northern whites capitulating during Reconstruction in the face of widespread violence against blacks. They talked about liberal whites who fought to end Jim Crow segregation practices during the civil rights movement, but then resisted desegregation efforts in their own neighborhoods and schools or interracial relationships or marriages in their own families. They cited those who had embraced "white flight," just like some of my white neighbors in Shaker Heights, as examples of white recalcitrance.

Because of the support of many good teachers and friends, white and black, as well as family resources, the consequences of the racist acts committed against me did not prevent college admission, but the frustration and despair were real. I can only imagine the anger and pain of other blacks who suffered more tragic consequences from racism.[35] It took me some time to realize how wrong it was to judge all whites according to the actions of some, but it was hard not to be bitter over such subtle and hidden, yet harmful, racist treatment.

The change in my attitude began to take shape during my freshman year in 1975 at Brown University. My white sociology professor[36] seemed to sense my anger, and he suggested I do a paper[37] comparing the experiences of a white friend from Beverly Hills, who was also a freshman at Brown,[38] with my own. In my research, I discovered that our families shared many struggles. While my friend's family had not undergone racism, they had experienced religious persecution and ethnic bigotry. The harm inflicted from the prejudice my white friend's family had endured was similar to the pain of racism my family had been subjected to and was deeply troubling to me, so much so that the realization of the similarity in treatment was transforming. Never again would I allow myself to become what I had despised so much in both blacks and whites—prejudiced. To the many whites who had befriended me, defended me, and been called a "nigger lover" because of me, separating myself from them would be misdirected, and harmful to me as well. At that point, I recognized that both racism and negative reactions to it must be prevented, as both contribute to isolation, ignorance, and, perhaps most damaging and permanent, inequality.

I reengaged with my white friends and made new ones, and, over time, most of my anger dissipated. Yet my new approach would be challenged quickly and, surprisingly, more often than I would have guessed.

In the fall of 1975, as a member of the freshman football team at Brown University, I learned about the complexities of race in the post–Jim Crow era. While there were sixty members on the team, only five players were black, two recruited players and three "walk-on," nonrecruited, players, including me.[39] Forty-four of the members played regularly during team scrimmages, including several white "walk-ons." None of the black "walkons" played in the preseason scrimmages. A week before the first game against Yale, it was announced that all members of the first and second teams would play an equal amount of time. All three black "walk-ons," including me, were third-string and would not play. However, the day before the game, the first-team flanker broke his ankle and was out for the season. As I was "suiting-up" for the game, the first-string quarterback and several other players said to me, "Now you are going to get your chance; let's see what you can do." On several previous occasions when a player quit or was injured, his back-up was automatically selected to replace the missing player. But, in this precedent-setting instance, when the depth chart listing starting rotations was posted three hours before the game's kick-off, I was still third-string. Despite not knowing the plays or having practiced in the position, a white player was moved from third-string defensive-back to second-string flanker three hours before the first game of the season. I did not play in the game against Yale, even though I was entitled to under the established criteria.

This is when I first realized that race was no longer the only factor in discriminatory treatment against blacks as it had been under Jim Crow laws; it was now one of several factors. Discrimination frequently involved race plus something else: race plus poverty, race plus lack of education, race plus lack of political power, or race plus not being recruited—all played a role in discriminatory treatment. Under this approach, not all blacks would be excluded from schools, neighborhoods, or participation in social activities, but most would. Recruited black players could play in games, but "walk-on" black players could not. When the five black players confronted the head football coach concerning the disparate racial treatment, he said, "One of the five blacks on the team is a starter, so why are you guys crying racism?" Our white coach truly believed that blacks could not be victims of racism if one of many was being treated fairly.

I hear this argument often today, to support the position that racism has ended. When one black is being treated fairly, how can denial of opportunities to other blacks have anything to do with racism? It is important to understand, however, that the mere fact that one individual black has been treated fairly does not warrant the conclusion that all others have been. In the post–Jim Crow era, individual assessment is critical.

During my junior year at Brown in 1977, thirteen years after Congress passed the 1964 Civil Rights Act prohibiting racial discrimination in public accommodations,[40] I was surprised to see that some whites would choose to lose profits rather than serve a black clientele. I attended the opening of Shamrock Cliffs nightclub in Newport, Rhode Island, located in a mansion on the beach of Millionaire's Row. On that first night, the club was packed; only three blacks were in attendance including the disc jockey, who played rhythm and blues music. Over the next several months, as word of the club's existence spread, there were progressively more black patrons, without any decline in overall numbers. By the sixth month of operation, the clientele was approximately 60% black. At that point, the white owner approached the disc jockey and requested that the format of the music be changed from rhythm and blues to rock. Given the high attendance, the disc jockey was surprised by the request and questioned the change. The disc jockey was told that while profits were high, and no security problems had arisen, the owner preferred rock music. The disc jockey quit rather than change the format; he recognized that the change in music was really meant to shift the racial makeup of the crowd. Attendance dropped significantly over the next several weeks, and there were few black patrons. The owner, however, was much happier with a lower profit and predominantly white clientele. Long after passage of antidiscrimination laws, some white proprietors resisted the spirit of those laws and adopted more covert practices, like drastic change in music format, which hindered interaction between blacks and whites, especially if whites were not predominant in numbers.

Eight years later, I experienced the apathy of white teammates to racial comment. In December of 1983, I received a Rotary Foundation scholarship to attend Cambridge University in England. In April of 1985, I was the only black American student at Cambridge. Earlier in the year, I had been elected president of the Cambridge University Basketball Club.[41] At Cambridge, basketball is one of the few sports where a majority of the players are American.[42] We were jovial the night of the team's annual banquet as we had recently defeated arch-rival Oxford for the first time in twenty-five years.[43]

During the dinner portion of the banquet, one of my British teammates told a "nigger" joke in which he spoke disparagingly about black people using the word "nigger" several times. Candidly, I like a good joke. The fact that a joke implicates race does not necessarily make it a bad one. But to tell a joke, at a large group function, that uses derogatory references and puts down an entire race should not be acceptable. None of the Americans laughed at the joke, but no one openly opposed it being made. At the banquet's finale, and after several other team members had spoken, I rose to speak as the team's next president. I contemplated what to say regarding the earlier racial references. I thought about the advice I had received from my parents, civil rights veterans who had fought against Jim Crow practices throughout their lives,[44] who said, "You can never run away from racism." However, given my experience at Beverly Hills High School in pointing out racism, I was reluctant to do so. As the banquet progressed, I kept hoping that one of my teammates would say something to express opposition to what had been said.

I made a short speech that night talking about the historic victory over Oxford and the bright prospects for the coming season, without ever referencing the racial incident. I had very mixed emotions about not wanting to spoil the festive atmosphere and the team camaraderie, while simultaneously desiring to stand true to my familial guidance. I felt as though I should publicly confront my teammate who had made the racist joke or walk out of the banquet, but decided to remain silent during the banquet and speak with my teammate afterwards in private. I asked him if he realized that the joke was derogatory to blacks and was offensive to me. He said it was "only a joke," that he did not mean to offend anyone, that I was just "too sensitive," and that after all we were "on the same team." Nothing further was said about this incident but, subsequently, every time I passed this teammate the ball during a game, I thought about the racist joke he had told and what it meant to be "on the same team" with such a person.

I have often thought about my decision to remain publicly silent in the presence of racially offensive language used by a teammate. It is deeply troubling to me, even today, that I kept silent at the banquet. What bothered me the most, however, was that none of my white teammates said anything publicly against this racist joke.

The silence of my teammates reminded me of the silence of my uncle's classmates while he experienced racism in a law school setting during a time of open discrimination. While my experience was much less harmful than my uncle's, the silence of teammates to racially insensitive treatment was equally disappointing. In 1951, as a second-year law student at Yale, my uncle, A. Leon Higginbotham Jr., won more oral advocacy honors than any other student in the history of the Yale Law School.[45] At the oral argument for the prestigious Honors Moot Court Prize, John W. Davis, head of one of the premier law firms in the country, Davis Polk & Wardwell, was one of the three judges in the competition. Just a few months later he would begin his representation of the Topeka, Kansas, Board of Education in its battle with seven-year-old Linda Brown over school segregation. My uncle was awarded the first prize for best oral advocate. After the ceremony, Davis congratulated the three other finalists and asked each one to come and interview at his firm. My uncle received neither a congratulatory handshake nor an invitation to interview.[46] The evening ended without one person expressing publicly or privately any condemnation for the racist treatment my uncle had endured.

In 1981, as a third-year student at Yale Law School, where 5% of the student body was black and where there was one black member of the faculty,[47] I received an invitation to interview at Davis Polk & Wardwell and accepted a position as an associate attorney. Having graduated from Yale without any of the honors my uncle had achieved, I was grateful for the opportunity to work at this prestigious firm even though its founder had discriminated against my uncle some thirty years earlier. In the late 1970s, Davis Polk & Wardwell had broadened its hiring practices to include racial minorities and women, as had Yale Law School with its admissions process. However, when I joined the firm, there were only five other black associates and no black partners out of three hundred lawyers.[48] Thus, while I benefited from affirmative action efforts in my admission to Yale Law School and a job offer from Davis Polk & Wardwell, at that time blacks were substantially underrepresented at both institutions.

Even so, I realize that few Americans, of any race, have been privileged with the opportunities that I have had. I was raised in an environment characterized by quality schools, beautiful neighborhoods, and racial integration. To suggest, however, that racism was not part of my experience because Jim Crow had ended and affirmative action programs had begun, or because I was economically privileged, defies reality. My experience in some ways may have been different from that of most blacks, particularly with respect to wealth status. Yet, I believe that when it comes to racism, many of my experiences are similar to those of blacks who do not have a high income. Further, I believe my unique background—having lived, gone to school, worked, socialized, and made lifelong friendships in integrated environments—gives me a perspective sorely needed to explore the issue of race in America today.

Currently, there are two types of racism that prevent equality—structural racism and cultural racism. Structural racism involves policies, laws, and programs that embed inequality within the entities of our society, and in so doing, reinforce cultural racism, those beliefs and actions that embrace racial hierarchy and isolation. Both structural and cultural racism must be ended in order to create equality and allow for integration. Ending structural racism without also changing the way Americans think will only perpetuate current inequalities because blacks will continue to be treated more harshly than whites, and the races will continue to be separated, resulting in further black victimization. Ending cultural racism without also altering those laws, policies, and programs that disproportionately impact blacks also will continue inequity, even without the intent to do so, because the negative impact on blacks from those rules will remain.

Many racially neutral laws, policies, and programs continue to negatively impact blacks in all aspects of society. Moreover, a process of racialization—negative connotations, actions, assumptions, and biases—still exists in the lives of middle-class and high-income blacks, as well as blacks who are impoverished. It typically lies just beneath the surface, lurking in the shadows but visible to those carefully attuned to post–Jim Crow racial interaction. Whether overt, as racial practices were under Jim Crow, or covert, as they tend to be in the post–Jim Crow period, the similarities in harmful impact remain present. Many of the racial incidents in my life reminded me of my dad's and mom's under Jim Crow—from the military police threatening to beat my dad if he did not move to the Jim Crow train car as he sat politely in his Army Air Corps uniform in the only available seat on the train, albeit one designated for whites only, to the movie theater usher requiring my mom to sit in the balcony of the theater reserved for black patrons who were prohibited from sitting anywhere else, to the insurance agent from Metropolitan Life Insurance Company who sent a letter to all University of Pittsburgh medical school graduates offering them a high-end policy but who upon arriving at my parents' home and seeing my dad abruptly rescinded the offer by informing my dad that high-end policies were reserved for whites only,[49] irrespective of the potential earning power of a black doctor—to name just a few examples. While many of the racial incidents that I experienced were covert, they resulted in harsher treatment than whites received and caused fear of bodily harm, denial of access, and lost opportunities just like those of my parents.

Most blacks, particularly the working poor, have endured discrimination more often and have suffered greater negative consequences than I have. But when it comes to such discrimination, if a black like me—residing in an upscale neighborhood, with an excellent education, financial resources, family support, and social skills—had to experience substantial racist incidents, how much more did blacks with far fewer advantages have to undergo? And while generational financial resources, family guidance, and many supportive teachers, both black and white, were able to lessen the harmful impact of such incidents for me, most other blacks did not have these options available.

This book demonstrates how racism plays a significant role in the lives of most blacks today. Unfortunately, sometimes these ghosts of Jim Crow are imagined, as when the "race card" is improperly played as it was in 2006, when a black female falsely claimed she was raped and verbally abused with racial epithets allegedly used by three white male lacrosse players attending Duke University.[50] At other times these ghosts are far too real, as in the disproportionate administration of the death penalty. This became all too evident on September 21, 2011, when the state of Georgia executed Troy Davis, a black man, for the murder of a white, off-duty police officer.[51]

Davis was executed despite the fact that evidence of witness coercion, intimidation, and fabrication of testimony by police had raised serious doubt as to his guilt.[52] As the Davis case reveals, a black person can still be executed in America today, as frequently occurred during Jim Crow, even though serious doubt exists as to whether he committed any crime.

The reality of racism today is highlighted by the apparent cold-blooded murder of a black teenager and the legal system's reluctance to indict and prosecute the white perpetrator. On February 26, 2012, Trayvon Martin was returning to a house in Sanford, Florida, where he and his father were invited guests.[53] Trayvon, a black seventeen-year-old male, had left the house just before the start of the NBA All-Star game in order to go to a local 7-Eleven convenience store.[54] After purchasing a bag of Skittles and a bottle of iced tea, Trayvon headed back to the house to watch the rest of the game.[55] On his way home, Trayvon was followed by George Zimmerman, a 28-year-old male of white and Hispanic descent, who was active in the neighborhood watch program.[56] At first, Zimmerman followed Trayvon from his vehicle.[57] He then called 911 and reported that Trayvon looked suspicious.[58] When the emergency operator asked Zimmerman to describe Trayvon, Zimmerman described him as black and wearing a hoodie.[59] The operator indicated that the police were on the way and told Zimmerman not to follow Trayvon anymore.[60] Zimmerman responded, "These assholes, they always get away."[61] Ignoring the operator's instructions, Zimmerman followed Trayvon on foot and a confrontation with the teen occurred.[62] A scuffle ensued, Trayvon yelled for help, and Zimmerman fired a 9 millimeter handgun and shot and killed Trayvon.[63]

Despite the clear evidence indicating racial motivation for Zimmerman's actions, Zimmerman has denied this and claimed self-defense.[64] No facts uncovered, thus far, from the incident support a self-defense justification, unless one views a hoodie and a bag of Skittles as inherently threatening. Evidence suggests that Trayvon was targeted because he was a young black teenager walking through Zimmerman's predominantly white neighborhood. Despite public outrage and protests by Americans of all races, grand jury charges were slow to be brought and an arrest appeared unduly delayed. As the initial facts in this case indicate, a black teenager can be gunned down by an overzealous white neighborhood watch volunteer and that act will be obfuscated, overlooked, condoned, or celebrated by many members of the legal system, as similar acts often were during Jim Crow.

While racism occurs with varying degrees of severity, most blacks are negatively impacted at some point in their lives. Rich blacks, as well as poor blacks and those in between, are harmed by racism. Of course, for some it is easier to overcome the racial barriers of today than it was to overcome those imposed by Jim Crow. For others, like Troy Davis and Trayvon Martin, the obstacles remain insurmountable. While things are better for blacks, they are still not equal. Subtle, yet pervasive, racism continues to prevent equality.

The improvements in race relations since Jim Crow ended have complicated explanations for today's inequality. With the decision in *Brown v. Board of Education*,[65] and the passage of antidiscrimination statutes in voting, housing, and employment,[66] American law prohibits much of the discrimination that was widespread up until 1954. Education and job opportunities have greatly increased,[67] interracial marriages are more readily accepted,[68] and blatant racial violence has been drastically reduced.[69] Despite these positive changes, cultural racism remains deeply entrenched in American media. In 2011, Fox Business host Eric Bolling, displeased with President Obama's decision to meet with President Odimba of Gabon, was roundly criticized for stating that it was not the first time Obama "had a hoodlum in the hizzouse."[70] In 2007, radio host Don Imus was fired by CBS after referring to members of the Rutgers University women's basketball team as "nappy-headed hos."[71] While the public outcry generated by these incidents is an encouraging sign that many Americans will condemn blatant racism, more subtle manifestations in the media largely go unchallenged.

The idea of the "welfare queen" was popularized by Ronald Reagan during the 1976 presidential race, when he would often refer to a fictional woman from Chicago's South Side who allegedly defrauded Medicare out of $150,000 and drove a Cadillac.[72] Reagan's welfare queen has never been identified, and some believe he grossly exaggerated the story of an Illinois woman who was indicted for defrauding Medicare of eight thousand dollars around the same time.[73] The welfare queen rhetoric proved an effective political strategy that helped conservatives drum up public support for welfare reforms, but the tactic left an indelible mark on the public's perception of the average welfare recipient, one that is as inaccurate as it is racist, reinforcing false perceptions of black inferiority.

Many of my daily experiences, and those of most blacks today, have nothing to do with race. Despite such progress, however, vast statistical disparities between blacks and whites exist, in all aspects of society, due to structural impediments and the process of racialization continuing, through unconscious discrimination, overt and covert bias, and self-inflicted harm. In 1957, my father was told by an insurance agent that the company did not issue high-end policies to blacks, even when they graduated from medical school and began successful medical practices. Seventeen years later, I was told that college inquiries to my white high school athletic director, after allegations of racism had been lodged against him, went unanswered. Nineteen years after that, Bari-Ellen Roberts, a black senior financial analyst at Texaco, was denied opportunities for professional advancement due to her race. Roberts's blackness prevented promotion as reflected by her superiors who joked that "all of the black jelly beans seem to be glued to the bottom of the bag."[74] Eighteen years later, in 2011, Sandra Green, a black woman, was denied service at a Denny's Restaurant in East St. Louis, Illinois, when a white waiter ignored her and then used racial slurs in response to her request for service. While the racist actions were different, in that the first and last were overt, and the middle two were covert, the end result—unequal treatment resulting in missed opportunity—was the same.

Personal responsibility issues afflict both blacks and whites. While exercise of responsibility can increase financial and educational opportunities for blacks, reducing the harmful impact of racism, a lack of such responsibility can equally diminish opportunities, exacerbating racism's negative impact. While current vast racial disparities would diminish if more blacks exercised such responsibility, the existence of such disparities today would continue due to structural and cultural racism. This unfortunate reality, after Jim Crow ended, after the passage of federal and state antidiscrimination laws, and even after the election of America's first black president, has served as my motivation for writing this book.

I have provided this brief glimpse of my experiences so that the reader understands my motivation. Racism was supposed to be a thing of the past for black children of the civil rights movement, especially in "upscale" neighborhoods and "good" schools. Yet, presumptions of black inferiority and embraces of black-separation and white-isolation notions seemed to be lurking just beneath the surface, everywhere. I hope this book will further a dialogue about our nation's racial experiences and facilitate an end to race-based discrimination so that vast racial disparities become a thing of the past.

I recognize that race is a difficult subject for many to discuss. Even Barack Obama, who delineated the issues so clearly in his 2008 speech on race, has been reluctant to discuss the subject on many subsequent occasions. Current conditions reflect that blacks are disproportionately unemployed, impoverished, and undereducated, and that conditions are worsening. While hopelessness, which can become a self-fulfilling prophecy, and poor choices by blacks themselves play a role in the statistical disparities, the prevailing embrace of racial-hierarchy notions and black-separation and white-isolation sentiments, and laws and practices that disproportionately harm blacks, prevalent throughout America, are primarily to blame. Despite my educational attainments and financial stability, and that of a small segment of blacks, I have experienced racism, and I continue to witness it happening to me and to other blacks—both educationally and financially successful blacks and those blacks who are not. Blacks must change, and so must whites, for this to end.

This book seeks to facilitate a new conversation on race by helping Americans understand the complex racial paradigm, a pattern or model, that continues. I submit that there is a vicious cycle. The false notion of white superiority/black inferiority ingrained through slavery led to whites separating themselves from blacks through Jim Crow practices. This racial isolation permitted the false notion to reinforce itself and continue, thus making it easier for blacks to be victimized by race-based and race-neutral policies, and further contributing to false notions of a racial hierarchy today; and there is also the impact of black self-victimization. This process has existed for centuries and continues to benefit whites and disadvantage blacks.

As this country was formed in 1789, blacks were viewed as inferior, thereby justifying their enslavement. Americans ended slavery in 1865 and replaced it with Jim Crow segregation, disenfranchising blacks and maintaining separation. Americans ended Jim Crow in 1954 and restored voting rights for blacks in 1965, but replaced previous burdens with severe limitations in creating parity. Large numbers of whites intentionally sought to escape from blacks, in schools and housing, by resisting desegregation efforts and engaging in "white flight." Their actions were sanctioned by laws continuing racial isolation, facilitating black victimization, and keeping the paradigm intact.

To fully understand the paradigm, one must acknowledge the relevance of our racial history, the breadth and depth of racism, the progress that has been made since the end of Jim Crow, the effect of education and wealth on reducing racism's negative impact, the effect of personal irresponsibility, hopelessness, and despair on increasing racism's negative impact, the blatant and subtle ways racism continues, and the empowering potential that eliminating these issues offers. The late Derrick Bell reasoned in his provocative book *Faces at the Bottom of the Well* that racism is permanent in America. I respectfully disagree. This book argues that, while difficult to overcome, racial inequality need not be permanent and, with the requisite effort and proper focus, can be eradicated.

There has been a lot of talk, since Barack Obama was elected president of the United States, about a post-racial America. Comments have been made such as, "Racism is over; we have elected the first black president."[75] Or, "I thought Obama's election heralded a new enlightenment, in America regarding . . . racism."[76] Incidents that have occurred, subsequent to his election, reflect a different reality. Congressman Doug Lamborn went so far as to say that being linked to President Obama would be "like touching a tar baby," during a July 2011 interview.[77] Lamborn is not the first to publicly use racially tinged language to refer to President Obama. Newt Gingrich has called Obama the "food stamp president."[78] Richard Cebull, a white federal judge, went so far as to generate an electronic message denigrating President Obama's mother by comparing blacks to animals in analogizing interracial marriage and sexuality to bestiality.[79] Donald Trump preferred "affirmative action president."[80] Such references occur far too often. Moreover, many who believe that America has entered a post-racial period focus on inequality resulting from economic disparities. They argue that poor blacks suffer from racial inequality due to their living in poverty. There is no doubt that the high percentage of black poverty significantly contributes to the widespread socioeconomic disparities. Yet, even if we examine blacks and whites in the same economic bracket, significant disparities and separation exist.[81] Therefore, even if black poverty is reduced, disparities and separation between blacks and whites will remain.

What causes these differences? What exactly is it today that happens to blacks, but not whites—in the workforce, when interacting with law enforcement, when purchasing houses or renting apartments, and while attending schools—that ensures racial inequality? This book argues that structural and cultural racism in America today is much more complicated than before, but continues to include bias against impoverished, working-class, and high-income blacks, just as it did during the Jim Crow period. Today's bias may be different in that it is less blatant and more subtle than it was under Jim Crow, yet its pervasiveness continues to hinder efforts to create racial equality in two ways. First, it reinforces the paradigm. Second, it undermines equality efforts. This book examines the impact of racism in America today on the vast majority of blacks who are working poor, working-class, high income, or wealthy—employed or actively searching for work, law-abiding or reformed, and productive citizens—but who continue to be harmed by disproportionate impact, unconscious negative reactions, overt racial bias, covert discriminatory treatment, or self-inflicted and unproductive reactions to racism.

Many whites seem to be in denial when it comes to recognizing racism, although it is still prevalent in many aspects of society, including employment practices. Black unemployment remains twice as high as white unemployment. Reduction or elimination of racism, not the entrance of some blacks into the middle and upper classes, is the only true measure of progress. Many blacks enter the middle and upper classes in spite of racism, not because of its demise. I encourage you to read further for evidence that Americans still have a long way to go to achieve a post-racial society.

When I refer to a post-racial society, I do not mean a color-blind society in which race is not recognized or identified. Rather, a post-racial society is one in which racial hierarchy notions, desires for isolation, and acts of victimization solely due to race are absent from the daily reasoning, judgment, perceptions, and practices of the majority of Americans. A society in which a black child is not placed, as an elementary school student, in a non-college-bound program because of negative presumptions of intellectual performance due to race. A society in which parents no longer need to tell their black children, especially their male children, not to run in public for fear that it might create suspicion of wrongdoing in the minds of white police officers. A society in which discretion by government personnel resulting in substantial racial disparities is presumptively prohibited. A society in which most whites do not move away from a neighborhood because an abundance of blacks have begun to move in. A society in which government encouragement and facilitation of racial integration is viewed as a compelling societal interest.

All Americans should be well motivated to begin the conversation on how to create a post-racial society.[82] Not only does racism's continuance harm blacks; it reduces America's competitiveness around the world. With China, Brazil, and other economic powers increasing their gross national product annually, it is more imperative than ever for America to maximize its human resources. Currently, Americans are fourteenth in the world in reading scores[83] and twenty-fifth in math scores.[84] Over the last decade, America has dropped from first to ninth in number of people with college degrees, first to eighteenth in number of people to graduate high school, and first to twenty-third in number of people with doctoral degrees.[85] Racism reduces America's chances of being number one in these categories. Eliminating racial inequality will create significantly more opportunities for a large segment of America's population. So, while ending racial inequality is ultimately about fundamental fairness, such a change will also benefit all Americans by increasing the country's economic competitiveness globally.

Unfortunately, today, many believe that if a few blacks are successful then the problem of inequality is not racism but the fact that unsuccessful blacks have done something wrong, have made bad choices, or are mentally incapable. Most blacks however, understand that a few blacks have always succeeded in the face of racist obstacles—during slavery, during the Jim Crow era, and today. Their success during slavery and Jim Crow did not equate to the absence of racism, and the success of a higher percentage of blacks today, albeit a woefully low percentage in comparison to whites, should not be seen as doing so either.

We must dismantle the paradigm—we must end black separation and its cyclical effects. The cycle will not stop until we relinquish our false notions of white superiority and black inferiority. We must tear down these false notions and acknowledge that a gap in perceptions exists between blacks and whites. Blacks cannot end white racism, but they can end the harm imposed due to feelings of hopelessness. Whites cannot end self-victimization by blacks, but they can end notions of racial hierarchy and desires for isolation. Both blacks and whites must change their behaviors and start dialogue to seek understanding. The interdependent features of the paradigm must be dismantled simultaneously, and that process will only be successful if we all work together, hand in hand.

Our current era presents an unprecedented opportunity for a nationwide dialogue on race relations. Our nation took a fresh, positive step when we elected Barack Obama as president. We must now take the next steps and directly confront the mistreatment and harmful reactions that continue.

Until each part of the racial paradigm is eliminated—(1) false notions of white superiority/black inferiority, (2) black separation and white isolation, and (3) black victimization—the process of racialization, discrimination, and disproportionate impact will continue preventing entry into a truly post-racial period. Changing laws to more readily deter racism—eliminating structural impediments—will help, but only by changing hearts and minds can the paradigm be permanently altered, eliminating cultural impediments as well. Conditions are ripe for progress.

I have witnessed, time and again, in a variety of racial interactions, the transformative effect diversity has on diminishing the racial divide. There is a tendency, in racially discriminatory treatment, to dehumanize the "other" as an abstract class, rather than deal with those of different races as individuals, with common, shared elements of humanity. The true value of diversity is that it prevents the biases that tend to dehumanize and allows each race to recognize the humanity of the other.

Racial diversity can be an amazing educational tool in destroying negative racial stereotypes. Studying, working, and socializing with members of different races, as a child and teenager, enabled me to learn early on that the racial stereotypes about blacks—that they're generally lazy, dumb, and prone to criminal activity and drug abuse—with which media portrayals bombard Americans are not grounded in reality. It also helped me to recognize that racism can be embraced by even the best-intentioned blacks and whites, so that all Americans must constantly and actively resist the racist notions that come to us from our history and our environment and that negatively influence our views and actions. In a racially diverse environment, one learns pretty quickly that the majority of blacks are hard-working, smart, law-abiding, and drug-free, and that some whites equally manifest negative tendencies that have erroneously been attributed primarily to blacks. One also learns that racism is wrong whether it is espoused or embraced by whites or by blacks. These are valuable lessons, easily learned by an exposure to racial diversity that too few Americans experience.

Via experiences in western Beaver County, Shaker Heights, Beverly Hills, Los Angeles, Providence, New Haven, and Cambridge, I learned that good neighbors come in all colors, as do bad ones. This premise has guided me through the difficult racial paradigm that continues. While my story reveals my motivation for choosing to teach race relations courses, for writing this book, and for desiring to shatter the racial paradigm, the need to have new dialogue goes much deeper. This book is about helping Americans live up to the promise of racial equality.

Introduction

Understanding the Racial Paradigm

"You may think you are seeing some new [stuff] out here but this ain't nothing but a rerun to me."
   —The character Melvin, played by Ving Rhames in the Columbia
Pictures/John Singleton film *Baby Boy*, 2001

FROM 1619, WHEN the first blacks arrived in the Jamestown, Virginia, settlement, racial inequality was imposed through law and maintained by practices.[1] In a long history of racial oppression motivated by white desires for economic exploitation and justified by false perceptions of inferiority, blacks were enslaved until 1865, were separated and victimized by law until 1954, and are separated and victimized by practice still, even when the president of the United States, the highest political official under the American constitutional democracy, is black.

What Does It All Mean?

At approximately 10:05 p.m., November 4, 2008, television news stations announced that Barack Obama had been elected president.[2] I was watching the election returns in the National Press Club in Washington, DC, surrounded by friends, members of the media, campaign volunteers, and political junkies. Most of those in attendance were jubilant at the news, slapping five, hugging, shouting, and dancing. As I ventured outside onto the Washington streets on a particularly warm November night, the celebratory festivities continued, the sidewalks crowded with people of different races congratulating one another on the historic election of the first black president. People on the streets seemed excessively friendly with strangers, greeting them as if they had been lifelong acquaintances, asking over and over, "Can you believe we finally did it?"

It was exactly the same when I witnessed whites and blacks in Johannesburg, South Africa, in 1994, as Nelson Mandela campaigned to become the first black president of the Republic of South Africa.[3] The image of achieving a long-term goal, in both settings, galvanized our notions of reconciliation and provided a springboard toward new social interaction. As I drove home late on the night that Obama was elected president, contemplating the day's momentous events, I began to ponder what it all meant, to me personally, to blacks specifically, and for Americans generally. With respect to racial equality, would my life, would black people's lives, would the lives of whites be significantly different because a black had been elected to the highest political office? Yes, blacks had been brought to America as slaves;[4] yes, blacks had been terrorized after the Civil War and denied political rights; and yes, blacks had been segregated by law in housing, education, and social activities throughout the first half of the 20th century.[5] But now, at long last, a black had ascended to the most powerful government position. Surely, that would change the perception that Chief Justice Roger Taney referred to in 1857, that blacks were identified in the public mind with the slave population rather than the free population.[6] Yet, as I drove along those same streets that U.S. presidents travel on inaugural day, I questioned whether this historic election would bring monumental change. In 1872, Ulysses Grant was elected president in a landslide on a radical Republican platform that primarily involved a commitment to black equality.[7] Yet, less than fifteen years later, that commitment had completely vanished, and with it all hope for just treatment. As I continued driving along the inaugural route, I kept wondering if this election would be different or merely a rerun of 1872. The euphoria that comes with hope for change can be short-lived. Meaningful change requires concerted work, over many years.

With the election of Barack Obama, many conservative academics have suggested that America has entered a post-racial period. For example, John McWhorter reasons that "racism is not black people's main problem anymore. To say that is like saying the earth is flat. Are there racists? Yes. But not enough to keep a black family out of the White House."[8]

McWhorter expressed the view that minorities have made so much progress since the civil rights movement of the late 1950s and early 1960s that blacks should stop blaming discrimination as the primary cause of their lack of success. He reasons that America has entered a new period of race relations in which one's race ceases to be a significant factor in op-portunities and obstacles to success. McWhorter and I can disagree as to whether racism remains a serious obstacle to black success, yet racial dis-crimination significantly impacts all blacks, both the successful and the un-successful. There are many aspects of racism. For example, there is racism in the criminal justice system that results in racial profiling of all blacks. There is tipping-point bigotry in the housing market that stigmatizes all blacks when residential real estate is being purchased, and there is racism in perceptions of intellect and character irrespective of socioeconomic status.

Today's racial dynamic not only negatively impacts blacks; it also posi-tively impacts whites. It involves overvaluing the presence of whites in schools, neighborhoods, and employment. Perhaps liberal television com-mentator Stephen Colbert demonstrated it best with his blind black char-acter who is convinced he is white because of the way he is treated by po-lice who call him "sir."[9]

Richard Ford characterizes current racial inequality as "racism without racists" because the inequities are the result of history, not current bias.[10] While I agree with Ford that our history reflects serious racial discrimi-nation, I question any assertion that racial biases do not significantly im-pact the lives of most blacks in America today. The results of a 2008 study, published in Du Bois Review: Social Science Research on Race, demonstrate how racial bias continues to shape the perceptions of many Americans. For example, academics examined representative households in Chicago and Detroit. Subjects were provided a computer monitor and asked to view pictures depicting different neighborhoods. While the neighborhoods re-mained constant, the pictures were altered to manipulate their racial com-position to show either whites or blacks living in the neighborhood. Law-rence Bobo explained the study's implication of racial bias:

> The results clearly show that whites rated the neighborhood much more favorably when whites dominated the make-up. And the more negative the stereotypes a white individual held of [blacks] generally, the more likely they were to negatively rate the identical neighborhood with a vis-ible black presence. . . . Sadly, it was the race cues that mattered, not the class cues.[11]

Over the past four centuries Americans developed a way of thinking about race—a paradigm by which we perceive our society. The racial paradigm in

America is the framework of mental concepts by which whites and blacks perceive and interact with one another, and it consists of three interacting, mutually reinforcing components. The first is the misguided belief in both white superiority and black inferiority. The second is the practice of separating blacks from the rest of the American community. The final piece is the continuing victimization of blacks, both by whites and by blacks themselves, through overt and covert practices including race-neutral laws and policies that have a disproportionate negative impact on blacks. This book explores the systematic formation of the paradigm and how it persists today, and it offers resolution to finally move America beyond race.

White superiority refers to the attitude that is expressed in law and private actions under which whites are treated better than others simply because they are white. This must be considered as a distinct problem from the related problem of black inferiority, the attitude expressed in law and private actions whereby blacks are treated worse than others simply because they are black.

The subtle, but important, difference was exposed by the famous doll experiments relied on by the Supreme Court in Brown[12] to prove the negative impact of segregation on black children.[13] Scientifically conducted tests revealed that, given a choice, black children consistently preferred to play with white dolls over black dolls, and consistently characterized the white dolls as "good" and "beautiful" and the black dolls as "bad" and "ugly."[14] The patterns of association were so highly consistent that they indicated an ongoing mental construct of inferiority. The doll study revealed that what the black children observed and felt on a daily basis, in the environment of school segregation, had a profoundly damaging effect on their self-image.

In finding that separate was inherently unequal by focusing on the associations made by the black children, the Supreme Court in Brown made a bold move forward, but an incomplete one. The Court focused on the negative impact of Jim Crow segregation on the psyche of black children, but this landmark decision failed to address the other side of the issue. It failed to identify the problem in the "other classroom," the impact such segregation had on the psyches of white children.[15] Studies revealed that white children of the same age group also preferred the white doll.[16] Segregation fostered two psyches in America: a feeling of inferiority among blacks and a feeling of superiority among whites. These two effects maintained the deep-rooted racial divide, which is still seen today. The concepts are connected: practices that separate blacks from the rest of society, such as legal and extralegal segregation, foster notions of both black inferiority and white superiority. No matter how often blacks proclaim that "black is beautiful" and support black empowerment initiatives, fundamental fairness in opportunities will not exist without an equal embrace of such concepts by whites as well.

Many young whites now embrace the hip hop culture through purchases of music, fashion, and other products created, developed, and owned by black entrepreneurs. This empowerment is a positive step in reducing notions of racial hierarchy, yet it is vastly incomplete. Such black empowerment must extend throughout society through more than just a segment of the music and fashion industries. It must be extended to other segments of the economic arena as well as to the educational, employment, housing, and political arenas.

Up until the civil rights movement of the 1950s and '60s, racial isolation was enforced by Jim Crow segregation laws that mandated the separation of blacks in every form of social activity.[17] Today, this isolation is maintained by a wide range of private practices, such as tipping-point bigotry in housing actions whereby whites flee from racially integrated neighborhoods. This is also known as "white flight."[18] Housing separation leads to educational separation in which many black schoolchildren in America attend schools that are predominantly black.[19] The funding of public education through local property taxes exacerbates hierarchy notions as most predominantly black schools are significantly underfunded in comparison to predominantly white schools. Even in integrated schools, tracking programs preserve black separation and racial hierarchy by placing most black students in non-college-bound classes while many more white students are placed in college-preparatory programs.[20]

Isolation permits perceptions of white superiority and black inferiority to continue, as there is little opportunity, especially for children, to meet and interact with people who can defeat historic stereotypes. Moreover, the separation makes it easier for blacks to be victimized.

The victimization of blacks can occur through direct discrimination, such as racial profiling or blatant racist decisions,[21] and also through seemingly race-neutral practices. For example, drug laws, like crack cocaine versus powder cocaine sentencing guidelines,[22] disproportionately impact blacks,[23] resulting in excessive incarceration rates.[24] Voter identification laws disproportionately impact blacks, resulting in suppression of the black vote. The victimization of blacks can also be self-inflicted, however. It can be seen in black-on-black crime, perpetrated because it is easier to get away with and may carry less severe consequences if one is caught. It can also be witnessed in self-destructive practices such as failure to value education, a trend that reduces opportunities for economic advancement.

The victimization of blacks leads to a society where black excellence is muted and undervalued. This, in turn, strengthens the false perceptions of racial hierarchy. Moreover, many whites rely on these strengthened perceptions of black inferiority as justification for further isolating themselves from blacks.

Today's complex matrix of racial inequality evolved over four centuries. We cannot understand the complexities of these problems without knowing the laws that sanctioned them and the societal practices that maintained them. Today's inequality is not a natural consequence of human behavior but the result of systematically limited choices based upon racially discriminatory laws of the past and policies and practices of the present.[25]

While most conservatives acknowledge the racism of our past, they often suggest that the problem of racism has passed. History will show that, indeed, our thinking and laws as a society have evolved. Slavery and Jim Crow segregation are prohibited, discrimination in many aspects of life has been outlawed, and many people are willing to accept people of different races as individuals, not simply as members of stereotyped groups. Nonetheless, many racial presumptions of the past continue to be embraced by far too many. Moreover, the lingering effects of our racial paradigm continue to harm blacks and society as a whole. We look to the past in order to help us figure out a better future.

Desires for economic exploitation that fueled false notions of racial hierarchy when blacks first arrived in American colonies were enhanced in laws and cases for the next four centuries. The Reconstruction Amendments in 1865, 1868, and 1870, *Brown*[26] in 1954, and civil rights antidiscrimination laws in the 1960s led to some gains but did little to destroy false notions of racial hierarchy or to reduce black separation. This failure fueled black victimization and further strengthened the racial divide, creating the monster of our race problem today.

"We're Voting for the Nigger"

Almost four centuries after the initial arrival of blacks, in the 2008 Pennsylvania Democratic presidential primary, a campaign canvasser for Barack Obama knocked on the door of a house in Washington, Pennsylvania, and asked the white woman there whom she was voting for. After consultation with her husband, she responded, "We're voting for the nigger."[27]

The response of this voter reflects both the progress that has been made in racial relations and the problem that still remains. A black person can run for president, and a white person can openly use a degrading racist term to describe him. The fact that substantial numbers of whites were willing to vote for a black candidate for the highest political office[28] suggests that racism in the political arena is decreasing. Yet, the characterization of Obama as "the nigger," as well as other pejorative images of Obama, indicates that, for some whites, willingness to vote for a black candidate did not negate their negative views about blacks.

The reference to Obama as "the nigger" is profoundly disturbing. Not only is the term derogatory; it conveys a deep level of disrespect for blacks in general and for Obama specifically. The term is disrespectful to Obama in two ways. First, he is stripped of his personhood through the substitution of an inflammatory racial epithet for his name. Second, he is referred to by race rather than any aspect of his personality or qualifications. Instead of being described as "the senator from Illinois" or "the Democratic presidential candidate," Obama is reduced to the term most blacks view, when it is used in a derogatory way, as the most hurtful word in the English language.[29] Historically, when the term "nigger" was used by a white person, most blacks would perceive this as the equivalent of throwing the first punch in a fistfight.[30]

This reference also demonstrates how the racial paradigm thrives in the 21st century. It is very unlikely that any of Obama's political rivals would have been objectified by racial labels such as "honky" or "redneck," but it was business as usual for racial characterizations of black candidates, even by those favorably disposed to vote for that candidate. This approach, of whites addressing blacks by a derogatory term or in a less respectful way, has a long history in the law going back as far as the 17th century.[31] In most cases prior to the Civil War, blacks were referred to by their first names only, or with a descriptive term of "negress" or "negro," while the full Christian name of whites was applied.

For Americans to heal the racial divide, artificial notions of hierarchy, white desires for black separation, and policies and practices victimizing blacks must be examined with a critical and objective eye. If we are to end racial inequality, it is imperative that Americans recognize how these notions, desires, policies, and practices continue to manifest themselves.

The Complexities of Race in the 21st Century

There are two vastly different ways to view American racial progress today. One is captured by the picture of those closely involved in assisting Congresswoman Gabrielle Giffords after she was shot and seriously wounded in 2011. Immediately after the shooting, the white congresswoman was comforted by her Latino legislative intern, was operated on by an Asian American surgeon, and received expressions of concern from a black president.[32] This combination reflects the tremendous progress that has been made since the end of Jim Crow. Opportunities are available for minorities to attain success in all walks of life. There is, however, a second, less positive way to view American racial progress. This is captured by the shocking statistical evidence indicating the ever-present and widespread socioeconomic disparities between blacks and whites. Whether one focuses on the achievement gap, employment gap, income gap, or wealth gap, each is alarmingly wide today.

The 2010 United States Census results indicates that more than one out of every ten people classifies himself or herself as black.[33] According to the census, large urban centers, including Atlanta, Houston, Detroit, Baltimore, and Washington, DC, house more blacks than whites.[34] The population of blacks continues to increase in other cities such as Charlotte and Miami.[35] At the present rate of growth, blacks, coupled with other minorities, will outnumber whites in some states by 2050.[36] The increased population of nonwhites continues to have a major impact on political appointments of blacks to high-level government positions. America has seen its second black Supreme Court justice,[37] second black secretary of state,[38] and a black attorney general.[39] But, most importantly, America has elected its first black president.[40]

Many view these milestones in political representation as indicative of racial equality. Yet, despite advances over the last fifty years in educational achievement, financial success, and national leadership, there are still astonishing gaps in socioeconomic indicators that divide blacks from whites. National statistics reveal that 75% of whites graduate from high school compared to less than 60% of blacks.[41] The median net worth of whites is ten times that of blacks,[42] and blacks earn only 66% of what their white counterparts receive for performing the same jobs.[43] As late as 2005, whites still accounted for 98% of CEOs and 95% of top earners in Fortune 500 companies.[44]   Twenty-five percent of blacks and 40% of black children live in poverty, compared to 8% of whites and 13% of white children.[45]

Moreover, though blacks comprise more than 12% of the United States population, the Senate has no black members.[46] Mortality rates for blacks are substantially higher than those of whites.[47] Even in this modern age, blacks are more likely to be undereducated, impoverished, and politically powerless, and to die prematurely.

The causes of those racial disparities are widely debated and discussed. Conservative arguments tend to explain the root causes in terms of personal responsibility. Familiar stereotypes about intellectual, cultural, or moral failings of blacks are blamed for inequality. Some, like Charles Murray, author of *The Bell Curve*, cite genetic intellectual deficiencies in blacks.[48] Amy Wax, author of *Race, Wrongs, and Remedies*,[49] cites personal irresponsibility, and Juan Williams, in *Enough*, cites failed black political leadership.[50] Inadequacies in the American legal process that permit or encourage false notions of white superiority and black inferiority, as well as black separation resulting in victimization, have been overlooked or diminished. Misguided judicial decisions and federal, state, and local laws have played a significant role in the development and maintenance of these erroneous views that serve to reinforce and widen this racial divide. Laws can play a role in reproducing inequality, even when no racial classifications are specified. While exercising personal responsibility may lessen the negative consequences of such laws on an individual level, black responsibility alone will not eliminate America's racial disparities.

America's Racial Paradigm

Today's racial disparities are rooted in a long-standing paradigm dating back well before the creation of the Constitution in 1789. Discrimination and physical separation of blacks, legally and extralegally, not only has become enmeshed in our social fabric but has prevented us from eliminating racial disparities. The paradigm is one of false beliefs of white superiority at one end and black victimization at the other, created by racial hierarchy notions and sustained by physical isolation of the races. Each part of the paradigm is interdependent on the other, and if we are to destroy it, each aspect needs to be eradicated. Addressing only one part of the paradigm will not solve the problem. The causes of disparities have to be dealt with in their totality in order for America to move to true equality for all.

The erroneous white superiority concepts, created in 1619 and embedded in state and federal law before and after the Civil War, continue to influence race-based disparities. These laws, separating blacks from whites in social activities, mandating harsher criminal punishment for blacks, and denying employment and housing opportunities to blacks,[51] supported false notions of racial hierarchy and constrained racial progress. If we look at distinct episodes in American history, we see how progress toward racial equality is marred by periods of resistance and retreat. Colonial talk, in the latter 18th century, of building a new nation on the principles of liberty and equality meant little to the millions of blacks forced into chattel slavery. At the end of the 1800s, the promise of emancipation following the Civil War was cut short when the Supreme Court adopted a "separate but equal" theory of constitutional equality in *Plessy v. Ferguson*.[52] Homer Plessy was arrested for riding in a "whites only" portion of a railroad car. In his 1896 case, the Supreme Court sanctioned the Louisiana state law that segregated train cars and social activities in general.[53] In the decades following *Plessy*, weak enforcement by federal officials of antidiscrimination laws, in the face of massive resistance to desegregation initiatives by many state and local governments, allowed Jim Crow segregation to flourish. This remained true even after such behavior was ruled unconstitutional in *Brown*, in 1954.[54] In the late 20th century, just as the civil rights movement was beginning to show results through race-conscious affirmative action programs adopted by government and private entities in school admission and employment hiring, the Supreme Court erected a myth of color-blind constitutionalism, limiting the government's ability to redress all but the most blatant examples of discrimination.

The Court made correcting racial disparities much more difficult in a series of cases—beginning in 1974 with *Milliken v. Bradley*,[55] in which the Court invalidated a Detroit, Michigan, area school desegregation plan, in 2003 in *Gratz v. Bollinger*,[56] in which the Court invalidated a University of Michigan admissions program that took race into account, and in 2007 in *Parents Involved in Community Schools v. Seattle School District No. 1*,[57] in which the Court invalidated a Seattle, Washington, school district desegregation plan. The stringent standards the Court requires for the correction of racial disparities, including a compelling reason for governmental action and a good faith effort at nonracial methods before initiation of race-conscious programs, severely limited government options designed to achieve equality. As a result, the most effective affirmative action programs were invalidated, abandoned or weakened.

Recent speculation, therefore, about the end of racism must be viewed in light of our cyclical history. The separation of blacks and whites that occurred as a result of slavery remained through the enforcement of Jim Crow segregation. The white superiority and black inferiority notions embraced by slavery were reinforced by the denial of political rights to blacks, in the post-Reconstruction period, through various devices sanctioned by law. These devices included grandfather clauses, which mandated that blacks could not vote because their grandfathers did not vote, and literacy tests, which prevented blacks from voting because they could not read or write (activities punishable by death during slavery), or poll taxes, which denied blacks the franchise because they could not afford to pay a fee. In the 1960s, when the Voting Rights Act was passed allowing the federal government to enforce voting rights that had been previously denied to blacks by many states, the Supreme Court, through its formalistic approach to prohibiting race discrimination, prevented the government from exercising the same authority in creating black access in neighborhoods and schools. In this way, federal government antidiscrimination efforts helped blacks vote, but at the same time, Supreme Court decisions severely curtailed access to housing and education, arguably areas just as important to notions of racial hierarchy as voting had been. Thus, the paradigm remained intact. While Americans may imagine that every watershed event on racial equality is the first such occurrence, each is merely another step in a long, and often disappointing, process.

Establishing a Racially Imperfect Union

In the 1700s, the legal regime of colonial America expressly permitted one person to own another person and to have complete and unrestricted dominion over that person, including the power and ability to take that person's life. The institution of indentured servitude that originally applied in a race-neutral way, to blacks, American Indians, and whites, had changed by the time the Constitution was ratified in 1789, into a system of race-based slavery implicitly sanctioned by that Constitution.[58]

The first two stated goals at the outset of our country's identity-defining, foundational document were "to form a more perfect union" and "to establish justice."[59] Yet, for blacks, the union could be neither "more perfect" nor "just." The original Constitution, therefore, encompassed a paradox. It sought to establish justice, and yet it recognized no rights for the black segment of the population. It sought to insure tranquility, and yet it preserved oppression. At a time when American national identity was being articulated, one's racial status within America determined whether the Constitution delineated or denied one's rights.

Although there were hundreds, if not thousands, of hours of discussion and debate at the Constitutional Convention about slavery,[60] there was no direct mention of the words "slave" or "slavery" in the Constitution until the institution was abolished, seventy-six years later.[61] The original Constitution was an exercise in nondisclosure, intentionally sanctioning black slavery while studiously excluding the word "slavery" from the document.[62] To assure creation of a national union, there was an overwhelming consensus that the new federal government would sanction slavery as the previous government had done. However, the framers sought the most artful method to quietly maintain black oppression. The Constitution should not patently reveal the sanctioning of an institution being increasingly morally questioned elsewhere, such as in England, where the *Somersett* case of 1772 opposed the practice of slavery.[63]

While the Founding Fathers displayed tremendous courage in opposing British colonialism and oppression, those who were opposed to slavery and racial inequality demonstrated cowardice in signing a document that embraced a racial hierarchy and laid the foundation for centuries of racial inequality. The Constitution, then, codified into law the myth of white racial purity, even though many classified as "white" were of racially mixed heritage, and it subjected those deemed "black" to lifelong captivity. Over seventy-five years later, the Thirteenth, Fourteenth, and Fifteenth Amendments, adopted after the Civil War, guaranteed freedom, equality, and full citizenship to newly freed slaves,[64] but the promise of emancipation soon collapsed in the wake of race-based segregation and discrimination designed to maintain the antebellum status quo.

By the mid-19th century, racial segregation would require a means of identifying those who were white and those who were not based solely on physical appearance. A person of mixed-race ancestry could still be considered white under the law as long as he or she bore European features.[65] Following Reconstruction, however, increasingly restrictive racial classification laws allowed fewer mixed-race persons to "pass" for white. In 1910, Tennessee and Louisiana adopted the "one drop rule," which classified as nonwhite any person with any nonwhite heritage at all. Labeled as the "one drop rule" because any bit of "black blood," or nonwhite ancestry, would classify one as black,[66] this rule became more popular after slavery ended as a way to separate more mixed-race people and prevent them from receiving benefits being afforded whites. These benefits, such as voting rights and access to a quality public education, supplied the impetus for many individuals of mixed race who looked white to claim to be white, or "pass," as many at the time referred to this practice.

Separating Blacks

The concept of racial separation—physically dividing blacks from whites—has played a significant role in the paradigm since its beginning. Slaves were set apart in manual labor, performing tasks that whites did not desire to perform. Slaves were set apart in housing, residing in "slave quarters" on plantations where they labored. Slaves were denied any personal rights, including education and travel, and socialized among themselves on the plantation.

When slavery ended in 1865, physical separation of blacks was maintained through Jim Crow segregation laws that separated blacks in all aspects of life just as during slavery. From birth in hospitals to burial in cemeteries, blacks were physically kept apart from whites. Jim Crow laws guaranteed the maintenance of separation in housing, education, public accommodations, and social activities.

Whereas slave status was determined by the status of one's mother at the time of birth,[67] after slavery, physical separation of blacks depended upon one's racial classification. Thus, race classification became even more important to the maintenance of the racial paradigm since the "slave" designation for blacks was no longer valid. Rights and privileges that formerly were tied to free status were now tied to a white racial designation.

By 1896, when the Supreme Court issued its decision in *Plessy v. Ferguson,* endorsing racial separation as a federally sanctioned policy,[68] blacks had already been separated socially, denied political rights, and terrorized by violence. *Plessy* established the misleadingly named "separate but equal" doctrine.[69] In reality, the facilities provided for blacks were never close to being equivalent to those provided for whites. As other states adopted the doctrine, *Plessy* provided a catalyst for states to enforce segregation and inequality well beyond public accommodations.[70] Throughout subsequent decades, a variety of state and local laws injected rigid segregation and discrimination into every area of life.

After *Plessy*, segregation became so pervasive that it was imposed in every possible context: California prisons, Mississippi courtroom oath Bibles, windows in government buildings with scenic views in Tennessee, and Louisiana brothels.[71] Florida and North Carolina even prohibited white students from reading textbooks previously used by blacks, so that white students would not have to "soil" their hands.[72] In some cases, only blacks were separated from whites; in others, all minorities were kept separate. Sometimes minorities would be further segregated into subgroups, all depending upon where the line would best serve the racial hierarchy. Usually, the larger minority groups would be targeted. In southern states, blacks were singled out; in southwestern states, Latinos were the focus, and in Northern California, Asian Americans bore the brunt of segregation efforts. While most whites viewed Asian Americans, American Indians, and Latinos as superior to blacks, these minority groups were still characterized as inferior to whites to justify keeping them separate.[73]

Segregation laws, though widespread, often contained exceptions that allowed black servants to accompany, or to reside with, whites. For example, on the Louisiana train where Plessy was prevented from riding in one of the designated "white cars,"[74] black wet-nurses were welcomed.[75] A wet-nurse could be allowed in a white car because her job openly defined her subservient role in society. The exception allowing her presence thus preserved the systematic notion of white superiority. These exceptions exemplify how segregation statutes left room for racial interaction, but only on terms that benefited whites and confirmed their alleged superiority.[76]

Under such circumstances like the designated "white" train car in Plessy,[77] the presence of dependent blacks could be endured because it maintained the racial hierarchy. The presence of blacks as social equals, however, was unacceptable, for it significantly undermined false notions of racial hierarchy. These two sets of rules reveal that segregation reinforced a system of white dominance. "Together if unequal" rules of dominance and subservience maintained white superiority notions just as effectively as outright separation.

The legacy of Plessy persists today, through limited racial interaction imposed by tipping-point bigotry, where whites prevent blacks from moving into a neighborhood that already has a small percentage of black residents, or policies such as school tracking programs, where black students are disproportionately placed in lower academic programs incommensurate with their academic potential. The end result, whether in 1896 or today, is the same—interaction between blacks and whites is stifled or made more difficult, even if some blacks and whites desire such interaction.

Nothing but a Rerun

In 1954, the Supreme Court ruled, in *Brown,* that government-mandated separate schools for whites and blacks were inherently unequal because the very act of separating the races made the black children feel inferior.[78] The justices acknowledged that separation even in "equal" facilities was "inherently" unequal.[79]

As school desegregation was implemented, state by state, and open manifestations of Jim Crow segregation ended, physical separation of blacks was still maintained by de facto segregation. Whites chose to flee urban areas where most blacks resided for all-white suburban areas. Schools, churches, restaurants, and all other social activities were made up only of whites because no blacks resided in the area. Physical separation of blacks was maintained through choices by whites, keeping the racial paradigm intact.

Indeed since *Brown,*[80] high rates of unemployment,[81] underachievement in school,[82] business, and politics, high infant and adult mortality rates,[83] and high incarceration rates[84] have continued to plague blacks, sustaining and reinforcing false notions of black inferiority. Despite the increase in black politicians, professionals, entertainers, and executives, a racial divide continues to exist for most Americans because physical separation continues through de facto segregation. Moreover, along with policies and practices that fuel white superiority and black victimization, such as inequitable public school funding schemes, drug laws resulting in a racially disparate impact on incarceration rates for blacks, voter identification laws resulting in a racially disparate impact on voter participation rates for blacks, and political machinations like the denial of senatorial representation for the District of Columbia, perpetuate the paradigm. As a result, many black children see themselves as part of a community with higher rates of political underrepresentation, incarceration, illiteracy, unemployment, and poverty.[85]

Unfortunately, forty years after the Kerner Commission warned that the nation was "moving toward two societies, one black, one white—separate and unequal,"[86] America has still made no direct efforts to confront notions of racial hierarchy and isolation. While blacks no longer are made to feel inferior by overt discriminatory laws, too many whites choose to live, attend school, work, worship, and socialize in all-white, or predominantly white, environments. With few exceptions, whites tend to avoid black-dominated activities, communities, and institutions. As in the past, today the same messages of black inferiority and white superiority are being sent by whites who still desire isolation. Exacerbating this problem is the fact that many blacks, now able to live in integrated environments, choose to self-segregate as well. By limiting their contact with whites, these blacks also inhibit their own opportunities. Segregation is harmful whether it is externally imposed or self-inflicted. At the same time, some blacks exacerbate disparities when they reject upward mobility through education, thereby enhancing erroneous views of black inferiority.

Today, American law on racial equality is at a crossroads. Unfortunately, the Supreme Court's approach of simply eliminating government racial classifications cannot prevent false notions of racial hierarchy, racial isolation, or black victimization. Whites must eliminate notions of superiority to stop the cyclical process whereby racist thoughts and actions lead to disparities. Not only must whites stop discriminating against blacks; they must also stop white privilege.

On February 18, 2009, Attorney General Eric Holder, the first black to head the Justice Department, said, "On matters of race, we have been and continue to be a nation of cowards."[87] On race we are a nation of many things—heroes and villains, warriors and pacifists, healers and destroyers, dreamers and realists, fighters and cowards—but we can change our future. We do not have to be a nation that continues the racial cycle. We should not ignore the widespread inequities that exist today as we hid the existence of slavery in the Constitution some 220 years ago. This indeed would be cowardly. We must demonstrate courage and bring our racial disparities to light, identify the causes, and begin to implement changes that will bring about reform, ending the racial paradigm forever.

Summarizing the Racial Paradigm

In this book, I aim to expose the damaging effects of discrimination by analyzing the three interlocking aspects of the racial paradigm: false notions of white superiority and black inferiority, the practice of isolating whites and separating blacks, and victimization of blacks. We will see how the racial paradigm was formed, encompassing notions of white superiority and black inferiority, and how that mindset spread through society and led to the separation and victimization of blacks. The first part of this book explores our nation's early efforts to legitimize the insidious notions of racial hierarchy and separation. Part II delineates the harmful effects of these notions, particularly black victimization after the decision in *Brown*.[88] Part III discusses steps by which we can dismantle the paradigm and end racial injustice in America.

Chapter 1 delineates the development of racial categories and classifications, the basis of laws and policies that enforced discrimination for hundreds of years. Mixed ancestry was common in early American culture, and so the system of race classification, which has no biological basis, was an artificial construct, developed by society and enforced by law. Chapter 1 demonstrates how legal decisions promoted the notion that physical appearance defines racial classification, and thereby assigns slave status.

Chapter 2 explores ways in which whites maintained their dominance over blacks during the Reconstruction period after the Civil War. This chapter illustrates how the Reconstruction Amendments to the Constitution led to some initial gains and shows how these were almost completely eroded, especially in southern states.

Chapter 3 documents how separation of blacks was used as a way to prevent them from gaining social and economic opportunities. This chapter reveals the failures of the Supreme Court, in a series of cases, to establish "justice" in our "more perfect union."

Part II of the book explores the years following the *Brown*[89] decision, demonstrating how systematic separation was used to victimize blacks. In chapter 4, the cycle of racial isolation in education is explored in detail. Although the holding in *Brown*[90] helped states make progress toward equality in schools, it failed to challenge whites to examine their notions of superiority. Chapter 5 explores how notions of white superiority and black inferiority formed a systematic subordination in politics and the economy. Stereotyped images in our society reveal pervasive false notions of black inferiority and continue to associate blacks with illiteracy, unemployment, crime, sickness, poverty, homelessness, political powerlessness, and personal irresponsibility.

Part III of the book discusses steps by which we can combat the racial paradigm and challenges individuals, the government, and courts to take ownership of the issues. Whites can repent the misdeeds of the past and confront the reality of present-day discrimination. Blacks can evaluate their priorities and move toward honest, trusting dialogue with whites. We must work together to end victimization, address injustices, deflate and expel the racial paradigm, and move toward a society where we value our differences. Diversity can and should be a source of strength. Structured dialogue can mend the racial divide and diminish the paradigm by which it persists. The key to meaningful dialogue begins with an apology and recognition of the benefits and burdens of Jim Crow. An understanding of the truths of our past and present leads to a better future for all.

PART I

Creating the Paradigm

Racial Hierarchy

1

Constructing Racial Categories from the Nation's Founding to the Civil War

[A]ll of them [blacks] had been brought here as articles of merchandise. The number that had been emancipated at that time were but few in comparison with those held in slavery; and they were identified in the public mind with the race to which they belonged, and regarded as a part of the slave population rather than the free.

—Chief Justice Roger Taney, 1856[1]

RACIAL CATEGORIZATION HAS been an invaluable tool for facilitating aspects of the paradigm. Without such categorization, aspects of hierarchy and separation could not be implemented. Under the law, slaves had no personal legal rights, and free blacks received limited government protection.[2]

The perception of blacks as inferior has affected laws governing American citizenship and criminal jurisprudence since the colonial period. From 1619, white lawmakers have pondered the question, "What should we do with them?" When slaves went from being considered "property" to becoming free persons, the legal system failed to protect them. The transition from "property" to persons should have been supported by the Constitution, which purported to ensure the equality, freedom, and liberty of all men. The most fundamental law of the land endorsed slavery, unleashing a perception by many whites that blacks were subhuman beings of an inferior order.[3] That endorsement has left America still struggling with the most intransigent issues of racial inequality today. To understand this negative perception of blacks and the desire to identify and separate them, we must first recognize what motivations preceded it.

The Beginnings of Racial Division

The first blacks taken from the west coast of Africa to North America by whites arrived in Jamestown Colony, Virginia, in 1619.[4] The surviving record suggests that while some blacks in this period may have been slaves, others were treated like indentured servants who earned their freedom after converting to Christianity or laboring for a term of years.[5] Many blacks during the period shared the same status as indentured whites.[6]

The early formation of the colonies and the use of slave labor were intertwined. Slave law developed in a piecemeal fashion, adapting to the needs and expectations of white settlers looking to build their territorial conquest with cheap, expendable labor. As slaves became more numerous, colonial legislators saw the need to regulate the terms and conditions of slavery—denying slaves the right to contract or hold property and conditioning an owner's ability to grant freedom to a slave.[7]

Numerous statutory restrictions were imposed on owners who wanted to free their slaves.[8] In Virginia, for example, procedural requirements for freeing one's slave, known as manumission—typically, a signed writing, witnessed by two persons, and recorded at the local county courthouse—prevented some slaves from realizing the freedom their owners had intended to grant them.[9] Slaves unlucky enough to have been manumitted orally, with unrecorded documents, or without the requisite number of witnesses were often denied their freedom by the courts.[10]

In some states, those slaves successfully manumitted were required to leave the state.[11] There was one exception to this harsh rule. Slaves emancipated for "extraordinary merit"—generally, providing information about slave revolts—were permitted to remain in the state.[12] The most severe statutory restrictions on manumission, however, concerned creditors' rights and the children of slaves.[13] These issues were especially difficult for courts because they involved the rights of third parties.[14] Some state legislatures allowed manumitted slaves to be resold into slavery in order to satisfy any debts incurred by their former owner prior to the manumission, and many courts strictly enforced such legislation.[15] The result was that a manumitted slave's freedom was perpetually contingent upon the financial solvency of his owner, former owner, or former owner's estate.[16] For example, Virginia courts ordered freed slaves to be resold into slavery as long as twelve years after their manumission,[17] providing the debt of the former owner had been incurred prior to the act of manumission.[18]

These manumission rules perfectly illustrate the absolute dichotomy of power between blacks and whites. These rules reinforced the notions of superiority in whites and inferiority in blacks, as well as the perceived need for physical separation. White slave owners were perceived as so far superior to their black slaves that they possessed the ultimate power to change slave status to free status. Black slaves were entitled to no personal privileges, except those that their owner chose to grant. Slaves manumitted were required to leave the state, for their mere presence as free blacks undermined the racial hierarchy. The presence of free blacks suggested that blacks may have been able to obtain a certain equality of status with some whites. While they may not have been as wealthy or educated as their former owners, they nonetheless were free, just like whites in general. Only those free blacks valuable to maintaining the paradigm were permitted to remain in the state, thus the exemption for those slaves who helped to prevent slave revolts. For free blacks, physical separation became critical, for if they remained in the state and prospered, the paradigm would have been jeopardized.

To what extent conditions of indentured servitude in the early colonies differed from slavery is unclear. By law, indentured servants contracted their services in exchange for transportation, food, shelter, and wages for an established period of time.[19] In practice, however, indentured servants were often coerced—by force, violence, and rape—to labor under harsh conditions against their will.[20] Many died in bondage.[21] Life as an indentured servant thus bore many of the hallmarks of slavery, though at least it offered the prospect of eventual freedom and was experienced by both black and white servants.[22] Over time, however, the system evolved into a race-based program of hereditary lifetime bondage for blacks.[23] Disparate treatment became the norm, and with it, the strengthening of the attitude that blacks were inferior.

From the colonial period forward, white supporters of slavery perceived blacks as slaves, not servants. Indeed, well before the founders agreed to the "Great Compromise" at the Constitutional Convention, legally sanctioning black slavery, white colonists had already laid the groundwork by assigning social rights, responsibilities, and punishments on the basis of race. An attitude that disparate treatment was acceptable is evident in a series of cases where, in each, the severity of punishment seems directly correlated to race—blacks were punished severely and whites were not.

Such severe punishment meted out by the courts was the fate of John Punch, a black indentured servant from Virginia. Punch was captured in

1641 along with two white servants, James Gregory and a man named Victor, while trying to escape to freedom.[24] A Virginia judge sentenced each of the three men to a public whipping and added additional years to their servitude.[25] James and Victor, who were white, received an additional four years, but John Punch, who was black, received a lifetime indenture.[26] John Punch committed the same crime and shared the same indentured status as James Gregory and Victor, but only he received lifetime servitude.[27] The judge did not provide an explanation, but the record suggests that the defendants were similar in every respect except race.

Singling out blacks for significantly harsher treatment would have probably emboldened impoverished whites by affirming their superior legal and social status over blacks, with whom they otherwise shared profound economic hardship. Poor whites were thus encouraged to bond with the merchant class on the basis of race,[28] instead of bonding with poor blacks on the basis of their socioeconomic class. This strategy served the economic interests of upper-class whites by uniting poor whites around a single cause—their racial superiority to blacks.[29] Whites living in poverty had less incentive to challenge their exploitation by an economic system that simultaneously disadvantaged black and white workers. Thus, a cycle began: white acceptance of racially disparate sentencing led whites to distance themselves from blacks. The separation reinforced social attitudes of segregation, which, in turn, led to more instances of disparate sentencing.

The more blacks and whites became increasingly isolated, both physically and socially, the more foreign each group became to the other. Negative stereotypes of each group by the other flourished, differences were magnified, and commonalities diminished. The more foreign each group became to the other, the more critical became the necessity to maintain physical and social separation, to prevent those differences from negatively affecting whites. Thus, legislation and case decisions reinforced the notion that racial divisions were more significant and inviolable than other divisions based on ethnicity, class, or religion. This focus on racial divisions influenced the evolution of law, which began to reflect racial divisions throughout the colonial period.[30]

Over the next century, colonists began to enact statutory laws that codified racial hierarchy, reinforcing common law decisions such as the one in Punch. They also formally tied social status to race by disregarding most legal distinctions between free and enslaved blacks.

Free blacks were treated harshly.[31] They were denied political, economic, and social rights under the law and, in most instances, were prohibited from interracial marriage or participation in the political process.[32] Even in the most progressive states, such as Pennsylvania, some free blacks, like William Fogg in 1837, who attempted to vote, were threatened, beaten, or killed.[33] They were prohibited from obtaining an education, from engaging in certain types of employment, and from enjoying certain kinds of property ownership.[34] Their travel was restricted, and they were required to pay extra taxes.[35] Finally, schools, churches, and public accommodations were subject to de jure racial segregation.[36] Flagrant segregation, by law, was widely practiced and unreservedly upheld, with judgments based solely on race, not on slave status. Statutes that defined racial classifications regulating the conduct of free blacks illustrate this dynamic.

Race classification provisions prior to the Civil War clearly embraced white superiority and were created to distribute political and economic rights. This system applied to free people, not slaves, and three major categories existed: white, American Indian, and black/mulatto, with whites on top of a hierarchal classification model and blacks on the bottom.[37] For example, in 1705, the Virginia legislature barred mulattos, blacks, American Indians, and criminals from holding "any office, ecclesiastical, civil or military, [or] of be[ing] in any place of public trust or power."[38] The mixed-race individuals defined as mulatto under the statute were "the child of an Indian, or the child, grandchild, or great grandchild of a Negro."[39] Whites had distinct legal advantages, but mulattos had no greater rights than blacks. Thus, the critical line of distinction was between whites and mulattos, not between blacks and mulattos. The fact that some people were classified as mulatto, rather than as black, seems to have been simply a matter of recognizing their visible differences in skin color.

The 1705 statute defines "mulatto" on the basis of racial proportions within one's ancestry.[40] A person with one American Indian parent and one white parent was a mulatto.[41] Someone with one American Indian grandparent and three white grandparents was, by implication, legally white and not barred from public office under the statute.[42] For black-white mixtures, it took two additional generations to diminish the effect of "black" blood to the point that it was legally insignificant.[43] A person with a single black grandparent or even a single black great-grandparent was still considered a mulatto.[44] The statute reveals the notion that remote black heritage still made an indelible stamp on one's status.[45] Moreover, the statute equated white criminals with law-abiding blacks, since it prohibited both from holding high political office.[46]

Free Blacks and Shades of Freedom

Free blacks shared the same formal status as whites, though they were treated, in many respects, much more harshly. While discrimination against free blacks occurred prior to the American Revolution in 1776, the big impetus came after the Constitution was created in 1789.[47] The combination of permitting blacks to be enslaved while at the same time proclaiming that "all men are created equal" unleashed states to pass a bevy of laws separating and restricting blacks.[48] Slaveholding states banished most free blacks from their jurisdictions, forbade them from assembling even in small groups, and prohibited them from owning firearms.[49] A Maryland law, passed in 1804, forbidding slaves from "strolling the streets at night, or frequenting the houses of persons other than their masters without permission," was applied against free blacks, who found themselves "subject to a moderate whipping" if caught breaking curfew.[50] Neither slaves nor free blacks were permitted to read or write in Georgia and other slave states. North Carolina even made it a crime for blacks to preach the gospel, fearing that black preachers would challenge the narrative of Christianity endorsed by whites—one that promised everlasting salvation to obedient and submissive slaves.[51]

Laws regulating free blacks discouraged them from plotting with slaves, while other laws reinforced the presumption of black inferiority. In many states, blacks could not testify against whites in a courtroom,[52] though whites could testify against blacks, and free blacks in North Carolina could buy or sell goods only in their own neighborhoods, unless they had a license.[53] Criminal codes were especially harsh. A black man who struck a white man in Mississippi was likely to have his ear chopped off.[54] In Louisiana, he might lose a foot.[55] Whites convicted of the same offense against another white or against a black were punished less severely, as were blacks convicted of this offense against other blacks.[56] These laws reinforced the racial hierarchy by demoralizing free blacks whose newly defined legal status challenged the notion of black inferiority.

Free blacks were constantly in jeopardy of being legally redefined as slaves. In Maryland, free blacks were peremptorily declared slaves under a statute passed in 1664.[57] That same statute also enslaved black children born to free women.[58] Most states, however, fashioned slave inheritance rules on the basis of maternal status. Racial identity statutes and slave inheritance laws were designed to propagate slaveholdings and reinforce the enslavement of persons who fit the presiding legal definition of "black." There was, of course, a significant likelihood that persons entitled to freedom under a slave inheritance statute would be unable to verify their status. When a purported slaveholder claimed ownership of such persons in a court of law, common law judges bore the responsibility of adjudicating the claim and establishing the rules of procedure for settling the dispute.

In 1806, for example, the Virginia court in *Hudgins v. Wright* heard a freedom suit brought by three mixed-race slave women whose owner threatened to "send them out of the State."[59] The case involved an American Indian woman named Wright, who sued her owner, Hudgins, for holding her, and several members of her immediate family, illegally as slaves.[60] Several facts were established at trial. First, the complexion, hair texture, and eye color of Wright's granddaughter (one of the plaintiffs) were shown to be "the same with those of whites."[61] Second, evidence at trial indicated that Wright's genealogy was traceable through the maternal line to an American Indian called Butterwood Nan.[62] Witnesses testified that Butterwood Nan's daughter, Hannah, had long black hair and a copper-colored complexion and was known in her community as being American Indian.[63] The legal question involved which party bore the burden of proof in the case—the litigants asserting their freedom on the ground that they descended from a free woman, or the defendant seeking to establish ownership over the women on the basis of their maternal slave ancestry.[64] Of all the statements in the case, it was Judge Tucker's concurring opinion that most clearly equates slavery with race and inferiority with blackness:

> Suppose three persons, a black or mulatto man or woman with a flat nose and woolly head; a copper-coloured person with long jetty black, straight hair; and one with a fair complexion, brown hair, not woolly nor inclining thereto, with a prominent *Roman* nose, were brought together before a Judge upon a writ of *Habeas Corpus*, on the ground of false imprisonment and detention in slavery: that the only evidence which the person detaining them in his custody could produce was an authenticated bill of sale from another person, and that the parties themselves were unable to produce any evidence concerning themselves, whence they came. How must a Judge act in such a case? I answer he must . . . discharge the white person and the *Indian* out of custody . . . and he must redeliver the black or mulatto person, with the flat nose and woolly hair to the person claiming to hold him or her as a slave.[65]

With this decision, Judge Tucker decreed that physical appearance determines racial classification, consequently establishing an indelible connection between race and slavery. Those who had flat noses and woolly hair were black; those with prominent Roman noses were white. But racial identity in antebellum Virginia was not so neat and tidy. Europeans, Africans, and American Indians had been mixing for over two centuries, producing offspring of varied features and complexions.[66] Racial identity was a more complicated endeavor than Judge Tucker proposed. Tucker created an artificially simplistic system of categorization embraced by those seeking a simple mechanism by which to assign race and enforce slavery.

Second, Judge Tucker's legal presumption held that litigants who physically appeared black were slaves. More than twenty thousand free blacks resided in Virginia at the time, yet Judge Tucker denied each of them the promise proclaimed by the Virginia Bill of Rights, "[t]hat all men are by nature equally free."[67] The ruling put many of these twenty thousand free blacks at risk of reenslavement. In *Hudgins*, the court implicitly rejected the traditional presumption in favor of liberty for all persons, replacing it with a presumption in favor of slavery for those with African features. Whites or "copper-coloured person[s] with long jetty black, straight hair,"[68] referring to American Indians, were presumed to be free. Accordingly, the burden always fell upon the black person to disprove the claim of an owner's right to enslave. Such a burden was impossible for most blacks with legitimate freedom claims to meet because of the difficulty of acquiring the documentation and testimony necessary to defeat this presumption. Moreover, these blacks would be subject to the provisions of Virginia law governing lawsuits by free persons illegally held as slaves.[69] These provisions were extremely favorable to slave owners and placed burdens inconsistent with notions of due process provided to white Virginians under the Virginia Bill of Rights.

The Freedom Suit Act required a petitioner to present himself or herself to a magistrate at the county court, and the magistrate would then summon the apparent owner to answer the complaint.[70] By requiring the freedom suit petitioner to present himself or herself at the courthouse, the 1795 act effectively asked slaves to obtain their masters' consent to be sued.[71] Recognizing the coercive power of owners to impede further proceedings, the law compelled a slaveholder to provide a deposit equal to the value of the alleged slave as a guarantee that he or she would allow the claimant to appear at the next court session.[72] If the owner refused to provide the deposit, the court held the petitioner and charged the owner for its expenses in holding the slave.[73] The primary purpose of the Freedom Suit Act, then, appears not to have been to facilitate freedom suits but to protect slaveholders and localities against the expense of legitimate requests for freedom by blacks.

Although similar in theory, freedom suits were not the same as habeas corpus suits.[74] The underlying rules of law and remedies available differed between the two types of claims. Habeas corpus actions were filed as real wrongful incarceration claims based on an invasion of existing legal rights.[75] Freedom suits were essentially fictitious actions in trespass, false imprisonment, or assault and battery—"fictitious" because at the time the suit was initiated the slave had no protected legal rights.[76] A freedom suit was based on the rights of the slave owner, not the slave.[77] During a freedom suit, the slave remained a slave subject to the complete control of his or her owner, limited only by the requirements necessary for resolution of the case.[78] A writ of habeas corpus, however, was available to a free person to restrain any further invasion of his or her rights.[79] Thus, in freedom suits, judges applied rules that favored slave owner defendants.[80] As a result, black slaves received considerably less protection in freedom suits than white persons who claimed wrongful incarceration in habeas corpus actions.[81]

Perhaps the most astonishing part of the Freedom Suit Act was its punishment provision. The Virginia legislature took great care to discourage abolitionists from exploiting the law by penalizing all persons who aided a slave in a freedom suit that failed.[82] The 1795 statute provided that "if any person aid or abet any person in such a claim for freedom and the claim is not established, he shall forfeit $100 to the owner of the slave."[83] The risk of losing a freedom suit was thus harsh not only for black slaves but also for whites who lent monetary or emotional support to that effort. Moreover, the legislature made clear its allegiances by determining that individual slave owners—not the state or the court—should collect the fine for frivolous suits. Such provisions indicate the seriousness with which the legislature took such challenges. Slaves—even illegally held ones—were property first, and consequently could expect very little aid or process from the law. What process they did receive was incidental to those safeguards the state provided owners in protecting valuable assets.

Under *Hudgins*, Virginia law presumed blacks were slaves, denoting their status as objects even when, in fact, they were free.[84] Judge Tucker undercut even the provisions in the statute that contemplated some mixed-race individuals as free, because they descended from either a white woman or a free black or mulatto female. Judges throughout the 19th century followed Judge Tucker's lead, creating presumptions of enslavement and other devices for limiting black freedom. These cases reinforced a subordinate role for blacks in American society, and in so doing, created a superior role for whites. This social construct of white privilege is unmistakably seen in the words of one South Carolina judge in 1836: "A slave cannot be a white man."[85]

Six years later, in *Prigg v. Pennsylvania*,[86] the Supreme Court reinforced the reasoning of *Hudgins*—that blacks located in slave states were presumed to be slaves.[87] The case revolved around a Maryland slave couple's daughter, who had never herself been previously claimed as a slave, and her children.[88] The woman had married a free black and moved to Pennsylvania, a free state, where some of her children were born.[89] After residing in Pennsylvania for five years, descendants of her parents' owner sought to have her and the children returned to Maryland.[90] Although the offspring's agent, Edward Prigg, obtained a warrant for arrest, the Pennsylvania court refused to provide a certificate for removal.[91] Prigg, nonetheless, took the woman and her children in violation of the state law.[92] Prigg was convicted and appealed to the Supreme Court.[93] The Supreme Court held that the federal Fugitive Slave Act was constitutional, the Pennsylvania antislave law was invalid, and private initiatives by slave owners to recapture fugitive slaves were permissible.[94]

For all practical purposes, the Supreme Court's ruling in *Prigg* provided an invitation for whites to kidnap free blacks, since so few blacks could rebut the presumption against freedom with appropriate documentation or witness testimony. On a national level, *Prigg* stood for the Supreme Court legitimizing kidnapping of free blacks through the intermingling of status and race.

Free blacks who were kidnapped and sold into slavery suffered years in bondage awaiting the freedom only a miracle was likely to deliver. Such was the fate of Solomon Northup, born in 1808 in New York, a free state, two years after *Hudgins* was decided.[95] Northup's father, though black and born into slavery, was able to accumulate enough property under a New York state law to earn his freedom and to marry a free black woman.[96] Both of Northup's parents were free, and therefore, Northup was born free. During his youth, he learned farming and carpentry as trades.[97] He was also an exceptional violin player.[98] In 1841, two white men, Merrill Brown and Abram Hamilton, convinced Northup to accompany them to Washington, DC, where they promised him work as a fiddle-playing circus performer.[99] Upon arriving in DC, however, Brown and Hamilton drugged Northup and sold him to a local slave trader.[100] The next day, Northup found himself chained in a holding facility waiting to be sold to the highest bidder.[101] For several years, Northup's friends and family searched for him in vain.[102] It was not until 1852, while enslaved on a cotton plantation in Louisiana, that Northup, with the help of a sympathetic abolitionist, succeeded in getting a letter to New York alerting his wife, Anne, to the kidnapping and enslavement.[103] New York happened to be one of the few states that allowed for the recovery of illegally enslaved free citizens.[104] At Anne's insistence, the governor intervened and succeeded in convincing the state Supreme Court in Louisiana to honor a writ demanding Northup's freedom.[105] Northup was returned to freedom, but only after twelve years apart from his family laboring as a slave.[106] Twelve years of his life had been stolen, and yet he was one of the lucky ones, because the federal government refused to protect kidnapped slaves, and federal laws made it difficult for states to do so. Thousands of free blacks, unlike Northup, remained illegally enslaved for the rest of their lives.

No Rights for Black Slaves

Life was mercilessly harsh for slaves. Unlike other societies throughout history that accorded slaves' varying degrees of rights, under American law, the slave owner possessed complete dominion over the slave. The owner was free to engage in any measure of oppressive practice against those held in bondage. For most slaves that meant long hours of arduous labor, minimal food and shelter, separation from parents or children, and physical beatings.[107] In addition, male owners often raped their female slaves.[108]

In June of 1855, a black woman named Celia killed a man for whom she worked as a slave and with whom she had been forced to have a sexual relationship for several years.[109] Celia killed him because, despite her numerous attempts to dissuade him, slave owner Robert Newsom forcibly and repeatedly sought to have and did have sexual intercourse with her.[110] Celia was convicted of murder in a Missouri trial court and subsequently hanged.[111] Her defense of justification, based on the fact that she was resisting an attempted rape, was rejected by the trial court.[112] The judge ruled that Celia was not entitled to resist the sexual advances of her owner due to her status as a slave.[113] As property of her slave owner, she had no rights of her own, including no right to defend her own well-being.[114]

It is important to remember that at the outbreak of the American Revolution in 1776, slavery existed in all thirteen colonies.[115] The prospect of being kidnapped into slavery was not a matter of concern for the majority of blacks; they were already held in bondage prior to the Civil War. The specter of inhumane treatment, however, did have an effect on them. Physical punishment, mutilation, and death threats proved to be effective weapons for slaveholders intent on coercing slaves into obedience and submission.[116]

Slaves had little recourse against the punishments of sadistic slave owners. To maintain submission of slaves, plantations were ruled by terror. Whippings and other physical cruelty constituted the ultimate form of punishment, and avoiding such treatment was a high priority for most slaves. Thus, even for slaves treated humanely, the threat to them, or to their children, of being torn from their slave community and sold to a more sadistic owner was enough to coerce obedience.

Submission was also enforced by the breaking up of families and social groups. For blacks, the family unit had always been a critical part of the social fabric, in Africa as free persons and in America as slaves. One of the cruelest aspects of slavery was that families on the same plantation often were broken up when owners sold family members to different owners.[117] Black mothers and fathers were traumatized by the sale of their children to owners in distant and remote locations.[118] Often, freed slaves would search for years to reunite with family members.[119] Even for those slaves who were lucky enough to find their families and able to reunite with them, the scars of slavery could be everlasting.

Enforced ignorance via bans to education furthered inferiority. Every southern state before the Civil War, with the exception of Tennessee, prohibited the education of slaves.[120] As a result, illiteracy topped 90% among the South's black population in 1860.[121] Some slaves did, however, learn to read or write through their own efforts.[122] Others received tutoring, in violation of the law, from slave owners who desired, out of either sympathy or economic interest, to promote learning and literacy among their slaves.[123] This is especially true where slave education would benefit whites such as house slaves working close to white women or plantation slaves given administrative responsibility over field operations.[124]

For the most part, however, whites preferred their slaves ignorant and uneducated. "It is a saying among the masters," one former slave wrote, "the bigger fool the better nigger. Hence all knowledge, except what pertains to work, is systematically kept from the field-slaves."[125] This attitude, openly embraced by white slave owners, reveals how education policy systematically propagated inferiority and dependence. The inability to read or write kept blacks subservient to whites by discouraging self-sufficiency. Illiteracy severely limited long-distance communication, making it difficult for slaves to organize revolts or escape with the help of blacks from neighboring plantations and also limited contact with far-flung family members. Educational impoverishment also fed the paternalistic narrative of slavery as an institution by which whites civilized otherwise hapless and helpless blacks.

Maintaining the Black/Slave Category

Through the 19th century, several legislative compromises attempted to define the balance between slavery and freedom in the states and territories. The Missouri Compromise of 1820 prohibited the introduction of slavery in the Louisiana territory above the line of latitude of 36 degrees, 30 minutes, while admitting Missouri as a slave state.[126] From the year 1820 on, in spite of the Missouri Compromise, slave states in the South vigorously attempted to secure new land and to expand their economic and political power.[127]

Opposition to the expansion of slavery, particularly among western settlers, was not founded on moral objections to slavery; rather, early settlers opposed competition with slave labor and many held contempt for blacks, whether free or slave.[128] Republicans in the 1840s and 1850s considered that the institution of slavery posed a threat to society. Yet, many still felt that association with any blacks degraded the white race.[129]

Prior to the Civil War, especially in the southern states, whites maintained absolute control over all social, political, and legal aspects of society. With the partial exception of the New England states, evidence indicates that up to the outbreak of the Civil War, and in fact through the outbreak of World War II, the dominant theme of American history, in the North and the South, was that this nation should be under the absolute control and dominance of whites—a government of white men in which blacks would occupy an inferior and subjugated position. In the South, slavery ensured dominance by whites. Conversely, in the western states, the prohibition of slavery was viewed as the best means of preserving white dominance by keeping blacks away altogether.[130] Legal equality for blacks did not exist.[131] Against the pervasive reality of white dominance, throughout the country, in which blacks were viewed as being fit only for slavery in the South,[132] the Supreme Court considered the questions presented by the *Dred Scott v. Sandford* case concerning the status of blacks and the expansion of slavery.[133]

The Supreme Court decision in *Dred Scott* ended any doubt that blacks and whites were viewed differently under American law, even though abolition of slavery in some states permitted free blacks to receive some rights and privileges such as voting and schooling.[134] The ruling in *Dred Scott* affirmed that blacks, even free ones, were perceived to be both different from whites and inferior to whites.[135]

On March 6, 1857, Chief Justice Roger Taney authored the Supreme Court's opinion declaring that it had no jurisdiction to hear Dred Scott's claim to freedom because he was black and, therefore, not a citizen of the United States.[136] The case had been set in motion almost twenty-five years earlier, when Dr. John Emerson, a physician in the United States Army, voluntarily took his slave, Dred Scott, from Missouri, a slave state, to the free state of Illinois.[137] After returning to Missouri, Scott filed suit claiming that by virtue of his time in Illinois, he had become a free person consistent with Illinois law.[138] In holding against Scott, Taney reasoned that residence in a free state did not automatically eliminate slave status.[139] That determination was left to the state having jurisdiction over the trial, and Missouri had already determined that, despite his stay in Illinois, Scott was still a slave.[140]

Dred Scott's legacy lies in the Supreme Court's determination that blacks, whether slave or free, were not citizens, and therefore were not entitled to constitutional protection.[141] Despite being born in the United States, possessing citizenship in a free state, or having served in the United States Armed Forces, blacks were viewed by the majority of justices as belonging to an "unfortunate race"[142]—unfortunate because, Taney reasoned, blacks were viewed by the Founding Fathers as socially and legally inferior to whites.[143] Accordingly, Scott's color, not his free status, determined his rights under the law. Whether slave or free, Taney declared blacks to be "so far inferior, that they had no rights which the White man was bound to respect."[144]

The *Dred Scott* decision embraced the racial paradigm by lumping free blacks and slaves together. Scott did not argue that slaves had rights. He argued that free blacks had rights and that he was free by virtue of having been brought voluntarily by his owner to a free state.[145] Scott viewed his transportation to a free state as an act of manumission, since Dr. Emerson had knowledge of Illinois law prohibiting slavery when he brought Scott to Illinois.[146] The Court ignored this argument, claiming that it did not matter whether Scott was slave or free because he was black.[147] Blackness, not slave status, was the mark of inferiority, thus making Scott unprotected by the Constitution.[148] Without providing any data, Taney concluded that it was universally recognized among civilized men that blacks were inferior.[149]

Taney began his opinion by linking all blacks, whether slave or free, to slavery.[150] He posed the question presented to the Court in the following way: "The question is simply this: Can a negro, whose ancestors were imported into this country, and sold as slaves, become a member of the political community formed and brought into existence by the Constitution of the United States . . . ?"[151] By formulating the question in this way, Chief Justice Taney drew the dividing line between blacks and whites, not between slaves and free persons, thus making it more difficult for Scott to win. As a slave, Scott's chances of winning were significantly lessened, for the justices would have had to go against the intent of the framers in sanctioning slavery, and rule on natural law grounds, rarely relied upon, that slavery was immoral. The justices could have easily reasoned, on the basis of precedent, that Scott, as a free person, had rights and privileges just like whites. Drawing the line on the basis of race rather than slave status allowed Taney to place free blacks with slaves, thus denying all blacks any constitutional rights.

To justify this conclusion, however, Taney had to make clear that blackness was the indicator of inferiority. He did so with twenty-one references to blacks as inferior and whites as superior.[152] These references indicated that blacks were inferior not because they were slaves but because they were black. Blacks were an "unfortunate race,"[153] an "inferior class of beings,"[154] and a "degraded" group[155] in Taney's racial order. Slavery was the appropriate place for such inferior beings, but even if blacks were free, they must be differentiated from whites through a racial classification scheme to put them in their proper place.

The twin pillars of the racial paradigm of white superiority/black inferiority and black separation began with the construction of racial categories subsequently sanctioned by the Constitution. The white category and the black category were defined differently—with political, monetary, and social privileges accompanying those classified in the white category, and slavery and a denial of personal rights to those classified in the black category. Differentiation in the rights and privileges between the two categories was appropriate because, in Chief Justice Taney's view, as well as many others', blacks were inferior to whites and not entitled to the same benefits.

Emancipation without Equality

As we have seen, prior to slavery's end in 1865, blacks were viewed by some of the Founding Fathers, by many white legislators, and by a majority of the members of the Supreme Court as inferior to whites. Slavery allowed blacks to be placed in an appropriate institution on the basis of their perceived inferiority. When some of those blacks became free, racial categories were created so that free blacks could remain in an appropriate inferior placement. Abraham Lincoln, who was a presidential candidate at the time of the *Dred Scott* ruling, said that the opinion made it seem that "[a]ll the powers of earth"[156] were combining against the black person, and "now they have him, as it were, bolted in with a lock of a hundred keys, which can never be unlocked without the concurrence of every key; the keys in the hands of a hundred different men, and they scattered to a hundred different and distant places. . . ."[157] In 1860, Lincoln was elected president, the first Republican to win the office and the first from a political party opposed to slavery.[158] On January 1, 1863, with the issuance of the Emancipation Proclamation executive order freeing slaves in territory held or controlled by the Confederacy, abolition became a formal part of Lincoln's federal policy.[159] Yet, just as with many northern states in the decades following the signing of the Constitution in 1789, the ending of slavery did not mean the demise of white superiority/black inferiority. On the contrary, the federal government under Lincoln maintained racial separation practices for free blacks, even those who served in the military.

During the Civil War, 186,000 blacks served in the Union Army.[160] Most fought as infantry, receiving less pay than white soldiers, but a few served in cavalry or artillery units.[161] As a rule, these blacks served in segregated units as the United States Colored Troops commanded by white officers, although a few blacks did become noncommissioned officers.[162] These few black officers did not command white troops.[163]

This military arrangement reflected the racial paradigm—free black soldiers had to be separated from white soldiers and commanded by white officers. Blacks were falsely perceived as inferior soldiers who could not be relied upon to make command decisions. Many white officers who commanded black troops viewed them as inferior to white troops. As one white Union officer put it, "There was as much of the soldier visible in the former slave as there was of an angel in a block of marble awaiting the touch of Michelangelo's chisel."[164] The military rules, even after Lincoln issued the Emancipation Proclamation, continued the racial paradigm perfectly.

While Lincoln evolved in his views on race and racial equality throughout his presidency, in 1858, candidate Lincoln explained,

I am not, nor ever have been in favor of bringing about in any way the social and political equality of the white and black races . . . I am not nor ever have been in favor of making voters or jurors of negroes, nor of qualifying them to hold office, nor to intermarry with white people; and I will say in addition to this that there is a physical difference between the white and black races which I believe will forever forbid the two races living together on terms of social and political equality. And inasmuch as they cannot so live, while they do remain together there must be the position of superior and inferior, and I as much as any other man am in favor of having the superior position assigned to the white race.[165]

Against this legal and social backdrop, blacks found themselves arrested, kidnapped, beaten, and enslaved due to physical characteristics of blackness.[166] The deep history and reach of racial profiling in the United States, reinforced and justified by the courts, legitimized this racial dynamic.

Thus, it is not surprising that on July 13, 1863, as the Civil War waged on some seven months after President Lincoln issued the Emancipation Proclamation[167] freeing all slaves in Confederate territory, white rioters in New York City targeted blacks as the cause of their economic and social problems.[168] Upset by challenges resulting from the war and imposition of the country's first conscription law requiring military service, thousands of whites demonstrated their anger with violence.[169] The bulk of those injured or killed were black, reflecting the racial focus of the rioters' rage. The *New York Times* described one particularly heinous act committed by the white rioters at the Orphan Asylum for Colored Children:

Hundreds, and perhaps thousands of the rioters, the majority of whom were women and children, entered the premises, and in the most excited and violent manner they ransacked and plundered the building from cellar to garret. . . . In it there are on an average 600 or 800 homeless colored orphans. . . .

. . . It hardly seems credible, yet it is nevertheless true, that there were dozens of men, or rather fiends, among the crowd who gathered around the poor children and cried out, "Murder the d——d monkeys," "Wring the necks of the d——d Lincolnites," etc. Had it not been for the courageous conduct of [several New York City firemen who rescued the children], there is little doubt that many, and perhaps all of those helpless children, would have been murdered in cold blood.[170]

Conclusion

During the early days of our nation, the hierarchal system of racial classification entrenched notions of white superiority and black inferiority.
Pivotal cases defined black inferiority as a legal construct, galvanizing the
notions already embraced by society. The racial paradigm pervaded society and was sanctioned by law. Discriminatory laws against free blacks and
denial of personal rights to enslaved blacks further reinforced the racial hierarchy and paved the way for violence against blacks who attempted to
exercise political rights during the Reconstruction period and who refused
to be separated during the Jim Crow period. The racial hierarchy and rampant violence against blacks melded together as a paradigm, a lens through
which whites could continuously assert superiority over blacks.

The germinal ruling in *Punch* in 1641 set the precedent for racial disparity that reverberated in subsequent cases, thrived under Jim Crow laws,
and persists in present-day America.

2

Maintaining White Dominance during Reconstruction

"This civil rights bill . . . is trifling. You talk about giving these [black] people the right to go to the theater, when there is not one of them in a hundred who knows what they are."

—Representative James Blount of Georgia, 1875[1]

AFTER THE CIVIL War, slavery ended in name only. Black servitude continued, as vagrancy laws and laws governing black apprentices were clever strategies to perpetuate slavery. Sharecropping and strategies to reduce black field hands to economic dependency precluded a genuine free labor system. The Civil War may have ended formal slavery, but it also set in motion a new racial schism of white superiority/black inferiority and black separation. The period between the end of the Civil War in 1865 and the end of Reconstruction at the turn of the 19th century reflected the initiation of white resistance to government efforts to reduce racial inequality. While slavery's demise would require new institutions and mechanisms to ensure maintenance of the three cornerstones of the paradigm, white superiority/black inferiority, black separation, and black victimization would continue, primarily through massive white resistance to change. At the end of the Civil War, supporters of the Confederacy were even more committed to ensuring that whites maintained the same level of privileges. Courts in southern states had endorsed notions of white superiority in cases like *Mann*,[2] *Hudgins*,[3] and *Punch*,[4] which set the stage for Reconstruction-era lawmakers to create policies that treated blacks more harshly than whites.

The passage of the Thirteenth Amendment in 1865 ended slavery in name only, as most southern state governments instituted the Black Codes—laws directed at newly freed blacks—effectively reenslaving them. The Black Codes[5] subjected blacks to vagrancy and curfew laws in an attempt to reenslave them through convict labor provisions once they were convicted and sentenced to prison. With the Confederate military disbanded in defeat, and the southern economy in chaos, unemployment rates were high. In this difficult economy, it was not a crime for whites to be unemployed, but it was for blacks. Under the codes, a black person could be arrested simply for being unemployed.[6] Once convicted, blacks were required to perform subservient labor tasks as they had done previously as slaves.[7] Moreover, the Black Codes applied to all blacks irrespective of whether they were former slaves or free blacks, making their physically apparent race, not their former slave status, the reason for their harsh treatment.[8]

The Black Codes were one of the core reasons why, despite slavery's demise, subsequent amendments were required to grant blacks rights following the passage of the Thirteenth Amendment. In 1868, the Fourteenth Amendment granted citizenship to newly freed slaves along with a right to "due process" and "equal protection of the laws."[9] In 1870, the Fifteenth Amendment passed, prohibiting race discrimination in voting.[10] The latter two amendments granted Congress the authority to enforce these rights through "appropriate legislation" that restrained the sovereign power of the states.[11]

These Reconstruction Amendments, and accompanying congressional enforcement statutes,[12] prohibited the Black Codes and other forms of economic and political race discrimination prevalent at the time. Yet, resistance to the letter and spirit of these laws by many southern whites would cause many northern whites to reduce and relinquish support for blacks, culminating in new practices that reinforced the racial paradigm.

Black Hope Begins

Even before the passage of the Reconstruction Amendments, blacks had reason to be hopeful as the Civil War drew to a close. As blacks gained their freedom through military liberation by Union forces, they began establishing small private schools.[13] Toward the end of the Civil War, Union major general Nathaniel P. Banks had established a Board of Education to organize and govern the spread of such schools.[14] At the war's end, 95 schools were operating under the board, with 162 teachers instructing 9,571 children and 2,000 adults.[15] By 1866, the Freedmen's Bureau, a federal government agency created a few months earlier to assist freed slaves with education, employment, and subsistence, assumed control over a majority of this school system throughout the southern states.[16]

As Freedmen's Bureau private schools began to open in the South after the Civil War, large numbers of blacks enrolled.[17] Members of the American Missionary Society, one of the largest abolitionist organizations in the country, most of whom were white and resided in the North, traveled south to teach.[18] These individuals were motivated by a firm belief that ex-slaves were entitled to civil and political equality.[19] They initially pushed for integrated schools,[20] but threats by southern white Democratic legislators to abandon public education efforts altogether forced them to settle for segregated Freedmen's Bureau schools.[21] These schools not only exposed blacks to academic subjects like Latin and Greek;[22] they also stressed that black children were the social and political equals of white children.[23] Indeed, the Freedmen's Bureau school system developed by the American Missionary Society may have been one of the earliest social programs that expressly promoted equality of blacks and whites.[24] In its April 1888 pamphlet *The Color-Line Question*, the Missionary Society asserted that the question of equality is not for men to decide but is "to be settled by the Divine authority."[25] They cited several passages of the Bible, including Acts 17:26, which state that God "hath made of one blood all nations of men."[26] Unfortunately, in 1870, the Freedmen's Bureau was terminated as an expensive war-related agency no longer justified.[27] From the outset in 1865, the Freedmen's Bureau had been viewed by Congress as a temporary entity.[28] As time passed and expenses mounted, Congress grew tired and did not renew funding after 1870.[29]

Many of the schools started by the Freedmen's Bureau were functioning successfully by 1870,[30] but without funding assistance, some of these schools would cease to exist. Private philanthropic groups based in the North provided some relief, and wealthy white industrialists from the North added financial assistance, allowing some of the schools to thrive during Reconstruction even after federal assistance had ceased. During Reconstruction, black success first took hold in the education context, and subsequently occurred in the political arena.

Leading the charge for black political equality was Hiram Revels of Mississippi, who was elected by black and white Republicans of the Mississippi legislature and sworn in as the first black United States senator in 1870.[31] Despite comments from some white senators, such as Willard Saulsbury of Delaware, who stated that "[t]here is not a Negro or mulatto or octoroon within the whole limits of the United States who is eligible to a seat in this body," Revels was confirmed by the United States Senate in a vote of forty-eight to eight.[32] Not only did his admission suggest the imminent possibilities of political equality for blacks, but the fact that he took the seat previously held by Jefferson Davis, who quit the Senate in 1860 to become president of the Confederacy,[33] reflected the radical political and constitutional change that had taken place.

With the loss of school funding due to the termination of the Freedmen's Bureau in 1870, blacks appealed to state governments to establish a system of public schools. This campaign challenged the then-prevalent ideology among most white southerners that neither state governments nor the federal government had a right to intervene in the education of children or to remedy the inferior status of blacks.[34] Blacks petitioned Republican politicians and Reconstruction legislatures to provide universal education in state constitutions.[35]

Some of these efforts succeeded,[36] in large part because legislatures of the South, for the first time, included black politicians. These politicians, such as John R. Lynch of Mississippi and Robert Smalls of South Carolina, played a crucial role in establishing universal education as a basic right.[37] Under the 1867 Military Reconstruction Acts, Congress empowered army generals to call for new constitutional conventions in which blacks as well as whites were to participate.[38] Black politicians and leaders joined southern white Republicans to place a mandate for public education in the constitutions of many of the former Confederate states.[39] In less than a decade, public school attendance for blacks had doubled, from less than 12% to approximately 25%.[40] While many southern whites resisted these black schools, support from blacks and most northern whites was particularly deep and widespread.[41] Perhaps because education of slaves had been so vociferously prevented by white slave owners, there existed an exceptionally strong willingness of black families to make sacrifices in order for children to be able to attend these schools. Many blacks perceived education as a way to erase the notion of black inferiority, so blacks went to great lengths to gain access to educational institutions.[42] As Republicans strengthened their political hold on southern state legislatures, government commitment to these schools increased. Many blacks began to receive a quality education for the first time in their lives, threatening the white superiority/black inferiority aspect of the racial paradigm.

Even more representative of change were the antidiscrimination laws that had been enacted via the Thirteenth Amendment in 1865, the Freedmen's Bureau legislation in 1865, the Reconstruction Act in 1867, the Fourteenth Amendment in 1868, the Enforcement Act of 1870, the Fifteenth

Amendment in 1870, the 1871 Ku Klux Klan Act, and the Civil Rights Acts of 1866 and 1875.[43] Combined, these laws ended slavery; provided food and educational assistance to freed slaves; awarded citizenship to blacks; prohibited race discrimination in contracts, property, voting, and public accommodations; cracked down on racially motivated violence by the Klan; and mandated equality of treatment, due process, and privileges and immunities of citizenship.[44] These were all important legal protections that would potentially, depending upon how they were interpreted and carried out, reduce racial inequality. While for the first time in American history blacks served in state legislatures and in Congress and one, P. B. S. Pinchback, served as governor of Louisiana for forty-three days in 1873, these changes would be fleeting. [45] Unfortunately, widespread and prolonged white resistance to most of the provisions, and a failure to sustain enforcement by state and federal officials, severely limited the impact these laws had on the racial paradigm.

Violent White Reaction

The Klan was founded shortly after the Civil War by Nathan Bedford Forrest, a Confederate, who on April 12, 1864, had refused to let black troops surrender after defeat in battle at Fort Pillow, but instead ordered them to be shot or burned alive as they surrendered.[46] The Ku Klux Klan's beginning was inauspicious, but its impact on black victimization would be long and severe. Professor Charles Lane describes the beginning of the Klan:

> Southern freedmen lived in poverty after the Civil War, but so did most of the region's whites, for whom economic misery was compounded by the shock and humiliation of defeat. Searching for companionship amid the devastation, some ex-Confederates formed clubs where they could drink, reminisce, and complain. One such group, founded in Pulaski, Tennessee, in late 1865, grew into a secret society with "dens" across the southeastern United States. By 1870, most white men in that part of the country either belonged to the organization or sympathized with it. "This is an institution of Chivalry, Humanity, Mercy and Patriotism, embodying in its genius and its principles all that is chivalric in conduct, noble in sentiment, generous in manhood and patriotic in purpose," the Ku Klux Klan declared. Its goals were to "protect the weak, innocent and defenseless,"

and "to protect and defend the constitution of the United States." Actually, the Klan aimed to terrorize all Negroes and the white Republicans who supported them.[47]

From the outset, members of the Klan worked to limit the educational, economic, and political opportunities of blacks. They did this by threatening and murdering black political leaders, disarming blacks who carried guns, burning down black schools, harassing and intimidating blacks who attempted to participate in the political process, and destroying black farms and business establishments.[48]

Professor Eric Foner explains the broad purpose of the Klan and its embrace of the racial paradigm:

> In effect, the Klan was a military force serving the interests of the Democratic Party, the planter class, and all those who desired restoration of white supremacy. . . . It aimed to reverse the interlocking changes sweeping over the South during Reconstruction: to destroy the Republican party's infrastructure, undermine the Reconstruction state, reestablish control of the black labor force, and restore racial subordination in every aspect of Southern life.[49]

At first, federal efforts to enforce civil and political rights of blacks in the South were quite successful. Arrests and prosecutions of Klan members were frequent and consistent, so much so that federal officials declared the Klan destroyed early in 1868.[50] This declaration, however, proved premature as events soon after in South Carolina would demonstrate.

In 1868, members of the Klan murdered three black Republican state legislators in South Carolina.[51] This followed a number of assassinations of other government officials in southern states, including a black Republican congressman from Arkansas.[52]

In response to this resurgent and organized violence against black elected Republican officials in the South, President Grant and Congress created the Justice Department in 1870[53] to oversee enforcement of federal laws and also enacted the Enforcement Acts of 1870 and 1871,[54] which increased federal authority and defined federal crimes. When these provisions proved insufficient to reduce Klan violence, Congress passed the Ku Klux Klan Act,[55] also known as the Third Enforcement Act, imposing more onerous punishments and giving the president the power to suspend the writ of habeas corpus when local governments had been infiltrated or taken over by the Klan.[56] The act protected black voters and increased penalties for anyone who interfered with federally delineated civil rights.[57]

This revised approach proved most effective. President Grant identified nine counties in South Carolina where Klan activity had overcome local governments.[58] President Grant suspended habeas corpus in these counties so that individuals suspected of racial crimes, or of actively supporting such crimes, could be detained and held for indefinite periods of time.[59] President Grant sent federal troops to these counties where hundreds of Klan members were subsequently arrested.[60] In addition, thousands left the state,[61] making Klan activity in the state almost nonexistent.

While federal troops were spread thin throughout the southern states during Reconstruction, they effectively controlled overt Klan violence when directed by the president to do so.[62] President Grant's approach proved quite effective in reducing Klan activity, yet his crackdown on the Klan earned criticism from both white southern Democrats and white northern Republicans.[63]

Representative of the opposition to Grant's crackdown on white racial violence against blacks was newspaper editor Horace Greeley, a former abolitionist, who believed Reconstruction had failed and blamed blacks for the failure.[64] Greeley characterized blacks as a "worthless race, taking no thought for the morrow."[65] Although Greeley's challenge to Grant's reelection in 1872 was unsuccessful, he created a schism in northern white Republican support for black political rights that would dramatically change the direction of Reconstruction and the privileges afforded blacks.[66] Ultimately, too many northern whites began to embrace the white superiority/black inferiority aspect of the racial paradigm, consequently sealing the fate of black politicians and their black constituency during Reconstruction.

President Lincoln's issuance of the Emancipation Proclamation in 1863 expanded northern goals in fighting the Civil War to include the abolition of slavery.[67] However, for many whites in the North, the conflict was about the Union victory in the Civil War and the right of the Republican Party to determine national policy, while for many whites in the South, the conflict was about states' rights and, particularly, whether blacks or whites would rule in southern states. These southern whites believed that blacks were incapable of governing because they were inferior. As was done during slavery, blacks had to be controlled, and if complete control could not be maintained over certain blacks, then those blacks had to be killed.

An example of such mass murder in order to prevent black political involvement was the Grant Parish Massacre, where on April 13, 1873, in Colfax, Louisiana, armed members of the Klan surrounded the courthouse where black Republicans were meeting in support of black elected officials, burned the courthouse, and killed those who were in it.[68] The United States attorney, James Beckwith, described the details surrounding the mass murder:

> The [white] Democrats of Grant Parish attempted to oust the incumbent parish officers by force and failed, the sheriff protecting the officers with a colored posse. Several days afterward recruits from other parishes, to the number of 300, came to the assistance of the assailants, when they demanded the surrender of the colored people. This was refused. An attack was made and the Negroes were driven into the courthouse. The court house was fired and the Negroes slaughtered as they left the burning building, after resistance ceased. Sixty-five Negroes terribly mutilated were found dead near the ruins of the courthouse. Thirty, known to have been taken prisoners, are said to have been shot after the surrender, and thrown in the river.[69]

For acts done at Grant Parish, William Cruikshank and three others were convicted of federal crimes under Section 6 of the Enforcement Act of 1870, which made it a crime for individuals to conspire or act together to deny others their constitutionally guaranteed rights.[70] On appeal to the Supreme Court, Cruikshank made a states' rights argument that under constitutional principles of enumerated powers and federalism, the crimes committed were punishable by the states, but not by the federal government.[71] He reasoned that Section 6 of the Enforcement Act was unconstitutional as beyond the scope of Congress. The Supreme Court agreed and Cruikshank went free.[72]

In the *Slaughter-House Cases* the Louisiana state legislature gave a 25-year monopoly to a particular slaughterhouse company to slaughter livestock.[73] This made it more difficult for previous slaughterhouse owners and butchers to practice their trade and profession. The plaintiffs relied upon the Privileges or Immunities Clause as a possible source of protection of fundamental civil rights.[74] These fundamental rights, in the plaintiff's view, extended to the right to practice one's profession. The Supreme Court accepted that these fundamental rights existed but suggested that the state, not the federal government, was the guarantor of basic civil rights generally.[75] As a result, the *Slaughter-House Cases* severely circumscribed the Privileges or Immunities Clause, reducing federal legal protections for blacks.

In a republican form of government with a constitution of enumerated powers, the federal government's effectiveness in eradicating racial injustices will seldom exceed the Supreme Court's definition of the limitations of federal power to intervene in such matters. As seen in the latter half of the 19th century, judicial decisions could be used to limit reconstructive efforts by the president and Congress. Going beyond checks and balances, these decisions by the Supreme Court systematically constrained freedom. Most often, the federal law's actual impact in racial spheres is considerably less than the theoretical or potential power of the federal government to intervene. Additionally, definitive rulings in Supreme Court cases that do not directly involve the issue of race frequently dilute the federal racial remedies or options. The *Slaughter-House Cases* are a prime example of such factors operating adversely on blacks.

The *Cruikshank*[76] case continued the approach the Supreme Court had adopted in the *Slaughter-House Cases,*[77] narrowing the scope and coverage of the Reconstruction Amendments. The Supreme Court gave a restrictive meaning to the Privileges or Immunities Clause of the Fourteenth Amendment. These decisions diluted the Fourteenth Amendment, which should have been the most likely of the Reconstruction Amendments to protect and extend the civil rights of blacks. The Supreme Court undercut the federal government's legal capacity to enforce constitutional rights, which had been expanded by the Reconstruction Amendments. Prior to the Reconstruction Amendments implementing statutes, the Constitution and federal law did not require the states to protect the rights of blacks. After their adoption, the Constitution and federal law, as the Supreme Court interpreted them, imposed a duty on the states to afford blacks equal protection of the laws. In fact, in the *Civil Rights Cases,* the Supreme Court held that the Fourteenth Amendment secured fundamental rights against state violations.[78] Unfortunately for blacks residing in southern states, the federal government was the only entity likely to enforce their legal rights as citizens.

Most revealing of the justices' views on black humanity was the way Chief Justice Morrison Waite, in writing the *Cruikshank* opinion, characterized the facts as to the acts perpetrated by Klan members on blacks exercising their newly guaranteed constitutional right to participate in the political process.[79] Waite obscured the reality of the horrendous crimes committed, before and after the blacks were murdered. Half of the blacks were gunned down as they fled the fire in the courthouse, unarmed.[80] The more than sixty blacks taken prisoner were tied up and shot in their heads, their bodies left to rot in a nearby field.[81] There was no mention of any of these despicable deeds in Waite's recitation of the facts.[82] Moreover, Waite failed to mention the racial hatred underlying these murders. He did not mention the history of the Klan, in general, nor did he mention the political circumstances in Colfax, Louisiana, that led to white members of the Klan killing the white Republican sheriff of Grant Parish as he attempted to protect black Republican elected officials.[83] This objectification of blacks was nothing new in Supreme Court jurisprudence. It had been done prior to Reconstruction in cases like *Dred Scott*, where slaves were portrayed as objects and as subhuman.[84] It is reflected in the Court's decisions—by the Court not providing blacks with legal protection, as it did in *Dred Scott*,[85] *Prigg*,[86] and *Cruikshank*.[87] It is apparent in its reasoning, in the indications that blacks were somehow less deserving than whites because they were "slaves," or members of "a degraded caste." And it is illustrated in the Court's statements of the facts, in which atrocities committed by whites against blacks were glossed over or left out—the Supreme Court reinforced the black inferiority notion by further demeaning blacks in the eyes of whites.

While Reconstruction offered the promise of racial equality, resentment by southern whites of black political empowerment, which could jeopardize white dominance of southern governments, caused widespread and often violent resistance to reforms. When the commitment to Reconstruction by northern whites wavered, federal enforcement of antidiscrimination provisions was significantly reduced. Fraud and violence eventually enabled supporters of the Confederacy to regain control of state governments, which, in turn, led these governments to institute Jim Crow segregation throughout the South while reaffirming the black separation aspect of the racial paradigm. Reconstruction efforts did not end suddenly as a result of government action but rather dissipated and ultimately ended through a long process.[88] The turning point came in 1876, when white Democrats supporting Samuel Tilden ceded the contested presidential election to Republican candidate Rutherford Hayes, on the condition that he remove federal troops from the South.[89] The "Hayes-Tilden Compromise" thus eviscerated the promise of Reconstruction by removing the protection of federal troops and surrendering blacks to the authority of former slave owners.[90] The compromise forced black politicians out of power and gave white politicians exclusive control of southern state politics.[91] Blacks lost power because the federal troops stationed in southern states were the only government entity that blacks could rely on for protection against Klan violence.

It is important to recognize that white supremacists, whether they were in power or out of power, were resolved to deny blacks political power. That was one of the primary goals of the Klan terror during the Reconstruction period, which began when the southern states were under Republican control and continued when they were under Democratic control. In 1877, the chairman of the Kansas Republican state committee, Henry Watterson, described the ominous but predictable consequences of white supremacist resolve: "As matters look to me now, I think the policy of the new administration will be to conciliate the white men of the South. Carpetbaggers to the rear, and niggers take care of yourselves."[92] The Civil War may have ended the institution of southern slavery, but Reconstruction failed to neutralize notions of white superiority and the ongoing exploitation and control of blacks.

Black Hope Denied

As the Grant Parish Massacre exemplifies, white supremacists, whether in or out of control of southern state governments, made it their mission to deny political power to blacks. Their determination and efforts to circumvent the Reconstruction Amendments occasionally resulted in Supreme Court intervention. In 1880, the Supreme Court struck down a West Virginia statute that excluded blacks from juries.[93] In *Strauder v. West Virginia*, Justice William Strong, delivering the opinion of the Court, concluded that blacks had been habitually discriminated against after the Civil War, and that such discrimination would probably continue.[94]

Strauder stood for the proposition that the Fourteenth Amendment could be used as a means of protecting some of blacks' political rights from overt racial discrimination, including jury service. But Justice Strong also stated, "We do not say that . . . a State may not prescribe the qualifications of its jurors, and in so doing make discriminations. It may confine the selection to males, to freeholders, to citizens, to persons within certain ages, or to persons having educational qualifications. We do not believe the Fourteenth Amendment was ever intended to prohibit this."[95]

While *Strauder* prohibited the outright exclusion of blacks from jury service solely because of their race, states found ways to circumvent the spirit of the ruling through property, level of education, and other juror qualification "standards" whose only real goal was racial discrimination. Though express racial discrimination in jury selection was prohibited, "race-neutral" devices that kept blacks off juries were not.[96] If a black citizen managed to clear the property and education jury pool requirements, the prosecutor could simply dismiss the survivor with a peremptory challenge. So successful was this scheme that by the start of the 20th century, although more than 75% of the Phillips County, Arkansas, population was black, no blacks had served on a jury for thirty years.[97] The Fourteenth Amendment took effect in 1868; *Strauder* was decided in 1880; and yet the effective protection of black political rights was still yet to be seen in the early 1900s.

As with jury service, states went to great lengths to disenfranchise black voters while ostensibly appearing to comply with the Fourteenth and Fifteenth Amendments' prohibition against race discrimination.[98] Most of these efforts grew out of state constitutional conventions convened to institutionalize barriers to blacks voting. Though many disenfranchisement provisions were challenged in court, few were struck down. In fact, in 1876, in *United States v. Reese*, the Supreme Court upheld states' use of racially exclusionary voting practices, such as literacy tests and poll taxes.[99] Those challenges that did succeed only marginally increased the number of black voters. One observer described the complex body of disenfranchisement laws as "devilishly complex, and no sooner did blacks succeed in striking down one discriminatory device, than whites substituted another."[100] Generally, the net effect was a decrease in access to voting as a correlation existed between the number of restrictions and the proportion of eligible blacks who voted.[101]

The 1890 Mississippi Convention led the way in increasing barriers for blacks to vote by amending the state constitution to include an annual poll tax.[102] This created an obvious obstacle for impoverished blacks who had been forced to work for no wages through centuries of slavery, and who subsequently earned very little as sharecroppers.[103] Mississippi required that voters pay the tax long before Election Day and show a receipt proving that they had paid the poll tax for the prior two years.[104] The two-year requirement made the poll tax insurmountable to all but the wealthiest blacks.

The poll tax was a formidable weapon[105] adopted within two decades by every state of the former Confederacy.[106] Reflecting the same racist hierarchy as the 1705 Virginia law that prohibited blacks, American Indians, and white criminals from holding public office, one delegate to the 1901 Alabama Constitutional Convention declared that the negro and the vicious element will not pay two months ahead of time a dollar and a half in order to exercise this privilege, but if the business man knows he is liable for the tax, although he will not give a dollar and a half to vote or exercise the franchise, he will put it on the list of liabilities like he does everything else and tell his clerk to pay it when it is due. . . .[107]

The poll tax provided a systematic means of defining eligible voters on the basis of race, and whites in power made every effort not to collect the tax from blacks. In some states, only property holders were reminded of their poll tax assessment. In other states, no reminders were sent at all to blacks or to whites, but whites were reminded in other ways.[108] Many states added their own supplemental restrictions as to when the poll tax could be paid.[109] Complexities were added to ensure absolute control over who was eligible to vote.[110] The cumulative poll tax imposed an added burden by requiring that an individual pay outstanding taxes from previous years before qualifying to vote.[111] Florida and Mississippi allowed poll taxes to accumulate for two years.[112] Virginia allowed them to accumulate for three years.[113] Poll taxes accumulated indefinitely in Georgia (after 1877) and Alabama (after 1901).[114] Generally, a voter who failed to pay taxes one year, for lack of financial ability, was effectively precluded from voting for life due to the accumulated weight of unpaid taxes.

The poll tax provisions conveyed an assumption that whites were responsible and blacks were irresponsible. Reflected in Horace Greeley's characterization, when he ran for president in 1872, that blacks were lazy and did not think about or make plans for the future,[115] the poll tax provisions—by sending reminders of payment only to property owners who were almost exclusively white—gave those whites an advantage to pay on time, thus reinforcing white superiority notions when whites paid on time and blacks did not because they had not received reminders. Similarly, by not sending reminders to whites or blacks, but continuing to show preference to whites by reminding them of the deadline through nefarious ways, government officials ensured that whites were again more likely to pay the tax in a timely manner than blacks. If whites were truly more responsible than blacks, in terms of tax payment, they would not need preferential treatment as to reminders. Viewed in that light, the preferential policy was an acknowledgment that blacks and whites were equally irresponsible and neither would pay the tax without a reminder. The laws, however, fueled notions of white superiority and black inferiority by reinforcing negative stereotypes that blacks were lazy and irresponsible and positive stereotypes that whites were hardworking and responsible. White legislators were embracing black inferiority by assuming black irresponsibility with the intention of harming black voting opportunities. Preventing blacks from voting, solely because they did not pay the poll tax due to not being informed or reminded of the payment deadline, fed the inferiority label by reducing black political power. This reduction in black political power correspondingly increased white political power, reinforcing the white superiority/ black inferiority aspect of the racial paradigm. Each fed off the other, for if whites paid the tax and blacks did not, each race must have had different levels of responsibility. If blacks were truly irresponsible, as evidenced by their failure to pay the poll tax, they did not deserve the franchise. On the other hand, if whites paid the poll tax, that was proof that they were responsible, and justified their right to vote. By implying that responsible voters paid their poll taxes on time and assuming that blacks would not pay such taxes on time, the poll tax laws obscured the embrace of white superiority notions behind the discriminatory tax notification requirements.

Literacy tests represented another way to disenfranchise large groups of black voters, as reading and writing had been legally denied to black people prior to the Civil War. Beginning in 1890, seven states of the former Confederacy (Alabama, Georgia, Louisiana, Mississippi, North Carolina, South Carolina, and Virginia) adopted literacy qualifications for voting, which required potential voters to prove their ability to read a portion of the state or federal constitution before being qualified to vote.[116] Blacks having been denied education during slavery and having had funding for education taken away in 1870, it was not surprising that in each of these states more than two-thirds of blacks were illiterate, compared to one-quarter of whites.[117] All seven states of the former Confederacy, with the exception of Mississippi and North Carolina, allowed an illiterate individual to qualify to vote if he or she owned a certain amount of property, thus providing an end run around the requirement and ensuring that illiterate whites who had access to wealth could still vote even if they could not read the Constitution.[118]

Some states, like Mississippi, also imposed comprehension tests requiring any voters not only to be able to read and write any section of the Constitution of the State of Mississippi but also to be able to "give a reasonable interpretation thereof to the county registrar"[119]—a real challenge when only several decades earlier it had been illegal for most blacks to read or write. More importantly, county registrars had discretion to judge a "reasonable interpretation," which they exercised to prevent even college-educated blacks from voting.[120]

Property and education restrictions specifically designed to exclude black voters always had the potential to affect poor white voters as well. Legislators thus created "escape clauses" to protect poor white voters while continuing to exclude rich black ones.[121] These escape clauses clearly reflected the same intentional effort to divide society along racial lines,[122] as found in earlier cases as far back as *Punch* in 1641.[123] An understanding clause, for instance, allowed an illiterate voter to demonstrate an understanding of a particular constitutional provision that was read aloud by the registrar.[124] County registrars exercised their discretion to allow illiterate whites to vote, but prevented even well-educated blacks from doing so. One delegate to the Constitutional Convention explained, "I expect the examination with which the black man will be confronted, to be inspired by the same spirit that inspires every man upon this floor and in this convention. . . . I would not expect for the white man a rigid examination."[125] For those blacks who managed to pass the examination, showing an ability to understand the constitutional text, other so called "race-neutral" requirements, such as the inability to afford the poll tax, virtually ensured that they could not participate in the electoral process.

Most blacks, no matter how well qualified, did not get to vote under these "race-neutral" schemes. Despite this mass exclusion of black voters, the Supreme Court continually refused to invalidate such provisions in state laws. For example, in the 1898 case of *Williams v. Mississippi*,[126] the Supreme Court held that the Mississippi Constitution and statutes did not intentionally "on their face discriminate between the races, and it has not been shown that their actual administration was evil, only that evil was possible under them."[127] As to Mississippi's poll tax provisions, the Court added, "[W]hatever is sinister in their intention, if anything, can be prevented by both races and by the exertion of that duty which voluntarily pays taxes. . . ."[128]

The Court's reasoning in *Williams* implied that blacks could avoid the harmful impact of such facially race-neutral laws with racially disproportionate impact simply by complying with them. While these laws were administered in a racially discriminating manner, and they were undoubtedly enacted to disenfranchise blacks, the Supreme Court displayed an indifference bordering on hostility to black equality in finding that no constitutionally protected right had been violated because the harmful acts were racially neutral on their face.[129] By faulting blacks as the cause of their own disadvantage, the Court was able to obscure the influence of white superiority notions behind discriminatory voting restrictions. This is a familiar rhetorical device commonly used to justify restrictions on racial progress. Fifteen years before *Williams,* the Court employed the same reasoning when it invalidated Congress's attempt to prohibit discrimination in places of public accommodation. Justice Joseph Bradley wrote in the *Civil Rights Cases,* "When a man has emerged from slavery, and by the aid of beneficent legislation has shaken off the inseparable concomitants of that state, there must be some stage in the progress of his elevation when he takes the rank of a mere citizen, and ceases to be the special favorite of the laws. . . ."[130]

There are two ways to interpret the meaning of Justice Bradley's language. Both reinforce the racial paradigm. The first way is to understand the language as recognizing that the former slaves were assisted in the transition from slavery to freedom by being made a "favorite of the laws."[131] Blacks were the intended primary beneficiaries of the Reconstruction Amendments and civil and political rights enforcement statutes. The Supreme Court recognized this in the *Slaughter-House Cases* and in *Strauder,* among other decisions. Bradley was reflecting the North's abandonment of blacks in declaring that they must now rely on and take care of themselves, like other Americans. Bradley's attitude underestimated the tremendous difficulty blacks faced in the transition from slavery to freedom, which was made all the more difficult by white supremacists determined to push them back into slavery, or at least servitude. Bradley was utterly insensitive to the plight of blacks, but he did not embrace the view that blacks were inferior to whites and do not deserve to enjoy equal rights. To the contrary, it is a mark of Bradley's formalistic legal reasoning that he believed, or at least claimed, that the adoption of legal guarantees of equal civil and voting rights was sufficient to place blacks on a plane of equality before the law. But, he was not different from most of his colleagues on the Court and most whites in this regard. To his credit, the former slaveholding justice, John Marshall Harlan, protested in his dissent in the *Civil Rights Cases* that Bradley and the majority were utterly unrealistic in their decision and had broken faith with the Fourteenth Amendment and the promise of equality it represented.[132] But, Harlan was alone in dissent. Sadly, the Court's decision in the *Civil Rights Cases,* leaving to the states the authority to permit racial segregation, was consistent with the attitudes of most whites in this era in which scientific racism was considered a respectable science.[133] To the contrary, it was consistent with the racial mores of its time.

A second way to interpret the meaning of Justice Bradley's language is to understand it as embracing the false perception of black inferiority. It is strange indeed that Justice Bradley believed that blacks had been the special favorites of the laws, when for two and one-half centuries they had been denied the right to vote, prohibited from acquiring knowledge, capital, or property, and designated as chattel. As a Civil War veteran, Justice Bradley presumably was familiar with the events leading to that conflict, but in the ruling he focused solely on Reconstruction-era civil rights legislation designed merely to grant blacks the same constitutional rights as whites. Justice Bradley's implication was a subtle one that, nonetheless, confirmed perceptions by many northern whites who were also war veterans. What Bradley suggested was that if blacks are indeed inferior, then treating them equally under the law would constitute special treatment. Under Justice Bradley's logic, those who, in fact, are equal should be treated the same, but those who are inferior should be given fewer rights and privileges. The natural reaction by those whites who embraced this reasoning was to defy laws that required equal treatment for blacks or to circumvent their requirements. Many southern states began to incorporate this approach into their constitutions.

From 1894 onward, the majority of states of the former Confederacy organized constitutional conventions[134] to adopt poll taxes, literacy tests, comprehension requirements, and complex registration systems. All-white Democratic Party primaries became the norm, as did disenfranchisement laws that withheld the vote from those convicted of certain crimes believed widely to be associated with blacks.[135] Consistent with the notion of white superiority, convicted white embezzlers who had completed their sentences could vote, but black petty thieves could not. These were just some of the ways "race-neutral" measures worked to circumvent the Fourteenth and Fifteenth Amendments' promise of political equality for blacks.

The impact on black political power was devastating. In 1867, in Mississippi, prior to these "race-neutral" measures, approximately 70% of eligible blacks were able to register to vote.[136] Less than two years after the 1890 Constitutional Convention, and the enforcement of its discriminating measures, that number declined to fewer than 6%.[137] With most southern whites joining the Democratic Party, there developed an absence of any meaningful Republican political power to oppose disenfranchisement schemes. The exclusionary measures being enforced against blacks became even more entrenched.

These schemes took an obvious toll and reversed early successes by some exceptional black politicians such as Robert Smalls. Smalls was born a slave in South Carolina twenty years before the Civil War began.[138] By his twenties, Smalls was serving aboard a steamship named *The Planter* that transported cotton.[139] When the Confederate government chartered the boat, in 1861, during the Civil War, Smalls was working as the wheelman[140] of the ship. On May 13, 1862, Smalls escaped from slavery by stealing the *Planter* from its southern dock and delivering his wife and two children, twelve other slaves, the boat, its cargo of weapons, and valuable papers to Union troops in Charleston, South Carolina.[141] The passage directly past Confederate naval ports required great courage and ingenuity. Smalls's de- livery of a Confederate warship to Union troops had a profound impact on Confederate morale.[142] To lose a ship to a black slave was bad enough. To lose it due to his ingenuity and cunning defied all notions of white superi- ority upon which slavery was based.

While working on board the *Planter*, Smalls had laid mines, intended for Union vessels, in South Carolina rivers and had surveyed Confederate forts.[143] After his successful escape to Charleston, he provided this confi- dential information to Union troops;[144] his information and his under- standing of Confederate military practices was invaluable, and resulted in several successful military missions by the Union.[145] Smalls fought in sev- enteen battles during the Civil War and was promoted to captain of the *Planter*, then a Union ship, in 1863—he was the first black captain of a ves- sel in the service of the United States.[146]

After the war ended and Reconstruction began, Smalls was elected to his first political office as a Republican delegate to the 1868 South Caro- lina Constitutional Convention.[147] Beginning in 1870, Smalls served in the South Carolina legislature for seven years.[148] In 1875, Smalls was elected to the United States House of Representatives, representing the majority- black Fifth District of South Carolina.[149] Subsequent to his election, many white Democratic politicians in South Carolina tried to impugn his charac- ter and ruin his credibility. In 1877, he was arrested on charges of accepting a bribe to vote for a bill; the unfounded charges against him were based on a check written more than one month after the bill was passed.[150] Then an attempt was made, by his political opponents, to attribute all of his ac- complishments to fraud, including his heroism on the *Planter*.[151] While Smalls's reputation did suffer because of such accusations, he continued to win elections to Congress.[152] Eventually, fraud, intimidation, and violence at the polls eroded black suffrage to such an extent that Smalls won his last electoral victory in 1884—he was defeated in 1886.[153] Robert Smalls, like all other black congressmen after Reconstruction ended, had his political career destroyed by racially discriminatory laws and practices that prevented blacks from reelecting him.

By 1876, supporters of white superiority were able to gain control of southern state governments and halt further progress of universal schooling efforts by decreasing taxation, opposing compulsory attendance laws, and blocking the passage of new laws intended to expand public school opportunities.[154] These newly constituted state governments also refused to protect blacks from violent acts by members of the Klan and other whites opposed to black education and racial equality.[155] As a result, many of the public schools for blacks were closed or destroyed. Consequently, the number of black children attending schools drastically decreased, from over 25% to fewer than 10%.[156]

In the event that legal devices failed, some of those who supported white superiority/black inferiority used fraud to prevent black progress. Those blacks who managed to attain educational success found that navigating the line of racial division was particularly tricky. Social norms required that blacks behave in a deferential manner whenever whites were present. For educated blacks, particularly officers in the military who were trained to be leaders, such a demeaning posture was difficult to maintain. Even when rules, customs, and norms were carefully followed, however, education and employment opportunities were denied, consistent with false notions of black inferiority.

Some whites would go to extreme lengths to prevent blacks from assuming positions of power. Henry Flipper, for example, was born into slavery in Georgia in 1856.[157] Flipper began his education by learning to read at age eight with the help of another slave.[158] He attended a succession of Freedmen's Bureau schools for newly freed slaves, the last of which was Atlanta University.[159] In 1873, Flipper wrote to Georgia Republican congressman James Freeman, asking for an appointment to the United States Military Academy in West Point, New York.[160] The two exchanged a series of letters, and Congressman Freeman eventually forwarded Flipper's nomination to the secretary of war.[161] Flipper passed the required examinations, officially entered the academy in 1873, and became its first black graduate in 1877.[162] Although over eighteen thousand black soldiers served with the Union forces during the American Civil War, and two blacks had entered West Point prior to Flipper's enrollment, none had served as commissioned officers until Flipper.[163] Upon his graduation, he was the first black commissioned officer, and served as a second lieutenant assigned to the 10th Cavalry at Fort Sill, Oklahoma.[164]

Flipper's first assignment at Fort Sill was to supervise the creation of a drainage ditch to keep water away from the camp, an effort that was necessary to combat malaria caused by the mosquitoes attracted to standing water.[165] Flipper's design of the ditch and his supervision of its excavation were a resounding success, immediately and noticeably improving the health of the troops.[166] The ditch was so effective that it was called "Flipper's Ditch," and was used as a model for other army projects.[167]

In 1880, Flipper was transferred to Fort Davis, Texas, where he was placed in charge of supplies as acting assistant quartermaster.[168] Despite his successes as a military officer, Flipper began to encounter officers who openly showed hostility toward the idea of having a black fellow officer.[169] These officers started falsifying reports.[170] Important communiqués were falsely reported as given to Flipper, but instead were hidden or destroyed.[171] Subsequently, Flipper was asked to produce the documents, and, when he could not, a bad conduct report was placed in his record.[172] When Colonel William Shafter, a self-declared white supremacist, became commander of Fort Davis, he relieved Flipper of his quartermaster duties.[173] Soon thereafter, Flipper discovered government funds missing from his trunk.[174] Fearing retribution from Shafter, Flipper attempted to conceal the loss, even lying to his commanding officer until the money could be found.[175] These actions resulted in charges recommending Flipper's court-martial for "embezzlement" and "conduct unbecoming an officer and a gentleman."[176] The court found him not guilty of embezzlement, but guilty of misconduct for lying to Colonel Shafter. President Chester Arthur approved his conviction, and he was dishonorably discharged from the army in 1882.[177]

Henry Flipper was a rarity during Reconstruction. While college-educated blacks were demeaned, degraded, falsely convicted of crimes, and wrongfully discharged from employment, most blacks were denied even the opportunity to take college preparatory courses. Consistent with erroneous views of black inferiority, blacks, irrespective of individual academic capability, were viewed as best suited for work as field hands or house servants. Consequently, opportunities for blacks to pursue higher education were rare.

Conclusion

During the early years of Reconstruction, the Freedmen's Bureau and southern state governments successfully established some schools for black students. We have seen, however, that Congress impeded these efforts, and state and local governments used Black Codes to maintain the separation of blacks in education and in all areas of life. In this way, the states sustained the racial hierarchy and perpetuated black victimization. There is a direct connection between these local laws, the Black Codes, and the spread of separation and victimization of blacks throughout our nation. White southerners used acts of violence against blacks and widespread disenfranchisement to completely erase black political power; funding reductions and threats of violence were used to undermine schools for blacks. As a result, white southerners strengthened the racial hierarchy and squandered opportunities by which they could have eradicated it. The Black Codes applied to all blacks, not just former slaves, and in this way, the racial hierarchy became all-encompassing, broadening the scope of its victimization. The downfall of black political power jeopardized educational opportunities for blacks, which, in turn, reinforced the false notions of white superiority and black inferiority. Poll taxes, literacy tests, and the rulings in *Strauder*,[178] *Cruikshank*,[179] and the *Slaughter-House Cases*[180] undercut and directly attacked the new protections that had been intended by the Reconstruction Amendments. These Supreme Court decisions opened the floodgates for blatant segregation and discrimination. Whites in southern states regained unchecked political power, and openly opposed educational, economic, and social opportunities for blacks. Southern state and local governments resisted integration and victimized blacks by destroying the quality and efficiency of their schools. In these ways, the notions of racial hierarchy were put into direct action, to separate and victimize blacks, to limit education, to deny voting, and to destroy economic opportunities. The Ku Klux Klan emerged as the institutionalized arm of the systematic victimization of blacks.

We have seen in this chapter that racist practices in education and politics undermined attempts by blacks to participate fully in society and to improve post-slavery conditions. Whites maintained complete control over political and educational systems, and offered few opportunities to blacks. After the Civil War and its Reconstruction Amendments, whites held onto all political and social power, and thereby reinforced black separation and victimization. In a time when blacks were hoping for equality and opportunity, Congress, local governments, and society maintained the racial paradigm, to perpetuate indefinitely the inequitable treatment of blacks in public accommodations, housing, employment, government services, and criminal justice. This inequitable treatment, in turn, further separated blacks and made them easier targets for continued victimization, propelling the cycle of inequality. The open, systematic separation of blacks would come to be known as "Jim Crow,"[181] and it flourished insidiously throughout the 20th century.

3

Preventing Black Excellence between
Plessy and *Brown*

"I am just as much opposed to Booker Washington as a voter, with all
his Anglo-Saxon reinforcements, . . . as I am to the coconut-headed,
chocolate-covered, typical little coon, Andy Dotson, who blacks my
shoes every morning. Neither is fit to perform the supreme function of
citizenship."

—Senator James Vardaman of Mississippi, 1903[1]

DURING RECONSTRUCTION, BLACKS had been promised the equal-
ity guaranteed in the Constitution.[2] Yet, by 1896, on the eve of the *Plessy*
decision, that promise seemed to have been completely destroyed. Black
political participation had been dismantled in southern states, where 90%
of blacks resided.[3] Post-Reconstruction governments had blocked political participation by blacks, and educational opportunities for blacks had
been greatly reduced.[4] In order to solidify and maintain false notions of
white superiority/black inferiority, blacks would have to be separated from
whites, unless they were obviously subservient. Laws were formulated
that reflected the notion that blacks were inferior, and demonstrations of
black excellence were suppressed because they stood to shatter the racial
hierarchy.[5]

Black opportunities to compete with whites were eliminated.[6] Racial
segregation, through physical separation, became the method by which
black excellence was denied.[7] During Reconstruction, having held absolute
power in America since the time of its colonization, whites felt threatened
by new laws and opportunities for blacks. They responded by crushing
those prospects even before they materialized.

Who Is Jim Crow?

"Jim Crow," the term identifying discriminatory laws and policies that separated blacks after Reconstruction, was, allegedly, named after a real person—an elderly, physically handicapped black slave on a horse farm in Louisville, Kentucky, owned by a Mr. Crow.[8] In 1828, a white entertainer, Thomas Dartmouth Rice, observed the elderly Jim Crow as he sang and danced with an unusual hopping and shuffling maneuver.[9] As Jim Crow danced, he sang in slave vernacular, "Wheel about, an' turn about, an' do jis so; eb'ry time I wheel about, I jump Jim Crow."[10]

Rice immediately memorized the song, added a few verses, copied the dance steps, and, apparently without any compensation or attribution to Jim Crow, tried out this new act on stage in Louisville. He dressed in blackface and called the routine "Jump Jim Crow."[11] It was an immediate hit. Soon, Rice was performing to sell-out audiences of whites in New York City's theater district.[12]

Rice's Jim Crow character propelled him to international fame and immense wealth, and inspired other white performers to create similar material. In 1842, four entertainers named the Virginia Minstrels[13] staged a full-length show focused exclusively on Jim Crow–type characters. For the next hundred years, minstrel shows were one of the most popular forms of entertainment in America.[14] The Jim Crow song was played so often that one foreign ambassador thought it was the national anthem.[15]

The Jim Crow minstrel shows demeaned and degraded blacks, while uplifting whites, through song, dance, and acting.[16] The shows created several stereotyped characters, including the happy plantation slave and the inept, corrupt, and foolish northern urban free black.[17] Every skit, song, joke, or dance reinforced these images.[18] Black minstrel characters in southern slave plantation settings were given endearing names like Uncle Remus and were portrayed as happy, healthy, obedient, and excessively loyal to their white owners, while the white masters were portrayed as compassionate, benevolent, and fair-minded.[19] In contrast, black minstrel characters in northern urban settings were given pompous names like Count Julius Caesar Mars Napoleon Sinclair Brown.[20] These characters were portrayed as ignorant fools or frivolous spectacles, often saved from disaster or self-destruction by whites who felt pity for them.[21] Such portraits of blacks and whites conveyed an unequivocal message that the proper place for blacks was a southern slave plantation, thereby asserting that freed blacks could not and would not be productive free citizens.[22] Minstrel shows were not only hugely profitable; they systematically promoted a message of white superiority.[23] These portrayals had an insidious effect: condoning public mockery and denying the humanity of blacks by relegating them to a "harmless" form of entertainment. Consistent with the creation and maintenance of black separation through de jure rules, minstrel shows were the first, and in some cases the only, exposure many whites would get to the black experience in America. Most did not know the actual conditions that blacks had to endure. The demeaning images created and reinforced superior attitudes toward blacks.

As minstrel shows saturated the country with notions of black inferiority, and as large audiences of whites embraced them, it is not surprising that racial segregation laws came to be named after the first and most famous minstrel character of all: Jim Crow.[24] The name of a handicapped slave was now recognized nationwide; it was a label, an entertainment sensation, and a mindset.[25] While there are no historical references identifying who first applied the term "Jim Crow" to segregation laws, the term caught on fast. By 1900, Jim Crow was widely used as the informal term to describe any law, custom, or practice that intentionally separated racial minorities from whites.[26] Physical separation allowed negative racial stereotypes to flourish, and Jim Crow laws mandated such separation.[27] For the next fifty years, Jim Crow laws proliferated in America.[28] The "harmless" humor on the minstrel stage created an atmosphere that accepted and justified segregationist laws. Those laws maintained and exacerbated physical and psychological distance between the races. Segregation spread and got ever stronger during the latter half of the 19th century, fueled by the notions of black inferiority celebrated in Jim Crow minstrel shows.

Jim Crow laws provided a combination of government hindrance of economic opportunities for blacks and empowerment for whites. The notion of white superiority/black inferiority was strengthened in many forms—eliminating blacks from sporting competition with whites; preventing educational opportunities for blacks; generating housing segregation such as all-white towns or designated black areas; excluding blacks from certain jobs; creating government programs, like farm assistance, of which poor and middle-class whites were the primary beneficiaries; and refusing to acknowledge or recognize black inventions and technological advancements.[29]

The Supreme Court Embraces Jim Crow: *Plessy v. Ferguson*

While black separation practices existed prior to Reconstruction, constitutional sanction of race separation, allowing for widespread and comprehensive coverage, would not occur until the end of the 19th century.[30] In 1896, the Supreme Court, in *Plessy v. Ferguson*,[31] upheld a Louisiana statute that prohibited black passengers from riding alongside whites in railway cars. In doing so, the Court placed its imprimatur on discrimination— even the justice who disavowed race separation embraced notions of white superiority.[32]

Complainant Homer Adolph Plessy was born in Louisiana in 1862.[33] His parents were free, French-speaking, and of mixed Spanish, French, Native American, and African ancestry.[34] Plessy had only one-eighth African ancestry and appeared to be entirely white.[35] By 1896, Plessy was a successful businessman, earning a substantial living by selling shoes.[36] He often traveled in the first-class car on trains; the Jim Crow car was usually dirty and in disrepair.[37] Plessy belonged to a citizens' group composed of leading blacks from New Orleans who opposed all forms of racial segregation, including the 1890 Louisiana statute that segregated passengers on local railway cars.[38] The group decided to challenge the statute under the Fourteenth Amendment.[39] They chose Plessy as their plaintiff, hoping that his white ancestry and appearance would reveal the arbitrariness of segregation laws in Louisiana.[40] By preapproval with the railroad company, which opposed the segregation law because it increased transportation costs, Plessy boarded a white train car and was arrested by the conductor and a railroad security guard.[41]

Plessy's lawyers argued that segregation violated the Fourteenth Amendment's equal protection guarantee.[42] The Court not only rejected this claim under a "separate but equal" theory of equality but scolded Plessy for attributing an invidious motive to Louisiana lawmakers.[43] Segregation, the Court said, was enacted "in good faith for the promotion of the public good, and not for the annoyance or oppression of a particular class."[44]

In the justices' view, the separation law did not discriminate; blacks who opposed the law were merely being too sensitive.[45] As Justice Henry Brown explained, "We consider the underlying fallacy of [Plessy's] argument to consist in the assumption that the enforced separation of the two races stamps the colored race with a badge of inferiority. If this be so, it is not by reason of anything found in the act, but solely because the colored race chooses to put that construction upon it."[46] Segregation, of course, was designed precisely for the purpose of demeaning blacks, and everyone, including the justices, knew it. Justice John Harlan referenced this reality in his dissent, where he alluded to the fact that such discriminatory intent was apparent to everyone.[47] Justice Harlan explained,

> It was said in argument that the statute of Louisiana does not discriminate against either race, but prescribes a rule applicable alike to white and colored citizens. But this argument does not meet the difficulty. Everyone knows that the statute in question had its origin in the purpose, not so much to exclude white persons from railroad cars occupied by blacks, as to exclude colored people from coaches occupied by or assigned to white persons. Railroad corporations of Louisiana did not make discrimination among whites in the matter of [ac]commodation for travelers. The thing to accomplish was, under the guise of giving equal accommodation for whites and blacks, to compel the latter to keep to themselves while traveling in railroad passenger coaches. No one would be so wanting in candor as to assert the contrary.[48]

Despite the transparency of the motives behind the effort to separate blacks, the Court declared that the Constitution sanctioned the racial divide in all social activities.[49]

According to the majority reasoning in *Plessy*, separate but equal facilities on the train did not imply legal inferiority but merely recognition of a social distinction.[50] According to the political/social rights distinction in the Equal Protection Clause first identified by the Supreme Court in the *Civil Rights Cases*, the clause guaranteed only political equality, not social equality.[51] Unlike racial distinctions in voting or serving on a jury, separation on a train did not constitute an infringement on any political right.[52]

Plessy's distinction between "social rights" and political rights also confirmed the true intent behind segregation.[53] This distinction, like the statutory exception for subservient blacks, provided whites with an opportunity to reaffirm superiority to blacks.[54] The argument that social segregation did not emanate from notions of white superiority but instead grew out of benign concern for the "natural affinities" of both whites and blacks to socialize separately enabled the Court to endorse discriminatory laws without having to acknowledge the racist presumptions behind them.[55] Even Justice John Harlan, who alone dissented from the majority decision, insisted that whites historically had been, and forever would be, socially superior to blacks:[56] "The white race deems itself to be the dominant race in this country. And so it is, in prestige, in achievements, in education, in wealth, and in power. So, I doubt not, it will continue to be for all time, if it remains true to its great heritage. . . ."[57] In truth, however, segregation laws were created by whites for the sole purpose of reaffirming such superiority by demeaning and degrading blacks and, thus, benefiting and uplifting whites.

The *Plessy* mentality of racial separation was also embraced by the highest elected government officials, including presidents, governors, and members of Congress.[58] For example, when the moderate black leader Booker T. Washington informally, and for the first time in history, had lunch with President Theodore Roosevelt, in 1901,[59] the public reaction revealed the extent of the nation's separatist mentality, as in the following indictment by the *Memphis Scimitar*: "The most damnable outrage which has ever been perpetrated by any citizen of the United States was committed yesterday by the President, when he invited a nigger to dine with him at the White House."[60] Similarly, Senator Benjamin Tillman of South Carolina said, "Now that Roosevelt has eaten with that nigger Washington, we shall have to kill a thousand niggers to get them back to their places."[61]

Jim Crow on Steroids

Perhaps no event better demonstrates the extent of violence by white supremacists in order to secure complete political domination, after Reconstruction ended, than the 1898 Wilmington race riot.[62] During the riot, white men in Wilmington, North Carolina, gunned down black men, seized the armory building, and burned down a local newspaper owned by blacks.[63] Two thousand white men assembled at the armory of the Wilmington Light Infantry and, led by former Confederate officer and United States congressman Alfred Waddell, proceeded to march through the city.[64] Blacks on the street were killed or wounded by the mob, with estimates of the death toll as high as one hundred.[65]

After a sweeping Democratic victory in the elections that followed the 1898 riot—victory that was achieved primarily by fraud and intimidation, including stuffing the ballot boxes and scaring black voters away from the polls—supporters of white privilege met at the Wilmington courthouse and presented a "White Declaration of Independence."[66] This declaration made demands of the black community, including the immediate resignation of Wilmington's black mayor, even though he had several months remaining in his term, as well as that of the police chief and the editor of the local newspaper.[67] Whites threatened violence if the demands were not met.[68] As a result, many blacks left the city,[69] which of course entrenched physical separation of the races even deeper.

For the blacks who remained in Wilmington, the intimidation continued in the elections two years later. After public threats of violence and bloodshed, black voters stayed away from the polls, resulting in resounding victories in support of the racist Democratic Party ticket.[70] The winner of the North Carolina gubernatorial election that year, Charles Aycock, vowed to prevent blacks from voting, making this the state's primary obligation to its white residents.[71]

By 1899, all southern state governments were comfortably in the hands of white Democrats committed to separation of blacks. Many members of Congress openly sought to exclude black politicians. By 1903, Congress had not one black member in its House or Senate. This disparity directly reflected the success of the schemes introduced decades earlier. At the 1901 Virginia Constitutional Convention, delegate Carter Glass accurately characterized the disparity: "Discrimination! Why, that is precisely what we propose. . . . That, exactly, is what this Convention was elected for—to discriminate to the very extremity of permissible action under the limitations of the Federal Constitution, with a view to the elimination of every negro voter. . . ."[72]

Over a dozen black members of Congress served during Reconstruction, but by 1903, that double-digit number had dwindled to zero.[73] In a democracy, how was that possible when in some states 40% of the population was black? The short answer, as we saw in chapter 2, is that the democratic process was perverted through the use of such devices as grandfather clauses, in which voting eligibility was limited to those who voted or whose grandfathers voted in 1867;[74] poll taxes, in which eligibility was based on a fee;[75] and literacy tests, in which blacks, who in the not-too-distant past had been executed for learning to read, were required to meet insurmountable reading comprehension standards.[76] When these devices failed, many who resisted voting by blacks preferred to kill them rather than allow them to vote.[77]

Presidents and members of Congress, like governors and state legislatures, were often either patently hostile or coldly unsympathetic to the muted and cautious requests by blacks for some slight improvement of their lot.[78] Even the false rumor that a black had been present at an official

White House function was sufficient to drive President Grover Cleveland into a frenzy.[79] He stated, "It so happens that I have never in my official position, either when sleeping or waking, alive or dead, on my head or on my heels, dined, lunched, or supped, or invited to a wedding reception any colored man, woman, or child."[80]

In keeping with his predecessors, Woodrow Wilson had no qualms about the plight of blacks. A black newspaper, *The New York Age*, warned that Wilson, "both by inheritance and absorption . . . has most of the prejudices of the narrowest type of southern white people against the Negro."[81] As president of Princeton University from 1902 to 1910, Wilson headed the only major northern school that excluded black students.[82] Moreover, when he was governor of New Jersey from 1911 to 1912, Wilson's "progressivism" did not embrace blacks. His "New Freedom" had been "all for the white man and little for blacks."[83] According to Professor Rayford Logan, President Wilson had not visited "any colored school, church, or gathering of colored people of any nature whatever."[84] During Wilson's administration there was a steady "expansion of segregation in the federal department buildings in Washington, a policy which President Taft had begun."[85]

Color was the mark of inferiority, and neither wealth, fame, education, nor skill altered that notion. As Thomas Dartmouth Rice so accurately portrayed in his minstrel shows, wherever blacks came in contact with whites, whether in public accommodations, schools, or job training programs, they were made to "weel about, turn about, and do jis so,"[86] resulting in segregation laws well into the next century. From the *Plessy* decision, in 1896, to the *Brown* decision, in 1954, most governments and private entities would separate blacks and whites except when black presence benefited whites, as when blacks performed services like cleaning or cooking on behalf of white employers.

Jim Crow Housing

In 1911, at a time when many blacks were trying to break away from rural poverty by moving into urban areas, Richmond, Virginia, passed an ordinance that legally sanctioned the segregation of all white and black residents.[87] Richmond was one of several Virginia cities to establish such requirements.[88] These laws gave municipalities the right to divide the land within their boundaries into segregated districts.[89] The city councils were authorized to prepare maps "showing the boundaries of all such segregation districts, and showing the number of white persons and colored persons residing within such segregation district[s]. . . ."[90] Thereafter, those newly defined Jim Crow districts were designated "white" or "black" depending on the race of the majority of the residents. Twelve months after the passage of such ordinances, it became a crime for any black person to move into and occupy a residence in an area known as a white district. Similarly, it was a crime for any white person to move into a black district. Many other states and cities across the country also instituted Jim Crow housing segregation in the early 20th century.[91]

For example, Baltimore passed the first racial housing segregation ordinance directed exclusively at blacks, in 1910.[92] Similar ordinances were passed in thirteen other cities, including Louisville, Winston-Salem, and Atlanta. The Baltimore ordinance's[93] passage was a direct response to attempts by blacks to move into neighborhoods that, by 1910, had become all white.[94] The plight of George McMechen and his family is a typical example.[95]

In 1910, George McMechen purchased a house in the previously all-white section of Baltimore known as Eutaw Place.[96] The family was subjected to harassment and required police protection.[97] Shortly after the McMechens moved into their new neighborhood, over ten thousand members of the community petitioned the city council in the hope of preventing any such future intrusions.[98] In response to this petition, the city council implemented the "Baltimore idea."[99]

The ordinance provided for residential segregation by street block. It prohibited blacks from moving into or assembling in residences located on blocks that were completely occupied by whites, prohibited whites from moving into or assembling in residences located in blocks that were completely occupied by blacks, and applied those same restrictions to schools and churches.[100] The ordinance was inapplicable to mixed blocks where both black and white persons lived.[101] Domestic servants, however, were exempted from this housing ordinance's coverage, just as they had been by segregation laws on trains.[102]

Residential segregation was not relegated to the South. Historically, Irish, Jews, and other white immigrant groups had been separated in housing in the North.[103] Ethnic colonies, or "ghettos,"[104] were created whenever new European immigrants arrived in large numbers. Typically, immigrants were impoverished, were poorly educated, and tended to crowd into low-rent areas with others of similar background or language.[105] As these immigrants accumulated money or became educated and informed about other opportunities, they left these ethnic areas and, no longer handicapped by their background, moved into more diverse communities.[106] However, the experience of the massive wave of blacks who entered the metropolitan North from the rural South in search of opportunity between 1905 and 1930 was altogether different. City and state laws relegated blacks to the least desirable areas and prevented them from meaningful opportunities to get out of those areas, while whites, even impoverished ones, were not separated.[107] Moreover, whites who improved their economic circumstances could move into wealthier white areas, thus moving up the ladder of success.[108] Blacks, however, were denied that opportunity under housing separation laws and practices.[109]

After the invalidation of residential segregation ordinances, many urban whites, in favor of black separation, turned to the Klan for help.[110] The Klan became extremely popular in northern cities like Detroit, Michigan, where a Klan member was elected mayor.[111] Violent Klan tactics were utilized in these cities, just as they had been earlier in southern rural areas, to maintain black separation.[112]

Other methods included steering, wherein real estate sales agents only show blacks houses for sale in black areas, and intimidation, wherein blacks who bought houses in white neighborhoods were threatened and harassed by white residents. One of the most popular methods was the racially restrictive covenant.[113] Of the myriad of devices implemented by whites to prevent blacks from buying property, the racially restrictive covenant received the first legal challenge.[114] As blacks tried to move from the less desirable areas of cities relegated to them through private and governmental practices, racial covenants were placed on houses in the more desirable areas.[115] Because of these covenants, the few blacks economically capable of owning such property were prevented or discouraged from doing so.

When housing segregation laws were prohibited by the Supreme Court, similar mandates were instituted by white vigilantism practices.[116] For example, certain cities excluded blacks from living within the city limits. After 1948, by practice, over three thousand "sundown towns" existed in the country. The term "sundown town" was derived from requirements that all blacks having business in the town had to leave by nightfall or risk bodily harm.[117] Blacks were not permitted to live or own property within the city or county limits. Some "sundown towns" prohibited only blacks, while others prohibited all minorities.[118] In a few towns and counties such as Pierce City, Missouri, and Anna-Jonesboro, Illinois, blacks were completely banished from the areas.[119] Confiscation of black-owned property was rampant, and such banishment was enforced by violence and intimidation.

Jim Crow Education

In response to demands by poor and middle-income whites in the beginning of the 20th century, most southern states began providing universal public education, albeit on a segregated basis.[120] The education provided to blacks was, keeping in line with *Plessy*, both separate and unequal. Affluent southern whites considered blacks cheap labor, good for one thing: the proper growing of cotton and tobacco.[121] These whites believed that education spoiled a good domestic or field hand,[122] preferring their laborers to be illiterate or semiliterate at best.[123] Southern white legislators claimed that blacks were not capable of higher learning and, therefore, were relegated to studying subjects dealing with manual labor. Money for educating blacks was often contingent on limiting their education to expansion of the manual labor force.[124] In 1900, the federal commissioner of education estimated that in sixteen former slave states, the average black child received half as much educational funding as the average white child.[125] Many states were worse.[126] South Carolina reports indicate that blacks, who represented 61% of the school population, received 20% of school funds (barely one-fifth as much as the average white child).[127]

Black children suffered other educational disadvantages as well. School terms in black institutions were significantly shorter.[128] Black schools were also fewer in number, and, therefore, were spread out, making travel to and from school more difficult, particularly in rural regions with poor roads and bridges.[129] Making it more challenging for blacks to acquire an education impeded the performances of those who tried. This reinforced inferiority notions, and provided false justification for expending fewer resources on black education.

The educational divide between black and white schools drastically increased as the 20th century moved forward.[130] By 1915, the funding disparity had grown so large that blacks received only one-twelfth as much money for education.[131] Moreover, most southern school boards, unlike those in the North, did not offer public secondary education to black youths.[132] Black school children, at best, received an elementary school education only. On the rare occasions when secondary schools were provided, those schools were drastically underfunded.[133] Typically, black southerners were not provided with public secondary schools until after World War II.[134] In 1909, Mississippi governor James Vardaman spelled out the white view of educating blacks:[135]

> Money spent today for the maintenance of public schools for negroes is robbery of the white man, and a waste upon the negro. You take it from the toiling white men and women, you rob the white child of the advantages it would afford him, and you spend it upon the negro in an effort to make of the negro what God Almighty never intended should be made, and which men cannot accomplish.[136]

Under the Supreme Court's "separate but equal" doctrine articulated in *Plessy*, states that adopted Jim Crow were obligated to provide separate educational facilities for blacks.[137] Many states in the North left the decision on whether to segregate public primary and secondary schools to local school boards.[138] While some local jurisdictions rejected Jim Crow, a majority, particularly the large urban school districts, chose to require racial separation.[139] Yet no state or local jurisdiction came close to satisfying the equality component of the doctrine, especially with regard to college, graduate, and professional school training.[140]

The Land-Grant Act, enacted in 1890, required that states using federal land-grant funds open their schools to both blacks and whites or allocate funds for black schools as an alternative to white ones.[141] The act gave states a choice, and the *Plessy* decision sanctioned that choice.

After 1896, most states provided an undergraduate institution for blacks to attend, but no states provided any graduate or professional schools for blacks.[142] Blacks who wanted to attend graduate or professional school had only two options: they could attend the limited number of private institutions throughout the country, like Howard University in Washington, DC, created by the federal government in 1867 to educate blacks, or they could hope to secure one of the token spots reserved for blacks at state, private, or federal institutions located in northern and western states.[143]

Many states attempted to satisfy the *Plessy* doctrine by choosing not to provide black students with an educational institution, and instead identified existing institutions in neighboring states as legitimate alternatives.[144] One of the most popular methods was providing scholarships for black students to attend Howard University, or another historically black institution located in another state.[145] These states reasoned that providing a scholarship to attend an out-of-state school was the same as providing a school within the state. Many black professionals, including a large number of black lawyers and doctors, were educated in this fashion.

Widespread use of this approach greatly limited the number of placements available for blacks at state schools. This explains why there were so few black professionals prior to the civil rights movement.[146] Graduate and professional placements nationally were limited to a couple of hundred per year.

This practice served to reinforce notions of black inferiority by limiting opportunities for blacks to become professionals. Those few blacks admitted, under a quota of one or two per year, to college or graduate and professional schools for whites, in northern or western states, were subjected to racist and discriminatory treatment.[147]

White students at military academies also pressed for black separation. In 1932, a young black male, Benjamin O. Davis Jr., entered West Point Military Academy in New York.[148] Like Henry Flipper before him, he was the only black cadet enrolled at West Point during that term, and just the fourth since the school had been established in 1802.[149] Shortly after his arrival, Davis accidentally witnessed a meeting of the other cadets in his class.[150] The subject of the meeting was, "What are we going to do about the nigger?" "From that meeting on," Davis recalled, "the cadets who roomed across the hall, who had been friendly earlier, no longer spoke to me. In fact, no one spoke to me except in the line of duty."[151]

The cadets at West Point "silenced" Davis for the duration of his four-year education.[152] This method of social exclusion meant that no cadet was permitted to speak or interact with Davis under threat of similar treatment by the rest of the academy.[153] Although the administrators at West Point, like most northern white leaders in the early 20th century, denied ordering, sanctioning, or even condoning this practice, the treatment Davis suffered was not prevented, nor were the culprits punished by academy officials.[154] Despite the "silent treatment," Davis became a skilled combat pilot during World War II and the commander of an all-black air corps unit called the "Red Tails" that achieved numerous combat records in spite of Jim Crow practices.[155]

Jim Crow Military

From the Spanish-American War in 1908 through the ending of World War II in 1945, blacks served in racially segregated units commanded by white officers.[156] Most often, black soldiers were excluded from skilled leadership positions and served overwhelmingly in labor and service capacities.[157] To discourage black participation, the military placed a strict cap on the number of black enlistments.[158]

When World War II began in Europe in 1939, only 3,640 black soldiers were in uniform.[159] By the time Pearl Harbor was bombed, that number had increased to 97,725.[160] By the end of 1942, the number of black soldiers had swelled to 467,833 men.[161] Despite this increase, the army pledged to maintain the practice of segregation and to keep the proportion of blacks in uniform the same as the proportion of blacks in the general population.[162] Thus, the military continued deliberately to relegate the vast majority of black soldiers to manual labor positions in support and supply units.[163] The primary task of the service troops included road building, stevedoring, laundering, and fumigating.[164]

The military's policies of parity in population percentage and racial segregation were difficult to maintain. Despite the cap on enlisted soldiers, the army did not have enough segregated facilities to house and train the unprecedented number of black recruits.[165] In addition to these logistical problems, most of the war was waged while black soldiers, a valuable and powerful resource, remained on the sidelines.[166] As in earlier wars, black soldiers were denied the right to fight until their manpower became a necessity.[167] Black infantry units were assigned to combat duty late in the war, but only when necessary to replace white units who had lost large numbers of soldiers.[168]

Eugene Bullard, a black American, fought with the French Foreign Legion in the early 20th century.[169] Bullard left the United States for France at the age of seventeen, after witnessing an attempted lynching of his father in Georgia in 1906.[170] A stellar soldier, Bullard was awarded the Croix de Guerre, the highest combat award, for heroics at the Battle of Verdun during World War I.[171] Opportunity presented itself when he was asked by French officers to volunteer for the Eagle Squadron, a group of American volunteers in the French Air Force.[172] Known as the "black swallow of death"[173] for his daring and courage, he was the first black aviator to fly successful missions for the French Air Force during the early stages of World War I.[174] In 1917, the United States entered World War I, and the United

States Army took over the squadron; Bullard applied to transfer to the newly formed American squadron.[175] Of the twenty-nine applicants, he was the only one denied transfer.[176] Instead, Bullard was ordered to report to a maintenance troop, a decision based solely on his race.[177] In spite of his decade of flying expertise, Bullard was excluded from serving his country in the way he was best qualified; instead, he was relegated to a low-level, menial position.[178]

Not one black was awarded the Medal of Honor, America's highest award for bravery during combat, in either World War I or World War II, even though several clearly qualified on the basis of meritorious and heroic deeds.

Jim Crow Employment

In the late 1800s, 75% of blacks lived in the South.[179] Most were undereducated and without capital. As a result, agricultural jobs served as the primary means for earning a living. Without money to buy land, blacks were limited to labor arrangements with low wages and no equity or equitable profit sharing. Such circumstances led to perpetual poverty.

Blacks who could not be coerced to work for unduly low wages were forced, through the legal system, to work without pay. Thousands of blacks, in the early 1900s, were arrested and convicted on false charges and leased out to corporations by southern state governments, as convict labor.[180] Unjustly forced to labor in coal mines, lumber mills, or road maintenance, these blacks were always exploited by being underfed and poorly housed, often injured or afflicted by illness, and sometimes overworked to the point of exhaustion and death.[181]

For those few blacks who could access capital, productive farm land was still not accessible. Few whites were willing to sell land to blacks. Where white purchasers existed, a sale of fertile land to blacks was less likely to transpire.[182]

Black employment in southern urban areas was not much better. Even as economic opportunities improved in the last decade of the 19th century, blacks were not permitted to benefit economically. Even in service positions such as maids, cooks, and barbers, blacks were refused employment due to the sentiment of many whites that these jobs were too good for blacks.[183]

For those blacks who remained in rural areas, the 1920s brought tremendous economic hardship. Agricultural cycles of overproduction and dwindling prices, coupled with frequent crop destruction from insects, caused widespread losses and infrequent payment to workers.

After the Civil War, most blacks lived in southern states.[184] By the turn of the 20th century, however, due to political and economic developments, including the denial of civil rights and high rates of unemployment, many blacks decided to leave the South for better opportunities in the North.[185] This process came to be known as the Great Migration.[186] Lasting twenty-five years, beginning in the late 1800s, it became the largest migratory shift in American history.[187] Blacks who participated encountered racist practices similar to those they had escaped in the South.

Intense conflicts occurred between white and black job seekers. Competition from skilled black laborers was particularly resented. Most blacks seeking employment as blacksmiths, furniture makers, or painters met hostility from whites who possessed similar skills.[188] This was exacerbated, within the union movement, when white workers attempted to organize to strengthen negotiating power with management over wages and hours, and black workers, denied union membership due to their race, were brought in as strike breakers. Companies exploited this dynamic to their own advantage. As far back as 1867, in Boston, Massachusetts, black ship-builders were brought from Virginia to undermine white laborers' efforts to obtain shorter working days,[189] demonstrating once again how those in positions of influence used race divisively. Black desires for employment and economic independence were used to reduce the economic clout of white workers, perpetuating racial division.

Many blacks headed for northern industrial areas, motivated by the same aspirations as white immigrants who came before them—to obtain better educations for their children and higher wages for themselves and to avoid brutal treatment from oppressive governments.[190] Black culture embraced a strong work ethic, and the Great Migration reflected blacks' strong desire for better employment opportunities.[191] Unlike white immigrants, however, black migrants were already Americans—they knew the language, understood America's social customs and class structure, and in a sense were at home in the North before they ever set foot in New York, Detroit, or Chicago.[192] Yet, blacks faced stronger opposition than white foreigners in many areas of life.[193]

Once white immigrants became "Americanized"—knowledgeable in the ways of America—they were allowed to become American citizens not subject to separation laws.[194] Despite the fact that European immigrants had much in common with black workers, as they were both exploited by employers with low wages, long hours, and poor work environments, white immigrants united along racial lines with their white employers to support discriminatory laws.[195] The lure of white privilege, it seems, was more unifying than common social or economic class characteristics.[196] Whites born in the United States, and those emigrating from Europe, united to withhold economic and other opportunities from black Americans.[197] From the start of the trade union movement in the late 19th century, blacks were excluded from membership. In 1915, immigration from Europe stopped suddenly with the outbreak of World War I.[198] As a result of white immigration being halted, many blacks were hired in war-related industries that had been heavily dependent on immigrant labor.[199] Blacks worked in industries from shipbuilding to iron and steel to automobile and trucks to electrical supplies to coal mines and to railroads.[200] Hundreds of thousands of blacks found employment during the war.[201] In 1917, as World War I came to a close, the American Federation of Labor (AFL), one of the largest labor organizations in the country, considered opening its membership to blacks in order to prevent them from being used as strikebreakers as they had been prior to the war.[202] Nevertheless, most AFL-affiliated unions denied black membership.[203]

The number of blacks and whites seeking employment in the urban North outnumbered available employment opportunities. Employers tended to favor white workers over blacks, so the latter had difficulty securing all but the most onerous and lowest-paying jobs.[204]

The racial divide in employment reflected the paradigm's racial hierarchy. Service and menial jobs were reserved for blacks, if they could get jobs at all. Most of the blacks who came to the North during the Great Migration were unskilled industrial laborers or farmers.[205] With only the most menial jobs available to blacks, these migrants formed the bulk of the working poor in cities throughout the North.[206] Black political leaders, like W. E. B. Du Bois and Booker T. Washington, encouraged business enterprise so that blacks could become their own employers and secure wealth and economic independence.[207] Blacks established a wide range of businesses located in northern cities, from restaurants to grocery stores to funeral homes and banks. The hair and beauty care industry was one of the most successful areas of black enterprise, producing the wealthiest black woman of the early 20th century, C. J. Walker, whose business employed thousands of black women as salespersons in the beginning decades of the 20th century.[208]

The lack of employment opportunities for blacks in white-owned businesses necessitated creative approaches on the part of blacks in order to further economic opportunities. One of the most successful approaches was to involve black churches in business enterprises in black neighborhoods. Because of limited access to capital from white-owned banks, black churches, the most prosperous entities of the time, exercised a more diverse responsibility than simply providing religious support. Black churches got involved in various economic enterprises to benefit the larger black community, such as building and loan organizations, newspapers, and restaurants.[209] Many of these church-affiliated businesses made steady progress and performed valuable economic services for blacks during the first three decades of the 20th century.

The economic depression of 1929, however, devastated most of these businesses; because they had little or no capital reserves, failure rates were high and only a few businesses survived. Black laborers were the first to lose their jobs or to have their wages lowered to poverty levels.[210] New Deal legislation in the late 1930s and early 1940s lowered unemployment numbers for blacks.[211] By 1940, over a million black laborers in the North owed their employment to New Deal work programs.[212] Nevertheless, in a majority of localities, blacks received less financial assistance than similarly situated whites, or no assistance at all.[213] In the early 1940s, industrial hiring began to pick up, particularly in war-related industries. Yet, first preference was given to white workers unemployed since the Depression.[214] Few black workers were hired until federal legislation required it in 1941.[215] As a result of this unequal treatment, whether skilled or unskilled, black workers in the North were subjected to discriminatory treatment if they were fortunate enough to be hired at all. In 1934, Paul Robeson, a black scholar and athlete, graduated from Columbia Law School.[216] As a member of Phi Beta Kappa at Rutgers University and as the College Football Player of the Year, he was a uniquely gifted individual.[217] Offered legal employment at a white law firm in New York City, a first for a black lawyer, he quit after several months, frustrated because a white secretary refused to take dictation from him.[218] Robeson would later become an internationally celebrated singer, opera performer, and movie star.[219] While "white-collar" blacks like Robeson were demeaned and degraded, most blacks, even those few who were highly trained or skilled, received no opportunities at white-owned or -controlled institutions, including federal and state governments.[220]

Jim Crow and Economic Growth

In the decades after World War I, business opportunities for blacks had worsened, with widespread disparities existing in government assistance programs. The Agricultural Adjustment Administration (AAA) sent millions of dollars to all-white county committees to pay for farm land retired from cultivation, thus reversing a drastic fall in prices caused by overproduction.[221] AAA subsidy checks never reached a sizeable percentage of black farm owners, and because white administrators and landlords kept the checks for themselves, when they did disperse funds appropriately, discriminatory discrepancies existed.[222] Comparable workers received widely disparate subsidies. A black sharecropper received an average of $295 from the AAA, while a white farmer received $417.[223] A black field hand received $175, while a white one received $232.[224]

While blacks were being forcibly displaced and denied housing opportunities, many whites were able to purchase their first homes with mortgages secured through the G.I. Bill, which was passed after World War II to allow veterans to secure government loan assistance. Many of the homes purchased in 1945 for ten thousand dollars were subsequently valued at more than one hundred thousand dollars, a tenfold increase in value.[225] The few blacks who qualified for assistance faced discrimination, with state government officials failing to deliver their earned benefits.[226] Even the G.I. Bill, which provided college tuition assistance for those who had served in the military, failed to provide benefits to most black veterans,[227] because racist southern state officials administered and controlled the distribution of the funds.[228] A substantial number of white males attending college after World War II did so with government assistance under the G.I. Bill.[229] That same opportunity was denied to many black veterans who had fought under the very same conditions.[230] Other government assistance programs, like Social Security and farmer assistance, had equally racist administration.

The Social Security program—designed to provide monetary assistance to retirees—excluded farm laborers and domestics from its coverage, due to concerns by white southern legislators that blacks would benefit from the program.[231] These legislators knew that 60% of all employed blacks nationwide fell within those two job categories.[232]

Jim Crow government programs and practices created a staggering discrepancy in wealth and resources among blacks and whites. Large numbers of whites, for example, were able to purchase homes or farm land while a majority of blacks remained renters in the North and sharecroppers in the South.[233] Approximately 75% of the black farmers in the South, in 1900, were sharecroppers or tenant farmers.[234] But in the Mississippi Delta, for example, Professor Leon Litwack explained that "black owners comprised only slightly more than 2% of the farm operators. . . ."[235] By 1940, 75% of white farmers owned their land while few blacks did so.[236] In the North, disproportionate white home ownership was maintained and perpetuated by racial covenants that prevented many whites from selling their homes to blacks.[237] By 1940, fewer than 5% of blacks owned homes in the North.[238] The lack of home ownership for blacks kept them in a weak economic state, especially during periods of inflation, when housing became easier to afford for those who owned real property and held a fixed-rate mortgage.[239] Renters, in contrast, usually saw their housing expenses increase. As a result, large numbers of whites would inherit valuable assets from deceased relatives. On average, one in four white families received an inheritance after a parent's death averaging close to $150,000.[240] In contrast, only one in twenty black families inherited valuable assets with an average worth of around $40,000.[241]

Jim Crow Sports

Separation in sports was necessary to prevent blacks from defeating whites, even if only in a game. Contrary to what most Americans have been led to believe today, there were integrated sports competitions as far back as the mid-1800s.[242] In fact, at that time, blacks participated in, and often excelled in, the major sports of the day—cycling, horse racing, and boat racing.[243] For example, in the first Kentucky Derby in 1875,[244] fourteen of the first fifteen jockeys were black, and ten of the Derby's first seventeen winners were black.[245] Soon after, in 1894, the Jockey Club was formed to license jockeys, and it denied licenses to blacks.[246] The main reason for this discrimination was that many horse owners believed that most whites did not want to see black jockeys winning races, making money, and getting newspaper coverage.[247] These owners felt that it would be more profitable to have white jockeys winning the races.[248] Similar separation practices were implemented in increasingly popular professional sports such as football, baseball, basketball, and in boxing after Jack Johnson[249] became the first black heavyweight champion of the world in 1910. After his defeat of Jim "The Great White Hope" Jeffries[250] inspired race riots, no black was allowed to fight for the heavyweight title from 1915 to 1937.[251] Some states even had statutes that prohibited whites and blacks from boxing one another in amateur bouts or social settings.[252]

The plight of Jack Johnson is particularly instructive as to the lengths that some white government officials would go to prevent black excellence.[253] As the first black heavyweight boxing champion, Jack Johnson was placed in one of the most high-profile positions symbolizing physical excellence. While he was heavyweight champion, members of the federal government targeted Johnson and attempted to have him incarcerated so he could not hold the title or fight anymore. Due to Johnson's extravagant lifestyle of traveling extensively and dating many women, including women who worked as prostitutes, government officials felt that he could be convicted under a recently enacted law, the Mann Act, which made it illegal to transport women across state lines for immoral purposes.[254] After a two-year investigation of Johnson culminating in his arrest in 1912, the case collapsed when it became clear that the woman in question, Lucille Cameron, had been a prostitute long before she met Johnson.[255] The government, however, refused to abandon their obsession with targeting Johnson for criminal investigation.[256] The government went to great lengths to secure a criminal conviction against Johnson.

Disappointed that Johnson had avoided conviction in 1912, Assistant United States Attorney Harry Parkin was determined to indict Johnson for his involvement with white prostitutes.[257] Parkin requested that the Justice Department investigate whether Johnson had ever transported any other women across state lines for allegedly immoral purposes.[258] Although the Mann Act was designed to apply to pimps and brothels or other business establishments promoting money for sex, Parkin insisted that the law could be used to convict Johnson.[259] One of Johnson's former companions, Belle Schreiber, whom he dumped for another woman, became a primary witness in the government's new case against Johnson.[260] Soon after Schreiber came forward, indictments were issued against Johnson for Mann Act violations relating to involvement in prostitution by transporting women out of state for sexual purposes in exchange for money.[261] Johnson was convicted and sentenced to a year in prison.[262]

Black Entrepreneurship under Jim Crow

Due to severe discrimination in education, housing, employment, and government benefits, the black entrepreneurial spirit was encouraged by black leaders as a way to combat discriminatory treatment. Many blacks established self-sustaining black towns in an attempt to minimize contact with and reliance on hostile and unresponsive state governments. Allensworth, California—along with Mound Bayou, Mississippi, and Nicodemus, Kansas—was one such place.[263] Started by Colonel Allen Allensworth in 1906, after he retired as an army chaplain, the thriving community grew to over four hundred residents and included a bakery, lumber yard, restaurant, livery stable, and blacksmith shop.[264] After being denied participation in a water cooperative agreement by neighboring white towns, Allensworth was abandoned in 1918.[265]

The National Patent Office was one of the few federal institutions that did not discriminate; it accepted patents irrespective of the race of the applicant.[266] As a result, thousands of blacks, including Elijah McCoy, who held fifty patents connected to automatic machine lubricators, and Granville Woods, who held several patents later assigned to the General Electric Company and American Bell Telephone Company,[267] successfully obtained patents between 1900 and 1954. Garrett Morgan was also one of the many black patent applicants.[268]

Morgan was born in 1877, the seventh of eleven children in his family.[269] As was typical of rural blacks, his formal education ended at grade five, and he subsequently sought work to help his family financially.[270] Eventually, Morgan found a job as a sewing machine adjuster for Roots and McBride, a clothing manufacturer.[271] Morgan became so good at repairing and fine tuning sewing machines that he found steady work fixing and adjusting them.[272]

Recognizing the high demand for his services, Morgan opened his own sewing retail and repair business in 1907.[273] This began a long and prosperous career of inventions, beginning with several patents that improved the sewing machine.[274] Morgan conceived his greatest idea in 1911, when he read newspaper reports of the tragic Triangle Shirtwaist Company fire in New York City.[275] The thick, deadly smoke prevented firefighters' efforts to save victims, which led to the death of 146 workers in the factory.[276] Shortly thereafter, Morgan designed and patented a helmet that could help firefighters survive in such dangerous environments.[277] Morgan named his invention the "gas inhalator," and it consisted of a durable hood that fit over the head and two long tubes that ran from the hood to the floor.[278]

Marketing his invention as "the Morgan Helmet," Morgan recognized that the best way to sell his invention was to demonstrate it.[279] Yet, when he traveled around the country displaying his invention in a dramatic tent demonstration equivalent to a magic show, where Morgan would use his device to amazingly survive a smoke-filled chamber, Morgan ran into hostility from white audiences due to his race.[280] Morgan realized that sales dropped off dramatically when he presented himself as the inventor.[281] As a result, Morgan staged a show where he had a white friend pose as the inventor, and Morgan posed as his assistant.[282] Sales improved dramatically when the invention was no longer associated with a black inventor.[283]

Garrett Morgan's experience is a prime example of how notions of white superiority/black inferiority hinder black excellence. It was difficult for Morgan to sell his invention to whites when Morgan identified himself as the inventor. The fact that Morgan was black caused many whites to question the quality of the device or the authenticity of the claims as to what the device could accomplish. Moreover, the lack of sales to whites may also reflect the sentiment that even if the device was effective and the claims were authentic, support of black businesses would undermine white competitors. In contrast, when Morgan posed as the assistant to the white inventor, sales to whites soared.[284] These whites could accept and embrace purchasing a technologically advanced product created by a white person but demonstrated by a black servant serving as the "guinea pig" for the experiment.

In the white mind, blacks were thought of as servants, cooks, maids, butlers, and field hands. Blacks could be successfully associated with products that reflected their rightful place in American society, such as "Aunt Jemima" selling pancakes or "Uncle Ben" selling rice—in those types of positions, blacks were serving whites in areas of labor where whites chose not to perform. But designing technology to be used in sophisticated mining operations or firefighting rescues moved into a realm deemed unsuitable for black control or supervision. Rejecting these inventions was the ultimate exhibition of racial insanity, for those whites would prefer to ignore or dispute the success of a device that could save thousands of lives, most of them white lives, rather than acknowledge that a black inventor may have accomplished a feat that whites had not been able to accomplish. Morgan had to acknowledge and make use of false notions of white superiority by having a white person pose as the inventor in order to get whites to even consider using Morgan's creation.

Unfortunately, this was not a rare occurrence. Notions of racial hierarchy were frequently reinforced through black/white interpersonal relations throughout the Jim Crow period. Many blacks had to falsely play roles inferior to whites in order to fit into the racial paradigm. Blacks whose activities or roles fell outside of the paradigm, by demonstrating excellence or beating white competitors, made many whites uncomfortable and undermined the notion of black inferiority.

Paul Williams, one of the first black architects in California, took a different approach from Morgan in overcoming white racism against black entrepreneurs.[285] Instead of camouflaging the fact that he was the building designer, Williams developed methods that would allow whites to utilize his services while maintaining a degree of black separation.[286] For instance, sensitive to white clients who might feel uncomfortable sitting next to him, Williams developed the ability to draw upside down.[287] This allowed clients to examine his designs right-side-up as he drew them from the opposite side of the table.[288] This tactic worked as Williams completed over three thousand projects, most of them for white clients.[289] Nevertheless, Williams was forbidden from visiting the Beverly Hills Hotel—a hotel he had designed—due to the hotel's policy excluding black customers.[290]

Often, denial of black excellence involved taking credit away from blacks and giving it exclusively to whites. In housing, schools, business, politics, and sports, the presence of and performances by blacks were devalued. Such devaluation occurred even in medicine, where lives were at risk. For example, Vivien Thomas, a black man with a high school diploma, created and perfected a complicated heart surgery procedure that saved thousands of lives.[291] In 1944, headlines across the world announced that Johns Hopkins University chief of surgery Dr. Alfred Blalock had repaired the heart of a nine-pound baby.[292] However, although Blalock actually performed the heart procedure, it was Thomas, his surgical assistant, who instructed him.[293] As Blalock scrubbed in for the procedure, he looked around the operating room and realized his guide, Thomas, was not present.[294] Despite the confusion of the other medical personnel in the room, Blalock insisted that Thomas be permitted into the operating room to advise him.[295] At the time of the surgery, Blalock had little experience with the procedure, while Thomas had successfully completed the procedure dozens of times on animals.[296] As the white doctor maneuvered the baby's heart, the black laboratory technician sat behind him, whispering instructions.[297] Because he was black, Thomas would not ordinarily have been permitted in the operating room, and was forced to use a separate door to enter the university hospital.[298] Furthermore, Thomas's official job title was initially "janitor."[299] But, Blalock's successful research and pioneering medical innovations were the result of Thomas's work.[300] Not only did Thomas perfect the procedure; he designed new surgical tools for Blalock.[301] Unfortunately, while Blalock was able to negotiate reasonable compensation for Thomas, he did little to acknowledge Thomas's contributions in the operating room—Blalock unfairly took credit for Thomas's work and innovations.[302] It was not until the 1970s, almost thirty years after the initial groundbreaking surgery, and several years after Blalock's death, that Thomas was finally recognized for his accomplishments—a portrait of Thomas was presented and hung at the hospital, and he was awarded an honorary doctorate by Johns Hopkins, as well as being appointed to a position on the Hopkins medical school faculty.[303]

When laws proved ineffective in suppressing black entrepreneurial excellence, economic incentives were offered for blacks to deny their excellence. During the early 20th century, A. Philip Randolph gained recognition as the head of the first black union, the Brotherhood of Sleeping Car Porters (BSCP).[304] Consistent with Jim Crow employment practices, national labor organizations, such as the American Federation of Labor, excluded black members. In 1925, Randolph agreed to help start and head a union for the black employees of the Pullman Train Car Company (Pullman Company), which provided the most expensive and luxurious accommodations for overnight train travel.[305] A majority of employees at the Pullman Company were blacks employed as service attendants.[306] Despite strong opposition by the Pullman Company's management, the employees voted to support the BSCP.[307] In 1929, the Pullman Company sent Randolph a check for ten thousand dollars as a thinly veiled bribe to discontinue his work as head of the BSCP.[308] Disgusted by the proposition, Randolph returned the check. In a later speech to the BSCP, Randolph said, "I will not take Pullman gold."[309] According to one BSCP member, in refusing the company's bribe, Randolph sent the message that "negro pride [was] not for sale."[310]

Preventing Black Excellence with Incarceration and Violence

Many blacks who challenged separation practices were either incarcerated or killed. During the first half of the 20th century, threats and intimidation against blacks were widespread.[311] Torture, used to coerce confessions, was prevalent in detentions of blacks,[312] and arrests for violating Jim Crow laws sharply increased incarceration rates. Under Jim Crow laws, in the early 1900s, blacks were arrested, imprisoned, and forced into labor.[313] Moreover, longer sentences for blacks were encouraged in order to extend their labor commitment. For example, 1913 court records from Arkansas indicate excessive sentences for convicted blacks—180 days for disturbing the peace; three years for stealing clothing from a clothesline; and thirty-six years for forging documents to buy whiskey.[314] If a local industry needed workers, vagrancy arrests increased proportional to the need for labor, in some cases rising by 800%.[315] Trials of blacks took place without legal representation, or with an all-white jury,[316] or without any jury at all. An offense such as hitching a ride on a train often quickly turned into years of forced labor on a prison-run plantation.

This is exactly what happened to John Davis, a black man from Goodwater, Alabama.[317] In 1901, Davis was arrested and convicted on a false charge of failure to pay a forty dollar debt.[318] The sheriff, Robert Franklin, claimed, as he did with numerous other blacks, that Davis owed him money.[319] A wealthy white landowner, John Pace, paid the fictitious debt plus a fine and, pursuant to Alabama law, Davis, under duress, signed an agreement to work for Pace for ten months in order to avoid a prison sentence.[320]

While vagrancy arrests could in theory affect both blacks and whites, officials generally targeted blacks. Many states had curfew laws that were applied to blacks only. The resulting disparity in incarceration was well documented. For example, in Texas in the early 1900s, blacks represented 20% of the state population but 60% of the prison population.[321] In 1917, in Mississippi, 90% of the prison population was black.[322]

Once convicted of a crime, blacks were frequently forced to work on chain gangs or prison-run plantations or factories. The largest and most notorious was Parchman Farm, a 20,000-acre prison camp plantation in Mississippi.[323] Life at Parchman Farm was particularly brutal.[324] Black prisoners would rise before dawn and march, at gunpoint, all the way to the fields, sometimes a mile or more, with prison guards trailing on horseback.[325] Once workers arrived at the fields, they were divided into squads and led by the fastest worker, who would "set the pace" for the entire group.[326] Any prisoner who did not keep up with the pace received severe punishment, and prisoners who tried to run or escape were shot on sight no matter what the reason.[327] Prisoners at Parchman Farm generally worked until they dropped dead or experienced sunstroke.[328] On several occasions, prisoners attempted to avoid work by "knockin' a joe," which referred to self-mutilation by cutting off a limb.[329] It was common to see a one-legged or one-armed man who had chopped off his own foot or hand with an ax or hoe to avoid the prison labor of the South.[330] Prisoners at Parchman realized that pardons were nonexistent, so self-injury became the only alternative available for them to get out of the laborious and torturous tasks.[331] Other prisoners drank poison, slit their wrists, or severed Achilles tendons to free themselves from the agony of working in the fields.[332] However, those who were unable to work due to severed limbs soon became guinea pigs for the state in medical experiments instead.[333]

Worse than incarceration and forced labor, the fate of death by white vigilantism befell some who challenged Jim Crow laws. One example was Lloyd Gaines, a black man who graduated from Lincoln University, in Missouri, in 1935 and wanted to go to law school.[334] Gaines sought to attend law school in Missouri, so he applied to the only law school within the state—the University of Missouri.[335] The university conceded that Gaines was qualified but would not permit him to enroll because he was black.[336]

The NAACP represented Gaines and sued the University of Missouri, alleging that Gaines had been denied admission in violation of equality provisions in the Constitution.[337] During the trial, the university claimed to have satisfied its obligation under the Equal Protection Clause of the Constitution by providing Gaines with a scholarship to attend a law school in an adjacent state that accepted blacks.[338] It was odd indeed to hear the lawyers for the University of Missouri advocating for the greatness of one of its competitors, the University of Illinois Law School.[339] The University of Missouri also contended that Gaines should have applied to Lincoln College, the Jim Crow school in Missouri, and asked Lincoln officials to create a law school for him and other blacks.[340]

The United States Supreme Court heard the case in 1938.[341] As Charles Hamilton Houston stood in front of the Court to argue the case, Justice James McReynolds, a declared supporter of white superiority, reversed his chair and turned his back to Houston.[342] Houston subsequently made his arguments and, not surprisingly, Justice McReynolds did not agree with Houston's position.[343] Yet, McReynolds's vote was inconsequential because seven justices agreed with Houston.[344] Led by Chief Justice Charles Hughes, the Court held that the University of Missouri had violated

Gaines's equal protection rights and affirmed that, unless an equal school in the state was available immediately, he had to be admitted to the University of Missouri.[345] On March 19, 1939, several months after the decision, but prior to his enrollment in law school, Gaines suddenly disappeared[346]— one afternoon, Gaines left the fraternity house where he resided to buy some stamps, and he was never seen again. Many believe that Gaines made the ultimate sacrifice, giving his life to bridge the racial divide.

While black separation was rigidly maintained under Jim Crow laws, those laws were frequently challenged within the judicial system and, sometimes, said challenges were successful. But even when those challenges succeeded, vigilantism by whites often prevented the racial divide from being bridged and black excellence from being fulfilled.

Crossing the Jim Crow Line

Throughout the first half of the 20th century, blacks who attempted to cross the racial divide of Jim Crow segregation or who demonstrated excellence while interacting with whites faced systematic atrocities. The practice of lynching—a form of public murder without trial—was frequently utilized against blacks who attempted to vote during Reconstruction and continued and expanded from the late 19th century well into the 20th century, especially in the South.[347] Perpetrators were rarely tried or convicted. Thousands of blacks were tortured and murdered through public spectacles held in town centers and attended by hundreds of spectators.[348]

Historians estimate that between 1880 and 1951, more than three thousand lynchings took place in America.[349] Lynching was supported by all levels of society, including law enforcement agents, who were sometimes active participants.[350] In nearly all historical records, the victim was falsely accused of a crime and assaulted by a violent mob, while police and the justice system made no efforts to restore order.[351] The key, however, in almost all lynchings, was the belief by some whites that a black perpetrator had wrongly crossed the racial divide, such as drinking from the white-designated water fountain, or committed an offense challenging notions of white superiority, such as engaging in sexual relations with a white female.[352]

It is important to note that lynchings were not unique to the South. In the summer of 1930, James Cameron, a sixteen-year-old from Marion,

Indiana, and two of his teenage friends were arrested and held in the Grant County Courthouse Jail, accused of murdering a white man and raping a white woman.[353] Over the course of several days a mob surrounded the jail, led by the Ku Klux Klan and urged on by local newspapers and radio broadcasts.[354] The sheriff and law authorities made no effort to control the crowd, which grew to several thousand and used sledgehammers to pulverize the brick frames around the iron doors of the jail.[355] For hours the unrelenting pounding of their hammers tore away at the brick frames, sending shock waves of terror into the souls of the prisoners within the holding cells.[356] The mob tore the iron doors from their frames, surged in, and began pounding down the inner doors.[357]

Reaching the cell of Thomas Shipp, the mob dragged him out, beat him into unconsciousness, and cheered as they hung him from a tree on the courthouse lawn.[358] As his lifeless body swung from the tree branch, they desecrated and mutilated it.[359] The mob reentered the jail to repeat the process on their second victim, Abe Smith.[360] In his cell, Cameron heard a second crescendo in the crowd outside, and he knew that Abe had been murdered. Smith was hung next to Shipp.[361]

The mob surged again into the jail, taking Cameron from his cell.[362] In his book, *A Time of Terror*, Cameron describes how he was punched, spit on, bitten, clubbed, and stabbed as his body was dragged through the crowd.[363] He recognized the faces of many of his attackers: some had been his friends during his lifetime in that town.[364] He noted how people urged each other on, teaching each other the expressions of hatred.[365] An adult told a child to bite Cameron's leg as he passed by.[366] The violent crowd dragged him toward the tree where the dead bodies of Tom and Abe hung.[367] As the rope was already placed around Cameron's neck to hang him, he heard a woman's voice above the din of the crowd, saying "Take this boy back. He had nothing to do with any raping or killing."[368] The booming voice knocked back the crowd, stopping them cold in their tracks.[369] They fell back stunned, suddenly motionless; time stood still for a moment.[370]

Though the crowd stopped momentarily, Cameron was not yet safe. A deputy and two assistants rushed him back into the jail and from there into a car that snuck him out of town.[371] For the next fifty hours Cameron had no food or rest, fleeing to safety in another prison.[372]

From the mid-19th century to the mid-20th century more than three thousand individuals were brutally murdered through lynching.[373]

Cameron is the only known survivor of such an attempt.[374] Although he was innocent, Cameron served four years in prison before gradually rebuilding his life.[375] Many years later, Mary Ball, the woman who had accused the boys of rape, testified that, in fact, she had not been raped.[376] More than sixty years later, in 1993, Indiana governor Evan Bayh granted Cameron an official pardon.[377]

In other cases, where the violence was planned well in advance, specific exemplars of black excellence were targeted, such as veterans, clergy, and especially civil rights leaders, whose actions were designed to change state and national laws and policies on discrimination and, thus, threatened Jim Crow segregation in all its forms. On Christmas night, 1951, Harry T. Moore, the head of the NAACP in Florida, and his wife were killed in a bombing that destroyed their home in Mims, Florida.[378] At the time, Moore was leading an investigation stemming from an incident in which a group of black men were accused of raping a white woman in Groveland, Florida.[379] At trial, the three defendants were found guilty.[380] However, in April of 1951, in a rare demonstration of judicial intervention, the Supreme Court overturned two of the convictions and death sentences on grounds that "Lake County's method of jury selection had 'discriminated against the Negro race.'"[381] The exonerated defendants' claim to innocence, however, was ignored when they were shot by the local sheriff.[382] He claimed they were trying to escape—behavior that would be rather illogical for a group whose conviction had just been overturned.[383] Witness accounts of the event affirmed that the sheriff shot without cause; evidence illustrated that it was highly unlikely that the two men were, in fact, trying to escape.[384] Moore spearheaded the investigation and, just months later, was killed.[385] The sheriff was never prosecuted.[386]

Conclusion

Woven through this rampant victimization, lynching, and exclusion, Jim Crow laws provided the systematic framework that expanded the separation of blacks and sustained the racial hierarchy. Black separation was maintained through government policies in education and housing, which perpetuated the physical separation of blacks and whites. The racial hierarchy was reinforced by preventing black advancements in virtually all walks of life: employment, housing, education, military service, sports, and business. The pervasive practice of separating blacks in these areas of life directly increased the proliferation of notions of black inferiority. By the early 1950s, the racial divide was rigidly maintained throughout the country by government enforcement and private acts. In this way, the second pillar of the paradigm—separation of blacks—became firmly entrenched in American society. The resulting long-term racial isolation made blacks extremely susceptible to economic and political victimization.

As we have seen throughout this chapter, blacks were kept separate in order to eliminate their competition with whites and to control the perceived threat of their integration into society. Central to this method of controlling blacks was the ruling in the *Plessy* case, introducing the harmful "separate but equal" doctrine.[387] This infamous case, in which the Supreme Court sanctioned segregation in public accommodations, resulted in decades of blatant segregation of blacks in public settings. In this way, the racial hierarchy was intensified and expanded, and segregation was given a false patina of judicial legitimacy.

Separation intensified throughout this grim period of history. Governments segregated education to separate blacks and to continue subjugating black labor to menial jobs. Segregated educational facilities were grossly unequal, and on the average, black schools received half the funding of white schools. Flagrant discrimination in housing saturated the United States, both in the South and in the North, sustaining the paradigm of black separation and white isolation. Such discrimination was legally sanctioned in most states, by laws, such as the Virginia statute on racial composition, or by policy, such as the "Baltimore idea."[388] By 1910, Jim Crow laws maintained black housing separation, even as blacks migrated out of southern rural areas. The paradigm persisted despite efforts to reduce it: courts invalidated housing segregation laws in 1917, but private racial covenants maintained black separation; as courts invalidated racial covenants, white flight maintained black separation. As a result, white isolation in housing persisted even as Jim Crow laws were invalidated. Black separation and victimization became more insidious, strengthening the paradigm. Gradual improvements in court rulings had no impact because the paradigm was so entrenched in the minds of individuals and the practices of society.

Throughout this period, government programs and societal practices openly excluded blacks from economic and educational opportunities. Whites refused to accept black inventions, unless they were attributed to whites, as we saw in the case of Garrett Morgan.[389] Whites took credit for the work done by blacks, as we saw in the case of Alfred Blalock taking credit for the discoveries made by Vivien Thomas.[390] Blacks were excluded from educational opportunities, by law and by violence, as we saw in the case of Lloyd Gaines.[391] During a period when positive growth could have been possible, victimization intensified. As victimization became ubiquitous, the paradigm took its most evil incarnation: lynching was the ultimate form of exclusion and violent victimization.

PART II

Sustaining the Paradigm

White Isolation and Black Separation and Subordination

4

Maintaining Racial Segregation in Schools and Neighborhoods from *Brown* to the 21st Century

"Hatred that rages in souls and suddenly loses its immediate object does not disappear without a trace."

—Anonymous, 1991[1]

FALSE NOTIONS OF white superiority/black inferiority fueled white desires for racial isolation that were supported by laws and case decisions beginning with Reconstruction. As blacks fought for integrated schools, housing, and public accommodations, white resistance increased. Most blacks would not be separated without resistance, and many whites would not cease creating policies and practices geared toward ensuring white isolation. While the famous 1954 Supreme Court decision in *Brown v. Board of Education*,[2] prohibiting state-mandated racial segregation in public schools, gave progressive Americans hope that racial isolation would be eradicated, not only in education but in all aspects of American society, this hope was misplaced. Unfortunately, *Brown* and its progeny neither altered notions of racial hierarchy nor prevented black separation.

Racial hierarchy and isolation did not end with the Supreme Court's decision in 1954, as commitment to both was evident even from the highest elected officials in the country. As president, Dwight Eisenhower explained, "[Segregationists] are not bad people. All they are concerned about is to see that their sweet little girls are not required to sit in school alongside some big, black bucks."[3]

President Eisenhower spoke these words to Chief Justice Earl Warren at a White House dinner in 1954.[4] Seated next to Warren was former presidential candidate and one-time congressman, Solicitor General John W. Davis, whom Eisenhower praised as a "great man" and one of the nation's most able lawyers.[5] It was not idle chitchat. Davis had argued more than

140 cases before the Court, most recently on behalf of southern school officials defending the right to exclude black children from white schools.[6] Meanwhile, Warren, with the rest of the Court, was deciding the fate of those schools in *Brown*.[7]

One Step Forward, Two Steps Back

There are two *Brown* cases, *Brown I*, decided in 1954,[8] and *Brown II*, decided in 1955.[9] The *Brown* cases involved a constitutional challenge by black primary school children segregated by the state due to their race. The Court in *Brown I* declared that racial segregation in public schools, at least when mandated by law, violates the principle of equality contained in the United States Constitution.[10] The Court rejected the "separate but equal" doctrine established in *Plessy*[11] on the basis that segregated schools were "inherently unequal."[12] Unlike segregated train cars, segregated schools created a sense of inferiority among black school children that time could not undo.[13] The Court in *Brown II* declared that the black school children were entitled to attend a desegregated school.[14] The Court empowered local school boards to implement the desegregation remedy and local federal courts to supervise the plans, all to be done "with all deliberate speed."[15]

The Court's striking down of school segregation came as a surprise to many. Separate but equal had been the law of the land since the ruling in *Plessy* in 1896, over half a century earlier.[16] The NAACP was asking the Court to strike down more than fifty years of practice built around that precedent, a precedent set by the very same court of law.

In discussing *Brown I* with the other justices, Chief Justice Warren admitted that "[t]he more I read and hear and think, the more I come to conclude that the basis of the principle of segregation and separate but equal rests upon the basic premise that the Negro race is inferior. . . . If oral argument proved anything, the arguments of Negro counsel proved that they are not inferior."[17] Justices William Douglas and Sherman Minton felt the same; the latter "saw segregation as the South's 'invidious' response to abolition and a substitute means for whites to degrade blacks in the absence of slavery."[18]

These striking admonishments, acknowledging the real purpose of segregation, no doubt played a role in the Court's decision. Yet, *Brown I* referenced none of them. Rather than acknowledge that segregation laws were premised on white superiority, the *Brown I* court focused solely on the psychological effect segregation had on blacks.[19] On the basis of testimony produced at trial, the Court concluded that segregated schools generated an irreversible "feeling of inferiority" among black children, regardless of any tangible equality between schools for black children and schools for whites.[20] The problem with the *Brown I* decision was that it did not address long-held notions of white superiority. While government-mandated racial segregation was prohibited, white choices of isolation and privilege were not. The justices condemned segregation because of the feelings of inferiority it generated in blacks; unfortunately, there was no mention of the feelings of superiority generated in whites.

Other aspects of the decision further limited *Brown I*'s potential to reduce notions of white superiority/black inferiority and black separation. The Court declined to overrule *Plessy* outright, settling instead for a "middling approach" that outlawed mandatory segregation only in the public schools.[21] In fact, in *Brown I*'s final draft, Chief Justice Warren intentionally deleted language that could have been construed as prohibiting all segregation outright.[22]

Since the decision was based on the unique psychological handicaps that grew out of public school segregation,[23] the question remained whether *Plessy* or *Brown I* controlled other[24] segregated institutions.[25] Relying on social science methodology and psychological consequences enabled the Court to sidestep the reality that segregation was designed, pure and simple, to degrade, humiliate, and exclude blacks, and to privilege whites.[26] Indeed, the Court held the view that the harm from segregation could be undone simply by providing blacks with an opportunity to associate with "the right" whites,[27] regardless of the prejudices those whites exhibited against blacks. The government would need to change the school environment, not to allow black children to identify more closely with the "white doll" but to create an environment in which they would see that the "black doll" is good and beautiful.[28] Changes would be needed to break down both notions of racial hierarchy.

Limiting the *Brown II* Desegregation Mandate

In *Brown II*,[29] the Supreme Court finally recognized the serious harm that state-imposed racial segregation in public primary and secondary schools had caused to black children over the course of several decades and indicated a remedy. Those black students who were subjected to such segregation would be entitled to a remedy for the harm imposed. Remedies that had been previously provided by states while maintaining the separate but equal doctrine were not really remedies but, in fact, reinforced segregation within society and exacerbated the sense of inferiority in those who were excluded.[30]

A major weakness of the Supreme Court ruling in *Brown II* was that while the goal was to reduce racial division, the decision allowed states to make exceptions to desegregation.[31] One court in Georgia ruled that *Brown I*'s concern with psychological injury did not apply to schools in its jurisdiction subject to *Brown II*'s mandate because, in its view, blacks in that district were already intellectually inferior to whites.[32] A district court in Texas went one step further, reasoning that if black children experienced a psychological injury "by not being allowed to sit in white classes in the school room," then white children necessarily suffered an "inferiority complex" when "required to sit in classes with the colored child."[33]

A second major shortcoming of *Brown II*, in its attempt at reducing black separation, involved the Court's failure to require immediate desegregation. The Court ruled segregated schools unconstitutional in 1954, but delayed over a year before providing remedial guidance and establishing an "all deliberate speed" measure of compliance in *Brown II*.[34] This slow standard did not mandate full and immediate action. Instead, the order required local school boards to make a "prompt and reasonable start" toward full desegregation,[35] but federal trial courts authorized with supervising compliance were not advised as to when desegregation should start, when it should finish, or what pace of progress to seek. They were instead told to move slowly and were permitted to halt any desegregation plan that merited "additional time."[36]

The justices thought this wait period might encourage voluntary compliance from reluctant school districts.[37] In fact, two justices agreed to invalidate segregation only if the opinion did not require immediate implementation.[38] The decision to promote voluntary compliance prolonged the delay in implementation by ceding control to "the most recalcitrant judge and the most defiant school board,"[39] the same individuals who either defended segregation before the Supreme Court or upheld it at the trial level. When *Brown II* was decided in 1955, Thurgood Marshall, a black lawyer and future Supreme Court justice who had organized the NAACP's litigation strategy, optimistically predicted that it would take no more than five years to fully desegregate America's public schools.[40] Yet between 1957 and 1959, only eight black students were assigned to white schools in North

Carolina.[41] Only one was assigned in Alabama.[42] By 1960, not a single black student attended a white school in South Carolina, Florida, Mississippi, or Georgia, and by 1965, just over 2% of black school children in eleven southern states attended schools with whites.[43] Even in the border states, almost half of the black students attended all-black schools until 1964.[44] Most black children entering southern schools when *Brown* was decided graduated twelve years later from schools that were still all black, and all segregated.[45] Much of this was attributed to resistance by school officials and refusals by district court judges to hold them accountable under the "all deliberate speed" standard. At least one justice had predicted this obstruction. Justice Black declared, during a meeting with other justices, that the Court had "no more chance to enforce [desegregation] in the Deep South than to enforce prohibition in New York City."[46]

Why was a set of justices so attuned to the harmful purpose and consequences of segregation willing to compromise the rationale and remedy in *Brown*? It is commonly understood that the Court mitigated the reach of *Brown II* to avoid a revolt in the South.[47] This was particularly important since the executive branch, as Chief Justice Warren came to understand after dining with President Eisenhower, sympathized with the concern over the impact of desegregation on whites.[48] In taking this approach, the Court ignored the true purpose of segregation, the notion of white superiority, and approved a strategy that would allow whites to circumvent desegregation efforts and maintain black separation. The justices themselves, like the nation at large, were struggling to reconcile their own biases with constitutional principles. After ruling against segregation in a case involving restaurants and interstate commerce, Justice Stanley Reed regretted the outcome—that a black man could, for example, walk "right into the restaurant [and] sit down and eat at the table right next to Mrs. Reed."[49] Justice Reed thought the "discomfort" whites would experience when sending their children to school with blacks was sufficient justification for upholding segregation, or at least eradicating it slowly.[50] Justice Robert Jackson expressed concern that desegregation would force whites to adjust "to the unfamiliar and the unpleasant" consequences of regular exposure to blacks.[51] Justice Felix Frankfurter wrote that while segregation might seem "invidious and irrational," the Court could "hardly deny the existence of sincerity and passion of those who think that their blood, birth and lineage are something worthy of protection by separatism."[52] Thus, it is not surprising that the justices would not expect or require that whites abandon their sense of entitlement to isolation.[53] The justices who decided *Brown II* were true progressives for their time, but conference discussions prove that the limits of the *Brown* decisions reflect notions of racial hierarchy. By portraying segregation as a problem of psychological consequences, the justices shifted the blame to blacks, just as the justices in *Plessy* criticized blacks who objected to "separate but equal" as overly sensitive.[54]

White Desires for Black Separation in Schools in the South

While *Brown* prohibited government-mandated segregation of schools, supporters of racial separation remained dedicated to white superiority and defiant of equality requirements in the Constitution. Much like white resistance to Reconstruction in southern states from 1868 to 1876, the revolt against *Brown* was swift and severe. The brutal murder of black teenager Emmett Till, in Money, Mississippi, just three months after *Brown I*, for allegedly whistling at a white woman, symbolized the "systematic racial terrorism" that continued in much of the nation.[55] Desegregation advocates, both black and white, experienced beatings, death threats, and house bombings when seeking to enforce *Brown*. For those blacks who successfully avoided the brunt of violent tactics, economic intimidation was used. "[W]hite citizens' counsels" and other grassroots resistance organizations promised "to make it difficult, if not impossible, for any Negro who advocates desegregation to find and hold a job, get credit, or renew a mortgage."[56]

Military troops were needed to defend desegregationists. It took six hundred armed troops and seven M-41 tanks to restore order in Clinton, Tennessee, after thousands of whites rioted against twelve black students entering the local high school.[57] In Sturgis, Kentucky, armed mobs, yelling for "nigger blood," roamed the streets when they learned that nine black students had enrolled in the local high school, until National Guard troops forced them back with an M-47 tank.[58]

Between 1956 and 1959, nine southern states revived the Civil War strategy of "interposition," claiming a sovereign right to ignore *Brown* because it upset the "proper" constitutional balance between federal and state power.[59] The Southern Manifesto, drafted by South Carolina Senator Strom Thurmond and Georgia Senator Richard Russell, accused the Court of political motivations and called upon legislators, school districts, and federal judges to defend the "humanity" of Jim Crow by resisting desegregation.[60] All but three southern senators signed the manifesto in March of 1956. Representatives, including Mississippi senator James Eastland, openly courted defiance by telling white supporters, "On May 17, 1954 [the date of the *Brown I* decision], the Constitution of the United States was destroyed because the Supreme Court disregarded the law and decided that integration was right. You are not required to obey any court which passes out [a desegregation] ruling. In fact, you are obligated to defy it."[61]

While many southern whites insisted on resisting desegregation mandates from *Brown II*, many black and white supporters of desegregation were pushing for integration in schools and in public accommodations. Martin Luther King Jr. introduced the concept of nonviolent resistance and civil disobedience to protest Jim Crow public accommodation laws, providing blacks with an effective method to push for racial integration and equal rights.[62] Nonviolent protest became the modus operandi of the early civil rights movement, which began with the Montgomery, Alabama, bus boycott in 1956, which took place after Rosa Parks, a black woman, refused to sit in the back of a bus.[63] In 1957, King founded the Southern Christian Leadership Conference (SCLC)—an organization of black ministers committed to using nonviolent actions to challenge Jim Crow practices.[64] One of the first protests was spearheaded by four college students in 1960, who conducted a sit-in at a lunch counter in Greensboro, North Carolina, with the goal of desegregating.[65] The sit-in was the first of many nonviolent actions initiated by the Student Nonviolent Coordinating Committee (SNCC), the student arm of the SCLC, which became one of the most active organizations of the movement.[66] By the end of 1960, the sit-ins had spread from lunch counters to beaches, parks, and other public places in every southern state.[67]

As blacks pushed for integrated facilities in interstate travel, white resistance increased and became more violent. The civil rights movement conducted Freedom Rides, initiated in 1961, with the goal of desegregating buses and terminals serving interstate travelers in the Deep South.[68] The riders fully anticipated being arrested and having to stay in jail as the cases came before the courts. As expected, they encountered hostility along the way, which culminated in a bloody attack in Birmingham, Alabama, in May—one of the buses was firebombed, and the riders were assaulted and chased by an angry mob.[69] President John Kennedy took a hands-off approach to avoid angering southern white supporters, but was finally forced to send in federal marshals to rescue the riders after a Justice Department official monitoring the incident was severely beaten.[70] The Freedom Riders movement grew over the summer of 1961, as hundreds of interracial volunteers from many civil rights organizations defied local segregation laws and rode interstate buses. The Freedom Riders aimed to force the federal government to enforce the existing laws and constitutional protections, which had been largely ignored by southern states. Only after the news media publicized the violence, arousing sympathy among many northern and western whites, did the Kennedy administration take action to enforce the court decisions outlawing segregation of interstate travel.

Even with enhanced federal enforcement, violent resistance in southern states increased. A bloodier civil rights campaign was waged in Birmingham, Alabama, in 1963, when King attempted to desegregate downtown businesses.[71] Children as young as six years old were assaulted and arrested.[72] Eugene "Bull" Connor, the police chief of Birmingham, unleashed water hoses and attack dogs on a group of one thousand student protesters who had gathered at a church.[73] Shortly thereafter, four young black girls were killed when the basement at the Sixteenth Street Baptist Church in Birmingham was bombed.[74]

A watershed event occurred in 1963, when hundreds of thousands of marchers converged for the famous "March on Washington," the largest political demonstration the country had ever seen.[75] The event received extensive news coverage, especially during Martin Luther King Jr.'s inspirational "I Have a Dream" speech at the Lincoln Memorial.[76] With over two hundred thousand in attendance,[77] King evoked a new era. That same year, encouraged by the March on Washington, President John Kennedy sent a sweeping civil rights bill to Congress.[78]

While black efforts to integrate were successful in that they resulted in new federal antidiscrimination legislation and enforcement, strong southern white resistance continued. Most white southern state executives and legislators rejected *Brown*. Georgia governor Herman Talmadge declared that the state was "going to resist mixing the races in the schools if it is the sole state of the nation to do so."[79] Of course, Georgia was not alone. Louisiana legislators publicly reaffirmed their commitment to segregated schools and enacted a statute that imposed a fine and prison time on any official who assigned a minority student to a white school.[80] Virginia governor Thomas Stanley enlisted legislators to defend that state's education system against the "insidious spread" of desegregation.[81] The legislature there passed a funding statute that guaranteed a district-wide shutdown whenever a single school within a district enrolled both minority and white students.[82] Ultimately, resistance bordered on the absurd. Alabama legislators demanded that public libraries remove a children's book because it illustrated an animal tale with black and white married rabbits.[83]

Southern school officials, with the consent of federal courts, devised mechanisms to preserve segregation as a matter of "choice." These mechanisms included transfer provisions, pupil placement laws, and step plans that resulted in token desegregation or extended the desegregation process over a period of years.[84] Pupil placement laws kept desegregation at token levels through broad discretionary admission qualifications, allowing officials to control the racial composition of their student body.[85] North Carolina's statute required officials to consider the "orderly and efficient administration" of the schools and the "health, safety and general welfare" of other pupils when making school assignments.[86] These laws encouraged opposition from whites by permitting school or community disruption to be a reason to deny cross-race assignments.[87]

Brown II's Failure to Prevent Black Separation in Schools in the South

After President Kennedy's assassination in 1963, President Lyndon Johnson advanced a bill through Congress that ultimately became the Civil Rights Act of 1964.[88] The package of reforms prohibited racial segregation and discrimination in employment, transportation, movie theaters, and other public places.[89] The statute also authorized federal officials to withhold funding from school districts that failed to comply with a court-ordered desegregation decree.[90] Implementation guidelines enacted over the next two years made clear that federal funding would be available only to schools that actually increased their enrollment of black students.[91] These monetary incentives became even more significant in 1965, when Congress enacted the Elementary and Secondary Education Act,[92] which allocated over $1.5 billion in local school aid for disadvantaged children.[93] The Civil Rights Act also relieved blacks of the emotional and financial burdens of confronting hostile school officials by empowering the attorney general to initiate desegregation lawsuits.[94]

The bill was signed into law on July 2, 1964, during a particularly brutal and violent summer for the civil rights movement in which three civil rights workers—one black and two white—were murdered in Mississippi by the Ku Klux Klan while trying to register black voters in the state.[95] The following year saw enactment of the Voting Rights Act of 1965,[96] which suspended poll taxes and literacy tests, and also authorized federal supervision of voter registration in districts where such tests were being used. The passage of the act was the culmination of a campaign by SNCC and SCLC to bring the plight of black voters in the South to the consciousness of the American people.[97] On March 7, 1965, a day often referred to as Bloody Sunday, SNCC and SCLC led a group of over six hundred protesters in a 54-mile march from Selma, Alabama, to the state capital of Montgomery.[98] The protesters had only gone a few blocks when local law enforcement officials attacked them with clubs, tear gas, rubber tubes wrapped in barbed wire, and bullwhips, causing sixteen of them to be hospitalized.[99] The march succeeded in accelerating the timetable for passage of the Voting Rights Act.[100] Under the law, black voter registration more than doubled in four years, and the number of elected black officials in the Deep South increased dramatically, thereby permanently changing the political landscape of the South.[101]

Despite state opposition, federal courts, without any empirical evidence, insisted that school officials would abide by constitutional standards. They were wrong. Using the same arguments made by segregationists during Reconstruction, school officials in Alabama, for example, threatened black families that their attempts to secure admission for their children to white schools would "invite the abolishment of the public schools."[102]

In reaction to decisions condemning obstruction and delay of desegregation, and legislative initiatives encouraging integration, many whites left school districts that were subject to desegregation decrees and relocated to all-white districts, thus ensuring the continuation of race separation in schools. Ultimately, even when courts held school districts to stringent standards, most school desegregation plans failed due to white flight. Blacks remained separated because whites fled urban areas subject to desegregation court decrees. Thus, just as it did during slavery and Jim Crow, physical separation of blacks and whites continued, albeit by white choices of where to live rather than by de jure requirements. Nevertheless, integration failed because too few whites remained in the district.

"Minority-to-majority" transfers were another way school boards, with the consent of district courts, limited interracial contact after *Brown II*.[103] Provisions that allowed students to withdraw from a neighborhood school previously designated for a different race spared whites from attending aged and dilapidated institutions once reserved for blacks.[104] A second facet of the transfer, which allowed whites to withdraw from a school where they were numerically outnumbered, guaranteed white students a dominant presence in the classroom.[105] Meanwhile, black students in predominantly white schools transferred back to substandard Jim Crow schools to escape threats, abuse, and violence from white students.[106] These one-way transfers even forced the status quo on "renegade" whites who wished to send their children to an interracial school. White students could transfer out of a school if they were outnumbered by blacks, but could not transfer into a majority-black school.[107]

The "minority-to-majority" transfer program recognized a right by white students never to attend a school where white students did not make up a majority. Such recognition reflects an embrace of white superiority. Whites must have been the dominant numerical group in any school where a white child was enrolled. If not, then white children would have been subject to domination by black children, an unacceptable outcome even in the midst of the desegregation mandate of *Brown*. Under this approach, integration could occur, but only when a numerical minority of blacks was subject to a numerical majority of whites. Thus, white numerical domination over blacks was acceptable, but black numerical dominance over whites was not. Racial integration meant a few blacks and a lot of whites but never a few whites and a lot of blacks. Under this definition, most blacks remained separated in schools, thus enforcing the white superiority/black inferiority rung of the paradigm.

"Minority-to-majority" transfers represented the exception swallowing the rule. If the purpose of desegregation, as the *Brown I* court indicated, was for black students to benefit from the presence of white students,[108] why would schools allow white students to transfer from majority-black schools to majority-white schools? Black students would have lost the benefit of *Brown I*'s mandate if such transfers had been permitted. Furthermore, permitting such transfers defeated the goal established in *Brown II* of desegregated schools. Although *Brown I* identified the constitutional violation as government-mandated segregation, *Brown II* imposed a desegregation remedy. So merely eliminating all school segregation laws would not satisfy *Brown II*; actual desegregation would require mass movement of both black and white students. Thus, allowing exceptions for white students served to maintain black exclusion and prevent desegregation.

Step plans, according to which schools would desegregate one grade or group of grades per year, reassigned large groups of black students in an entire grade or series of grades to formerly all-white schools, but stretched out the process of desegregation over a number of years.[109] Only black students were assigned to white schools, but no white students were assigned to black schools. School districts delayed completion of step plans that, for Nashville, Tennessee, would not achieve systemwide desegregation until

1976—an incredible twenty-two years after *Brown I* recognized a "personal and present right" to desegregated schools.[110] District courts excused these long delays on the rationale that "[f]ull desegregation is not denied. It is merely postponed"—though that was not true for the large number of black students who would graduate without ever attending a single class with white peers.[111]

After thirteen years of delay and obstruction by many local school boards to the *Brown II* desegregation mandate, the Supreme Court took a more committed stance on desegregation. In *Griffin v. Prince Edward County*,[112] the Court struck down the private school voucher program Virginia had used to circumvent a district court's desegregation order in Prince Edward County. In 1962, state legislators had closed the county schools while offering tax breaks and tuition credits to white parents who sent their children to private schools that were not subject to constitutional "equal protection" standards.[113] The Court had already ruled that "[d]elays in segregating school systems [would] no longer [be] tolerable,"[114] and in ruling against Prince Edward County, the justices reasoned that the "time for mere deliberate speed had run out."[115] The Court indicated that school districts had an obligation to implement meaningful and "immediate" desegregation[116] that brought about actual changes in the racial composition of segregated schools. Three years after *Griffin*, the Court voided a Virginia school system "freedom of choice" plan in *Green v. New Kent County*[117] that allowed parents to decide which school their child would attend. County officials implemented the plan knowing that white parents would continue to send their children to white schools where few black parents would dare seek admission for their children.[118] The Court flatly rejected the argument that school officials had no responsibility to circumvent "voluntary" segregation.[119] School officials had an "affirmative duty to take whatever steps might be necessary to convert to a unitary system in which racial discrimination would be eliminated root and branch."[120] The Court reaffirmed the requirement for immediate and meaningful integration announced in *Griffin*, declaring that a desegregation plan must be one that "promises realistically to work, and promises realistically to work now."[121]

Though the Supreme Court grew less tolerant of obstructionist tactics, the justices did not repudiate the notion that whites should have a choice in and the determination of the racial makeup of the students with whom their children went to school. Such choice could severely limit the effectiveness of desegregation efforts by courts.

Brown II's Failure to Prevent Black Separation in Schools in the North

The realities for desegregation differed little in the North and the South. When district courts began enforcing desegregation in northern school districts, the public outcry made clear that demands for racial isolation were not unique to the states of the Old Confederacy. White northerners, especially in urban areas like Boston, New York, and Chicago,[122] vehemently opposed mandatory school desegregation. White government officials opposed mandatory busing plans, and civil rights organizations were forced to litigate those cases, just as they had been forced to sue school districts in the South. An area does not need formal Jim Crow practices to be impacted by notions of superiority or to reflect a commitment to black separation.[123] Boston provides a stellar and disturbing example.

In 1972, fifty-three black parents in Boston sued the Boston school system to desegregate the schools. This case, which became known as *Morgan v. Hennigan*,[124] was named after one of the parents, Tallulah Morgan, and the School Committee chairman James Hennigan. On June 21, 1974, a federal court judge for the district court in Massachusetts found that Boston had "intentionally brought about and maintained" racial segregation.[125] Judge W. Arthur Garrity concluded that the school committee had the power to end desegregation,[126] but it allowed the ongoing resistance to desegregation. Garrity ordered the schools to be desegregated by the upcoming September of 1975.[127] Black children would be bused to predominantly white schools, and white children would be transported to predominantly black schools.

Specifically, he ordered that the entire junior class from the mostly poor, white school, South Boston High, be bused to the black Roxbury High School.[128] Half the sophomores from each school would attend the other, and seniors were left to make their own decision. Roxbury High and South Boston High were regarded as the two "worst schools in Boston."[129] Many wondered what educational purpose would be served by mixing two low-performing schools and most feared widespread violence. Few knew this better than Judge W. Arthur Garrity who, in 1974, received death threats at the federal courthouse when he issued a busing order to desegregate Boston's public schools.[130] Protesters picketed outside his home and scrawled graffiti on walls, bridges, and roadways that read "Bus Garrity," "F—— Garrity," and "Kill Garrity."[131] Street violence by whites left one black reporter beaten on a sidewalk, and buses and cars overturned in the streets.[132] Fearful of what might happen once the busing order went into effect, more than one-third of Boston's public school students stayed home for the first weeks of school.[133] Many of those students who did attend school engaged in violent resistance.[134]

As a result of the judge's orders, many Boston communities reacted so violently that President Gerald Ford put the 82nd Airborne Division on alert, in preparation for duty on the streets of Boston.[135] When school started in September, black children who were bused to the community of South Boston were met with angry, rock-throwing mobs, which resulted in injuries. One community leader remembers that the children "were crying. They had glass in their hair. They were scared . . . they wanted to go home."[136] Of the 550 juniors who were to go to Roxbury from South Boston, only thirteen showed up on the first day.[137] The football season was canceled, parents protested daily, and black and white students entered the school through different doors.[138] For the remainder of the 1974-1975 school year, black parents organized escorts to get their children to school safely as violence remained prevalent.[139]

Even though the busing plan was revised the next school year, white families in South Boston still boycotted and continued directing violence toward black students. Four years after the plan, many classes were still underpopulated.[140] Many white families moved out of the neighborhood or sent their children to private schools. The busing experiment ended in 1988, and by then, the Boston school district had decreased from one hundred thousand students to fifty-seven thousand, only 15% of whom were white.[141] Today, although the city of Boston is still predominantly white (56.3%),[142] the public schools are 76% black and Hispanic, and only 13% white.[143]

Just as South Boston experienced severe racial backlash, Yonkers, New York, similarly resisted desegregation. In 1980, nine years after *Swann*[144] examined a wide range of judicial options allowing for great latitude by school districts to eliminate the remaining vestiges of de jure segregation, the U.S. Justice Department and the Yonkers branch of the NAACP filed a civil lawsuit against the city of Yonkers, the school board of Yonkers, and the Yonkers Community Development Agency.[145] The lawsuit charged that those entities had been allowing "systematic segregation" for the previous thirty years.[146] The case, which alleged that the city had placed new subsidized housing projects in predominantly black neighborhoods, marked the first time that a charge of racial segregation had been brought against both school and housing officials.[147]

The United States district court found that Yonkers had, in fact, engaged in racial segregation in housing and schools.[148] After a series of appeals and additional trials,[149] in January of 1988, the parties agreed to a Consent Decree that established a new housing plan.[150] The plan included building low- and middle-income apartments in largely white neighborhoods across the city.[151] "Under the plan, public housing tenants were moved from large projects into smaller, scattered low-rises. The idea was to sprinkle, not dump, blacks into suburban neighborhoods and, hopefully, avoid the backlash that crippled integration plans in other cities."[152] Yet, the city failed to pass legislation outlining the new housing plan by the mandatory deadline.

In 1993, the NAACP and the Yonkers Board of Education reactivated the original case, alleging that segregation was still prevalent even though the city schools were not actively pursuing policies that promoted racial segregation.[153] This time, the plaintiffs decided to include the state, claiming that it had a responsibility to make sure the schools in Yonkers were not underfunded.[154] This claim against the state, while not holding up in trial court, was upheld in the Second Circuit, on appeal, finding that the state had a fiscal obligation to help end segregation in Yonkers.[155] Even so, another trial was held, where the court also found the state responsible and ordered the city and the state to share the financial cost of the second segregation plan devised by the court—the "Educational Improvement Plan."[156] In 2002, an agreement was reached that would provide $300 million in state funding to the school district over a five-year period. The funds would be used to fund programs that boost academic achievement for all city students. The pact called for the assignment of a monitor who would ensure that the school district was following the agreement. In March 2003, the monitor position had yet to be filled, and many questioned the school district's commitment to the pact.[157]

It all finally ended in 2007, when the United States district court signed off on a settlement agreement that was approved by officials in Yonkers and the Yonkers NAACP.[158] The settlement included protections against housing discrimination by the city of Yonkers through two programs: (1) the existing housing maintenance program and (2) the affordable housing program. Through these two programs, blacks would receive government assistance in renting and purchasing homes in Yonkers.[159] The city of Yonkers would also reserve a certain number of houses and rental properties for blacks on the basis of income levels, and make sure mortgages and loans were monitored, thus providing additional protection against racial discrimination.[160] With this decision, the court put an end to twenty-seven years of "often hostile litigation—a battle that turned out to be so costly it almost drove Yonkers into bankruptcy."[161] Yonkers officials were so committed to housing and school segregation they were willing to risk financial solvency to protect them.

A New Method of Racial Isolation in Housing: "White Flight"

As federal judicial enforcement closed mechanisms for slowing down school desegregation, resistant whites found ways of dealing with residential housing patterns to circumvent the courts throughout the 1970s. "White flight," a phenomenon first named in the United States, is a term for the demographic trend in which whites move away from suburbs or urban neighborhoods that are becoming racially desegregated.[162] Some attribute the evolution of white flight to the effects of World War II, when blacks, who began entering the middle class with good jobs and education, were trying to establish homes in cities across America and white residents moved out of the cities and into the suburbs.[163] Others believe that the contributing factor was the *Brown I* Supreme Court decision, which led to the desegregation of public schools across America.[164] To avoid having their children go to school with black children, many whites moved out of the cities into the suburbs.[165] Whichever characterization one relies upon, white relocation was motivated by an effort to ensure white isolation and black separation.

White flight has taken place in nearly every major city in America, although it has affected some cities more than others. The structure of local government in America provided a vehicle for people to move to suburbs, affording them the ability to create new cities apart and away from the jurisdiction of the original city without any legacy expenses for sustaining existing infrastructure.[166] This resulted in the building of suburban roads, new schools, water and sewer lines, and other entities that are necessary in any city.

In addition to the establishment of these new "cities," restrictive zoning requirements were enacted.[167] These restrictive requirements made it virtually impossible for the poorer residents of the inner cities to afford to move to the suburbs.[168] The NAACP alleged that the federal government induced middle-class whites to move to the suburbs by allowing the inner-city neighborhoods to decay.[169]

For example, around 1960, just after desegregation began, Clifton Park Junior High School, in Baltimore, Maryland, had 2,023 whites and 34 blacks; ten years later, it had 2,037 blacks and 12 whites.[170] Comparable numbers resulted at Garrison Junior High School, also in Baltimore, which saw its population go from 2,504 whites and 122 blacks to 297 whites and 1,263 blacks in the same period.[171] Similar outcomes occurred at schools around the country.[172]

White flight was another manifestation of white desires to maintain racial isolation by separating blacks. With the end of Jim Crow, due to the *Brown* decisions in 1954 and 1955, and the subsequent judicial crackdown on desegregation slow-down tactics by local school boards, increased integration in schools of blacks and whites began to occur in the late 1960s and early 1970s. Whites opposed to such desegregation simply continued efforts toward black separation. While the primary method for achieving racial isolation utilized prior to the Civil War was enslavement, white choices continued to prevail. With this manipulated physical separation, desegregation became more difficult and costly. Yet, judicial approval was needed in order to determine whether the white flight choice was beyond the *Brown II* desegregation mandate.

Civil rights advocates argued that the only way to delay white flight was to allow desegregation across city and suburban district lines. In 1974, the Supreme Court undermined desegregation by refusing to allow a Michigan district court to enforce an urban desegregation order.[173] The lower court had ordered a regionwide desegregation plan because most whites had moved outside of Detroit to its surrounding suburbs.[174] In *Milliken v. Bradley*,[175] the Supreme Court held that for a court to set aside school district lines by imposing a cross-district remedy, "it must first be shown that there has been a constitutional violation within one district that produces a significant segregative effect in another district."[176] The Court held that intentional segregation by city officials within Detroit's urban schools did not implicate suburban school officials in any way.[177] Since Detroit was a majority-black city, best estimates showed that without suburban participation, even the most ambitious citywide desegregation plan would result in most schools being 75 to 90% black.[178] Recognizing the similarities between "white flight" and "Jim Crow" created by whites isolating themselves in all-white neighborhoods, the Sixth Circuit declared, "The instant case calls up haunting memories of the now long overruled and discredited 'separate-but-equal' doctrine of *Plessy*."[179] Rich whites could always send their children to racially isolated private schools. *Milliken* now allowed middle-class whites who desired racial isolation in schools to avoid desegregation decrees simply by moving from racially diverse urban public school districts to exclusively white suburban districts.[180] *Milliken,* like *Brown II,* fostered the continuation of black separation. As a result, most urban school districts today have very few white students, and suburban school districts have very few black students.[181]

One might ask why so many whites would desire to abruptly sell their homes and relocate from urban areas to neighboring suburbs. Perhaps they perceived the services and living conditions in the suburbs as better than what was offered in cities. Perhaps they were attracted to the aesthetics of the suburbs, with more open space and undeveloped tracts of land. Yet it would be a mistake to ignore the notion of white superiority that had fueled white desires for separation from blacks for hundreds of years. Why would those desires have suddenly ceased just because some segregation laws were changed? Unfortunately, notions of white superiority remained.

The Failure of Antidiscrimination Laws to Prevent White Isolation in Housing

A similar resistance was reflected in congressional laws concerning housing desegregation. Demands by whites for white isolation were higher in housing than in any other arena because so many activities—like education and entertainment—were connected to where one lived. Consequently, fair housing laws, reflecting those white demands, have traditionally been weaker than laws in other areas such as voting, employment, and public accommodations, which, literally, do not hit whites "where they live." Indeed, fair housing did not become a public issue until four years after fair employment and public accommodations actions and three years after voting rights actions had peaked.[182] The Fair Housing Act (FHA) of 1968 prohibits discriminatory housing practices but exempts sellers who do not advertise or use real estate agents, and it also exempts landlords who maintain living quarters on the premises and are renting fewer than three units.[183] The act's coverage is limited by its broad exemptions, and its impact is weak due to its reliance on private action for enforcement.[184] Many whites fall within one of the exemptions, and private enforcement tends to be unreliable and inconsistent. Moreover, the standard of proof required by the Supreme Court places great demands on any potential housing discrimination plaintiff.[185]

Whites continue to embrace the "tipping point" notion in housing integration. As with school desegregation, many whites feel they must maintain neighborhood dominance and will abandon the area or resist further integration as soon as such dominance is threatened.[186] This approach reflects two aspects of the racial paradigm: white superiority and black separation. It is important to whites who subscribe to the tipping point notion that whites remain numerically dominant, consistent with white superiority notions. When numerical dominance is threatened, efforts at black separation must be intensified, resulting in white flight or violent resistance.

Traditionally, after Jim Crow laws ostensibly ended, discriminatory mortgage practices, selective public housing placement, racially skewed zoning restrictions, and redlining—whereby banks provided mortgages for home purchases only to individuals whose race matched the racial makeup of the neighborhood—became common and encouraged resegregation.[187] Well into the late 1960s, discriminatory mortgage and real estate practices prevented black families from purchasing homes in white areas, and at the same time contributed to the continued separation of blacks.[188]

In almost every urban area in the country, blacks were separated in housing. These black areas, known as "ghettos," were the product of all three aspects of the racial paradigm. Because of white superiority/black inferiority notions, many whites viewed blacks as different. Consequently, whites treated them more harshly and separated themselves from blacks. Once separated, they could victimize blacks more easily. This is exactly what happened to create the ghetto.

The impact of black separation and white isolation in housing remains the same as it was in 1954 when *Brown I* was decided. The general health of blacks suffers. They are the victims of economic exploitation, and opportunities for educational, political, or business advancement are limited. The ghetto is reflective of overcrowded and dilapidated housing, lack of government and private business services, and deficient educational institutions.[189]

Social science research identifies the connection between black separation in housing and its negative impact on employment opportunities, susceptibility to crime and violence, educational options, health care access and quality, and access to credit.[190] The connection between opportunity and race is irrefutable. Black separation in housing results in black separation in schools. Segregated schools result in reduced employment opportunities. Limited employment opportunities result in income and wealth ceilings. Income and wealth ceilings result in diminished health care and credit options. Lack of credit options increases racial separation in housing, thus perpetuating the cycle and reinforcing the paradigm.

Conclusion

Throughout this period, segregation in education and housing caused the separation and victimization of blacks to intensify throughout America; segregation pervaded all segments of society and all geographic regions, urban and rural. The Supreme Court's decisions in *Brown* ended government-mandated racial segregation, but the rulings had no power of enforcement: they neither altered notions of racial hierarchy nor significantly reduced racial isolation. The holdings in *Brown I* and *II* failed to prevent black separation and white isolation in education, and failed to address the false notions of white superiority and black inferiority that had created pervasive education disparities. *Brown I* and *Brown II* forbade government-imposed discrimination but did not actually require integration, and as a result the paradigm of racial separation and isolation gained an even stronger foothold. States such as Louisiana and Virginia brazenly enacted statutes to prevent integration,[191] and the "minority-to-majority" transfer program was used to reverse any existing integration.[192] The judicial decision in *Brown I* was a milestone but was ultimately ineffective because society clung to its false notions of white superiority and black inferiority. The paradigm of black separation was so deeply entrenched in our social identity that as a nation, we once again squandered an opportunity for significant progress. In a bitterly ironic twist, the incomplete, ineffective decision in *Brown I* was the key factor that set the stage for intensified discrimination in education.

Open resistance to integration in education led to further acts of resistance to integration in housing, which in turn further exacerbated the separation of blacks. White flight maintained white isolation even after Jim Crow laws subsided. White flight was an intentional, active effort to limit racial integration. Antidiscrimination laws in housing did not reduce racial isolation because those laws were not enforced consistently. In fact, to the contrary, local laws were used to encourage segregation, and maintain the separation of blacks. An opportunity to effectuate positive change was squandered because we actively chose to perpetuate the racial hierarchy. These decisive discriminatory acts reinforced the paradigm, which continued to take root in more insidious forms, further preventing blacks from opportunities in education and housing.

Whites fought tenaciously to keep blacks out of their schools and neighborhoods, both openly and indirectly. The next chapter illustrates the continuation of black separation through practices such as "tracking systems" and predatory lending schemes. Widely accepted practices of white superiority and black inferiority in education and housing allowed the paradigm to strengthen and spread in the arenas of criminal justice, politics, and economics.

5

Victimizing Blacks in the 21st Century

> Job applicants with identical resumes, qualifications, and interview styles still experience different receptions, depending on their race. White and black consumers still encounter different deals. People of color looking for housing still face discriminatory treatment by landlords, real estate agents, and mortgage lenders. Minority entrepreneurs sometimes fail to gain contracts though they are the low bidders, and they are sometimes refused work even after winning contracts.
>
> —Justice Ruth Ginsburg, 1995[1]

DESPITE PRONOUNCEMENTS TO the contrary, as Justice Ginsburg reminded us as the 20th century drew to a close and more than a half-century after *Brown I* declared an end to Jim Crow segregation, the desire by some whites for racial isolation, and the opportunity to victimize blacks, persists. These desires manifest themselves in a wide variety of areas such as education, criminal justice, housing, economics, and politics. In the 21st century, while Jim Crow laws have been eliminated, the white superiority/ black inferiority beliefs remain, resulting in choices by both whites and blacks that maintain black separation and white isolation, and that make black victimization an ongoing, frequent reality.

While blacks continue to be victimized by overt racism, other racism today is covert, but still just as harmful. Where private choices exist, it is difficult to determine the true reason for disparity. Polls are notoriously inaccurate in measuring attitudes about race.[2] People tend to camouflage racist views in surveys because Americans have agreed, collectively, that racism is morally wrong.[3] As a result, those attitudes are hidden and not discussed openly. Thus, the reality is that racist views are likely to be more severe and widespread than the polls reveal, festering in hidden spheres. The following story further illustrates this type of thinly veiled racism thriving in modern America.

Rogers Washington, a black male from Boca Raton, Florida, had been fishing when high winds capsized his boat in 2005.[4] He treaded water for six hours in seven foot waves, evaded sharks, and watched helplessly while his coworker drowned.[5] He suffered a heart attack before finally being rescued.[6] Two white male boaters from Maryland spotted Washington struggling and saved him.[7] Occupants of two other boats had spotted Washington earlier, but they did not stop or radio for assistance.[8] They saw him waving frantically, and Washington suspects they "thought he was a refugee attempting to flee from Haiti to the United States."[9] No one has come forward to dispute Washington's claim.

We may never know for certain the reason Washington was not rescued by the first two boats hours earlier. One cannot help but wonder, however, if aspects of the racial paradigm were not underlying this incident, in that Washington was ignored initially due to his being black.

The Valley Swim Club is a predominantly all-white, members-only, private swim facility located in a suburb outside of Philadelphia, Pennsylvania.[10] In order to generate additional revenue, the club allows local day camps to pay a fee for access for their campers to swim.[11] Creative Steps Day Camp is a Philadelphia-based camp that provides activities for fifty black children ages eight to ten.[12] In July 2009, the Creative Steps Day Camp made arrangements for its children to use the Valley Swim Club facility once a week, during the summer, by paying nineteen hundred dollars in advance.[13] When the black children showed up on the first day to swim, the white children in the pool immediately exited the water, and one of the white parents commented, "What are all these black kids doing here?"[14] The Valley Swim Club attendant asked all of the Creative Steps Day Camp children to leave.[15] Very disappointed, the black children exited, some, including nine-year-old Marcus Allen, in tears.[16] The next day, the Valley Swim Club director told the Creative Steps Day Camp director that their access was being suspended and their money refunded.[17] The president of the Valley Swim Club, John Duesler, indicated that the reason for the suspension was that "there was concern that a lot of kids would change the complexion . . . and the atmosphere of the club."[18]

Desires for white isolation today are not limited to whites in private establishments. A similar mentality has been displayed by white owners of businesses open to the public. In December of 2010, Mark Prior, a white resident of Clark County, Wisconsin, placed a sign on the front window of his gentleman's club that read, "No Negroes Allowed."[19] When asked why he posted the sign he explained that "he had some problems with black people in the past and needed to make a policy against them."[20]

Black and white attitudes concerning notions of white superiority and black inferiority are interconnected, as Washington's suspicion, Duesler's concern, and Prior's feeling reveal. Attitudes held by whites are interdependent on actions and attitudes by blacks; one cannot exist without the other. Each is fueled by the other, and both are exacerbated by the other. Whether focusing on disparate school funding schemes, black political disempowerment, economic exploitation of blacks, false allegations of blacks committing crimes, profiling of blacks for criminal activity, harsher criminal sentences for blacks, black-on-black crime, unproductive values adopted by blacks, or self-destructive choices blacks make, black external and internal victimization continues.

Progress and Setbacks

There have always been rich blacks, even during slavery and Jim Crow segregation. I do not disavow the many amazing individual black success stories today—like Oprah Winfrey, one of the wealthiest entertainers and entrepreneurs in the world, or Bob Johnson, a successful media and business mogul—nor do I fail to recognize the tremendous progress that has been made over the last century in educational, business, and social opportunities. Black presence—in higher education as students and teachers, in politics as members of Congress and governors, in business as chief executive officers and board members of Fortune 500 companies, and as entrepreneurs—is at an all-time high.[21] While much progress has been made, white desires for black separation continue to harm many blacks like the Creative Steps campers.[22]

While *Brown I*[23] prohibited government-mandated segregation, and civil rights legislation prohibited race discrimination, both failed to ensure racial equality. First, not all racial discrimination was prohibited, only race discrimination dealing with housing, voting, employment, public accommodations, and federally assisted programs.[24] Other substantive areas, such as private clubs, are, to this day, not covered by federal antidiscrimination laws or state laws. Private establishments, not open to the general public, where no state action is implicated, can legally discriminate. Second, most antidiscrimination laws contained exemptions that allowed a significant amount of discrimination to continue even in the substantive areas covered by the laws. Antidiscrimination housing laws exempted those sellers who did not employ public advertising or a broker, and rooming housing in which the owners lived with three or fewer units.[25] These exemptions cover 20% of the housing market.[26] Antidiscrimination employment laws continue to exempt small employers of fifteen persons or less.[27] This exemption left more than 16% of the national workforce (more than nineteen million employees) unprotected.[28] Third, enforcement of antidiscrimination laws has been inconsistent and weak. For example, enforcement of housing discrimination laws falls mostly on private individuals rather than the government. Private enforcement mechanisms tend to be much less effective.[29]

The statistics are alarming. Black unemployment is nearly twice that of whites, regardless of whether one is examining white-collar or blue-collar jobs,[30] and education does not reduce the gap. Black high school graduates have a higher unemployment rate than whites who did not finish high school.[31] Black college graduates have a higher unemployment rate than whites who did not complete college.[32] At all income levels, blacks with the same educational degrees make less than their white counterparts.[33]

What could possibly explain this alarming gap? Education, while improving standard-of-living indices for blacks, does not eliminate disparities between whites and blacks who possess the same educational attainment. Perhaps the answer can be found in notions of white superiority and black inferiority.

Notions of white superiority manifest themselves in two ways: (1) intentional discrimination against blacks; and (2) choices that disproportionately impact blacks adversely. Many Americans have a strong sense of fairness and decency that prevents them from displaying overtly racist behavior. Yet, some continue to harbor notions of superiority. This is why, while the laws no longer require racial separation and discrimination, racist choices continue to cause disparities that persist in many aspects of society. While the vast majority of whites are not intentionally and knowingly racist, too many make choices—by supporting policies, practices, and procedures—that maintain white isolation and privilege. The final step toward equality must address both of these problems because while "race is only skin deep, notions of superiority run to the bone."[34]

It is crucial not to discount or ignore the extent and degree of present embraces of white superiority/black inferiority. For example, upon his retirement in 2001, Bob Scott, a middle-class, white midwesterner who had worked as a blue-collar employee for forty years, moved to Harrison,

Arkansas, a town from which blacks had been banished in the early 20th century.[35] When asked why he had chosen Harrison, Scott responded, "the low cost of living, the low cost of real estate, and, probably more importantly than anything else, the lack of blacks."[36] Many would not openly admit that bias. People who conclude that issues concerning race in America are fine, due to the tremendous progress made toward equality, are just as wrong as those who conclude that equality is impossible.

The support of slavery, segregation, and "white flight" by many whites demonstrates that the United States was founded explicitly, has thrived implicitly, and continues to live uneasily on erroneous beliefs in white superiority. As described by President Bill Clinton near the end of his presidency in 1999, "While we may have torn down the walls of segregation, there are still a lot of walls in our hearts and in our habits. And sometimes, we are not aware of those walls in our hearts, but we have to test them against our habits."[37]

Surveys indicate that while a majority of whites believe that racial discrimination is largely a thing of the past, most blacks believe it still seriously impacts their lives.[38] Whites tend to focus on individual black success stories, such as Super Bowl–winning football coach Tony Dungy[39] or political phenomenon President Barack Obama, as proof that the racial divide has been dismantled. Blacks, on the other hand, tend to focus on widespread statistical disparities or personal experiences, as proof the racial divide still exists.

When whites focus on the select, statistically few, thriving blacks, and thereby reject the notion that discrimination still exists, they commit what statisticians have termed a "type I error" or a "false positive."[40] This refers to the mistaken conclusion that something has had an effect, while, in fact, no effect has taken place.[41] Initial data and evidence erroneously suggest that there was an effect, but later evidence proves there was none. For example, initial observations might suggest that blacks have gained equal access to economic opportunities, but later, more complete information shows that there has been no significant improvement.

Statisticians also frequently find another type of error called a "type II error," also known as a "false negative."[42] With a "false negative" we think there has been no improvement or no change, but later, with more complete evidence, we find that our conclusion was premature.[43] We rush toward a negative conclusion based on initial negative results, which turn out to be incomplete information. For example, based on initial perceptions, some blacks may think there have been no gains in education for inner-city youth, but closer inspection may reveal gains in math and reading skills.[44] If we fail to look past the first impression, we may be negatively influenced by a false perception of failure, when in fact, there has been some success. When blacks focus on the overwhelming disparities in education and employment, and thereby reject the notion that individual effort may overcome racism, they are influenced by a false negative. False positives and negatives occur all the time and provide a framework in which to analyze racial misperceptions. Whites tend to perceive a false positive, seeing improvement on the basis of isolated, incomplete data. Blacks tend to make a false negative by failing to acknowledge improvements.

For large numbers of blacks, the past century has brought few significantly improved opportunities in education, housing, and jobs. We miss the mark if we conclude that laws and practices are fair simply because some blacks have succeeded, failing to ask why many others have not. Any adequate evaluation of progress must examine how the average black person, not the "best and the brightest," is treated. Not all whites are wealthy or educated; many struggle with obstacles to success. Blacks face all the same obstacles and must also overcome perceptions of inferiority. This "double whammy" explains some of the alarming disparities that exist today for high-income and middle-class blacks, as well as poor ones.

We should not be shocked that whites who watched *The Cosby Show* on television in the 1980s or the Thomas confirmation process in the 1990s were being exposed to images of prosperous, successful, and educated blacks for the first time.[45] Physical separation of blacks and whites prevented such knowledge for the vast majority of Americans.

Negative perceptions cut both ways.[46] Many blacks, particularly blacks with little exposure to whites, view whites with suspicion of racist motives.[47] A white person may treat some blacks harshly without race being a motivating factor. In today's complex world, when should one yell racism? The answer is not clear. But what is clear is that this nation has come nowhere close to eliminating discrimination. Those who claim the election of Obama, the nation's first black president, is proof that racial discrimination no longer exists in this country are preaching a very damaging notion. Not only are we far from a post-racial America, but we will diverge even further from such an ideal if people falsely claim that equal opportunities are already being afforded to all blacks. Disparities and division in education, housing, the criminal justice system, economics, and politics must be addressed directly.

Tracking Blacks for Failure in Schools

The education system is less racist today than it was under Jim Crow. No longer are black children taught a different curriculum, no longer are books designated for whites only,[48] and no longer are college and professional schools off limits for most blacks. Yet, racial division and inequality in schools continues and is getting worse.

Whether one is comparing grade point averages, test scores, or placement in advanced classes, the gap between blacks and whites is large. For example, 17% of white students receive a high number of As, but only 7% of black students receive such high numbers.[49] While the number of black high achievers has increased yearly, the change is not dramatic—the gap between whites and blacks continues.[50]

The 2005 Census Report reveals that only 17% of blacks twenty-five and over have a bachelor's degree or higher,[51] and in 2008, it was reported that fewer than 5% of blacks are master's or doctoral degree recipients.[52] The National Center of Education suggests that the low percentage of blacks in graduate school is due to the fact that "minorities are less likely to aspire to attend graduate school, are less likely to complete high school, and are less likely to attend a four-year college immediately after finishing high school."[53]

Educational tracking, instituted in the late 1960s following the *Brown* decisions, is largely to blame for black separation in the 21st century in schools that would otherwise prove "integrated."[54] Students who are tracked into different classrooms based on perceived differences in academic abilities are disadvantaged in lower-level courses, which are generally taught by less experienced teachers.[55] This has an adverse impact on black students. Even when controlling for achievement scores and social class, research shows that whites are more likely to be tracked into advanced placement and honors courses than blacks.[56] Even in diverse schools, most lower-track classes are disproportionately black.[57] This disparity is due, in part, to erroneous placements of black students, without their knowledge, into lower tracks than their proven ability warrants.[58] Racial bias regarding the performance of black students and the disproportionate influence white parents have over school policy decisions impact student placement.[59] Research has shown that white parents often insist on tracking in response to increased desegregation, and administrators are willing to comply in order to minimize complaints and galvanize support from whites.[60]

In this respect, tracking is a flashback to 1954, when the practice of assigning students to different classrooms on the basis of race was a strategy used after *Brown* to avoid the effects of court-ordered desegregation.[61] The practice continues to impede integration today. Nearly 65% of white students benefit from high school advanced placement classes, while 5% of black students benefit from such programs.[62] Students assigned to different classrooms based on perceived academic ability lose important opportunities for interracial contact, which social scientists agree helps reduce stereotypes and racial friction.[63]

The same negative impact of segregation on black children, recognized by the justices in *Brown*, is present today where black children are separated by tracking. If the justices in *Brown* were correct, we should not be surprised that black children, separated out due to tracking and placed in remedial classes with other, mostly black, children, develop feelings of inferiority[64] just as black children did during Jim Crow segregation. All of the harmful factors identified by the justices in *Brown*, such as creation of a sense of inferiority and deprivation of educational benefits available in integrated environments, are present in the tracking practices that exist today. Under tracking, black children are placed in remedial classes primarily with other black children.[65] Remedial classes create a similar sense of inferiority, just as Jim Crow segregation in schools did, since most of the remedial classes are not racially diverse, stigmatize those assigned to them, and result in underachievement in comparison to other classes at the school.

In 2003, the Supreme Court affirmed, for the first time, the value of integration for all students when it approved the use of an admission program to establish law student diversity.[66] In *Grutter v. Bollinger*,[67] Justice Sandra Day O'Connor's majority opinion drew on research finding that student body diversity promotes cross-racial understanding, advances learning outcomes, "better prepares students for an increasingly diverse workforce and society, and better prepares them as professionals."[68] The Court reasoned that the skills needed to succeed in a global marketplace could develop only through "exposure to widely diverse peoples, cultures, ideas and viewpoints."[69] Leaders in business, government, and the military had made this very point, arguing that success requires a workforce that is both qualified and diverse.[70] The problem is that the *Grutter* court was not clear as to whether its rationale extended beyond higher education to secondary education, as well as to other activities such as employment and housing. The *Grutter* reasoning easily can be applied in these other contexts. For example, diversity in the workplace, both public and private, or in neighborhoods, would serve the same operational needs as it does for institutions of higher learning, namely, enhancing problem solving and fostering creative solutions, as well as enhancing institutional legitimacy.[71]

Unfortunately, however, the Court diverged from this understanding, in 2007, in *Parents Involved in Community Schools v. Seattle School District No. 1*.[72] In *Parents Involved*, the Supreme Court of the United States reviewed the question of whether the Equal Protection Clause of the Fourteenth Amendment allows public schools to voluntarily adopt student assignment plans that utilize race in order to remedy de facto segregation and achieve racially diverse student bodies within each school.[73] The Court struck down the public school assignment plan.[74]

The decision is problematic because the reasoning and holding embrace the concept of racial isolation and contradict the reasoning of *Grutter*. A local government's interest in accomplishing racial diversity in the realms of elementary and secondary education, as well as in providing students with the inherent "intangible socialization benefits" of a racially integrated school environment, are consistent with the Court's recognition of the value of diversity in higher education.[75] Such consistency is evident by the way diversity promotes cross-racial understanding, reduces racial stereotypes, and enriches classroom discussion.

As the *Grutter* court recognized, education does not merely encompass the teaching of mathematics and deciphering of Shakespeare, but serves the intrinsic purpose of exposing students to other students of diverse backgrounds.[76] The exposure is less valuable and beneficial if it is unreflective of the diversity in our society. Authored by Chief Justice John Roberts, the plurality's reasoning in *Parents Involved* forgoes the vital importance that diversity serves; disregards a history of race segregation and the difficulties in overcoming black exclusion; neglects the complex issue of racial separation in private housing in relation to its effect on the integration of public schools; and, consequently, embraces the concept of white and black separation by striking down school assignment plans aimed at remedying de facto segregation and creating racial diversity in public secondary and elementary schools. By characterizing the Seattle school assignment plan as simple racial balancing,[77] when the history of desegregation efforts in Seattle was extensive,[78] and the plan did, in fact, result in increased racial diversity, the Court, once again, hindered integration efforts.

Its failure to recognize the intangible benefits that flow from a racially diverse student body embraces white and black separation. Justice Stephen Breyer best foreshadowed the decision of *Parents Involved* as one "that the Court and the Nation will come to regret."[79] This statement is accurate because, through its reasoning, the Court has willfully forgotten that it "was not long ago that people of different races drank from separate fountains, rode on separate buses, and studied in separate schools."[80] This willful blindness disarms public schools from addressing the effects of private segregation and demeans efforts to create racial diversity by terming any plan that strives to make public schools racially reflective of the entire community unconstitutional racial balancing. By suggesting that diversity might not be a compelling interest outside the university context, the Court drew a distinction between law schools and secondary schools.[81] The justices failed to recognize that the problem of racial inequality is not only caused by the way blacks feel but also, more fundamentally, by limitations that notions of white superiority impose on the nation's potential. Whites benefit from integration too through exposure to different cultures, viewpoints, and ideas and through reduction of beliefs in negative racial stereotypes.[82]

Unfortunately, little has changed as to funding discrepancies in the nation's public schools. During Jim Crow, funding for white schools was sometimes as high as ten times that of black schools.[83] Thirty years after Jim Crow ended, the funding differences were still significant.[84]

Today, blacks are victimized by a school funding system that creates inequality in a de facto segregated system. Resegregation, however, tells only part of the story. More than half of the students attending intensely segregated black schools live at or below the poverty line.[85] Because public schools are funded through local property taxes, disproportionate poverty rates among black communities limit the programs and services most black schools can provide.[86] New textbooks, college-prep courses, and instruction in art, music, and physical education are, for the most part, unavailable in schools that are both segregated and poor.[87] A study published in 2008 found that resources vary dramatically across schools depending upon income level and race of students in attendance.[88] The study found that schools in the highest-poverty settings tend to be in the worst physical condition and experience the most overcrowding.[89] Additionally, the percentage of classrooms wired for the Internet in predominantly black schools is twenty-one percentage points below the rate for predominantly white schools.[90]

Moreover, intensely segregated poor schools often lack experienced teachers. Studies prove that schools serving low-income and black students typically have the largest percentage of inexperienced and noncredentialed teachers,[91] which clearly has a significant impact on the quality of education provided to the children in attendance. According to a report released by the U.S. Department of Education, Maryland elementary schools in wealthy areas have 94.8% of classes taught by highly qualified teachers, while poor districts have only 66.2% of classes taught by such teachers, a gap of 28.6%.[92] Secondary schools show a gap of 25.7% between rich and disadvantaged schools.[93] These disadvantages may explain why white students outperform black students on national reading, math, and science tests and are generally more likely to graduate from high school and attend college.[94] The 2008 results of the National Assessment of Educational Progress Tests reveal a score gap between black and white twenty-year-olds of twenty-nine points in reading and twenty-six points in math.[95] The statistics show that the average gap in graduation rates between black and white students in 2006 was approximately 18%.[96] The numbers are even more shocking at the graduate school level, with black women earning 4.4% and black men earning only 2.1% of all doctoral degrees awarded at American universities in 2008.[97]

By 2003, data analyzed by the Harvard Civil Rights Project showed that public school integration had fallen to its lowest level in thirty years.[98] In the nation's five largest school districts, whites make up less than 15% of the student body.[99] Nearly equal numbers of black and white students attended public school in Detroit, Michigan, just before *Milliken*[100] lifted the city's desegregation decree in 1974. By 2000, less than thirty years later, white enrollment had dropped to 4%.[101]

The sad reality is that some fifty years after the Supreme Court outlawed Jim Crow schools, most black students remain in all-black or predominantly black schools. In 2004, New York *Newsday* entitled its fifty-year retrospective on *Brown* "Still Separate, Still Unequal," concluding that "[t]he dream of the racially harmonious world that *Brown* inspired in 1954 has dissolved in the cold daylight of racism,[102] troubled schools, [and] white flight."[103] Gary Orfield, of the Civil Rights Project, repeated that sentiment in 2005, asking how America could celebrate "a victory over segregation at a time when schools across the nation are becoming increasingly segregated."[104] But it was Jonathan Kozol, in 1991, who most accurately captured the forgotten legacy of desegregation, explaining that "the struggle being waged today, where there is any struggle being waged at all, is closer to the one that was addressed in 1896 in *Plessy v. Ferguson*, when the Court accepted segregated institutions for black people, stipulating only that the facilities must be equal to those open for white people."[105] America has yet to fulfill the equality mandate of *Plessy*, much less the desegregation promise of *Brown*, in schools or in other areas such as employment.[106]

Black Economic Inequality

As President Barack Obama explained in 2007, when he was still a senator, in a foreword for the National Urban League's publication, *The State of Black America 2007*,[107] there were "two stories to tell about the state of Black America in 2007."[108] The first of those stories celebrated the economic, social, and political accomplishments of black Americans—the "fulfillment of the hopes and dreams of black Americans who marched, bled, sat-in, voted and toiled against all odds and obstacles."[109] The second story, however, served as a "stark reminder that the long march toward true and meaningful equality in America isn't over."[110] Poverty and lack of access to resources continue to be acutely felt by black communities.

A study conducted by Brandeis University over the past twenty-five years shows that the wealth gap between blacks and whites has increased fourfold.[111] These statistics are a stark reminder of the economic realities many blacks face. If left unchallenged or ignored, they will continue to reinforce poverty in black communities.

A closer examination of economic disparities between blacks and whites since 2000 illustrates this point. In a report entitled *Invisible Men: The Urgent Problems of Low-Income African-American Males*, authors Renee Hanson, Mark McArdle, and Valerie Rawlston Wilson of the National Urban League Policy Institute refer to unemployment rates among black men as representing a "canary in [a] coal mine"—an early warning of danger for black men.[112] Referencing a report by the Bureau of Labor Statistics that tracked unemployment among whites, Latinos, and blacks from 1997 through 2006, Hanson, McArdle, and Wilson explain that, while unemployment rates across racial or ethnic classifications generally track economic cycles of recession and recovery, unemployment among black men consistently remains at a level higher than that among most groups and generally twice the rate of unemployment experienced by whites.[113] More specifically, with regard to the relationship between age and unemployment, nearly one-third of black teenagers were unemployed in 2006, compared to only 15% of white teenagers during that same period of time.[114] Similarly, although unemployment is typically said to decline as men age, white men experience unemployment at a rate one-half that of blacks in each age group.[115]

In times of economic downturn, black women are hit particularly hard. While black women fared slightly better than black men during the recession that lasted from December 2007 to June 2009, they continued to lose jobs during the recovery period, while black men recouped some of the previous losses.[116] Over the course of the recovery period, black women lost more jobs than any other group in the American workforce.[117] The disproportionately high unemployment rate for black women is particularly alarming, not only because of the dual racial and gender bias implications but also because more than half of all black families with dependent children are headed by black women.[118]

The acute impact of unemployment on blacks does not appear to be lessening over time. Algernon Austin, writing for the Economic Policy Institute, recounts how, despite periods of growth in the American economy, blacks were harder hit by lower incomes, lower wages, unemployment, and poverty in 2007 than they were in 2000.[119] According to Austin, while the black family poverty rate fell by 8.5 percentage points between 1989 and 2000, black family poverty increased by 2.8 percentage points between 2000 and 2007, with poverty among black children increasing by 3.3 percentage points during that same time.[120] Recognizing that many analysts discount official poverty rates as insufficiently reflecting changes in the cost of living, Austin further details how the percentage of families and children falling below "twice" the poverty level—a calculation standard used by poverty researchers to more accurately reflect financial struggles among those not officially counted as the "poor"—reveals an even more disturbing picture.[121] Using this lens, Austin explains that, in 2007, 46.5% of all blacks fell below the "twice the poverty level" bar, representing an increase of 0.9 percentage points from 2000.[122] Moreover, 60.6%, or nearly two-thirds, of black children fell below this level, an increase of 1.8% from 2000.[123]

These numbers reflect a historical trend of both unemployment and poverty disproportionately impacting black communities and the unique way in which economic downturns hit blacks harder than their white counterparts. Such alarming economic disparities are a historic reality[124] and have not abated in recent years. Statistics compiled by the Department of Labor's Bureau of Labor Statistics, tracking unemployment by race, gender, and age from July 2008 through July 2009, reveal that while unemployment rates for whites in the civilian, noninstitutional population ranged from 5.4% in August 2008 to 8.8% in August 2009, unemployment rates for blacks in the same population ranged from 10.7% in August 2008 to 15% in August 2009.[125] The black unemployment rate was almost double that of whites.[126] Additionally, the New York Times detailed the results of a study by the New York City Comptroller's Office demonstrating that, in the first quarter of 2008 and for the first three months of 2009, black unemployment increased at a rate four times the unemployment rate among whites.[127] As a result, the usual two-to-one ratio of joblessness among blacks and whites "widened substantially," in New York City, over that year.[128] The starker-than-usual disparity was attributed, in part, to the fact that certain sectors—including manufacturing, retail, and service sectors—are vulnerable to layoffs.[129] Blacks, traditionally holding a larger number of those jobs, are thus at greater risk of becoming unemployed.[130]

In today's bad economy, many Americans have a renewed sense of the value of having and retaining a job. For unemployment to be twice as high for blacks as it is for whites in a time of serious economic devastation is alarming. When many Americans are hurting economically—when middle-class families are struggling to make college tuition payments for their children, monthly rent and mortgage payments for their housing, summer trips for their relaxation, and dining out for their enjoyment—the disproportionate hardship for black families seems particularly unjust.

This bleak economic picture may partially explain why black women experience domestic violence at higher rates than their white counterparts. One in three American women will experience domestic violence at some point during her lifetime, and recent studies indicate that the number is higher among black women.[131] For example, while black women comprise just 8% of the total United States population, in 2005 they accounted for 22% of intimate partner homicides.[132] Socioeconomic status plays a significant role in these racial disparities, as domestic violence is generally more common in communities with lower income levels and high unemployment rates. However, a deep-seated distrust of law enforcement and health-care providers persists in many black communities and prevents both men and women from seeking treatment and protective services.

Even in the post–Jim Crow era, this distrust is not entirely unfounded, particularly for women who have children. In some states, a black mother who seeks medical treatment for drug abuse is ten times more likely to be reported for child neglect than a white mother.[133] The unfortunate result is that battered black women are often reluctant to utilize the resources available to protect women and families because they are afraid of losing their children and potentially facing criminal prosecution.

Wealth and race in America continue to be connected in a way that reinforces Jim Crow economic inequality against blacks. Many barriers to the long-term economic health and stability of blacks are systemic, institutionalized, and deeply rooted in historical trends of inequality that continue to challenge new generations of blacks. Moreover, these barriers are interdependent. Unemployment, dwindling home ownership, homelessness, lack of access to education, and incarceration attack black communities with devastating consequences. There are, indeed, two stories to tell about the state of black America. A significant minority of blacks have achieved middle-class status, including job stability, home ownership, and equity wealth.[134] Yet, even these achieving blacks continue to lag behind their white counterparts in the indices of wealth such as income, net worth, and debt accumulation.[135] Moreover, for the vast majority of blacks, economic stability is an increasingly elusive attainment due to policies and practices that have a disproportionate impact on black economic upward mobility.

Certainly, individual merit through hard work plays a significant role in wealth accumulation today. Yet, it is important for Americans to also recognize that blacks, through government policies and practices by some whites, have been historically excluded from certain methods of wealth accumulation that continue to have a significant impact on economic status. For most Americans, 75% of individual wealth is concentrated in home ownership, which has been the case for six decades.[136] Unfortunately, government policy limited black access to home loans.[137] Discriminatory practices of state officials authorized to administer $1 billion in federal government home loan funds, with over $1 billion of loans given to veterans of World War II in 1945, resulted in less than 1% being distributed to black veterans.[138] Though the registration laws at the time severely limited black service in the military, 467,833 blacks served in World War II.[139] Yet, few of these deserving blacks received the benefits of home ownership that many white veterans did. As a result, most black veterans were not able to pass wealth on to the next generation as many white veterans had done.

This discriminatory treatment has had a significant impact over the years on wealth disparities between blacks and whites. While America prospered economically in the post–World War II economic boom, the gap between white wealth and black wealth widened,[140] even after Jim Crow segregation ended, partly as a result of lack of black home ownership. Perhaps former senator and cochair of President Obama's Debt Commission, Alan Simpson, said it best, in November of 2010, when he reasoned that the disproportionate impact on blacks from the current debt crisis results from "emotion, fear, guilt, and racism."[141] As long as racialized barriers remain in employment and home ownership, true and meaningful economic equality remains elusive for blacks and will carry over into other activities.

Black Stereotypes in the Criminal Justice System

On his *Morning in America* radio program, in October 2005, former secretary of education William Bennett stated, "If you wanted to reduce crime, you could, if that were your sole purpose, you could abort every black baby in this country, and your crime rate would go down."[142] If we carry his thesis one step further, aborting every baby, irrespective of color, may also reduce the crime rate. Why did Secretary Bennett feel the need to inject race into his analysis? While many Americans are aware that criminality is based upon individual actions and may be produced in white households as well as black ones, many, like Secretary Bennett, continue to embrace notions of black inferiority and to assume that crime and blacks are synonymous.

In a 1990 General Social Survey from a University of Chicago report, 52.8% of respondents considered violence a characteristic closely associated with blacks, while only 18.8% associated violence with whites.[143] These survey results revealed that beliefs in black inferiority persist.[144] That same belief, that blacks are prone to commit crimes and, therefore, should be separated and watched carefully, led to Jim Crow criminal practices.[145] Today, disparate racial stereotyping remains prevalent and leads to blacks being "profiled" randomly, and an increased likelihood of their being searched, harassed, arrested, threatened, and killed.[146] These disparities reflect the same prejudices formed centuries ago.

There is no question that the criminal justice system is less racist than it was under Jim Crow. No longer do laws mandate harsher sentences for blacks convicted of crimes; no longer are blacks incarcerated to provide menial labor for private business interests, and no longer are innocent blacks lynched without a trial.[147] Yet, racism in the criminal justice system still exists. The myth of racial inferiority pervades the criminal justice system through discretionary acts by legislators, law enforcement officials, prosecutors, witnesses, jurors, and judges. Today blacks, whether male or female, rich or poor, adult or juvenile, are still treated more severely by the legal system.[148] Nationally, blacks are imprisoned at more than five times the rate of whites,[149] thus resulting in a loss of certain civil rights and employment,[150] since opportunities in many states, such as voting rights, are denied to those with felony records.[151] Few states allow prisoners to vote while incarcerated, but prisoners are counted under the census for voting representation in the jurisdiction where the prison in which they reside is located.[152] The high percentage of black incarceration and the vast number of prisons located in predominantly white areas, coupled with severe black separation in housing, consequently results in reduced electoral power in some predominantly black districts and increased electoral power in some predominantly white districts.[153] Fourteen states permanently bar voting rights for ex-felons, including Alabama, where 31% of the black male population has lost the right to vote as a result.[154] Blacks serve longer prison sentences, have higher arrest and conviction rates, receive higher bail amounts, and are more often the victims of deadly police force.[155] Black interaction with police often carries the risk of lethal force. Studies indicate that black males are killed by police at a rate six times that of white males.[156] In addition, blacks are more likely to be stopped, searched, arrested, and subjected to force by police.[157]

According to the testimony of Bryan Stevenson, "one-third of black males born today likely will spend at least some part of their lives behind bars; nearly one-tenth of black males in their twenties already live in prison; and almost one out of three black males in their twenties currently remains in jail, prison, on probation or parole, or otherwise under criminal justice control."[158] Overall, blacks are prosecuted and imprisoned at a rate more than five times that of whites.[159]

In 1995, almost a decade after the Anti–Drug Abuse Act[160] was adopted, the *Los Angeles Times* reported that no white defendant had ever been charged with a crack cocaine offense in any of the federal courts in Los Angeles, Boston, Denver, Chicago, Miami, or Dallas, or in seventeen state courts.[161] In 2000, less than 6% of crack cocaine offenders were white, and more than 80% were black.[162] By 2006, for every ten blacks tried for crack cocaine possession, one white defendant was charged with a crime involving crack cocaine, even though 65% of crack cocaine users are white.[163]

The racial disparity is further magnified because black drug offenders have a greater chance of being sentenced to prison than white drug offenders, given the average quantities involved in a drug offense.[164] The median amount of crack cocaine a defendant is charged with is fifty-two grams, which triggers the statutory ten-year sentence.[165] Conversely, the median amount of powder cocaine is 340 grams, which is insufficient to warrant a prison sentence.[166]

The excessive incarceration of blacks today, primarily due to excessive sentences for certain types of drug possession, is just another way to separate blacks. Blacks are the victims of these racially disparate impact drug laws, resulting in their disproportionate incarceration. Through incarceration, these blacks are physically separated from their communities and from other Americans. Thus, the black separation aspect of the racial paradigm is reinforced.

Prosecutors have wide discretion in determining whether and how to charge defendants, as well as in plea bargaining.[167] As a result, wide racial disparities exist due to notions of black inferiority pervading the decision-making process. One example is provided in the story of Richard Thomas and Tim Carter, both arrested in 2004, ninety days apart, in the same area of St. Petersburg, Florida.[168] Police discovered one rock of cocaine on Carter, who is white, and a crack pipe with cocaine residue on Thomas, who is black.[169] Both claimed drug addictions, neither had any prior felony arrests or convictions, and both potentially faced five years in prison.[170] Carter, the white defendant, had his prosecution withheld and the judge sent him to drug rehabilitation.[171] Thomas, on the other hand, was prosecuted, convicted, and sent to prison.[172] Carter and Thomas committed the same crime, had similar arrest and conviction histories, and made the same claim of extenuating circumstances due to drug addiction.[173] Their only obvious difference was race.

What could possibly have caused this disparate result? Racial bias permeates the discretionary acts of members of the criminal justice system from beginning to end. Whether it is the initial stop by the police, or a decision by the jury to convict, or a determination by a judge to impose the death penalty, the opportunity for racial bias is pervasive.

Consequences of this racial bias for blacks are severe. Long-term incarcerations impose serious financial burdens on families of the incarcerated, as well as psychological ramifications for the incarcerated individual and his or her family members. Moreover, felony convictions, even after sentence completion, sometimes exclude participation in voting and public assistance programs.

The racial bias that occurs in the criminal justice system today is the same bias that existed in the criminal justice system during slavery and Jim Crow. Grounded in notions of black inferiority, the system consistently treats blacks differently and more harshly. Slavery and the slave codes that governed slave conduct were justified because blacks were viewed by slave owners as objects—more reminiscent of animals than human beings. Jim Crow separation was justified because blacks were viewed by white segregationists as morally corrupt, disease ridden, intellectually deficient, lazy, irresponsible, and dishonest. Higher suspicion levels against blacks by law enforcement officers after Jim Crow reflect an embrace of the Jim Crow stereotypes. The racial bias that manifests itself today in racial profiling, laws targeting black behavior, and harsh sentencing, and that subsequently results in widespread disparities, has existed for centuries and appears motivated by the same false notions of black inferiority that justified slave codes, Black Codes, and Jim Crow criminal practices.

False allegations by whites against fictitious blacks also reflect the embrace of black inferiority. In 1989, Charles Stuart of Boston, Massachusetts, claimed that he and his pregnant wife had been carjacked by a black assailant.[174] In 1994, Susan Smith, of Union, South Carolina, claimed that she and her children had been carjacked by an armed black man.[175] In 2009, Bonnie Sweeten, of Bucks County, Pennsylvania, claimed that she and her nine-year-old daughter were kidnapped by two black men and held in the trunk of their Cadillac.[176] In 2011, Bethany Storro, of Vancouver, Washington, claimed that a black woman threw acid on her face. In each highly publicized account, facts subsequently revealed that the whites themselves committed the crimes, and no black persons were involved.[177] When the perpetrator is fictitious, what plausible reason could a white person have for blaming a black person, except for the white person's belief that Americans are more likely to accept the false allegation when it implicates a black perpetrator? Bethany Storro apologized to the black community in Washington State for making a false allegation.[178] Storro's apology was an appropriate individual response, yet this phenomenon of guilt for implicating fictitious black predators reflects a larger notion in our society than simply sorrow for lying. Implicating a fictitious black perpetrator takes advantage of the continuing perception that blacks predominantly commit criminal acts and provides yet another example of how blacks continue to be victimized in the criminal justice system by an enduring false notion of excessive black criminality.

Conversely, whites often avoid prosecution when their victims are black. The famous 1983 study by Professors David Baldus, Charles Pulaski, and George Woodworth, introduced by the defendant in *McCleskey v. Kemp*,[179] studied two thousand murder cases during the 1970s in Georgia and concluded that blacks convicted of killing whites had the greatest chance of receiving a capital conviction.[180] The raw numbers collected by Professor Baldus indicate that defendants charged with killing white persons received the death penalty in 11% of the cases, but the defendants charged with killing blacks received the death penalty in only 1% of the cases.[181] The study took account of thirty-nine nonracial variables and found that defendants charged with killing white victims were 4.3 times as likely to receive a capital sentence as defendants charged with killing black victims.[182] The court in *McCleskey* found that the defendant's statistical evidence did not establish an Equal Protection Clause violation.[183] The justices reasoned that statistical evidence of a racial disparity alone was insufficient to demonstrate racial bias.[184] While the justices recognized the possibility of the presence of racial bias, they refused to assume that what was not clearly admitted may have been the intentional manifestation of racially discriminatory treatment.[185] While theoretically that standard may sound reasonable to some, the reality for most defendants was an insurmountable burden for proving an Equal Protection Clause violation. To prevail, they would need to show that decision makers had acted with a discriminatory purpose.[186] The *McCleskey* case and the significant findings of the Baldus study support the notion that in the value system of the average jury in Georgia, the life of a white person is more valuable than the life of a black person. While the criminal laws of Georgia no longer expressly state that the life of a black person is less valued, the Supreme Court's ruling implicitly endorses the continuation of this belief.

More recent studies reveal that attorneys general seek the death penalty at much higher rates when the victim is white, while white federal defendants are more likely to have death charges reduced to life sentences through plea bargaining.[187] Almost 80% of persons on death row have been convicted of crimes against white victims, despite the fact that blacks are more likely to be victims of homicide and other violent crimes.[188] Such disparities prove that white lives and safety remain more protected than black ones, thus reinforcing notions of white superiority.

Blacks are victimized in the criminal justice system due to the fact that many laws identify criminal activities predominantly associated with blacks and provide harsher penalties. The substantial sentencing disparity between powder cocaine and crack cocaine convictions, provided for in the Anti–Drug Abuse Act of 1986,[189] reflects this racist discretion.

The sentencing guidelines for crack cocaine, more popular with black users, are much more severe than those for powder cocaine, consequently resulting in a 100-to-1 ratio in sentencing.[190] A defendant caught with fifty grams of crack will be subjected to the same sentence as one caught with five thousand grams of powder.[191] The sentencing guidelines for crack cocaine result in first-time offenders getting jail time with no option for plea bargaining.[192] Conversely, first-time offenders for powder cocaine can plea bargain or even get parole and rehabilitation.[193] Crack cocaine is a derivative of powder cocaine made by adding baking soda and cooking it.[194] While crack cocaine and powder cocaine have the same physiological and psychotropic effects, the disproportionate sentencing guidelines impact much higher numbers of blacks.[195] Statistics suggest that overall incarceration rates of blacks, which have risen as much as 70% in some states, are due to this disproportionate treatment in drug sentencing.[196]

One high-profile case is that of professional baseball player Willie Mays Aikens, the first baseman for the Kansas City Royals, who in 1994 was sentenced to twenty years for possession of 2.2 ounces of crack cocaine.[197] Aikens, who is black, had nationwide acclaim in professional baseball—his record still stands as the only player with two home runs in two games of the same World Series.[198] For a defendant to receive Aikens's same twenty-year sentence would require possession of fifteen pounds of powder cocaine— over one hundred times the amount he had.[199] Aikens spent fourteen years in prison and was finally released in June 2008.[200] A recent review of sentencing disparities helped lead to his release and the early release of nearly twenty thousand others who had been imprisoned with similarly disproportionate sentences.[201] In contrast, the same year Aikens was sentenced to twenty years for 2.2 ounces of crack cocaine, a white Kansas federal court defendant with seventeen ounces of powder cocaine (as well as a handgun and alleged intent to distribute across state lines) was sentenced to only five years in prison.[202]

Prosecutorial racial discrimination against black juveniles resulted in six black teenagers (the "Jena Six") being jailed in Jena, Louisiana, which is 85% white and only 12% black.[203] The Jena Six, all students at Jena High School, were indicted on charges of attempted murder and conspiracy to commit murder for the December 2006 schoolyard beating of a white male student, who allegedly used racial taunts against them, including "nigger."[204] All six students were football players and school leaders.[205] None had prior criminal records or had ever been in trouble with the law before this incident,[206] except for Mychal Bell, who had four juvenile convictions for assault and burglary. The beating incident that led to the arrests was the culmination of three months of racial tension at Jena High School.[207] After a spate of national publicity and outpouring of support for the Jena Six from around the world,[208] the charges were reduced to aggravated battery and conspiracy to commit aggravated battery consistent with the fact that it was a school fight.[209] The potential sentences were reduced from eighty years to twenty-two years.[210] The deadly weapons alleged by the state to elevate the incident from simple battery to aggravated battery were not guns or knives but tennis shoes.[211] District Attorney Walters charged the Jena Six as adults, even though they were all minors.[212] Eventually, five of the six charged pled guilty to battery.[213] As this case reflects, black juveniles are often treated much more harshly than white juveniles through prosecutorial discretion in determinations as to whether to issue a charge, how to characterize the seriousness of the offense, and whether to recommend leniency for those convicted.

Although blacks make up only 15% of juveniles in the nation, they account for more than 26% of juvenile arrests, 32% of delinquency referrals to juvenile court, 41% of juveniles detained in delinquency cases, 46% of juveniles in corrections institutions, and 52% of juveniles transferred to adult criminal court after judicial hearings.[214] High rates of sentencing and incarceration indicate that black juvenile offenders are given much longer sentences, sometimes as much as twice as long, than white ones for the same crimes.[215] Black juveniles are over six times more likely than whites to be prosecuted and sentenced to prison or tried as adults.[216] As a result, black juveniles are sentenced to prison, whereas white juvenile offenders, such as those at Jena High School who hung nooses from a tree, have criminal actions dismissed as "pranks," or youthful indiscretion, and are more often referred to treatment programs than to prisons.[217] Another startling statistic is that 77% of juveniles who receive life sentences, both with and without the possibility of parole, are black or Hispanic.[218]

The widest racial disparities are reserved for capital punishment cases. While blacks only make up 12% of the general population in the United States, 42% of persons on death row are black.[219] In contrast, whites account for 67% of the population, but only 56% of persons on death row.[220]

One illustrative story began in December 2001, when Cory Maye was at home in a poor black neighborhood in Prentiss, Mississippi, with his eighteen-month-old daughter.[221] Maye's daughter was asleep in the bedroom, and he had fallen asleep in the living room while watching television.[222] Suddenly, Maye was awakened by pounding at the door and loud yelling.[223] Fearing for his child's safety, he ran into the bedroom and loaded a gun he used for hunting and self-defense.[224] He then crouched behind the bed with his daughter, hoping the intruders would leave.[225] Instead, they broke down the rear door of the duplex apartment and rushed through the bedroom door.[226] Maye fired three shots, hitting one of the men, who turned out to be police officers conducting a raid in search of illegal drugs.[227] The officer, Ron Jones, who was white and the son of the Prentiss police chief, died on the way to the hospital.[228] Maye was charged with capital murder, the only charge that carries the death penalty, despite the fact that no drugs were found, and that he had no history of violence, no previous trouble with the law, and no motive for purposely killing the officer.[229] Under Mississippi law, the only way Maye could be found guilty of capital murder was if he knew or should have known that the person he shot was a police officer.[230] No evidence supported that basis, and the prosecutor's theory of the case defied logic—a man with no criminal record, who was trying to build a new life for his family, looked out his window to see a team of police officers at his door and purposely decided to shoot them.[231] The jury rejected Maye's defense of mistaken self-defense, found him guilty of capital murder, and sentenced him to death.[232] On appeal, and with a new lawyer, Maye succeeded in overturning his death sentence.[233] The Mississippi circuit court vacated Maye's death sentence on the grounds of incompetence of counsel, and the new district attorney agreed to no longer seek the death penalty when the sentencing phase was retried.[234] However, on December 2, 2010, a decision was issued by the Mississippi Supreme Court granting Maye a new trial on the grounds that the trial court judge had failed to provide proper jury instructions regarding Maye's right to self-defense.[235] Furthermore, Maye pled guilty to reduced charges of manslaughter.[236] On July 1, 2011, Maye received a ten-year sentence which the judge declared "time served."[237] This unexpected change of events, that allowed Maye to return home, is the exception rather than the rule for blacks wrongly convicted of first-degree murder.[238]

While the death of a police officer in the line of duty is tragic, sentencing Maye to capital punishment under circumstances of possible mistaken identity and self-defense makes absolutely no sense without racial hierarchy overtones. One might suggest that Maye received the death penalty because the victim's father was the chief of police. This explanation is just a proxy for white superiority notions since few blacks serve as police chiefs in the South.[239]

Blacks are even more likely to get the death penalty in cases where the victim is white. One national study illustrated that blacks who killed whites were sentenced to death over fifteen times the rate of blacks who kill blacks.[240] A Maryland study found that not only were eight of the thirteen total inmates on death row black, but all thirteen were sentenced to death for killing whites despite the fact that 55% of the victims in all cases in which the death penalty could be or was sought were not white.[241] When courts consistently apply the death penalty in cases where the victims are white, but not when the victims are black, it reveals a systematic value judgment: a greater value is being placed on white life. Furthermore, the diminished punishment for black-on-black murder also reveals white superiority notions within the system, suggesting that the loss of black lives is not considered as significant as the loss of white lives. Differing treatment in the value of life is also visible outside of the criminal justice system, particularly in the housing arena.

Black Housing Separation

Today, most whites reside in majority-white neighborhoods, as they did before housing desegregation efforts began in 1968.[242] Even after such efforts began, racism has contributed to a shortage of affordable housing, resulting in barriers to community integration. Many predominantly white suburbs resist efforts to build affordable housing due to concerns that blacks will occupy such housing, resulting in a decrease in property values for white area residents.[243] Local government entities often require affordable housing requests to acquire community approval, thus preventing most of these projects.[244] Even when a project receives community approval, bureaucratic resistance can increase costs, dissuading many developers from pursuing such projects.[245]

Hurricane Katrina globally demonstrated the extreme lack of racial integration in housing when it hit Louisiana in 2005.[246] Racial segregation in New Orleans demonstrated patterns of housing for blacks in less desirable, flood-prone areas.[247] The aftermath of the flood revealed that blacks lived in the most vulnerable areas.[248] As a result, the storm victims were predominantly black.[249] In addition, the worst discrimination occurred after the hurricane hit, as blacks sought shelter and alternative housing. According to a survey conducted by the National Fair Housing Alliance, black apartment seekers, evacuated due to Katrina, were discriminated against in two-thirds of the apartment complexes in seventeen different cities.[250] White rental seekers were quoted lower rates, received higher incentives, and were more likely to have security deposits waived.[251] Frequently, blacks were falsely informed that no vacancies existed.[252] One predominantly white suburb of New Orleans passed a law that allowed only family members of residents to rent houses in the area.[253] This unusual provision appeared to be directed toward limiting black renters, displaced by Hurricane Katrina, from entering this suburb through the rental housing market. As these examples from New Orleans after Hurricane Katrina indicate, the commitment among some whites to black separation in housing remains high even in the midst of an emergency.

Blacks repeatedly resisted white attempts to maintain black separation. Historically, the more blacks sought to avoid racial isolation, whether in public accommodations, housing, or schools, the more whites violently reacted. Blacks are often the victims of violent reactions from whites when they challenge racial isolation efforts or undermine white superiority/black inferiority notions. When blacks move from inner-city areas to outlying suburbs today, white resistance is frequently high. Tipping-point bigotry inspired Jeremy Parady, who pled guilty in 2005 to conspiracy to commit arson in a series of fires in a new housing development in southern Maryland.[254] The fires caused over $10 million in damages.[255] Parady admitted to the police that he set fire to this development because many of the buyers were blacks, and the surrounding neighborhood was mostly white.[256]

Today, blacks remain excessively separated in housing.[257] Residence determines a myriad of opportunities in America today, including the school one attends, safety and security levels, access to public transportation and roadways, employment options, and access to credit and finance considerations.

Due to such rigid housing separation, institutions can target blacks for harsh treatment, without specifically identifying race, by targeting a neighborhood, area, zip code, or district. As a result, insurance companies may charge extra premiums for life, auto, or health insurance on the basis of location of residence rather than individual merit. Oil companies may charge more for gasoline at service stations on the basis of location of business rather than individual performance of the station, leading to further economic exploitation of blacks.[258]

Blacks and Predatory Lending

Broad indicators of poverty, such as unemployment, lack of education, and incarceration, all combine to create a set of forces that disproportionately affect blacks. This intersection can best be illustrated through a focus on one aspect of institutionalized or entrenched practices—predatory lending practices targeting lower-income, black communities with high-interest, subprime mortgages.

The term "subprime" refers to a category of loans used to buy, improve, or refinance homes that are offered to borrowers who, because of their underdeveloped or blemished credit histories, do not typically qualify for mortgage loans at the "prime," or lowest available, rate.[259] In exchange for the loans, subprime borrowers are asked to pay higher interest rates, points, and fees and are often subject to prepayment penalties.[260] Subprime loans are also often associated with adjustable rate mortgages (ARMs) and other variable-interest or interest-only loans.[261] In May 2000, the Department of Housing and Urban Development (HUD) issued a report entitled *Unequal Burden in Baltimore: Income and Racial Disparities in Subprime Lending*, one of a series of HUD reports examining subprime lending throughout the country.[262] Using data collected as a result of the reporting provisions of the Home Mortgage Disclosure Act, the HUD report concluded that the rapid growth, on a national level, of subprime refinance lending during the 1990s was characterized by a disproportionate concentration of such lending in low-income and minority communities.[263]

Focusing, in part, on the Baltimore metropolitan area, the HUD study revealed that subprime loans were six times more likely in predominantly black neighborhoods as compared to white neighborhoods.[264] Moreover, racial classifications accounted for a prevalence of such loans where class and income were constant variables.[265] According to the HUD study, homeowners in predominantly black middle-income neighborhoods were nearly four times as likely to have subprime loans as homeowners in predominantly white middle-income neighborhoods.[266] Similarly, across neighborhoods, low-income blacks represented 45% of subprime borrowers.[267] By comparison, white, low-income borrowers accounted for 13% of subprime borrowers.[268] In predominantly black areas, subprime mortgages accounted for 57% of foreclosures, compared to a subprime market share of 42%.[269] While recognizing the positive aspects of banking practices that provide loans to those traditionally excluded from obtaining mortgages, the HUD report cautioned that subprime lending often operated "outside federal regulatory structure," running the risk of breeding predatory lending practices that resulted in disastrous consequences for less financially savvy borrowers.[270]

Nine years after HUD's report, the devastating impact of these lending practices has come to light on a mass scale. Blacks are approximately 34% more likely than whites with similar income and credit histories to receive high-rate and subprime loans with prepayment penalties.[271] Nor have these loans resulted, as some predicted, in sustained increases in black home ownership, which, as a result of historical redlining[272] and racial discrimination, has lagged in substantial ways behind home ownership trends among whites.[273] Rather, the massive wave of foreclosures resulting from the resetting of interest rates, which priced variable-rate and interest-only mortgages outside of the financial capacities of those mortgage holders, hit black and low-income homeowners the hardest, reversing the modest, but steady, increase in black home ownership that had occurred between 1995 and 2004.[274] Disproportionately for blacks, sustained home ownership remains an elusive dream.[275]

Race, poverty, and subprime lending, and the devastating impact that these intersections created in terms of foreclosures in low-income black communities, are due, in part, to large-scale and deliberate efforts by banking industry giants to make a profit off vulnerable communities. In July 2007, the NAACP filed suit in a Los Angeles federal court against fifteen of the country's largest mortgage lending institutions, alleging systemic and institutionalized racism in subprime mortgage lending, in violation of the FHA of 1968, the Equal Credit Opportunity Act (ECOA) of 1974 and the Civil Rights Act.[276] Similarly, in March 2009, the NAACP filed separate lawsuits in California federal district court against Wells Fargo and HSBC

Bank, alleging systematic, institutionalized racism in their subprime home mortgage lending practices.[277]

The NAACP is not the only group to attempt to hold lenders accountable for deliberately targeting the most vulnerable communities for the most volatile lending. In January 2008, Baltimore became the first city in the nation to take legal action on this issue by filing a federal lawsuit against Wells Fargo Bank, alleging deliberate discrimination in subprime mortgage lending that has resulted in a foreclosure rate in black neighborhoods four times that of white neighborhoods and twice that of the city's average.[278] In support of the lawsuit, former Wells Fargo bank employees have alleged that the bank systematically singled out blacks in Baltimore for subprime mortgages, providing detailed accounts of deliberate racial targeting in the marketing of these loans, including pushing individuals to assume subprime mortgages when they qualified for loans at the prime rate.[279] City officials further released data, as part of their lawsuit, indicating that more than half the properties subject to foreclosure on a Wells Fargo loan from 2005 to 2008 were vacant, with 71% of those located in predominantly black neighborhoods.[280] According to city officials, the conclusion is clear. City Solicitor George Nilson stated that the bank's practices "confirm[ed] our worst fears: that this is not just a case based on a review of numbers and a statistical analysis," adding: "You don't have to scratch your head and wonder if maybe this was just an accident. The behavior is pretty explicit."[281]

These numbers are reflected throughout the country.[282] Although blacks comprise 12% of the population over the age of eighteen, 52.4% of loans awarded to black borrowers are subprime loans or high-cost loans.[283] One in thirty-three homeowners is expected to lose a home due to foreclosure, primarily because of subprime loans made in 2005 and 2006.[284] The estimated blow to the financial health of Americans is in the billions.[285] While no single factor accounts solely for the enormous economic impact this will have on black communities, discriminatory lending practices played a substantial part.[286] Black neighborhoods have, as a result, been stripped of substantial equity wealth; and far too many individuals and families have been displaced from their homes and financially ruined.[287]

Disparities in Homelessness

In addition to being disproportionately impacted by foreclosures and predatory lending practices, blacks constitute a disproportionate number of America's homeless. In December 2008, the U.S. Conference of Mayors issued a report compiling the results of a one-year, 25-city survey of hunger and homelessness.[288] The cities surveyed for the report identified a lack of affordable housing, poverty, and unemployment as the three main causes of family homelessness.[289] Additionally, the top three cited causes of homelessness among single individuals were substance abuse, lack of affordable housing, and mental illness.[290] Thus, it should come as no surprise, in light of the foregoing discussion, that although blacks were estimated to comprise approximately 12.8% of the population as of 2008,[291] in 2007 they accounted for approximately 45.7% of sheltered homeless singles and unaccompanied youth and 47% of sheltered members of households with children.[292] By contrast, whites comprised approximately 79.8% of the U.S. population as of 2008[293] but only 47% of members of households with children in shelters and 50% of sheltered homeless singles in 2007.[294]

Joblessness, homelessness, and poverty among blacks do not exist in a vacuum. They are attributable to a host of social and economic factors, all combining to perpetuate debilitating cycles of poverty. According to the Bureau of Labor Statistics, in 2005, the unemployment rate among those without high school diplomas was nearly three times higher than unemployment among college graduates.[295] Hanson, McArdle, and Wilson, discussing statistics compiled by the U.S. Census Bureau, explain that almost 20% of all black men over the age of twenty-five do not have a high school diploma, compared to only 10% of white men in the same age group.[296] They further explain that more than half of all black men in America's "inner cities" do not finish high school.[297] In 2004, 72% of black men in their twenties who did not complete high school were unemployed.[298] Clearly, public school education, long thought to be the great equalizer, has yet to achieve parity among black and white students. In the absence of effective, educational interventions in the lives of young, poor blacks, the risk of their dropping out of the system—and falling through the cracks—increases at a dramatic rate.

These factors, in addition to the disproportionate incarceration of blacks, combine in a way that acutely affects poor black children. Marian Wright Edelman, president of the Children's Defense Fund, writes compellingly about a "cradle-to-prison pipeline" that "funnels tens of thousands of poor children every year down life paths that lead to arrest, conviction, incarceration and death."[299] Indeed, black children, comprising 16% of American youth, end up representing 28% of juvenile arrests, 30% of adjudicated youth, and 58% of youth admitted to a state adult prison.[300] Far from being easily defined, Edelman explains that the cradle-to-prison pipeline is "made up of a complex combination of social and economic factors and political choices," including "stressed, poor and often single-parent families," "disparities in access to health and mental health care," "underperforming schools," and "broken child welfare and juvenile justice systems," all converging to disadvantage poor black children who receive few protections from elected officials.[301]

Racial Bias in Politics

Before the federal government passed the Voting Rights Act in 1965,[302] few blacks could vote, making the promise of democracy as hollow as was the promise of liberty to slaves in the Declaration of Independence. The Fifteenth Amendment to the Constitution,[303] adopted in 1870 specifically to address this issue, did very little, because it was not enforced due to white resistance efforts. In signing the Voting Rights Act into law, President Lyndon B. Johnson termed it "a monumental law in the history of American freedom."[304] He was right. The impact has been substantial. Shortly after the law was enacted, eight hundred thousand blacks registered to vote. Today, there are about ten thousand elected black officials;[305] in 1965, there were approximately three hundred.[306] These advancements in the political arena did not, however, result in black political successes on the national level.

Historically, black candidates have not been successful in national elective politics because appeals to white racism have been effective. The racially charged language used by Geraldine Ferraro and others during the 2008 presidential primary campaign,[307] referring to candidate Barack Obama as an affirmative action candidate, reflects such an appeal, and many assumed that these appeals would work once again.

Americans must acknowledge this history and recognize that racism in politics persists. While there has been a significant improvement in black representation in Congress since the civil rights movement, race continues to play a significant, sometimes insurmountable, role in the political arena. With Obama being the rare exception thus far, white reluctance to support black candidates has made successful statewide and national black candidacies rare. Massachusetts governor Deval Patrick and New York governor David Patterson, who was elected as lieutenant governor[308] and ascended to power when Eliot Spitzer resigned,[309] are the notable recent exceptions. The United States does not have one black senator.[310]

Many thought Harold Ford Jr. would serve as the junior senator from Tennessee in 2008.[311] Ford served in Congress and represented Tennessee's Ninth District.[312] Following in his father's legacy, he was elected to five terms in the district and was seen as a new type of Democrat, one who was fiscally and socially conservative and who knew how to reach out to Republicans to build much-needed bipartisan coalitions.[313] Perhaps due in part to Ford's moderate political viewpoint, President Bill Clinton referred to him as "the walking, living embodiment of where America ought to go in the twenty-first century."[314] Yet, his years of experience and moderate political positions could not save Ford from the deleterious effects of race baiting.

A little more than two weeks before Election Day, in November of 2007, with Ford leading in most Tennessee polls, the Republican National Committee ran an advertisement that played on racial fears.[315] The ad featured a provocative white woman who claims to have met Ford at "the playboy party" and ended with the woman asking the candidate to call her.[316] The ad drew national attention and scorn from Republicans and Democrats alike,[317] as the commercial targeted the many whites and blacks who are uncomfortable with interracial dating. The ad not only painted Ford as a party boy but also fed on traditional fears by many whites of black males who date white women. While it was not widely known, at that time Ford was dating Emily Threlkeld, a white woman, who would later become his wife.[318] Ford lost the election, in a very close race.[319]

Black candidates continue to be hyperscrutinized out of a fear that they may have hidden racial biases. Black politicians have the added onus of not only needing to appear completely race neutral in their everyday lives but also preventing the appearance of a black agenda. The subconscious fear of many (and the conscious fear of a few) whites, that blacks will band together to advance a specifically "black" agenda, is too great for black candidates to ignore and still capture a significant amount of white votes.

Even their supporters face questions. For example, in 2008, when Republican and retired general Colin Powell announced his endorsement of Barack Obama on *Meet the Press*, host Tom Brokaw questioned whether race played a role in Powell's decision.[320] When television star Oprah

Winfrey endorsed Obama, many assumed racial bias.[321] Yet, the racial motives of Obama's high-profile white supporters, like conservative columnist David Brooks,[322] went unquestioned.

National and statewide black political leaders are rare and are put under intense, race-based scrutiny that often draws on the black inferiority rung of the paradigm. Much of this scrutiny is incredibly insulting and degrading to blacks.

After Obama announced his economic stimulus plan, one that could prove to be a hallmark of his presidency, the *New York Post* ran a cartoon depicting Obama as a monkey.[323] This was only the beginning. Obama has been called a "Nazi"[324] and a supporter of "white slavery,"[325] and his American citizenship continues to be questioned by those who call themselves "the birthers."[326] Some of Obama's political opponents appear particularly disrespectful, such as Congressman Joe Wilson, who disrupted President Obama's 2009 State of the Union Address by shouting "you lie" in response to Obama's characterization of recent immigration legislation.[327] While no overt reference to Obama's race was made in the outburst, the fact that such disrespect had never occurred at a State of the Union Address, and that Obama was the first black to give such an address, causes one to consider the magnitude of race-based superiority and inferiority assumptions in behaviors in America.

This attitude echoes *Plessy*,[328] in which blacks in subservient roles are acceptable, but blacks in roles of equality are not. President Obama was highly criticized for what some perceived as arrogance during the 2008 presidential election campaign.[329] This reflects false notions of white superiority requiring black politicians to be careful when they interact with whites not to appear too smart, sophisticated, or confident. There is a real risk that white sensibilities may be negatively impacted if black politicians do not appear humble, gracious, and deferential to whites.

Karl Rove made a statement to an ABC reporter that Obama was "coolly arrogant."[330] In response, columnist John Ridley wrote an article in the *Huffington Post* that offered a different perspective of what critics were actually implying by the word "arrogant."[331] Ridley wrote that a majority of well-to-do blacks are called "uppity" and "arrogant" when "a select section of privileged white guys fear that the silver spoons are about to be snatched from their lily white places."[332] In retrospect, Ridley wrote, white people are asking themselves "how dare they think they can work jobs like ours or live in neighborhoods like ours or send their children to schools like ours? These people are just damn arrogant."[333] Additionally, he stated that "the only arrogance Obama is guilty of is unforgivable blackness."[334] The bias, evident in acts such as viewing confident black candidates as "uppity" or hyperscrutinizing the associations of black candidates, that many whites display against black political candidates is grounded in the paradigm and its false notion of white superiority and black inferiority and a dynamic, as we have seen in this book, that goes back to the nation's founding.

Most revealing of the racism against President Obama are the labels placed on him by political opponents. Racially tinged language is often used to describe or refer to Obama. Newt Gingrich referred to President Obama as "the food stamp president,"[335] Donald Trump questioned his academic credentials and whether he deserved to get into Columbia and Harvard universities[336] when he referred to Obama as the "affirmative action president," and congressman Doug Lamborn questioned his veracity when he compared Obama to a tar baby.[337]

These references, while not overtly racist, seem to have an underlying implication of race. These references tap into the widely held and racist notions that Obama wants a free ride just like all those blacks on welfare; that Obama couldn't possibly, as a black man, be smart enough to earn those degrees; or that Obama, because he is black, is politically inept. Not even George W. Bush, whose college and business school performances were said to be marginal,[338] has ever been requested to produce transcripts. Yet, President Obama, who was the elected leader of a prestigious law school organization, has been asked to show such proof.[339] Just as innuendo was used during the 2008 presidential campaign to suggest that Obama was different from whites by emphasizing his middle name of "Hussein,"[340] his Hawaiian roots,[341] or his attendance at a Muslim school, innuendo is also used against President Obama to attempt to characterize him as "the other," not American, not Christian, and not white. While his religious faith was questioned during the first presidential campaign, his citizenship and educational achievements have been challenged since he became president.

Moreover, some whites oppose Obama's policies because they believe his motives behind the policies are designed to harm whites. For example, conservative commentator Rush Limbaugh indicated his opposition to Obama's health-care legislation because Limbaugh reasoned that it was a way for Obama to redistribute wealth from whites to blacks.[342] Limbaugh's reasoning was based on the fact that higher percentages of whites (90%) retained health insurance coverage than blacks (81%) and Obama's legislation would provide, at taxpayer expense, free coverage for many of those previously uninsured blacks.[343] Similarly, conservative television host Glenn Beck characterized his opposition to Obama's health-care plan as grounded in the basis that the policy was racial "reparations" in disguise.[344]

Research suggests a correlation between white racial prejudice and opposition to President Obama's policies.[345] Implicit racial prejudices corresponded with a reluctance to vote for Obama and with opposition to his health-care reform legislation. When Obama's plan was attributed to former president Bill Clinton, opposition from some whites lessened as a result,[346] in part, of Obama being black and Clinton being white.

Of course, not all criticism of President Obama or opposition to his policies, not even a majority of it, is racist. But when the criticism deviates significantly from the normal criticism of a president, such as in the request for production of a birth certificate when no previous president ever had to present such credentials, causes most thoughtful and objective Americans to question whether Obama's race, not his politics, is the critical factor in the deviation of treatment. In southern states during Reconstruction under the Black Codes and in South Africa under apartheid, blacks were required to present proof of who they were and whether they rightfully belonged where they were. In a similar manner Obama, even as president, is being treated as black political leaders have always been treated—he's being required to prove his legitimacy. Whether it be that they were willing to die for their country in military service like many white Americans, whether they despised communism as much as most white Americans, or whether they were just as smart as their white counterparts, black leaders have been subject to presumptions of illegitimacy. Even Thurgood Marshall, at his Senate confirmation hearing for the United States court of appeals in the mid-1960s, spent an inordinate amount of time refuting questions concerning his patriotism and whether he was a communist sympathizer.[347] The same racially biased questioning of patriotism occurred in 2011 when Governor Rick Perry of Texas responded to a question of whether he thought President Obama loved his country by answering, "Ask the President."[348]

As a law student at Harvard, Obama was elected president of the *Harvard Law Review*,[349] an honor reserved for only the most accomplished of law students. If he were white, no one would question his legitimacy to claim that he belonged at Harvard. Apparently, successful black law students who run for political office must provide additional proof of intelligence.

Black Self-Victimization

As presidential candidate Obama recognized, to get to a racially "more perfect union,"[350] both blacks and whites will need to contribute and to change. While many whites continue to embrace false notions of black inferiority, reactions by some blacks to such notions have been unproductive, thus exacerbating the tenacity of the racial paradigm. While it is dangerous to overgeneralize, far too many blacks have embraced unproductive values or made harmful choices that help to maintain, in a self-destructive manner, negative racial stereotypes.

One is the antieducational embrace known as "acting white." The term characterizes academically inclined but allegedly snobbish black students, who are often shunned by their black peers.[351] Studies confirm this sentiment, finding a "race to mediocrity" occurring among black students.[352] Using academic achievement as a measure of "acting white," Harvard professors Paul Torelli and Roland Fryer found that as academic achievement rose, so did peer-group separation.[353] Simply put, blacks who academically achieve are less popular with black students and have fewer black friends.[354] By contrast, white students' popularity grew with higher grade point averages.[355]

Blacks succeeding in areas historically reserved for whites have been chided as "acting white" as well. When he was a presidential candidate, Barack Obama faced such criticism.[356] The implication is that there is one particular way to be black and that contemporary conceptions of blackness do not leave room for achievement in areas traditionally inaccessible to blacks or for divergent views. The "acting white" label belies an antieducational sentiment that many blacks embrace, contributing to a false perception that whites are more academically inclined.

Another harmful reaction is a failure to maintain strong family units. Bill Cosby pointed to a problem with single-parent households consisting of "five or six different children, same woman, eight, ten different husbands or whatever, pretty soon you're going to have to have DNA cards so you can tell who you're making love to."[357] Black families, it seems, increasingly do not fit the favored image of the traditional two-parent family unit. Many, including Cosby, attribute this to a black acceptance of out-of-wedlock children, promiscuous behavior by black youths, and a failure of black parenting.[358] With our nation's jails overwhelmingly filled with young black men, generally from poor urban communities, there is a dearth of stable, "successful" black men to provide role models and create stability in impoverished black communities. As a result, those who are left in the community are forced to turn elsewhere for guidance. It should come as no surprise that gang members who still have a presence in these communities are, for better or for worse, filling that void. These men create a "street culture" complete with its own sense of justice and morality, often encompassing the drug trade and other illegal enterprises as means of income, glorifying violence, and devaluing education. With no place left to turn, since many mothers are busy working, adolescent males in particular come to idolize those who provide any sort of structure or authority in their neighborhoods. It is not surprising that these young men also turn to lives of crime and continue the cycle of incarceration and illegal activity that afflicts too many urban blacks.

Perhaps the most detrimental aspect is the victimization thinking that some blacks embrace, erroneously blaming racism for all of their failures. In the words of Bill Cosby, "even with lingering discrimination, there are more doors of opportunity open for black people than ever before in the history of America."[359] Blacks have the opportunities to earn a college and postgraduate degree, pursue entrepreneurship, join the military, and become educators, doctors, or lawyers. Thus, there is a strong argument that blacks can no longer blame white racism for every unsuccessful venture.

Black conservatives, and some moderates too, have asserted for years that black disparities are generally due to the adoption of the victim mentality. Bill Cosby calls it "one of black America's most disabling problems."[360] Prominent blacks such as Barack Obama, Cornel West, and Juan Williams have endorsed Bill Cosby's viewpoint. They too have stressed the correlation between personal responsibility and success. Juan Williams stated that the call for personal responsibilities did not just start with Bill Cosby:

> [His] views mirror those of the civil rights greats of old. Booker T. Washington similarly urged education and self-reliance and cautioned that "we should not permit our grievances to overshadow our opportunities."[361] W. E. B. Du Bois, despite differences with Washington, shared his "goal of black self-reliance."[362] Martin Luther King said he "wanted above all else to get black people to shed the idea that they did not control their destiny."[363]

In his book, *Affirmative Action Debate*, Cornel West and his coauthor George Curry contend that those who promote the victim mentality are supporting a concept that not only endangers and demeans blacks but also allows blacks to claim "exemption from personal responsibility."[364]

Obama emphasized the importance of personal responsibility throughout his 2008 presidential campaign, and particularly in his Father's Day speech of that year. He continuously reassured Americans that all things are possible and that anything can be achieved if one just works hard.[365] He used his own life story to illustrate how various possibilities and opportunities are available to those who work hard,[366] and has stated that it is incumbent on each American to work hard and take personal responsibility for his or her success.[367] A generally accepted principle among many successful blacks is that being black requires that "you work twice as hard to be just as good." All blacks should subscribe to this philosophy. Even the most motivated blacks have encountered situations where they almost had to become indispensable in order to be given an opportunity. This principle recognizes that opportunities are available to blacks even if those opportunities may be significantly harder for blacks to access than whites.

Conclusion

Discrimination persists in all areas of present-day society: tracking programs impede integration in our schools; restricted opportunities in employment and housing maintain black separation; rates of unemployment, homelessness, and incarceration reveal racial inequities; imbalances in the criminal justice system perpetuate black victimization; and unfair economic practices, such as predatory lending, perpetuate economic disparity. These expressions of discrimination demonstrate that the paradigm persists to the present day. As a society, we intentionally sustained the false notions of white superiority and black inferiority, despite advancements in civil rights, despite amended laws, and despite the gradual integration of our communities. Discriminatory practices, though less open, continue to separate and victimize blacks. Many of these practices, such as lower salaries for blacks in comparable positions, reveal that hidden racist attitudes in modern times have the same harmful effects as blatant victimization and exclusion under Jim Crow. As society continues to cling to notions of white superiority and black inferiority, we maintain the racial hierarchy in covert forms. Judicial decisions continue to perpetuate segregation in insidious forms, as we see in the 2007 *Parents Involved* decision. The Baldus study of 1983 demonstrated the prevalence of hidden racial bias in criminal convictions. The paradigm persists and thrives, mainly in reduced opportunities and continued division for blacks in education, employment, criminal justice, housing, and politics.

Martin Luther King Jr. reminded us that all people, black and white, control their own destiny. President Obama's life story is an excellent illustration. The next chapter explores how the election of President Obama can be a key to breaking down notions of white superiority and black inferiority in our society. When we elected Obama, we, as a society, looked beyond racial differences and focused on our needs as a whole. Our unity is evidence that many of us desire to no longer embrace the paradigm of isolation and victimization. Earlier, in chapter 2, we saw that the Military Reconstruction Acts of 1867 helped create forums in which states could review and revise their constitutions, improving civil rights and access to education. We will explore whether, in the Obama era, a similar process could be used to foster discussion and analysis of current laws and state practices. We will begin to look at steps toward breaking down the racial paradigm.

PART III

Ending the Paradigm

Building a Post-Racial America

6

Black Empowerment and Self-Help

"Not everything that is faced can be changed, but nothing can be changed until it is faced."

—James Baldwin, 1963[1]

ERASING THE FALSE image of black inferiority will require increased economic, educational, and political empowerment of blacks, and massive black self-help efforts, particularly in emphasizing the importance of education and limiting the use of racism as an excuse for not trying or for misdirected efforts. This chapter challenges us to break down false notions of racial hierarchy through a new emphasis on massive self-help efforts.

By believing that failure is inevitably the result of racism, some blacks create the false and dangerous notion that their futures are out of their own control. As Debra Dickerson explained, "The last plantation is the mind, and . . . blacks can't see that they have the ultimate power in post–[civil rights movement] America—the power to disregard the nonsense and refuse to be sidetracked from accomplishing what's important. . . ."[2] Indeed, it is this sentiment—that it's time to stop blaming racism—to which Bill Cosby referred when he said, "Now look, I'm telling you. It's not what [whites are] doing to [blacks]. It's what [blacks are] not doing."[3] It is high time that blacks avoid playing the race card in error and accept responsibility for both their successes and their failures. This means change for many blacks who view their own destinies as out of their control, at least to some extent, due to white racism. This does not, however, mean ignoring the actual racial discrimination that continues.

White conservatives like Rush Limbaugh accuse advocates of affirmative action of creating a culture of victimhood, yet those fighting such policies also have a tendency to play the victim. A classic example is the infamous 1990 television advertisement used by Jesse Helms in his North Carolina Senate campaign against Harvey Gantt, a black candidate. The ad shows the hands of a white man as he reads a letter rejecting him for a job purportedly given to a black beneficiary of affirmative action. A voice says, "You needed that job, and you were the best qualified. But they had to give it to a minority because of a racial quota. Is that really fair? Harvey Gantt says it is."[4] Helms won a close race that political experts suggest turned on the ad's effectiveness in convincing some whites, who otherwise would have opposed Helms, to vote against Gantt.[5] The irony of the ad is that it revealed the tendency of whites to transfer responsibility for their own personal failures. All individuals—black or white—have the power to exercise significant control over their destinies in this imperfect world. It is this imperfection, however, that makes it necessary for remedial programs designed to reduce the harm caused by ongoing racism to target only those in need of a remedy.[6]

Avoiding negative racial presumptions by blacks and whites would represent a huge step forward in bridging the racial divide. Charges of bigotry must be avoided when race inequity is absent. And when inequality does exist, it is important to identify its cause.

The tendency for some blacks to overestimate the role of racism is harmful.[7] Political activist Jesse Jackson Sr. has been rightly criticized for his reaction to the highly publicized rape case involving the white Duke University lacrosse players and a black dancer, Chrystal Gail Mangum.[8] After the accusations surfaced, Jackson immediately jumped to the aid of Mangum, eventually accusing the Duke players of wanting to act out a slavemaster fantasy with a woman because of her race.[9] All of the accused men eventually had the charges dropped, and those charges were found to be baseless.

Conservatives such as Professors Shelby Steele and John McWhorter believe that substantial numbers of blacks use racism as an excuse for failure and an entitlement for undeserved benefits.[10] These academics believe that such blacks view themselves as victims of racism when, in reality, they are victims of their own deficiencies. Steele defines "race-holding" as "any self-description that camouflages a person's weaknesses, insecurities, fears or inadequacies."[11] Race-holding, according to Steele, occurs when a black person uses race to keep from looking at himself or herself.[12] He goes on to say that it is the tendency for black people to reject whites before whites can reject them.[13]

In Steele's view, once blacks start "race-holding," it "ensnares [those] blacks in a web of self-defeating attitudes that end up circumventing the new freedoms [blacks] once won over the past several decades."[14] According to Steele, the solution to overcoming failure due to "race-holding" is to take personal initiative by exercising individual responsibility.[15] Steele believes that through lack of accountability "race-holders" wrongly perceive that failure is inevitable and refuse to engage in positive actions to improve opportunities.[16] In his view, the reason some blacks resort to characterizing themselves as victims is to avoid the inevitable necessity of examining their own culpability in their lack of success.[17]

According to Steele, the difference between race-holders and people who complain honestly about conditions is the reality of who or what is to blame.[18] Some blacks deny culpability for their lack of success. Other blacks accept responsibility for their opportunities, or lack thereof, and demand fair treatment even if it is not immediately forthcoming.[19] For Steele, the ability of blacks to achieve success is connected to their overcoming psychological burdens of dependency that prevent them from choosing to exercise personal responsibility, which they alone control.[20]

While Steele sees the cause of current racial inequalities in America as an intentional self-defeating attitude,[21] McWhorter claims that "victimology" is an unconscious characteristic that afflicts many blacks.[22] McWhorter acknowledges that race continues to impact opportunities throughout our society today, but not in the negative way that it did under Jim Crow.[23] McWhorter reasons that "victimology"—the belief that racism continues to significantly harm blacks—is ingrained in blacks through aspects of black culture.[24] McWhorter concludes that these aspects of black culture involve "myths, exaggerations, or distortions about the continued existence of racism, avoidance of personal responsibility, and the fueling of the 'victimization' mentality in blacks."[25] Certainly, evaluating the cause of racial inequality is a valid concern, but focusing solely on deficiencies in blacks seems clearly misguided.

I do not believe that the overwhelming majority of blacks suffer from "victimology" thinking or an unconscious or intentional negative cultural ideology. Just like most whites, most blacks are responsible, hard-working, honest, law-abiding, and fair. In fact, the history and culture of blacks in America is one of overcoming barriers, making individual sacrifices, and exhibiting undeniable patriotism and incredible resiliency. It is a story of which all Americans can be proud. So while personal responsibility may help some blacks improve their circumstances even though they continue to suffer challenges due to racism, ignoring the hardships that racism continues to inflict will only exacerbate the problem.

The following suggestions offer ways to reduce false notions of black inferiority, as well as prevent opportunities for black victimization. As with the proposals in the following chapter, these would significantly reduce one or more aspects of the racial paradigm and could be implemented within the current legal and structural framework of the American constitutional democracy.

Empowerment of blacks educationally, economically, and politically will undermine stereotypical views that blacks are uneducated, impoverished, and politically powerless. Moreover, such empowerment will provide real checks against black victimization through increased diversity in the political, business, and educational arenas, resulting in the passage of new preventive laws and increased consumer purchasing power. Black self-help methods will enable blacks to better offset the harmful effects of ongoing racism.

Educational Empowerment

Education remains indispensable to meaningful movement toward racial equality in the United States. Among the many strategic reasons Charles Hamilton Houston and Thurgood Marshall may have had for choosing to litigate education cases, one obvious practical rationale stands out: education is fundamentally important for racial progress.

In order to allow all individuals to rise to full expression of their abilities, we need to provide the best educational facilities, resources, and options for every child, irrespective of color. According to Richard Kahlenberg, "black and Hispanic students . . . were eight times as likely as white students to be stuck in high poverty elementary schools (those with more than 75% of students from low-income families) and fifteen times as likely to be in high poverty middle and high schools."[26] Most black children, who are not from high-income families, receive inadequate educational services. This must change. We must spend money wisely but fairly. Economic disparity in education will only be corrected when there is equal funding. While equal funding will not automatically result in improved standardized test scores for black students, requiring equal funding will at least enable black students to avoid starting their education at such a severe disadvantage.[27]

Equalizing public school funding will help destroy the racial paradigm in two ways. First, equal funding will inject poorer districts—many of which are predominantly black—with much-needed funds that can be used to improve facilities and services. Years of inequitable funding have created large gaps in the quality of facilities, teachers, and services.[28] It will take time for poor districts to catch up, but an equal funding requirement will prevent the gap from getting larger each year. As funding is equalized and quality improved, black students will be better prepared to improve their academic performance. Over time, improvement in knowledge, capabilities, and test scores should occur.[29] Second, equal funding will decrease black victimization by providing poor black districts with a chance to compete with wealthy white districts. Although adequate funding is only one of several components, including concerned parents and quality teachers, essential for a high-quality school, equal funding is a component outside of the control of parents and teachers. Equal funding would put more of an onus on parents and teachers to deliver a quality education. Evidence of the positive impact from such a change is provided in the many successful magnet school programs throughout the country.[30]

Moreover, I propose a constitutional amendment guaranteeing the right to education.[31] This amendment would ensure that a higher minimum standard of education be maintained by all state governments and that facilities and services be improved to ensure compliance with that higher standard. This proposed constitutional amendment would have both substantive and symbolic benefits in the struggle for racial equality. The substantive benefits include (a) the establishment of a comprehensive and nationally uniform definition of "minimally adequate education"; (b) the ability of underserved populations to assert an enforceable right to parity in access to minimally adequate education; and (c) constitutionally mandated equity in funding across school districts nationwide. The symbolic, consciousness-raising benefits of a constitutional right to education include (a) placing education squarely at the center of national debate; (b) linking the issue of education to that of overall advancement; (c) asserting the centrality of quality public education to the vibrancy of our democracy.

The Supreme Court has repeatedly declined to decide whether a state's failure to provide a minimally adequate education is a denial of a right guaranteed under the federal Constitution. It is theoretically possible that the Supreme Court could recognize "a right to education emanating from (1) the First Amendment; (2) participation in the political process; (3) the concept of liberty; and (4) substantive due process."[32] It is also theoretically possible that progress in education reform will continue in the states, where positive constitutional rights have been adjudicated and, in some cases, well defined. The problem with a state-by-state approach, however, is the inevitable inconsistency. Some jurisdictions will simply refuse to recognize and uphold the kind of guarantee that is necessary to afford every American child at least a minimally adequate education and, ideally, educational opportunities commensurate with the child's competence.

One could be optimistic about the chances of reform at the state level, given recent state court decisions on educational reform. On the other hand, any reform realized through a state court, or state constitutional amendment, is more susceptible to attack than a federal ruling or constitutional amendment. So while malleability of state law makes the states a desirable arena for seeking change, it also makes any gains vulnerable to attack.

It seems, then, that a federal constitutional amendment guaranteeing the right to education would be a more stable and feasible option for progressive educational reform than continued litigation at the federal level or advocacy and activism at the state level.

If framed as a racial remedy, or even as a measure that would primarily benefit blacks, a constitutional amendment guaranteeing the right to education would almost certainly fail. American conservatives have mastered the science of framing public debate to their advantage,[33] and they would undoubtedly find a way to frame the issue as yet another government handout for people who do not pull their weight. Progressives must anticipate and preclude this argument by framing the debate themselves. Why not couch the argument in terms of domestic economic interest and American primacy in technology and culture? To this end, the proposed amendment must contain a guarantee of a basic minimal education that should include a guarantee of the requisite facilities, materials, and teaching staff necessary for delivering that education.

Tying together the basic rights to adequate education and assistance in advanced education, and a federal funding requirement for basic education, could achieve a standardized level of access to educational resources with the support of middle-class whites, who could otherwise be persuaded that their educational options would be diminished by this approach. Moreover, many states would have an interest in such an approach because their education budgets are severely burdened.

Presidents and Congress must maintain a strong commitment to funding public education and must ensure that current funds are not diverted from public education to the detriment of impoverished students. Increased educational opportunities can be transformational. These programs must start early; pre-kindergarten would be ideal. These programs must involve hands-on instruction and one-on-one counseling. Studies show tremendous success in schools located in impoverished black urban areas like Harlem, in New York City, when such techniques are employed.[34] There needs to be a widespread application of these techniques in other urban areas around the nation. These programs must have tangible and guaranteed benefits attached to successful completion by enrollees, such as guaranteed college tuition upon acceptance at a university, or guaranteed employment upon successful completion of a job training program. Only by maximizing human resources can the programs actually help enrollees to secure the knowledge and skills necessary to compete. Only through concrete guarantees of college tuition and jobs will the programs attract those who need the help. While these kinds of programs, which maximize human resources and provide mandatory guarantees, are expensive, they are essential.

Creating a uniform definition of "minimally adequate education," establishing the ability to assert the right to such education, and instituting an equitable federal funding regime would ensure that the quality of a child's education would never fall beneath a certain threshold level, regardless of the economic circumstances of the state, county, or municipality where the child is educated. States, of course, could provide more educational resources than the federal minimum, as long as they did so on an equitable basis. While blacks would certainly not achieve instant parity under such a regime, they would have a valuable, enforceable, constitutional right not only to adequate education but also to assistance in achieving the highest level of education attainable.

Economic Empowerment

The current retrenchment of government employment and massive downsizing in the private sector has decimated blacks in the middle class and further entrenched low-income blacks in poverty.[35] As millions of blacks have become jobless or faced a reduction in wages, the black community has been affected by home foreclosures and a widening wealth gap with whites.[36] This widening racial wealth gap contributes to the growing disparity in wealth distribution between high-income wage earners and poor persons in the country.

Racial hierarchy has always been, in part, about the maldistribution of wealth. Denial of home ownership, credit, employment, and adequate income, combined with overcharging for services provided to whites for less, have all contributed to economic challenges for blacks. A bold and comprehensive plan is needed to improve three financial indicators for blacks: employment, home ownership, and credit.

Despite the home mortgage crisis that surfaced in 2008, home ownership remains one of the primary mechanisms for creating wealth and equity. Jim Crow laws and practices prevented most blacks from owning homes until the mid-1960s.[37] Due to antidiscrimination laws, the rate of black home ownership rose to almost 50% by 2004.[38] White ownership at that time was 76%.[39] It is very difficult to accumulate wealth without credit.[40] Home ownership is an excellent way to establish and gain access to credit. Even after the recent mortgage crisis, increased home ownership remains a laudable societal goal. Home ownership can improve neighborhood quality, strengthen individual financial stability, and aid family cohesion. Congress must understand the racially discriminatory aspects of the wealth gap and focus resources on establishing parity in home ownership.

Since black unemployment is twice that of whites, additional steps are necessary to reduce racial inequity. One such step should be a federally funded jobs program, focused on rebuilding the country's infrastructure (roads, bridges, and urban areas), that is open to those who are unemployed and in the greatest financial need. A needs-based infrastructure jobs program would help reduce racial disparity in employment while providing jobs for many Americans desperately seeking employment and help to spur economic recovery. The 2011 proposal by President Obama, known as the American Jobs Act, contains several components that would reduce racial inequality in employment. First, the act is aimed at revitalizing and rebuilding communities where unemployment has risen most sharply, especially urban areas. (Many such areas have a high percentage of black unemployment). Second, the act is aimed at neighborhoods where the foreclosure rates are highest. This includes many areas with high concentrations of blacks. Third, the act is aimed at decreasing youth unemployment by creating summer and year-round jobs for impoverished teenagers and young adults. Many of these youths are black with little chance of finding employment under current economic circumstances.

The private sector may also contribute to black economic empowerment through improved employment prospects. The largest corporations could implement a hiring plan to give interviews to at least one qualified black candidate for every high-level and mid-level management position that becomes available. This approach, known as the Rooney Rule—first implemented by the National Football League and recently championed by black billionaire Robert Johnson—has resulted in significant improvements in equal hiring.[41] Since the Rooney Rule's implementation, in 2003, the National Football League has increased the number of black head football coaches by seven, and the number of black general managers by four.[42] These are substantial increases, tripling and quadrupling, respectively, the number of high-level black hires in the span of a few years. Large private-sector companies should emulate this practice, which does not mandate hiring any specific person but encourages companies to be more inclusive in their hiring process.

Political Empowerment

Political power has two aspects: (1) negotiating and coalition building between factions, and (2) increasing factional strength. Having a seat at the table of political power is important. Having a voice that is heard can be transformational.

In addition to improvements in education, housing, and economic opportunities, black political empowerment represents another critical aspect in destroying the pillars of discrimination. The Voting Rights Act of 1965 facilitated a significant increase in black voters through antidiscrimination protections against voter suppression.[43] It is one of the most transformative laws ever passed. Another positive development, since 1965, is the increase in majority-minority districts. A majority-minority district is a congressional district where the majority of constituents are racial minorities.[44] At the time of this writing, there were thirty-two majority-black districts and five districts where blacks represent a significant plurality. There are few black members of Congress who represent majority-white districts.[45]

The diversity in the House of Representatives resulting from an increase in black voter registration and majority-black districts is commendable. Yet, these increases are in serious jeopardy. For example, a Georgia state law that requires voters to show government-issued photo identification before they can vote is emblematic of the racially discriminatory impact of supposed "race-neutral laws."[46] Eleven percent of American citizens (roughly five million potential voters) do not possess government-issued photo identification.[47] Black voters are eight times less likely to possess such because significantly higher percentages of blacks use public transportation and therefore have no driver's license, or were born at home instead of in a hospital and therefore have no birth certificate. Most do not travel abroad and therefore have no passport. The alleged justification for the provision is to reduce voter fraud. However, because absentee ballots are exempt, the fraud justification is clearly a facade since most fraud occurs in absentee voting.[48] The racial divide is implicated further when one considers that most black voters in Georgia do not vote absentee.[49] The Georgia law is reminiscent of past Jim Crow voter suppression practices, such as poll taxes and literacy tests— provisions whose supporters camouflaged the real reason for their implementation and that were also characterized as race neutral but clearly had a discriminatory intent (unfortunately not acknowledged by the Supreme Court), as well as discriminatory impact.

In 2009, the United States Department of Justice (DOJ) rejected the Georgia law.[50] A letter released by the DOJ noted that "[t]housands of citizens who [were] in fact eligible to vote under Georgia law [had] been flagged" by the state's voter verification process and denied their right to vote.[51] While the DOJ subsequently approved the Georgia law when the fee requirement was dropped, thirty-one other states, such as South Carolina, Mississippi, Alabama, and Texas—all states with high percentages of black voters—instituted or proposed discriminatory voter identification laws that applied to elections held in November 2012.[52] Even without the fee requirement, voter identification laws constitute more than a minor inconvenience for those many blacks currently without designated identification who are elderly, handicapped, impoverished, or isolated from public transportation routes. If these laws, even without a fee requirement, continue to be implemented in future elections, potentially more blacks will be prevented from voting due to voter identification laws than were prohibited from voting due to literacy requirements and poll taxes during Jim Crow. One way to increase black political empowerment is to end all discriminatory voter identification laws.

A second way to create black political empowerment is to end felony voting prohibitions. Today, all but two states disenfranchise felons in some way.[53] Only Maine and Vermont allow inmates to vote, while fourteen other states restore voting rights after release from prison.[54] Four states

(Kentucky, Virginia, Iowa, and Florida) have a "voting death penalty," denying all convicted felons the right to vote, even after they complete their prison terms, probation, and parole.[55] Several other states distinguish among felonies, denying voting rights to ex-offenders on the basis of the category of felony committed.[56] The Sentencing Project estimates that 5.3 million Americans—3% of the population of the United States, many of whom are black—are currently barred from voting as a result of a felony conviction.[57]

Most states that disenfranchise felons take intermediate approaches in denying the voting rights of probationers and parolees.[58] Arizona, for example, disenfranchises the currently incarcerated, probationers, and parolees, but only after they commit a second felony.[59] Nevada does not disenfranchise first-time nonviolent offenders once they leave prison.[60] In Wyoming, first-time nonviolent offenders can regain voting rights five years after completing their sentence, while repeat offenders and violent offenders are permanently barred.[61]

Many of the state felon disenfranchisement provisions require pardons for individuals to regain the right to vote.[62] The process for restoring voter rights can be quite confusing and onerous, making it even more difficult for ex-felons to regain the right to vote, even when they are legally allowed to do so.[63] Hundreds of thousands of eligible voters are continually being prevented from exercising their right to vote, due in part to the complicated, state-specific nature of felon disenfranchisement laws.[64] Election officials and criminal justice officials often have very little training in these complex laws.[65] One of the simplest solutions is to restore voting rights automatically upon an individual's release from prison.[66] This would reduce bureaucratic complexity and allow many more blacks to exercise the right to vote.

The incarcerated population has increased sixfold in the last thirty years, even as the crime rate has fallen.[67] Furthermore, blacks are disproportionately represented in this incarcerated population. In 2003, black inmates comprised 43% of the prison population, but only 12% of the American population as a whole.[68] At the same time, white inmates comprised only 20% of the prison population, but more than 70% of the American population as a whole.[69] These numbers create a large variance between the number of whites and blacks who are disenfranchised.

Over the last several decades, while legal challenges to felon disenfranchisement have been largely foreclosed due to current judicial acceptance of facially neutral laws, voting rights advocates have been somewhat successful in achieving legislative reforms. These reforms have included removing the "voting death penalty"[70] and extending the right to vote to probationers, parolees, and felons who have completed their sentences.[71] For example, in 2007, Maryland's legislature repealed its lifetime voting ban and implemented an automatic restoration of voting rights upon completion of sentence.[72] Similarly, in 2005, Nebraska removed the lifetime ban on voting rights for all felons and now has a two-year ban after completion of sentence.[73]

Unfortunately, some states have moved backward toward lifetime voting bans. In 2011, Iowa's Governor Branstad rescinded a previous governor's executive order automatically restoring voting rights to felons.[74] Similarly, Florida's Office of Executive Clemency reversed a decision automatically approving reinstatement of rights for nonviolent offenders.[75] All state legislatures should at least ensure that felons can vote when finished with their probation.

A third way to create black political empowerment is through reforming the redistricting process. After every decennial census,[76] each state is responsible for redrawing their state and federal district lines consistent with changes reflected in the census count.[77] First, the federal head counters—in a related process called reapportionment—figure out how many congressional seats each state will have according to population gains and losses over the past decade. Thus, states with a shrinking population may lose seats, while those gaining new residents could increase their representation in the House of Representatives. For example, Florida's population grew from 15.9 million in 2000 to 18.8 million in 2010, resulting in a two-seat increase to its congressional delegation; it had twenty-seven for the 2012 elections.[78]

Most states then rely on state legislatures to redraw the lines.[79] In order to reduce the politicization of the redistricting process, a number of states have shifted responsibility for revising district lines from the legislature to a board or commission.[80] The use of state legislatures to create and execute redistricting maps exacerbates racial redistricting concerns.[81] Many state legislatures committed acts of race discrimination in voting[82] during the first half of the 20th century. They also resisted federal efforts to protect voting rights for blacks and continue to do so today.[83] Leaving the redistricting process in the hands of state legislatures increases the likelihood that racial redistricting problems will continue.[84] Although most states still use state legislatures to draw the lines, that is the most dangerous and least controlled option.[85] Even states that use commissions or boards to redraw the district lines seldom give the final decision to these entities.[86] Currently, only twelve states give initial and final authority for redistricting to an entity other than the legislature.[87]

There is a difference between an independent commission and a legislative board.[88] Independent commissions are made up of nonpartisan individuals who draw the lines subject to approval by the state legislature.[89] Iowa is the only state that follows this method.[90] Before the legislative vote, maps are drawn for the Iowa House and Senate, as well as United States House of Representatives districts, without the independent commission ascertaining any political or election data, including the addresses of incumbents.[91] Using this method reduces the likelihood that race will be used in the redrawing of district lines.[92] Nonpartisan map drawers are used so that race hierarchy and isolation need not be reinforced through the deliberative process.[93] Although Iowa may have a small black population, this method can work in more diverse states throughout the country.[94] As long as the map drawers have no significant and overriding political interests, developing a district map that does not reinforce the paradigm can occur anywhere.[95] The best way to assure that this occurs in the redistricting process is through the use of independent commissions.[96]

I propose that all states, especially those states with a significant number of black voters (15% of the state population or more), reform the redistricting process by creating independent commissions. The composition of the independent commissions should be balanced on the basis of political affiliation, including those who have independent party, minor party, or no party affiliations. Nevertheless, irrespective of what kind of entity is selected to determine redistricting, it is critical that it be guided by a diversity-in-representation mandate that will draw districts to maximize diversity in the selection of a state's elected officials.

There are two primary issues for concern: (1) too few majority-minority districts, where blacks make up a majority of the eligible voters in the district, may be created; and (2) black voters may need to spread out in order to benefit individual candidates or particular political parties. Actions by an independent commission would reduce the likelihood of racially biased judgments. Independent commissions, with a creation of diversity-in-representation mandate, are more likely than legislative bodies to make decisions in a racially equitable manner. The role of legislators is not to be objective but to reflect the will of their constituents. Nonelected members on independent commissions would have a more objective role to provide the equality mandate contained in the Constitution.

It is critically important to have a mandate to destroy the paradigm. Part of that mandate would include directions to commission members to include encouragement of racial diversity in political representation as a significant factor in the drawing of political boundaries. This diversity mandate could only be implemented successfully through independent commissioners who are not legislators, since elected representatives by designation vote their own interests and not those of society.

As a result of race prejudice manifested in the political machinations discussed in previous chapters, blacks as a group were shut out of representation in the two national legislative chambers, the House of Representatives and the Senate. Consequently, approximately 12% of the population was underrepresented.[97] With the developments in voter protection over the last fifty years, this lack of representation has changed in the House of Representatives. More than forty blacks serve in Congress, most of them from majority-black districts.[98] Because of the way the House of Representatives' districts are formed, about 10% of them are majority-black.[99] While there are more than forty black members in Congress, black presence in the Senate has been severely lacking.[100]

The Senate has no majority-black "districts"; all senators are elected statewide. Mississippi has the largest percentage of black population at 38%.[101] No state is majority-black. As a result, few blacks have ever been elected to serve in the Senate, and none is currently serving. Thus, the number of blacks in the Senate today is the same as it was during Jim Crow.

In order to fulfill both aspects of empowerment, black elected officials must come from and represent majority-black districts, as well as majority-white districts. This will permit the black electorate to exercise both aspects of empowerment in the Senate, as it has done in the House of Representatives over the last five decades.

A fourth way to increase black political power would be to create a predominantly black state. This could be accomplished quite efficiently by granting statehood to Washington, DC.[102] Establishing statehood for the District of Columbia would give the citizens of Washington, DC, full representation in the United States Congress, including two members in the Senate. Statehood could be achieved by an act of Congress exercising the powers granted in the Constitution.[103] For the first time, black voters would have an opportunity to vote for senatorial or gubernatorial candidates in a state where blacks comprise the majority of voters. While from a legal standpoint, nothing prevents a majority-black state except demographics, the current reality is that no existing state boundary is close to creating a majority-black electorate. Granting statehood to Washington, DC, would help to empower blacks politically.

Voting rights of United States citizens who reside in the District of Columbia differ from those of citizens living in the fifty states. District of Columbia residents do not have voting representation in the United States Senate, but DC is entitled to three electoral votes for president.[104] In the U.S. House of Representatives, the District is permitted one elected representative, who cannot vote on legislation.[105]

The Constitution authorizes congressional voting representation to the states, but not the District, because it is a federal territory and not a state. Congress holds political power over the District.[106] The absence of voting representation in Congress for residents of the District has been debated for decades. Several recommendations have been made in recent years, including congressional legislation and constitutional amendments to grant DC residents voting representation, to return the District to the state of Maryland, or to make the District of Columbia into a new state.[107] All recommendations have received strong resistance. Consequently, no voting representation for the District currently exists in Congress.[108]

The DC Statehood movement has often downplayed the most important benefit of statehood. While certainly there are many benefits from autonomy and local control, the most important for achieving equality and diversity is that the District of Columbia would probably elect two black senators. What is critical to undermining notions of racial hierarchy is black political empowerment. That will only happen with senatorial representation for a majority-black electorate. That majority-black electorate could choose to elect senators who are not black, but that would be their choice, a choice that truly reflects political empowerment.

Thus, senatorial representation for majority-black districts is crucial. Since the District of Columbia is a majority-black district, senatorial representation there would involve less disruption of the current electoral map and structural allocation of government power. Nevertheless, the creation of majority-black electoral districts for senatorial representation is vital. That is the only way the black electorate's voice can be heard through negotiation of important positions and through the building of coalitions with other powerful factions to influence policy. Most significantly, by enabling blacks to have a presence in the Senate, the black electorate's voice would be heard through a factional voice of political strength.

Allowing the black electorate to remain voiceless in one of the highest legislative bodies in the country helps reaffirm notions of black inferiority in the political arena. The crux of the issue is not the absence of blacks in the Senate, although diversity would help to undermine black isolation; the most harmful aspect of this lack of representation is the black electorate's inability to influence it. Political power means, at a minimum, the ability to voice one's opinion even if others disagree. Unfortunately, the black electorate has no voice at all in the Senate today.

Self-Help

Black victimization occurs in four ways: racially neutral laws that disproportionately harm blacks; intentional acts specifically designed to harm blacks; unconscious acts that harm blacks; and wounds self-inflicted through the adoption of unproductive choices and values by blacks themselves. Each contributes to current racial inequality. Improving personal responsibility can help end self-inflicted black harm by (1) reducing black-on-black crime; (2) increasing the value placed on education; and (3) avoiding victimization thinking.

Blacks in America have endured racism since before the nation's founding. While racism has always been a problem, it should never be an excuse. Black victimization can occur not only from whites but also from blacks. For example, while blacks comprise 12% of the nation's population, 47% of all murder victims in 2005 were black, and 94% of their killers were black.[109] Criminologists at Boston's Northeastern University released the results of a study, on December 29, 2008, showing that the number of murders among young black males had dramatically increased since 2000, despite the fact that the total number of murders among all Americans had decreased during that time period.[110] Victimization of blacks by other violent crimes, not resulting in death—including rape/sexual assault, robbery, aggravated assault, and simple assault—totaled 24.3% in 2007, with the highest percentages of victimization (over 38%) within the age range of fifteen to twenty-four.[111] Despite warnings of the consequences of black-on-black crime more than twenty years ago, many blacks have not heeded the warn-ings and have subsequently destroyed their lives and those of countless others in the process.

Violent black offenders typically find a reduced likelihood of convic-tion and punishment for offenses against other blacks.[112] This disparity em-braces the racial hierarchy of the paradigm and is deeply rooted in our his-tory. Slaves who committed crimes against other slaves were not punished as harshly as slaves who committed crimes against whites.[113] Today, many violent black offenders seem to have recognized this disparity. While crime is deplorable whether it is interracial or intraracial, we should not allow racial disparities to encourage one or the other.[114]

The focus on education, emphasized earlier, is one of the most effec-tive ways to reduce black-on-black crime and promote opportunity. Blacks must make education an important priority. Family resources must be allo-cated to provide money for college, tutors, exam preparation courses, and housing in neighborhoods with good schools. Even if a family is impov-erished, without the money for these services, time management is criti-cal. Time must be managed so that children focus on homework, under supervision when necessary. Extracurricular activities, such as sports, must be more closely tied to academic performance. By emphasizing academ-ics, blacks will demonstrate that they value academic excellence even more highly than success in sports. Blacks, as well as whites, need to see an as-sociation between blacks and academic excellence.

Far too many black youths devalue education, which seriously under-mines their options for success. This must change by parents altering the way they allocate both money and time. Certainly, this will necessitate sacrifice for some families. Nevertheless, more equity in allocation of soci-etal resources toward education demands a corresponding change in black families making wiser choices. Blacks must be willing and able to take ad-vantage of the increased educational programming that will result from more equitable funding in public schools.

Resistance to assimilation manifests itself in ways that can make suc-cess more difficult. Assimilation is not necessary for success, but knowl-edge is. Failure to master traditional English language rules contributes to poor performance on standardized tests. Although some blacks may choose to speak in dialects informally, they must learn correct word usage and syntax. Black students must reject the notion that success in school, particularly enrollment in advanced placement or honors classes, equates to "acting white." In this respect, critics of black irresponsibility are correct.

Success in school must not be synonymous with a single racial group. To accept the notion that educational achievement is a characteristic of whites and not blacks further embraces the premise of white superiority.

Slave states prohibited blacks from learning to read and write because education is empowering.[115] Slave owners knew that once enslaved persons learned to read and write, they had taken a big step toward breaking the chains of bondage. Similarly, most Jim Crow schools were not permitted to offer advanced math, science, or language courses, because those classes led to college.[116] Black children must be made to understand that post–Jim Crow America can be a land of opportunity, and that one of the best vehicles for upward mobility is a quality education.

Many authors over the last two decades have identified the causes of disparities between blacks and whites.[117] Causes examined included racism, deficiencies in the legal system, personal irresponsibility, and negative cultural influences.[118] Recently, one study changed the focus from why blacks fail to why they succeed. One of the primary reasons for such success was the influence of family, friends, peers, and adult role models.[119]

One of the ways blacks can empower themselves is to create support programs so that every black child in a school designated as impoverished has a support network of educational role models, both older peers and adults, to provide guidance, encouragement, and reinforcement. A national mentoring program, privately funded, that would help every child in need gain entry to college or a career by providing that child with the necessary support for success would be helpful.

Improving personal responsibility on the part of impoverished blacks will have a significant impact on the racial paradigm in two ways. First, it will enable substantial numbers to attend college and/or secure jobs with decent salaries to get out of poverty. As a result, the widespread socioeconomic inequalities between blacks and whites will be reduced. Reduction of these inequities will allow more blacks to avoid the housing isolation of certain urban areas, affording more options based upon newly attained economic security. Second, these new options will foster increased integration, not only in housing but also in schools and social activities. Such increased interaction will serve to undermine racial hierarchy notions which, in turn, will lessen recalcitrance and resistance to increased integration.

Poverty is not an excuse for personal irresponsibility, yet the burden of overcoming poverty and racism simultaneously increases the difficulty of the task. This increased difficulty must be offset by government programs in education, as well as the creation of employment opportunities that can be accessed through increased personal responsibility.

Those who argue for the "bootstraps" theory that racial inequity will be eliminated by blacks pulling themselves up by their bootstraps are missing a large part of the problem. Racial disparities will not go away, even if blacks commit fewer crimes or focus more on educational attainment, if we do not also prevent harms from ongoing racism. Black self-help is necessary, but it alone is insufficient as a solution to the problem of racial inequity. This is especially true for impoverished blacks without the means to offset the detrimental effects of racism that continue.

Racism imposes additional burdens on blacks from all economic classes, however. These burdens inflict harms, regardless of the level of personal responsibility exercised by blacks. It will take a concerted effort, for all parts of society, to destroy the paradigm of race once and for all.

Conclusion

Jim Crow was a false image. In minstrel shows across America throughout the 19th century, the mockery was acted out with song and dance. The insidious effect of those mocking images of black inferiority became deeply engrained in our psyche as a nation. Now, well into the 21st century, we are challenged to displace those negatives with positive truths. Empowerment in areas of education, economics, and politics will enhance our perceptions, thoughts, and behavior. We must break the images of the past. We must shift from the centuries-old racial paradigm to a new framework of thinking, in which all Americans are equal.

We must take bold steps toward equity in housing, employment, and political representation, in order to break down all aspects of the racial divide.

The challenges we face may seem insurmountable. Yet, empowerment of all Americans is essential to eradicate the ghosts of Jim Crow. Only then can America fulfill the constitutional promise and achieve its full potential.

7

Integration and Equality

[W]e remain imprisoned by the past as long as we deny its influence in the present.

—Justice William Brennan, 1987[1]

FOR BLACKS TODAY, opportunities are much better than they were under Jim Crow. The opportunities to attend college and professional schools have significantly increased. During Jim Crow, no opportunities existed in major colleges and universities in the South. Only a token number of spots opened annually at schools in the North, causing most to rely on a small number of historically black colleges and universities. Today, almost all schools of higher education actively recruit blacks for admission, and most have significant percentages of black enrollees.

Employment opportunities, both in the public and private sectors, have also greatly expanded from the days when black applicants, for the most part, were limited to menial positions, if they were given any positions at all. Today, blacks are employed in significant numbers at all of the major corporations in the United States and throughout federal and state governments in all employment capacities—from executives to clerks and from managers to maintenance workers. We have made dramatic steps toward equality. Blacks also serve as police officers and are welcome in labor unions, which rarely occurred during Jim Crow.

Protection of black voting rights has been enhanced, and political opportunities through elective office have greatly increased. While in the early 1960s there were only a few hundred black elected officials throughout the country, there are more than ten thousand today,[2] including the highest elected official.

Access to public accommodations for blacks is accepted throughout the country. Many exclusive private clubs now have black members who would have been refused just a few years ago.

Compared to the grandparents of the current generation, who faced many racial barriers, blacks today have very different attitudes about race. As Ellis Cose notes in his book, *The End of Anger*, blacks under the age of forty were never exposed to the Jim Crow racism of the pre-1960s or to the civil rights movement that helped end it.[3] Some of these blacks do not view America exclusively in racial terms, as did prior generations.[4] They have become more receptive to interracial relationships, more positive about the potential for reducing racial divisions, and more optimistic that racism will be eradicated in the future.[5]

But while some Americans feel more positive about race relations today, too few have grown up in such an atmosphere. Even with all of these advances, not all racial barriers have been destroyed. Ghosts of Jim Crow continue to divide and diminish. Racial isolation, particularly in schools and neighborhoods, is a blatant reminder that racial hierarchy notions persist.

The wealth gap between whites and blacks has reached a twenty-to-one ratio, its widest level in a quarter-century.[6] Ghosts of Jim Crow walk among us in nearly every aspect of American life. Society is permeated with not only the remnants of discrimination but the active perpetuation of those practices, often in subtle expressions, making it difficult to measure. However, concrete evidence illustrates its existence, perpetuated by whites and blacks alike. America can ill afford such domestic infighting in today's competitive global market. The time to begin taking steps toward that post-racial America is now.

The following suggestions offer ways to reduce racial separation and hierarchy. These proposals are broad in coverage, targeted in scope, feasible in implementation, and practical in nature. The proposals satisfy two criteria: (1) each would significantly reduce one or more aspects of the racial paradigm: black separation and victimization and white isolation and racial hierarchy, as well as false notions of black inferiority and erroneous assumptions of white superiority; and (2) each could be implemented within the current legal and structural framework of the American constitutional democracy. The solutions include changes that emanate from individual growth, governmental policy, and judicial decision making.

All change begins with dialogue and understanding. Accordingly, this chapter begins by exploring ways for blacks and whites to increase interaction, particularly in housing and education. Next, we consider the criminalization of race-based discrimination in its pervasive, insidious forms.

Further, the chapter encourages Americans to redefine discrimination and reaffirm affirmative action efforts in order to reduce racial isolation. It then challenges the nation to confront the notion of white superiority through racial reconciliation efforts.

Solving the problem of white superiority will entail a combination of intensified legal prohibitions against private racial discrimination, including the criminalization of some discriminatory acts, and drastic alterations of notions of white privilege and entitlement. Erasing the image of black inferiority will require substantial reforms in the criminal justice system and school tracking.

Race-conscious policies benefiting blacks have received increasing opposition in Congress and many state legislatures. While still constitutional, such policies have been severely restricted by recent Supreme Court decisions. Yet, given the persistence of racial isolation and inequality, more must be done. Not only will each proposal bring blacks closer to integration and equality; each will benefit society as a whole as well.

Foster Racial Integration in Schools and Neighborhoods

Racial integration is a powerful tool for shattering the paradigm. Integration in housing reduces black separation, which, in turn, impedes the external victimization of blacks. Integration in schools significantly impacts racial hierarchy notions for both blacks and whites.[7]

Integration in Schools

Racially integrated schools yield a myriad of benefits, including increases in academic achievement, cultural competency, appreciation of diversity, and access to opportunity, for both whites and blacks.[8] Integrated school settings prepare students to navigate an increasingly diverse and intertwined world and can also reduce racial biases.[9] Those skills are becoming increasingly important in an interconnected world and in a country that will significantly increase in racial diversity in the coming decades.[10]

One of the best ways to reduce both explicit and implicit racial bias is to let young children interact with children from different backgrounds.[11] Racial integration in the early years has a profound, positive impact on perceptions of people of different races in adulthood.[12]

By dispelling racial stereotypes, integration may also help whites better understand the challenges that blacks face in America. This could lead to whites taking a more active role in advocating for social change.[13] For example, there is a positive correlation between the willingness of white adults to live in diverse communities and the years of integrated schooling those whites have had.[14] Furthermore, whites who experienced early integration are less likely to harbor negative racial stereotypes.[15] Integration may also increase whites' enjoyment of the racially diverse metropolitan areas in which they live.

Any federally funded government program attempting to improve quality of education, such as the Obama administration's Race to the Top[16] program, can encourage racial integration in schools in several ways. The program should include effective racial integration as a factor to be considered as states compete for funding.[17] Federal funding should be provided to states making significant advances in integrating public schools.

Additionally, Race to the Top should include more funding for magnet school programs.[18] Magnet schools are public schools that provide a specialized, enhanced academic environment, seek to attract and enroll students from multiple school districts who have different social, economic, ethnic, and racial backgrounds, and have a track record of high academic achievement in racially diverse settings.[19] Charter schools are public schools that receive government funding and operate under government guidelines pursuant to the school's charter. These guidelines provide charter schools with greater flexibility than other public schools in choosing textbooks, selecting teachers, adopting programs, and deviating from curriculum requirements. Although magnet schools still educate more children in the United States than charter schools, they continue to receive less federal funding.[20] Support for magnet schools from the federal government has remained stagnant over the past few decades.[21] Given the potential for magnet schools to increase integration and provide strong academic outcomes, the federal government should renew efforts to provide resources for magnet schools.[22] Nevertheless, whether a charter or magnet school is being considered, diversity should be a key factor in determining federal financial support for such schools.

Integration in Housing

School integration is closely tied to neighborhood integration, especially since attendance at many public schools is determined by residency.[23]

Better government enforcement against housing discrimination is needed. To reduce black separation in housing, there are five possible remedies. First, the capacity of federal and private agencies to effectively address housing discrimination must be increased. The Federal Fair Housing Act (FHA) of 1968 was greatly strengthened by changes in the Fair Housing Amendments Act of 1988.[24] These amendments gave the Department of Housing and Urban Development (HUD) and the Department of Justice (DOJ) additional power to enforce the law.[25] The National Fair Housing Alliance notes that the "Fair Housing Act . . . [is] one of the most powerful tools in our civil rights arsenal. But [it] is only effective when wielded with skill and intent. . . ."[26] Additional funding is needed to provide sufficient staffing and training to increase the agency's ability to screen, identify, and address discriminatory acts.

Private fair housing organizations in the United States assist these federal agencies with education and enforcement activities.[27] Better enforcement against housing discrimination is also needed. Congress and states should enact provisions to allow standing for fair housing organizations by reducing standards of proof of injury. While the courts have taken the initial step to grant standing, judges have generally required a high standard of proof of injury resulting from discriminatory housing practices. This approach must be reversed. Courts should accept a lower standard of discrimination in housing practices, including sales and leases of property.

Second, the Supreme Court should require all communities to provide their "fair share" of low-income housing. Currently, many communities avoid providing such housing as a result, in part, of false racial beliefs that such housing will be provided mostly to blacks. Third, a density bonus allowing builders to include more units in a project than the zoning for the area would otherwise permit, if they construct a certain number of low-income dwellings, could address this issue.[28] The popularity of density bonuses stems from their ability to create low-income housing without requiring additional expenditures by a municipality.[29] However, officials must avoid providing low-income housing exclusively in overcrowded areas. That only perpetuates the problem of low-quality housing conditions for blacks, reinforcing false notions of black inferiority, as well as increasing black separation.

Fourth, unfair and predatory lending practices must be identified and stopped. Some blacks are at increased risk of losing their homes, and most of their wealth, as a result of discriminatory and negligent lending practices. Several states and Congress have passed new progressive anti-predatory-lending legislation.[30] In 1999, North Carolina was the leader in this legislative effort, passing a number of provisions that have reduced the foreclosure rate in the state. In 2010, Congress followed North Carolina's direction by passing several provisions designed to protect consumers against risky loans. These provisions prohibit loan refinancing without creating a net tangible benefit to the borrower (also known as flipping) and expand the definition of and the protections for high-cost loans.[31]

For more comprehensive and consistent application of these protections, however, additional federal law is essential. Congress should strengthen federal comprehensive predatory lending legislation that requires initial disclosure of costs and fees and prohibits prepayment penalties.[32] These protections will help, but it is critical that any new legislation maintain credit availability for qualified black borrowers.

Fifth, public housing should facilitate racial integration. Government-provided housing exists in every state.[33] Federal, state, and local governments spend over $25 billion annually subsidizing or supplying housing.[34] Most of the government-provided housing maintains the racial status quo.[35] Housing developments located in black areas have primarily been filled with black occupants, and housing developments located in white areas have primarily been filled with white occupants.[36]

Integration can be accomplished through new fair housing laws that encourage it. Preference should be given to qualified applicants who increase the racial diversity of the area. That is, preferences should be given to white applicants in predominantly black areas and to black applicants in predominantly white areas. Moreover, government-backed mortgage regulations should provide an incentive for mortgages that contribute to the racial integration of the neighborhood. Economic incentives, such as lower interest rates, should be offered for new homeowners who benefit the neighborhood by enhancing racial diversity.

For true integration to be achieved in housing, blacks and whites must embrace diversity as adding value, and support housing policies and practices that encourage and foster integrated options, like "live where you work" programs.[37] The government should create economically diverse living options near large employers located in or near urban areas. Black separation in housing can be reduced if white employees who live in isolated white suburbs are encouraged to move to urban employment locations.

Housing laws should require publicly financed housing projects to be strategically located to facilitate racial integration. Location of new housing projects should be prioritized in antidiscrimination laws for highly segregated areas first, in order to maximize integration impact. Moreover, these laws should be vigorously enforced. Integrated housing is essential to reducing the racial divide, because so many of life's activities, especially education, revolve around communities. If Americans are racially divided in housing, they are likely to be divided in other activities such as schools and employment.

Criminalize Private Race-Based Acts of Discrimination

In order to reduce false notions of white superiority, there must be a change in the way discrimination is identified and legally defined. A new definition of constitutionally prohibited discrimination must include private acts. In the 1883 *Civil Rights Cases*,[38] where the majority reasoned that the Fourteenth Amendment empowered Congress to outlaw only government discrimination and not private acts, the Supreme Court invalidated an antidiscrimination law prohibiting race discrimination by hotels, theaters, restaurants, and other public accommodations. Like government-imposed discrimination, race discrimination by private entities and individuals contributes to racial hierarchy and black separation and victimization.

The Supreme Court's erroneous interpretation of the Constitution as not prohibiting private discrimination must be remedied. The law prohibits government-mandated racial discrimination and private discrimination that is attributable to the state. Unfortunately, the Court's current approach defines most private activity as beyond attribution. Only government subsidization of private racial discrimination is attributable to the state. Subsidization requires substantial state involvement such as ownership of the property where discriminatory treatment is occurring. To truly address the ill effects of a country divided on racial lines, the federal government must be permitted to make laws that address private discrimination condoned by some communities.

Certain types of racial discrimination should be made criminal offenses. Currently, racial discrimination is a civil offense, and violators of antidiscrimination laws are subject to fines. Criminalization would subject violators to both fines and imprisonment, or some other limitation on liberty. This would both discourage discrimination and also send the message that those who engage in such practices pose as much a threat to society as other criminals.

Several states and the federal government have established laws to punish perpetrators for hate crimes—crimes that have been committed with racial, religious, gender, or sexual orientation animus. Such laws stop short of criminal punishment for race discrimination alone, however, on the ground that intentional discrimination is difficult to prove. The language that triggers the penalty enhancement under hate crime statutes is either literally or functionally the same as language that triggers liability under hundreds of civil rights and antidiscrimination laws. These laws also impose liability when an actor takes some action "because of" the race, religion, or other specified status of the affected person. Whether a criminal act is a hate crime depends on the perpetrator's intent. If the act was motivated by a racial intent, additional punishment may be appropriate. The racial animus itself is not a crime, but it can be the basis for enhancing the punishment for the resulting criminal act.

I suggest going even further. As Derrick Bell first suggested, in his book *Faces at the Bottom of the Well*, why not make race discrimination a criminal offense itself? I recognize the difficulty in establishing the requisite intent for a crime due to the high evidentiary standards of "beyond a reasonable doubt" necessary for a criminal conviction. Nevertheless, race discrimination harms not only the individual victim but society as a whole.

What makes something a crime is that it is harmful to the state. A crime is a wrong that is viewed by society as wrong. It should not matter that the harm was emotional, rather than physical. Emotional harm can be just as devastating to a person's ability to contribute to society as physical harm. The law recognizes this by characterizing intentional or negligent infliction of emotional distress as an offense, albeit a civil one.

States are authorized, under their police powers, to prohibit any conduct they choose providing that conduct is not constitutionally protected. While Americans have a constitutional right to freedom of speech, they should not have a constitutional right to discriminate on the basis of race.

In its 2003 *Grutter* decision, the Supreme Court indicated that the creation of racial diversity in higher education was a compelling societal interest.[39] The reasoning articulated the value of such diversity. States should use their police power to prohibit racially discriminatory acts, thereby fostering beneficial integration.

There are already a number of laws that provide supposed protections from race discrimination. An equal right to housing is guaranteed by two major pieces of legislation: the FHA of 1968 and the ECOA of 1974. The Civil Rights Act of 1964 (Title VII) prohibits employment discrimination based on race, color, religion, sex, or national origin. Unfortunately, these federal laws only have civil penalties. It is clear that civil penalties are an inadequate deterrent. The Equal Employment Opportunity Commission (EEOC) fielded 82,792 employment discrimination complaints in 2007.[40] In 2009 it fielded 99,922.[41] If the civil penalty structure served as an effective deterrent, a downward trend would be expected.

The Supreme Court has upheld Congress's authority, under the Commerce Clause, to enact federal antidiscrimination legislation in federally funded programs in housing, lending, and employment. Any effort by Congress to enact a federal criminal penalty for racial discrimination should coincide with existing civil statutes that have withstood constitutional challenges. Amending the FHA of 1968, the ECOA of 1974, and Title VII to include criminal penalties for violations would be an effective approach.

Imposing criminal penalties for certain types of racial discrimination will pose challenges. First, a decision would need to be made regarding what substantive violations should have criminal penalties. Second, it would need to be determined who should be held responsible for violations in the corporate setting. Race discrimination in hiring, promotions, demotions, and firing should have criminal penalties. The normal rules for criminal and civil wrongdoing in the corporate setting are appropriate. Those who have committed the wrong, and those who could have and should have prevented the wrong, would be subject to criminal action. The more widespread and systematic a violation, the higher up the management chain the prosecutors should be able to go. This will ensure that those responsible for the discriminatory behavior will be severely punished, even if they are senior-management-level employees.

Will a criminal penalty work to deter isolated incidents of discriminatory behavior? In isolated incidents of discrimination, the EEOC and other agencies enforcing federal antidiscrimination regulations currently encourage mediation or some other form of alternative dispute resolution, allowing satisfactory results for both the victim and the employer. However, imposing a criminal penalty takes the process out of the victim's hands and puts it in the hands of federal prosecutors. While such an approach may reduce the number of settlements between victims and employers, the criminal sanction should serve as a deterrent against prohibited conduct resulting in harmful treatment. Adequate protection against abuse of employers and supervisors would be maintained because the burden of proof for proving discrimination in court would be "beyond a reasonable doubt," substantially higher than the standard in a civil case.

The degree of penalty also poses a challenge. Should a manager who discriminates at the behest of his superiors be subject to the same penalty as his superiors? And, if so, what should the penalty be? The civil penalties allow for a company to mediate a settlement with the victim of discrimination and handle the perpetrator as it sees fit—perhaps through firing, suspension, or workplace training. Criminal penalties may be a viable option. Congress should mandate that, depending on the severity and breadth of the violations, a first-time violator need not be subject to imprisonment but rather required to pay a fine or perform community service. Mediation or arbitration for first-time offenders would be appropriate. Private settlement could also work for a first-time offender but not for a second-time or subsequent offender. Just as other crimes allow for escalating penalties as the number of violations increase, so too should a criminal violation of federal antidiscrimination statutes. Prosecutors should be free to adjust the penalties depending on the egregiousness of the offense. Such an approach would demonstrate the appropriate government commitment to the compelling societal interest of promoting racial diversity in realms beyond higher education.

Rethinking the Value of Racial Neutrality

End Racial Profiling

Race-based thinking is usually dangerous. Racial profiling is a perfect example. Two types of law enforcement practices involve selecting a suspect on the basis of race: racial profiling and description reliance. Racial profiling—race-dependent assessments of suspicion—involves making decisions on the basis of a stereotype of the criminal propensities of blacks, thus resulting in discriminatory treatment of blacks.[42] Suspect description reliance accepts a description of a criminal suspect when the witness has seen the suspect and knows the suspect's race.[43] Suspect description reliance is rational and should be permissible. Racial profiling should be prohibited. It invokes the notion of white superiority because of its inherent implication that apparent whiteness implies innocence of criminal conduct.[44]

While racial profiling may seem reasonable where the potential for societal harm is great—such as when law enforcement profiles terrorists for national security reasons or drug traffickers for crime prevention reasons—it is nevertheless racially discriminatory and should be prohibited under the Equal Protection Clause of the Fourteenth Amendment. Behavior-dependent assessments of suspicion, rather than race-dependent assessments, should be standard practice for law enforcement personnel. Racial profiling, whether done consciously or unconsciously, merely reinforces false notions of black inferiority.

Racial profiling is emotionally harmful. The experience of being stopped because of one's skin color is not only inconvenient; it is also frightening.[45] Innocent individuals subjected to such police abuse feel as though they have to change their daily activities, the cars they drive, the clothes they wear, and/or the places they frequent.[46] The impact of racial profiling is widespread. Not only has the practice led to increased distrust and animosity by blacks toward law enforcement, as well as increased tensions between the police and blacks; it has also impeded the effectiveness of community policing. A focus on behavior rather than racial characteristics is the key. If innocent individuals are treated like criminals, they will lose trust in officers as investigators of crime or as witnesses in court.[47] Victims of racial profiling are less likely to confide in officers and inform them of criminal activity,[48] allowing guilty people to go free because of lack of cooperation.

End Laws with a Severe Disproportionate Impact

Today, most racism is not as overt as racial profiling is; it is covert and takes many insidious forms. The majority of whites are opposed to overt discrimination, but many support programs and policies that severely burden blacks to the same degree as would overtly discriminatory practices. Justice William Brennan, in the 1987 *McCleskey* case, referred to this reluctance by whites to prevent less overt discriminatory practices as emanating from "a fear of too much justice." This fear jeopardizes racial equality in the United States.

Unintentional government-imposed discrimination contributes to racial hierarchy and black separation and victimization just as intentional discrimination does. Yet, the current Supreme Court interpretation fails to recognize this reality. This reluctance ensures that today's racism remains a steadfast aspect of American life. The Supreme Court should reject the current formalistic approach to preventing race discrimination and articulate a new standard of equality that strives to eliminate racial disparity.

Not all intentional race-based action is bad, and not all "race-neutral" action is good. The Supreme Court must reject the notion that race-neutral laws and actions cannot be as harmful as laws or actions that are overtly discriminatory. Race-neutral laws with significant disparate impact can be just as damaging to equal rights for blacks as laws that expressly discriminate against blacks, if not more damaging. Such race-neutral laws may, for example, unintentionally foment ideas of racial inequality. Recent examples include the qualification test for firefighters, where no proof has been provided that the test actually evaluates ability to do the job, and where no black test takers qualify;[49] or the funding of public primary and secondary schools through property taxes, with most blacks residing in low property tax districts; or capital sentencing, with the death penalty being imposed primarily on black defendants but not white defendants if the victim is white. The end result is the same—unequal treatment that reinforces notions of white superiority.[50]

Laws implicate race in three ways: origin, application, and effect. *Origin* refers to express terms that legally classify blacks for different treatment, such as traditional Jim Crow laws that said "whites only" or "no dogs, no blacks, no Jews, no Mexicans."[51] *Application* means that a neutral law is being administered with different degrees of severity for blacks, such as can occur with discretionary traffic stops when only blacks are stopped. *Effect* refers to the impact of the law, as when a neutral law imposes different burdens on blacks than on whites. Laws that discriminate by race in origin or administration are currently prohibited by equality provisions. Laws with only a racially discriminatory impact, however, are usually permitted, even though the resulting harm may be the same as an openly racist law.

The crack/powder cocaine sentencing disparity has been repeated in thousands of cases since the Federal Sentencing Guidelines were introduced in 1987. The disparate impact these guidelines have on black and white defendants has been well documented. The disparity in sentencing persons convicted of crack cocaine possession, predominantly blacks, and persons convicted of powder cocaine possession, predominantly whites, reflects a serious problem of inequality. Treating individuals differently when they are in fact situated the same will almost always result in continued inequity. Given the widespread knowledge of their disparate racial impact, each successive application of those guidelines reflects knowledge of harm. For the government to knowingly act with a severe racially disparate impact strongly suggests that the government is willing to disregard that harm. Under my approach, if it is clear that a law has a substantial discriminatory effect, and that law is continually upheld and applied, proof of discriminatory intent should be irrelevant. Knowledge should be enough to show discrimination. While this may seem a stringent standard, in order to break the paradigm, more is required than the status quo.

The Obama administration introduced renewed efforts to change crack cocaine sentencing policy.[52] Congressional hearings examined the 100-to-1 ratio, finally provoking a response.[53] The Fair Sentencing Act of 2010 was intended to completely eliminate this disparity, but it was amended in committee in an effort to build bipartisan and unanimous support in Congress.[54]

The adoption of the Fair Sentencing Act was a positive step but will not alone resolve the racist impact of twenty-five years of a disparate crack cocaine policy. Many drug offenders punished under the previous laws, primarily blacks, will not see their sentences reduced or dismissed, because the Fair Sentencing Act will not be retroactively applied to all who were sentenced more severely under Federal Sentencing Guidelines.[55] This should be corrected through the reduction of sentences or elimination of the mandatory minimum sentence for all of those sentenced under the previous law, not just those sentenced for low amounts of crack cocaine possession and distribution, as the current amendments to the Federal Sentencing Guidelines provide.

Additionally, many facially neutral laws have a disproportionate impact on blacks because blacks and whites are not similarly situated due to racial inequality that was created and reinforced for four centuries. The Supreme Court in *Washington v. Davis* reasoned that without proof of intent, no constitutional violation of equality could occur. This approach reinforces the paradigm.

The "disparate impact doctrine" is a theory of discrimination that recognizes a legal wrong on the basis of the disproportionate negative effect of a practice affecting individuals in a protected class.[56] The disparate impact doctrine was first implemented after Congress passed Title VII, which prevented race-based discrimination in the employment arena and in federally funded programs.[57] From the outset, courts disagreed over whether the law prohibited disparate outcomes for blacks.

The Supreme Court clarified the scope of the disparate impact doctrine in *Griggs v. Duke Power Company*, reasoning that "practices, procedures, or tests neutral on their face, and even neutral in terms of intent, cannot be maintained if they operate to 'freeze' the status quo or prior discriminatory employment practices."[58] The justices further reasoned that Congress "directed the thrust of the [Civil Rights] Act to the consequences of employment practices, not simply the motivation."[59] Through this reasoning, the Court acknowledged that facially neutral employment practices could nonetheless have an "unjustifiably exclusionary effect on protected groups."[60] Consequently, in disparate impact claims raised in the employment context, a plaintiff must only establish sufficient evidence to illustrate the disproportionate impact of the employment practice to state a claim.[61]

After *Griggs*, in *Washington v. Davis*, the Supreme Court refused to apply the disparate impact doctrine to equality claims under the Fourteenth Amendment.[62] In *Davis*, the black plaintiff challenged the District of Columbia Police Department's use of a written test that "blacks failed at a rate roughly four times that of whites."[63] Because there was no evidence that the test scores predicted job performance or measured success in job training, the plaintiffs argued that the disparate impact on blacks was discriminatory in violation of "the guarantee of equal protection implicit in the Fifth Amendment's due process clause."[64] The Court of Appeals found the *Griggs* standard applicable and held that the racially disproportionate impact of the test should shift the burden to the defendant to show the legitimacy of the device.[65] The Supreme Court, however, reversed this holding on the ground that statutory and constitutional standards differ, and in constitutional cases plaintiffs have the burden of proving intentional discrimination.[66] This burden of proof requires that a plaintiff must present evidence that the defendant purposely subjected the plaintiff to disparate treatment because of race; the plaintiff must actually prove the intent of the defendant.

I propose that Congress enact the "Racial Equality Act" to prohibit practices that lead to substantial disparities between blacks and whites in activities that are of fundamental importance in American life. These would include, but would not be limited to, employment, housing, education, and the criminal justice system. Under this proposed law, a prima facie case of illegal racial discrimination would be established if any facially neutral practice resulted in significant disproportionate effects and reinforced one or more aspects of the racial paradigm: racial hierarchy, black victimization, or racial isolation. We must go beyond employment actions and capture all racism that reinforces the paradigm.

Previous approaches to race-neutral laws with disproportionate impact are problematic. Rather than applying the current *Washington v. Davis*[67] intent test, I propose a test that is based upon our racial history and the laws that continue to support disparate impact. Any neutral practice by the government causing a significant disparity in an important activity that reinforces or is related to racial hierarchy, results in black separation, or directly causes black victimization would be prohibited unless proof of a nonracial reason was established. This would be similar to the Supreme Court's approach to determining activities relating to "badges and incidents"[68] of slavery under the Thirteenth Amendment and Congress's approach to preventing employment discrimination under the 1964 Civil Rights Act.

Federal antidiscrimination laws on employment protect against disproportionate impact by shifting the burden of proof to an employer to demonstrate that race discrimination was not the reason for the harmful treatment once disproportionate impact is established. This approach provides much better protection for blacks against inequitable treatment and should be applied more broadly to discriminatory treatment in housing, education, and the criminal justice system through congressional legislation and Supreme Court reinterpretation.

The Truth about Affirmative Action

Many Americans misperceive the meaning of diversity. They frequently define or conceptualize it as a few blacks and an overwhelming number of whites. However, as Justice O'Connor reasoned in the *Grutter* majority opinion, diversity requires more than mere tokenism.[69] It requires a critical mass of blacks to have the positive effect of reducing negative stereotypes.[70] Significant numbers of blacks must be present in order to derive considerable social benefits from diversity.

Diversity in schools offers many advantages to students. Diversity enriches the educational experience by helping students learn from peers and mentors whose experiences, beliefs, and perspectives differ from their own. Additionally, diversity strengthens personal growth by helping students learn to communicate effectively with many different people, and to see the full spectrum of career goals as realistic possibilities.

Moreover, diversity benefits the country financially. The percentages of racial minorities in the population are steadily increasing. In some states, such as California, racial minorities will make up 50% of the work force in the near future.[71] Failure to provide adequate education and employment opportunities to such a large portion of the population will harm the country's economic competitiveness and productivity. Thus, providing education and business opportunities to blacks will help the country's financial health. Diversifying the work force will help to maintain a strong economy.

Contrary to what many believe, the country still needs affirmative action, the most effective way to guarantee diversity. State and local governments must be free to adopt affirmative action programs. However, such freedom can only be achieved through a new approach by the Supreme Court in interpreting the constitutionality of affirmative action.

Throughout our nation's history, education and employment laws have valued and protected whites. Now, those same laws must equally value and protect blacks. The courts must embrace a constitutional interpretation that values racial diversity over racial separation. In *Grutter*,[72] the Supreme Court ruled that the creation of racial diversity in higher education is of such importance that it is a "compelling governmental interest."[73] The Court, however, must go even further. Given our long and disappointing cyclical history of black separation and inequality—from slavery to Jim Crow segregation to de facto segregation—the creation of racial diversity in core aspects of American life is imperative. The Court must recognize that racial diversity is not only "compelling" in higher education, but it is also compelling in primary and secondary education, housing, employment, politics, and business.

American society readily accepts the use of certain preferences in decision making in employment and academic settings.[74] For example, the

Court has approved, without much public complaint, preferences for those who served in the military[75] or belonged to a union.[76] Moreover, preferences are given to tenured professors, alumni legacies, and "the old boy network."[77] For example, at Harvard University, children of alumni are three times more likely to be accepted than nonlegacy applicants.[78]

We must recognize that many preferences exist in our society today. Preferential treatment that benefits the children of college-educated whites is not necessarily more justifiable than diversity-based affirmative action. Some states, such as California, have forbidden the use of race as a factor in public college or university admissions.[79] Yet these same states allow a preference for children of alumni even at schools where blacks were excluded in the past or did not attend in large numbers. The justification for the alumni preference, or legacy admissions, is fundraising. Reducing negative racial stereotypes should be seen as just as important. Prohibiting a preference for underrepresented blacks while permitting a preference for children of mostly white alumni may appear to be race-neutral on its face, but in fact this practice embraces the notion of white superiority. Inequity continues due to the lingering effects of slavery and segregation. In order to level the playing field and guarantee equality of opportunity for all Americans, affirmative action must be maintained at private and public institutions.

There are arguments against affirmative action, including the idea that it will stigmatize and demean those individuals who receive "preferential" treatment. Yet, without reducing ongoing discrimination, the preferential label seems misplaced as blacks who are admitted through affirmative action programs at colleges and universities perform well academically and improve graduation rates. Opponents of affirmative action often view black recipients of affirmative action as inferior to other matriculants, even though the evidence refutes that assumption.

A 1998 study of doctors trained at the University of California at Davis over a twenty-year period illustrated that the beliefs about the inferiority of those admitted to medical school under affirmative action programs are unfounded.[80] The study found that medical students admitted with special consideration for factors such as race, ethnicity, or national origin had remarkably similar postgraduate records and careers to those admitted on academic merit alone.[81] The study proved that "the two groups graduated at essentially the same high rate and, following graduation, they followed parallel paths, completing residency training at the same rate, receiving similar evaluations by residency directors, selecting their specialties in the same percentages and establishing practices with almost the same racial mixes."[82]

Despite this and other evidence to the contrary, some opponents of affirmative action still view black recipients as inferior. Thus, while affirmative action creates access to opportunities in education and employment, it also reinforces false notions of white superiority and perceptions of black incompetence.

In weighing the benefits and drawbacks of affirmative action, leaders must consider both the opportunities created for blacks and the advantages for everyone that accrue from a diverse environment. These benefits far outweigh the drawbacks resulting from negative perceptions. Congress and state legislatures must recognize the effectiveness of affirmative action in creating diversity and must continue to support it, even though, like most racial issues, it is politically divisive.

Prior to its decision in *Grutter*,[83] the Supreme Court unduly restricted race-conscious remedies such as affirmative action; it must reject that formalistic approach. Justice O'Connor's reasoning for the majority in *Grutter*,[84] her last decision before she retired in 2003, strongly tipped the scales in favor of affirmative action. The majority's position was clear: the creation of racial diversity in higher education is compelling because it reduces negative racial stereotypes,[85] and that compelling government interest outweighs the combined arguments against affirmative action. In future cases, the Court should make clear that its reasoning applies to all levels of education and to all important aspects of society.

In order to reduce racial isolation, federal and state governments must have broad discretion to impose affirmative action programs. This flexibility will be possible if the Supreme Court adopts either an expansive interpretation of the *Grutter* rationale, applying it to other substantive areas, or an intermediate standard of scrutiny for all affirmative action programs. This intermediate standard would ensure the government's ability to foster equal opportunity for blacks, while simultaneously protecting whites from harm.

Acknowledge the Existence of Racism and Apologize for Its Harmful Effects

Notions of white superiority continue to hinder racial integration in the United States. The eradication of white superiority should include compensation for individuals who uniquely suffered under Jim Crow laws, such as those who lost property, were harmed physically, or were denied educational opportunities. People like Recy Taylor, of Abbeville, Alabama, deserve to be compensated. In 1944, after attending a church service, Taylor, a 24-year-old black wife and mother, was abducted at gunpoint by seven white men and gang raped. While an investigation by the Alabama governor's office produced admissions of guilt from the seven perpetrators, an uncooperative local sheriff refused to accept the evidence, and an all-white jury refused to convict any of the accused assailants.[86] People like John Hurt, of Prince Edward County, Virginia,[87] also deserve to be compensated. Hurt had only finished first grade when, in 1959, the county closed its public schools rather than desegregate.[88] At seven years old, Hurt took a job on a dairy farm while court challenges were initiated.[89] Five years later, he was allowed to resume his education with children his own age, even though he could only read at a first-grade level.[90] While Prince Edward County had issued vouchers to white children to attend private schools, black children were provided no such option.[91] Hurt eventually dropped out of school.[92] Blacks like Taylor, who have been physically and mentally harmed by racist acts, or like Hurt, harmed by denial of educational opportunities, should pursue legal recourse.

States should provide monetary compensation and apologies. Taylor received an apology, in 2011, from Alabama's governor but no money.[93] Other blacks similarly wronged should be compensated. The states can help ameliorate the harmful effects of past education discrimination through scholarship programs similar to one enacted in Virginia. In 2004, the Virginia legislature created scholarships for people like John Hurt, harmed by white resistance to desegregation, to resume their education.[94] The fact that other states did not close schools does not mean that blacks were not harmed. Individuals who can prove harm must be afforded an opportunity to do so. Once heard, these individuals must be helped.

The Virginia legislature was very careful not to characterize these scholarships as reparations. Payment for past racial discrimination has been one of the most controversial issues of recent decades. Although not unprecedented in American history, talk of reparations has become more controversial due to the vast economic consequences associated with compensation for millions of blacks. Smaller amounts paid to American Indians, and a few other numerically smaller groups, have drawn little attention. When lawyers use creative legal theories to seek compensation for centuries of racial exploitation, there is a great outcry from even disinterested observers of racial issues. No matter what we call the compensation, those harmed should be compensated. Once imposed, any remedy should take the form of economic and educational empowerment through community-based and institution-based assistance, not merely through individual cash payments.

One common argument opposing reparations is that persons harmed by slavery are "dead and gone," and to compensate their descendants would somehow constitute an "unjust enrichment."[95] Other arguments emphasize the difficulty of identifying who should be compensated and calculating how much they should receive.[96] The courts routinely struggle with these matters, as they resolve questions.

There is a need for government to acknowledge culpability in the racial paradigm that exists today. Governments, like Virginia, that profited from slave auctions;[97] insurance companies, like Aetna, that profited from slave cargo;[98] and families, like the Vernons of Newport, Rhode Island, or the DeWolfs of Bristol, Rhode Island, whose generational wealth was built directly on the use of slave labor,[99] must condemn the acts of their forebears in the strongest possible terms. Anyone whose father attended college on the G.I. Bill should be aware that he or she benefited from this policy in a Jim Crow era, when racism prevented most black veterans from taking advantage of this benefit to which they should have been entitled. Although the act of apologizing is often mocked as meaningless, it is a good starting place, as repentance is a powerful catalyst for reconciliation.

The first formal apology by the United States government, for slavery and Jim Crow, was a 2008 resolution passed by the House of Representatives.[100] This was a step in the right direction. Congress has issued apologies in the past—to blacks for failing to pass antilynching laws, to Japanese Americans for their incarceration during World War II, and to native Hawaiians for the overthrow of the Hawaiian king in 1893.[101] The purpose of apologizing for historical wrongs is not to generate guilt or false blame, but rather to acknowledge wrongs in an attempt to make things right.

Most whites are aware that slavery and segregation have harmed blacks tremendously over the past centuries. As part of the dialogue, whites should recognize how white families benefited from slavery and discrimination, and continue to enjoy the benefits today. Awareness and contrition are important for an effective conversation. Effective dialogue cannot begin without it.

If a majority of whites step up and acknowledge post–Jim Crow mistakes—such as "white flight," tipping-point bigotry, racial profiling, disparate drug and voter identification laws, and inequitable school funding schemes, to name a few—that would send a strong and clear message to blacks that they need to similarly evaluate their post–Jim Crow culpability. In order to begin effective dialogue, blacks and whites must understand the benefits and burdens imposed as well as the choices that now preclude America from being the land of equality.

Conclusion

In recent years, proactive steps have helped us move away from the negative racial paradigm toward unity and equality as evidenced by improved opportunities for blacks in education and employment. As we continue to strive toward equality, we must continue to integrate schools and neighborhoods, reduce race-based discrimination, support affirmative action, exercise racial reconciliation, and value diversity. This would improve huge criminal and economic disparities and strengthen the nation as a whole. We have witnessed division topple governments, threatening nations across the globe.

Dialogue about the value of our diversity will help to confront the racial paradigm. Bold action and racial reconciliation will help to eradicate it. Only then will America enter a post-racial society and be rid, once and forever, of the ghosts of Jim Crow.

Notes

Preface

1. Charles Dickens, *A Christmas Carol* (Forgotten Books, 2008) (Chapman & Hall, 1843).

2. For a brief biography of Professor F. Michael Higginbotham please visit the University of Baltimore website at http://law.ubalt.edu/template.cfm?page=582.

3. *See generally* Dickens, *A Christmas Carol.*

4. *See Red Tails,* a George Lucas Film about the 332nd Fighter Group during World War II (2012).

5. According to NPR, "The Legacy of Medgar Evers," *All Things Considered,* June 10, 2003, http://www.npr.org/templates/story/story.php?storyId=1294360,

> On June 12, 1963, Evers was killed by an assassin's bullet. He was buried at Arlington National Cemetery. The accused killer, a white supremacist named Byron De La Beckwith, stood trial twice in the 1960s. Both cases ended in mistrials because the all-white juries could not reach a verdict. De La Beckwith was convicted in a third trial in 1994, and sentenced to life in prison.

6. The Cleveland Browns defeated the Baltimore Colts 27-0 in the 1964 NFL title game. Steve King, "History: 1964," Cleveland Browns, http://www.clevelandbrowns.com/team/history/year-by-year-results/1964.html.

7. "Stokes, Carl B. (21 June 1927–3 April 1996) became the first black mayor of a major U.S. city when he was elected mayor of Cleveland in November 1967. He later became a news anchorman, judge, and a United States Ambassador." Case Western Reserve University, "Stokes, Carl B.," *The Encyclopedia of Cleveland History,* http://ech.cwru.edu/ech-cgi/article.pl?id=SCB2.

8. Memories of 1964-65, Lomond Elementary School Yearbook (on file with author). *See generally* Shaker Heights Schools, "Lomond Elementary School," http://www.shaker.org/lomondschool_home.aspx.

9. *Id.* In 1964-65, district enrollment was 7,737 and minority enrollment was 814. Shaker Heights City School District Racial/Ethnic Report 1964-79, www.roederconsulting.com/files/100621_Shaker/.20schools_facts_Review.pdf.

10. *Id.*

11. Derrick A. Bell, *Race, Racism, and American Law,* 6th ed. (New York: Aspen, 2008), 92.

12. For the 2008-2009 school year, the black (non-Hispanic) students at

Lomond comprise 63% of the entire student body. Lomond Elementary School, "2008-2009 School Year Report Card," Ohio Department of Education, http://www.ode.state.oh.us/reportcardfiles/2008-2009/BUILD/021279.pdf.

13. According to "The Boxer: Controversy," Ali: The Official Site of Muhammad Ali, http://www.ali.com/legend_boxer_controversy.php,

> In 1967, as the Vietnam War was escalating, Ali was called up for induction into the Armed Services. Ali refused induction on the grounds of religious beliefs. He was, in fact, a practicing Muslim minister. This refusal led to the now-famous Ali quote, "I ain't got no quarrel with them Vietcong. . . . No Vietcong ever called me nigger." The national furor over that comment, combined with Ali's refusal to be inducted into the Armed Services, caused virtually every state and local entity in America to cancel Ali's boxing licenses.

14. Johnny Cochran, *A Lawyer's Life* (New York: St. Martin's, 2002).

15. The number one network television show the previous year had been "The Beverly Hillbillies," a show about an impoverished white family from the Ozark Mountain region of the United States that strikes oil on their land and moves to Beverly Hills. The show's theme song noted Beverly Hills for having many swimming pools and movie stars. Despite their newly acquired oil wealth, the family is very much out of place in terms of values and way of life. While they were white, I often felt a kinship with those "Beverly Hillbillies" for I, too, had similar feelings of difference ("The Beverly Hillbillies," Museum of Broadcast Communications, http://www.museum.tv/eotvsection.php?entrycode=beverlyhillb).

16. In 1970, there were few black families with school-age relatives or children living in Beverly Hills. Most of these blacks, such as Berry Gordy Jr., owner of Motown Records, Diana Ross, one of Motown Records' biggest recording stars, and Greg Morris, who starred in a hit network television series called *Mission Impossible*, derived their wealth from the entertainment business. Others were successful business owners such as Lovey Yancey, founder of a chain of fast-food restaurants called Fatburger, or professionals like my father, Robert Higginbotham.

17. Jim Brown appeared in well over thirty films and television programs. Among some of his more famous titles were *The Dirty Dozen* (1967); *100 Rifles* (1969); *I'm Gonna Git You Sucka* (1988) and *Any Given Sunday* (1999). For a complete listing of Jim Brown's film and television credits visit "Jim Brown: Filmography," Fandango, http://www.fandango.com/jimbrown/filmography/p83235.

18. Created by Paul Henning, *The Beverly Hillbillies* aired on CBS from 1962 until 1971. "The Beverly Hillbillies," Museum of Broadcast Communications, http://www.museum.tv/eotvsection.php?entrycode=beverlyhillb.

19. Not long after my request, my parents relocated the family to the View Park section of Los Angeles, an upper-middle-class and predominantly black section of Los Angeles. Even though residing outside of Beverly Hills, I was permitted to

finish my schooling at Beverly Hills High to avoid academic disruption. Unfortunately, not much seems to have changed since 1970, when I was repeatedly profiled in Beverly Hills. Jeff James, a black football star at Beverly Hills High School
in the 1980s, complained about repeated profiling. *See* John Mitchell, "Minorities
Making It at Beverly Hills High," *Los Angeles Times*, June 19, 1983, part IX, p. 1. In
the 1990s, Kirk McCoy, a black *Los Angeles Times* employee who lived in Beverly
Hills in 1992, complained of profiling. McCoy was returning home after covering
the day's events for the paper, including a photo story on the riots, fires, looting,
and curfew that had taken place throughout the area immediately following the
announcement of the Rodney King verdict. McCoy was stopped by Beverly Hills
police officers and California National Guard troops and asked, "What are you
doing in this neighborhood?" McCoy responded, "I am going home." "City of
Fear," MSNBC Special, Aug. 18, 2007.

20. For more information on "tracking" in schools *see* George Anselone, "Getting Our Schools on Track: Is Detracking Really the Answer?" *Radical Pedagogy* 6,
no. 3 (2005), http://radicalpedagogy.icaap.org/content/issue6_2/ansalone.html.

21. Black students with the same test scores as white students are less likely
to be placed in accelerated courses and more likely to be placed in low-track academic courses. "Race Matters: Unequal Opportunities in Education," Annie E.
Casey Foundation article citing Jeannie Oakes, "Two Cities Tracking and Within-
School Segregation," *Teachers College Record* 96, no. 4 (1995): 686.

22. In 2009 at a Beverly Hills High School Athletic Hall of Fame reunion dinner, I asked Michael Suter, one of two other blacks who attended the eighth grade
with me at Horace Mann Elementary School in 1970, what he thought about
the school's tracking program. He responded, "What tracking program?" I then
turned to Randy Stonehill, who is white and was also a classmate, and asked him
if he knew about the tracking system. Randy responded, "Of course I did, didn't
everybody?" Videotape on file with author.

23. "After nearly a week of rioting, 34 people, 25 of them black, were dead and
more than 1,000 were injured. More than 600 buildings were damaged or destroyed. Thriving business districts, their stores mostly white-owned, were burned
to the ground." Valerie Reitman and Mitchell Landsberg, "Watts Riots: 40 Years
Later," Aug. 11, 2005.

24. While I never viewed myself as "rich" since my dad worked for a living (he
is an orthopedic surgeon), many of my black friends or sports competitors classified me as such.

25. According to "Landmark Cochran Cases," *Jet Magazine*, April 18, 2005,

In the first legal proceeding in California history to be broadcast live,
Johnny Cochran represented Leonard Deadwyler and his widow, Barbara,
at a coroner's inquest after Deadwyler, a black motorist, was stopped and
killed by Los Angeles police as he raced his wife, then 8 months pregnant,

to the hospital. She was in labor. The officer stuck his cocked weapon into the car and it discharged, killing him. A nine-member jury found it was an accidental homicide, and a jury failed to rule for the plaintiffs in a $3 million civil suit.

26. In what is known as the "Howard Beach Incident," four blacks were attacked in the Howard Beach section of Queens after their car broke down on their way back to Brooklyn. For a detailed account of the incident please read Leslie M. Alexander and Walter C. Rucker, eds., *Encyclopedia of African American History* (ABC-CLIO, 2010), vol. 1, p. 815.

27. Rochester High School year book (1975).

28. After finishing first and third in the 200-meter finals in 1968 at the Summer Olympic Games in Mexico City, Tommie Smith and John Carlos donned a black glove and raised their fists on the medal stand while the "Star Spangled Banner" played. Jeremy Larner and David Wolf, "Amid Gold Medals, Raised Black Fists," *Life Magazine*, Nov. 1, 1968. For a more in-depth analysis of this important event please read Tommie Smith and David Steele, *Silent Gesture: The Autobiography of Tommie Smith* (Philadelphia: Temple University Press, 2007) and Dave Zirin and John Wesley Carlos, *The John Carlos Story: The Sports Moment That Changed the World* (Chicago: Haymarket Books, 2011).

29. Official Program, Beverly Hills Babe Ruth League 43 (1973); Watchtower Yearbook 188 (1972) (on file with author).

30. F. Michael Higginbotham, "Soldiers for Justice," *Wm & Mary Bill Rts. J.* 8 (2000): 273.

31. Bernard C. Nalty, *Strength for the Fight: A History of Black Americans in the Military* (New York: Free Press, 1986), 145.

32. Highlights, Beverly Hills High School Newspaper (Senior Edition, June 1975), 27. *See also* Beverly Hills 90008.com; "Normans Open Gridiron Season," *Beverly Hills Post*, Sept. 14, 1974, 1.

33. Yale's head football coach at the time was Carmen Cozza. "1974 Yale Football Roster," Fanbase, http://www.fanbase.com/Yale-Bulldogs-Football-1974/roster.

34. According to Ronald Davis, "From Terror to Triumph: Historical Overview," The History of Jim Crow, http://www.jimcrowhistory.org/history/overview.htm,

The term *Jim Crow* originated in a song performed by Thomas Rice, a white minstrel show entertainer in the 1830s. Rice covered his face with charcoal to resemble a black man, and then sang and danced a routine in caricature of a silly black person. By the 1850s, this Jim Crow character, one of several stereotypical images of black inferiority in the nation's popular culture, was a standard act in the minstrel shows of the day. How it became a term synonymous with the brutal segregation of blacks in the late nineteenth-century is unclear. What is clear, however, is that by 1900, the term was generally identified with those racist laws and actions that deprived blacks of their civil rights by defining blacks as inferior to whites, as members of a caste of subordinate people.

35. For example, Shirley Sherrod, a black woman wrongfully terminated by the USDA in July 2010 due to an erroneous belief that she discriminated against white farmers, witnessed her father's murder in 1965 in Newton, Georgia, when he was shot in the back by a white farmer in a dispute over a few cows. Investigation by an all-white grand jury resulted in no charge being brought. Will Bunch, "Hosie Miller: Shirley Sherrod's Dad, and a Casualty in a Forgotten War," Philly. com News, July 21, 2010, http//www.philly.com/philly/blogs/attytood/Hosie_ Miller_Shirley_Sherrods_dad_and a casualty_in_a_forgotten_war.

36. Professor Martin Martel.

37. On file with author.

38. David Gross was a neighbor of the author's in Beverly Hills and a classmate at Horace Mann Elementary School, Beverly Hills High School, and Brown University.

39. Rick Troncelliti, "Cardiac Kids Do It Again," *Brown Football Association Newsletter*, Oct. 29, 1975, 6.

40. For full text of the Civil Rights Act of 1964, Document Number: PL 88-352. Date: 02 JUL 64. 88th Congress, H. R. 7152, visit https://www.civilrights.dot.gov/page/civil-rights-act-1964.

41. Cambridge University Basketball Team photograph, April 1986 (on file with author).

42. *Id.*

43. Cambridge University Basketball Team photograph, April 1985 (on file with author).

44. My mom, Margaret Higginbotham, hosted a television show, *Let's Talk about Art*, that ran on WVIZ, the public television station in Cleveland, Ohio, from 1965 to 1968. She was the first black woman in the state to host her own television show. My dad, Robert Higginbotham, enlisted in the Army Air Corps in 1944 and was involved in protests to desegregate the military. *See* Michael Higginbotham, "Soldiers for Justice: The Role of the Tuskegee Airmen in the Desegregation of the American Armed Forces," 8 *Wm & Mary Bill Rts. J.* 8 (Feb. 2000): 273.

45. *See* F. Michael Higginbotham, "An Open Letter from Heaven to Barack Obama," *U. Hawaii L. Rev.* 32 (2009): 5 n.15.

46. *Id.*

47. Yale Law School Directory (1980-1981).

48. Firm Directory, Davis Polk & Wardwell (1984) (on file with author).

49. Insurance companies routinely charged blacks more than whites for burial coverage. Normally the cost was a third more for blacks. *See* Jeff Donn, "Insurance

Firms Repenting of Race Discrimination," *Deseret News*, Oct. 10, 2004, http://www.deseretnews.com/article/595097273.

50. *See* Duff Rucker and David Barstow, "All Charges Dropped in Duke Case," *New York Times*, April 12, 2007.

51. *See* Melanie Eversley and Larry Copeland, "Georgia Proceeds with Troy Davis Execution," *USA Today*, Sept. 22, 2011, http://www.usatoday.com/news/nation/story/2011-09-21/troy-davis-georgia-execution/50491648/1.

52. *See* Nathan Thornburgh, "Troy Davis's Clemency Denial: The Failure of a Legal 'Safety Valve,'" *Time*, Sept. 20, 2011, http://www.time.com/time/nation/article/0,8599,2094103,00.html#ixzz1jubHiAp3.

53. *See* Philip Caulfield, "Trayvon Martin Case: Screams on 911 Tape Aren't George Zimmerman's; Experts," *New York Daily News*, April 1, 2012, http://articles.nydailynews.com/2012-04-01/news/31271471_1_voice-screams-experts.

54. *See* Dan Barry, Serge F. Kovaleski, Campbell Robertson, and Lizette Alvarez, "Race, Tragedy, and Outrage Collide after a Shot in Florida," *New York Times*, April 1, 2012, http://www.nytimes.com/2012/04/02/us/trayvon-martin-shooting-prompts-a-review-of-ideals.html?_r=1&ref=us&pagewanted=print.

55. *Id.*

56. *Id.*

57. *Id.*

58. *Id.*

59. *Id.*

60. *Id.*

61. *Id.*

62. *Id.*

63. *Id.*

64. *Id.*

65. *Brown v. Board of Education of Topeka*, 347 U.S. 483 (1954). There are two *Brown* cases, *Brown I* (347 U.S. 483) and *Brown II* (349 U.S. 294 (1955)). The *Brown* cases involved a constitutional challenge by black primary school children segregated by the state due to their race. The Court in *Brown I* declared that racial segregation in public schools, at least when mandated by law, violates the principle of equality contained in the United States Constitution (*id.* at 493). The Court rejected the "separate but equal" doctrine established in *Plessy* (163 U.S. 537 (1896)) on the basis that segregated schools were "inherently unequal" (347 U.S. at 495). Unlike segregated train cars, segregated schools created a sense of inferiority among black school children that time could not undo (*id.* at 494). The Court in *Brown II* declared that the black school children were entitled to attend a desegregated school (349 U.S. 294 (1955)). The Court empowered local school boards to implement the desegregation remedy and local federal courts to supervise the plans, all to be done "with all deliberate speed" (*id.* at 301).

66. *See* the Civil Rights Act of 1964, 1965, and 1968 (Pub.L. 88-352, 78 Stat. 241, enacted July 2, 1964).

67. John Hope Franklin and Evelyn Brooks Higginbotham, *From Slavery to Freedom: A History of African Americans,* 9th ed. (Columbus, OH: McGraw-Hill, 2010), 585.

68. David A. Love, "Interracial Marriages in U.S. Rise to All-Time High, Pew Study Finds," February 16, 2012, http://thegrio.com/2012/02/16/interracial-marriages-in-us-rise-to-all-time-high-pew-study-finds.

69. Robert A. Gibson, "The Negro Holocaust: Lynching and Race Riots in the United States, 1880-1950," Yale-New Haven Teachers Institute, 1979, http://www.yale.edu/ynhti/cirriculum/units/1979/2/79.02.04.x.html.

70. "Fox's Eric Bolling: Obama Is Hosting 'Hoodlum[s]' in 'The Hizzouse,'" *Media Matters,* June 11, 2011, http://mediamatters.org/blog/201106110002.

71. "CBS Fires Don Imus over Racial Slur," CBS News, Feb. 11, 2009, http://www.cbsnews.com/stories/2007/04/12/national/main2675273.shtml.

72. David Zucchino, *Myth of the Welfare Queen: A Pulitzer Prize–Winning Journalist's Portrait of Women on the Line* (New York: Scribners, 1997), 65. *See generally,* Melissa Harris-Perry, *Sister Citizen: Shame, Stereotypes, and Black Women in America* (New Haven, CT: Yale University Press, 2011).

73. *Id.*

74. *See* Bari-Ellen Roberts, *Roberts vs. Texaco: A True Story of Race and Corporate America* (New York: Avon, 1998).

75. Michael Higginbotham, "Michael Higginbotham: A Request from Heaven Asks Obama Not to Forget the Race Issue," Noozhawk, http://www.noozhawk.com/noozhawk/print/021010_michael_higginbotham.

76. *Id.*

77. *See* "Rep. Lamborn Apologizes after 'Tar Baby' Remark," *CBS News,* Aug. 2, 2011, http://www.cbsnews.com/stories/2011/08/02/national/main20086724.shtml.

78. *See* Philip Rucker, "Gingrich Promises to Slash Taxes, Calls Obama 'Food Stamp President,'" *Washington Post,* May 13, 2011.

79. *See* "Judge Cebull's Racist Joke," *New York Times,* March 5, 2012, A26.

80. *See* Beth Fouhy, "Trump: Obama a 'Terrible Student' Not Good Enough for Harvard," NBC New York, Apr. 26, 2011.

81. Stan A. Kaplowitz, Clifford L. Broman, and Bradley J. Fisher, *Soc. Psychol. Q.* 69, no. 4 (Dec. 2006): 367-79 (discussing the perceived racial difference of blacks by whites. Economic achievement by blacks has had little effect on the belief that blacks do not work as hard as whites). *See also* Tom Hertz, "Rags, Riches, and Race: The Intergenerational Economic Mobility of Black and White Families in the United States." In *Unequal Chances: Family Background and Economic Success,* Samuel Bowles, Herbert Gintis, and Melissa Osborne, eds. (New York: Russell Sage and Princeton University Press, 2005); *see also* Julia B. Issacs of the Brookings

Institute, "Economic Mobility of Black and White Families," part of the Economic Mobility Project, an Initiative of the Pew Charitable Trusts, 2007, http://www.brookings.edu/~/media/Files/rc/papers/2007/11_blackwhite_isaacs/11_blackwhite_isaacs.pdf (offering statistical evidence that, in similar household economic conditions, children of whites are more likely to surpass their parents' income than children of blacks). My focus, in this book, on the black/white binary of race relations, while reflecting similar notions of inferiority imposed on other racial minorities, is not a characterization that the stories, contribution, suffering, and spirit of other racial groups are not equally as important. Their stories are uniquely valuable and certainly as rich and complex. My focus is on the more familiar, extreme black/white issues(s).

82. Several authors have correctly recognized that we have yet to enter a "post-racial" period. For example, Touré, in his book *Who's Afraid of Post-Blackness?* reasoned that today's racism is invisible, unknowable, but always present. Touré concluded, "There's a sense of malevolent ghosts darting around you, screwing with you, often out of sight but never out of mind." See Touré, *Who's Afraid of Post-Blackness: What It Means to Be Black Now* (New York: Free Press, 2011). In addition, Randall Kennedy, in his book *Persistence of the Color Line: Racial Politics and the Obama Presidency*, reasoned that race continues to play a role in American politics and that in 2008, candidate Obama had to understate the extent of the country's racial divisions and falsely blame blacks and whites equally for them, in order to secure adequate support from the white electorate. See Randall Kennedy, *Persistence of the Color Line: Racial Politics and the Obama Presidency* (New York: Pantheon, 2011). Moreover, Gregory Parks and Matthew Hughey, in their book *The Obamas and a (Post) Racial America?* argued that implicit bias by whites, against blacks, continues to influence whites' receptions of, attitudes about, and interactions with blacks. See Gregory Parks and Matthew Hughey, *The Obamas and a (Post) Racial America?* (New York: Oxford University Press, 2011). Furthermore, Tim Wise, in his book *Colorblind: The Rise of Post-Racial Politics and the Retreat from Racial Equity*, argues that current race-neutral responses to racism make stopping it more difficult. See Tim Wise, *Colorblind: The Rise of Post-Racial Politics and the Retreat from Racial Equity* (New York: New York University Press, 2010). Finally, H. Roy Kaplan, in his book *The Myth of Post-Racial America*, reasoned that racism continues to prevent equality between black and white in corporate, educational, and social settings throughout America. See H. Roy Kaplan, *The Myth of Post-Racial America: Searching for Equality in the Age of Materialism* (Lanham, MD: Rowman & Littlefield Education, 2011).

83. See Jessica Sheppard, "World Education Rankings: Which Country Does Best at Reading, Maths, and Science?" *The Guardian*, Dec. 7, 2010, guardian.co.uk.

84. *Id.*

85. "Benchmarking for Success: Ensuring U.S. Students Receive a World-Class Education," National Governors Association, 2008, http://www.nga.org/cms/

render/live/en/sites/NGA/home/nga-center-for-best-practices/center-publica-
tions/page-edu-publications/col2-content/main-content-list/benchmarking-for-
success-ensurin.html.

Introduction

1. *See* A. Leon Higginbotham Jr., *In the Matter of Color: Race and the American Legal Process* (New York: Oxford University Press, 1978), 20.

2. *See* Adam Nagourney, "Obama Elected President as Racial Barrier Falls," *New York Times*, Nov. 4, 2008.

3. *See* F. Michael Higginbotham, "The Price of Apartheid," *How. L.J.* 38 (1995): 371.

4. Howard Ball, *A Defiant Life: Thurgood Marshall and the Persistence of Racism in America*, 1st ed. (New York: Crown Publishers, 1998), 1.

5. Harlon L. Dalton, *Racial Healing: Confronting the Fear between Blacks and Whites*, 1st ed. (New York: Doubleday, 1995), 19-20.

6. *The Journal of Negro History* 59, no. 2 (Apr. 1974): 133 (published by Association for the Study of African-American Life and History).

7. *See* Geoffrey Perrett, *Ulysses S. Grant: Soldier and President* (New York: Random House Digital, 1998).

8. Lydia Lum, "The Obama Era: A Post-Racial Society?" Diverse, Feb. 5, 2009, http://diverseeducation.com/article/12238.

9. "The Colbert Report," Wikipedia, http://en.wikiquote.org/wiki/The_Colbert_Report.

10. Richard Ford, *The Race Card: How Bluffing about Bias Makes Race Relations Worse* (New York: Farrar, Straus, Giroux, 2008).

11. Lawrence Bobo, "Not in My Neighborhood," The Root, Dec. 2, 2008, http://www.theroot.com/views/not-my-neighborhood; *see also* Marianne Bertrand and Sendhil Mullainathan, "Are Emily and Greg More Employable Than Lakisha and Jamal?A Field Experiment on Labor Market Discrimination," June 20, 2004, http://www.economics.harvard.edu/faculty/mullainathan/files/emilygreg.pdf.

12. In *Brown v. Board of Education*, 347 U.S. 483 (1954), the Supreme Court decided that the segregation of children in public schools solely on the basis of race deprived the minority children of the equal protection of the laws guaranteed by the Fourteenth Amendment.

13. K. B. Clark, *Effect of Prejudice and Discrimination on Personality Development* (Midcentury White House Conference on Children and Youth, 1950).

14. In the "doll test," psychologists Kenneth and Mamie Clark used four plastic, diaper-clad dolls, identical except for color. They showed the dolls to black children between the ages of three and seven and asked them questions to determine racial perception and preference. Almost all of the children readily identified the

race of the dolls. However, when asked which they preferred, the majority selected the white doll and attributed positive characteristics to it. The Clarks also gave the children outline drawings of a boy and girl and asked them to color the figures the same color as themselves. Many of the children with dark complexions colored the figures with a white or yellow crayon. The Clarks concluded that "prejudice, discrimination, and segregation" caused black children to develop a sense of inferiority and self-hatred.

15. Jan Donaldson, "The Latest DUH Study: CNN Experiment Shows Black and White Children Have Bias toward Light Skin," Blackvoices, May 17, 2010, http://www.bvblackspin.com/2010/05/17/cnn-doll-study.

16. Morton M. Hunt, *Profiles of Social Research: The Scientific Study of Human Interactions* (New York: Russell Sage Foundation, 1985), 58.

17. C. Vann Woodward, *The Strange Career of Jim Crow* (New York: Oxford University Press, 2001) (1982).

18. Arthur, Mikaila Mariel Lemonik, *Student Handbook to Sociology: Social Change* (New York: Infobase Publishing, 2012).

19. Tim Lockette, "The New Racial Segregation at Public Schools," *Teaching Tolerance*, Feb. 4, 2010.

20. For more information on "tracking" in schools *see* George Anselone, "Getting Our Schools on Track: Is Detracking Really the Answer?" *Radical Pedagogy* 6, no. 2 (Winter 2005), http://radicalpedagogy.icaap.org/content/issue6_2/ansa-lone.html.

21. *See* A. Leon Higginbotham Jr., *In the Matter of Color* (New York: Oxford University Press, 1978), 60-61, 306.

22. "As a result of the Anti–Drug Abuse Act of 1986, Congress set forth different mandatory penalties for powder cocaine and crack cocaine, with significantly higher punishments for crack cocaine offenses." "Crack vs. Powder Cocaine: A Gulf in Penalties," *U.S. News and World Report.* Oct. 1, 2007, http://www.usnews.com/news/national/articles/2007/10/01/crack-vs-powder-cocaine-a-gulf-in-penalties.html.

23. For an in-depth analysis of the disparity of sentencing guidelines between powdered and crack cocaine, *see* "Testimony of Judge Reggie B. Walton Presented to the United States Sentencing Commission on November 13, 2007, on the Retroactivity of the Crack-Powder Cocaine Guideline Amendment," http://ebook-browse.com/walton-testimony-pdf-d115559353.

24. Although the two types of cocaine cause similar physical reactions, the sentences that users and sellers of the drugs face are vastly different. For powder cocaine, a conviction of possession with intent to distribute carries a five-year sentence for quantities of five hundred grams or more. But for crack, a conviction of possession with intent to distribute carries a five-year sentence for only five grams. This is a 100:1 quantity ratio. Crack is also the only drug that carries a mandatory prison sentence for first-offense possession.

Approximately two-thirds of crack users were white or Hispanic in 1994, yet the vast majority of persons convicted of possession in federal courts in that year were black. Defendants convicted of crack possession in 1994 were 84.5% black and 10.3% white. The result of the combined difference in sentencing laws and racial disparity is that blacks are serving longer prison sentences than whites for, essentially, committing the same offense. The Sentencing Project, "Crack Cocaine Sentencing Policy: Unjust and Unreasonable," http://www.prisonpolicy.org/scans/sp/1003.pdf.

25. While this book uses history to demonstrate the origin and depth of existing dilemmas, it is not a history book. This book is about identifying the sources and extent of current inequality and the means to eradicate it.

26. 347 U.S. 483 (1954).

27. James Hannaham, "Racists for Obama," salon.com, Nov. 3, 2008, http://www.salon.com/opinion/feature/2008/11/03/racists_for_obama.

28. "Obama did not win a majority of white voters; no Democrat has since Lyndon Johnson in 1964. But he ran equal to the last three Democratic candidates for president among white voters, and even slightly better than the party's 2004 nominee, according to an Edison/Mitofsky exit poll conducted for a consortium of TV networks and the Associated Press." Peter Walliston, "Red and Blue, Black and White," *Los Angeles Times,* Nov. 5. 2008, http://articles.latimes.com/2008/nov/05/nation/na-assess5.

29. Randall Kennedy, *Nigger: The Strange Career of a Troublesome Word* (New York: Vintage, 2002).

30. *Id.*

31. *Id.*

32. Mixed Race America by Jennifer, http://mixedraceamerica.blogspot.com/2011/01/tgif-mixed-race-america.html.

33. In the total population, 34.7 million people, or 12.3 %, reported only black. An additional 1.8 million people reported black and at least one other race. U.S. Census Bureau, http://www.census.gov/prod/2001pubs./c2kbr01-5pdf.

34. As of 2000 blacks comprise 64.3% of the population of Baltimore and 60% of the District of Columbia. As of 2012, Baltimore remained the same but the District of Columbia dropped. U.S. Census Bureau, State and County QuickFacts, "Washington (city), District of Columbia," http://quickfacts.census.gov/qfd/states/11/1150000.html, and "Baltimore (city), Maryland," http://quickfacts.census.gov/qfd/states/24/2404000.html.

35. "Census Estimates Show More U.S. Blacks Moving South," February 15, 2011, http://www.usatoday.com/news/nation/census/2011-02-15-census-black-migration_N.htm.

36. By 2050, the minority population — everyone except for non-Hispanic, single-race whites—is projected to be 235.7 million out of a total U.S. population of 439 million. The nation is projected to reach the 400 million population milestone

in 2039. U.S. Census Bureau, http://www.census.gov/Press-Release/www/releases/archives/population/012496.html.

37. The Supreme Court of the United States has had two black justices: Thurgood Marshall, appointed from New York by President Lyndon Johnson, judicial oath taken Oct. 2, 1967, service terminated Oct. 1, 1991; and Clarence Thomas, appointed from Georgia by President George H. W. Bush, judicial oath taken Oct. 23, 1991. "Members of the Supreme Court of the United States," Supreme Court of the United States, http://www.supremecourt.gov/about/members.aspx.

38. Colin Powell was the first, appointed in 2001, and Condoleezza Rice was the second, appointed in 2005. http://www.infoplease.com.

39. Eric H. Holder Jr. was sworn in as the eighty-second attorney general of the United States on February 3, 2009. "Office of the Attorney General," U.S. Department of Justice, http://www.justice.gov/ag.

40. Barack Obama was elected the forty-fourth president of the United States on November 4, 2008, and sworn in on January 20, 2009. "President Barack Obama," The White House, http://www.whitehouse.gov/administration/president-obama.

41. "There is a wide disparity in the graduation rates of white and [black] students. In the class of 2002, about 78% of white students graduated from high school . . . compared to 56% of [black] students. . . ." Jay P. Greene and Marcus A. Winters, "Public High School Graduation and College Readiness Rates: 1991-2002," Education Working Paper no. 8, Feb. 2005, http://www.manhattan-institute.org/html/ewp_08.htm. "Non-Hispanic whites gained 4 percentage points in the decade examined [1996-2006], rising to a graduation rate of 76.1%; the Hispanic rate rose 1.7 points, to 55%; the rate among blacks rose 2.4 points, to 51.2%." Stacy Teicher Khadaroo, "U.S. High School Graduation Rate Climbs 69.2 Percent," Christian Science Monitor, June 9, 2009, http://www.csmonitor.com/USA/2009/0609/p02s13-usgn.html.

42. 2006 State of Black America Report, National Urban League, 2006, http://www.nul.org/estore/content/state-black-america-soba-2006.

43. "Wage Gap Still Separates Black Baby Boomers from Whites," Jet, Jan. 17, 2005, 6.

44. See Marilyn Gardner, "Is 'White' the Only Color of Success?" Christian Science Monitor, Oct. 31, 2005 (discussing research by Sylvia Ann Hewlett and Cornel West).

45. Reported on CNN Television, American Morning Show, Feb. 21, 2007, 2006 U.S. Census.

46. Jennifer Manning, "Membership of the 112th Congress: A Profile," Congressional Research Service, Mar. 1, 2001, http://www.senate.gov/reference/resources/pdf/R41647.pdf .

47. Table 105. Expectation of Life and Expected Deaths by Race, Sex, and Age: 2006: White Male: 75.7 years from birth; Black Male: 69.7 years from birth; White

Female: 80.6 years from birth; Black Female: 76.5 years from birth. U.S. Census Bureau, http://www.census.gov/compendia/statab/2010/tables/10s0105.pdf.

48. Richard J. Herrnstein and Charles Murray, *The Bell Curve: Intelligence and Class Structure in American Life* (New York: Free Press, 1996).

49. Amy Wax, *Race, Wrongs, and Remedies: Group Justice in the 21st Century* (Lanham, MD: Rowman & Littlefield, 2009).

50. Juan Williams, *Enough: The Phony Leaders, Dead-End Movements, and Culture of Failure That Are Undermining Black America—and What We Can Do about It* (New York: Broadway, 2007).

51. For examples of Jim Crow laws isolating blacks *see* "Examples of Jim Crow Laws," Race, Racism, and the Law, http://racism.org/index.php?option=com_content&view=article&id=501:jcrow02&catid=114:legal-apartheid-jim-crow&Itemid=140.

52. 163 U.S. 537 (1896).

53. *Id.*

54. 347 U.S. 483 (1954).

55. 418 U.S. 717 (1974).

56. 539 U.S. 244 (2003).

57. 551 U.S. 701 (2007).

58. *See* U.S. Const., Article I, Section 2 & 9., U.S. Const., Article IV, Section 2.

59. U.S. Const., Preamble (1789).

60. A. Leon Higginbotham Jr., "The Bicentennial of the Constitution: A Racial Perspective," *Stanford Law Magazine*, Fall 1987, 8.

61. U.S. Const., Amendment 13.

62. *See* U.S. Const., Article I, Sections 2 & 9, U.S. Const., Article IV, Section 2.

63. *R v. Knowles, ex parte Somersett* (1772) 20 State Tr 1.

64. U.S. Const. Amendment 13, 14, 15.

65. F. Michael Higginbotham, *Race Law: Cases, Commentary, and Questions* (Durham, NC: Carolina Academic Press, 2005), 23.

66. The first state to legislate the one-drop rule of endogamous group membership as statutory law was Tennessee in 1910. Citing Pauli Murray, ed., *States' Laws on Race and Color* (Athens: University of Georgia Press, 1997), 428.

67. December 1662-ACT XII. Hening, ed., *The Statutes at Large*, vol. 2, p. 170.

68. 163 U.S. 537 (1896).

69. *Id.*

70. "Plessy v. Ferguson (1896)," The People's Vote: 100 Documents That Shaped America, usnews.com, http://www.usnews.com/usnews/documents/docpages/document_page52.htm.

71. Michael J. Klarman, *From Jim Crow to Civil Rights: The Supreme Court and the Struggle for Racial Equality* (New York: Oxford University Press, 2004), 48.

72. *Id.*

73. Higginbotham, *Race Law*, 50 (citing *People v. Hall*, 4 Cal. 399 (1854)).

74. 163 U.S. 537 (1896).

75. Higginbotham, *Race Law*, 374.

76. Susan M. Glisson, *The Human Tradition in the Civil Rights Movement* (Lanham, MD: Rowman & Littlefield, 2006), 37.

77. 163 U.S. 537 (1896).

78. 347 U.S. 483 (1954).

79. *Id.*

80. *Id.*

81. According to Dion Haynes, "U.S. Unemployment Rate for Blacks Projected to Hit 25-Year High," *Washington Post,* Jan. 15, 2010, http://www.washingtonpost.com/wp-dyn/content/article/2010/01/14/AR2010011404085.html,

> Unemployment for blacks is projected to reach a 25-year high in 2010, according to a study released by an economic think tank, with the national rate soaring to 17.2 % and the rates in five states exceeding twenty %. Blacks as well as Latinos were far behind whites in employment levels even when the economy was booming. But throughout the recession, the unemployment rate has grown much faster for African Americans and Latinos than for whites, according to the study by the Economic Policy Institute.

82. Only 70% of all students in public high schools graduate, and only 32% of all students leave high school qualified to attend four-year colleges. Rates for black students are significantly lower. Jay Greene and Greg Foster, "Public High School Graduation and College Readiness Rates in the United States," Manhattan Institute for Policy Research, Sept. 2003, http://www.manhattan-institute.org/html/ewp_03.htm.

83. Blacks have 2.3 times the infant mortality rate as non-Hispanic whites. They are four times as likely to die as infants due to complications related to low birth weight as compared to non-Hispanic white infants. Blacks had 1.8 times the sudden infant death syndrome mortality rate as non-Hispanic whites, in 2005. "Infant Mortality Statistics from the 2005 Period Linked Birth/Infant Death Data Set," *National Vital Statistics Reports* 57, no. 2, table 2, http://www.cdc.gov/nchs/data/nvsr/nvsr57/nvsr57_02.pdf.

84. Paul Butler, *Let's Get Free* (New York: New Press, 2009), 23-25; Michelle Alexander, *The New Jim Crow* (New York: New Press, 2010), 58-94. Statistics as of June 20, 2004, from Prison and Jail Inmates at Midyear 2004, Tables 1, 14, and 15 and U.S. Census (Graph: Peter Wagner, June 2005), http://www.prisonpolicy.org/graphs/raceinc.html.

85. Poverty rates for blacks greatly exceed the national average. In 2008, 24.7% of blacks were poor, compared to 8.6% of whites. Poverty rates are highest for families headed by single women, particularly if they are black. In 2008, 28.7% of households headed by single women were poor, while 13.8% of households headed by single men and 5.5% of married-couple households lived in poverty. "Poverty in

the United States: Frequently Asked Questions," National Poverty Center, University of Michigan, http://www.npc.umich.edu/poverty/#_ftn3.

86. *Report of the National Advisory Commission on Civil Disorders* (New York: Bantam, 1968), 5. President Lyndon Johnson established the National Advisory Commission on Civil Disorders, known as the Kerner Commission, named after its chair, Otto Kerner, to investigate the 1967 race riots in Detroit, Michigan, and Newark, New Jersey. Milton Kleg, *Hate, Prejudice, and Racism* (Albany, NY: SUNY Press, 1993), 13.

87. Pierre Thomas and Jason Ryan, "The Stinging Remarks on Race from Attorney General," *ABC News*, Feb. 18, 2009, http://abcnews.go.com/TheLaw/story?id=6905255&page=1.

88. 347 U.S. 483 (1954).

89. *Id.*

90. *Id.*

Chapter 1

1. *Dred Scott v. Sandford*, 60 U.S. 393, 411 (1856).

2. A. Leon Higginbotham Jr., *In The Matter of Color: Race and the American Legal Process; The Colonial Period* (New York: Oxford University Press, 1978), 19-60.

3. 60 U.S. 393, 404-5 (1856).

4. Frank E. Grizzard, *Jamestown Colony: A Political, Social, and Cultural History* (ABC-CLIO, 2007), 107.

5. Higginbotham, *In the Matter of Color*, 20-21. For an examination of slavery, *see generally* David Brion Davis, *The Problem of Slavery in Western Culture* (Ithaca, NY: Cornell University Press, 1966).

6. Gwendolyn Mink, *Poverty in the United States: An Encyclopedia of History, Politics, and Policy* (ABC-CLIO, 2004), 403.

7. *See, for example,* Ch. XXI, 11 Laws of Va. 39 (Hening 1823) (enacted 1782).

8. *Id.*

9. A. Leon Higginbotham Jr. and F. Michael Higginbotham, "Yearning to Breathe Free: Legal Barriers against and Options in Favor of Liberty in Antebellum Virginia," *N.Y.U. L. Rev.* 68 (1993): 1213.

10. *Id.*

11. *See Hening's Statutes at Large (1816)*, chap. 24, p. 51 (enacted 1815).

12. Higginbotham and Higginbotham, "Yearning to Breathe Free," 1267. *See also* Act of January 24, 1816, *Hening's Statutes at Large (1816)*, chap. 24, p. 51 (enacted 1815) (giving regulations under which slaves emancipated since May 1, 1806, could obtain permission to reside within a county of the commonwealth).

13. Higginbotham and Higginbotham, "Yearning to Breathe Free," 1255-56.

14. *Id.*

15. *Id.*

16. *Id.*

17. *Id.* at 1256.

18. See *Woodley v. Abby*, 9 Va. 336 (1805).

19. Mink, *Poverty in the United States,* 402-3.

20. *Id.*

21. *Id.*

22. *Id.*

23. *Id.*

24. H. R. McIlwaine, ed. *Minutes of the Council and General Court of Colonial Virginia* (Richmond: Virginia State Library, 1924) (July 1640), 466.

25. *Id.*

26. *Id.*

27. *Id.*

28. Mary Beth Norton and Paul F. Boller, *A People and a Nation: A History of the United States.* Vol. 2, *Since 1865* (Independence, KY: Wadsworth, 2011), 425-27.

29. Jeff Ferret, *Race and Relations at the Margin: Slaves and Poor Whites in the Antebellum Southern Countryside* (Baton Rouge: Louisiana State University Press, 2006), 21.

30. Higginbotham, *In The Matter of Color,* 33.

31. *Id.* at 288, 310.

32. *Id.*

33. A. Leon Higginbotham Jr., *Shades of Freedom: Racial Politics and Presumptions of the American Legal Process* (New York: Oxford University Press, 1998), 170-71; see also *Hobbs v. Fogg,* 6 Watts 553 (1837).

34. Higginbotham, *Shades of Freedom,* 168.

35. *Id.* at 156, 176.

36. *Wake Forest L. Rev.* 35: 671, 683.

37. *See, for example,* A. Leon Higginbotham Jr. and Barbara K. Kopytoff, "Racial Purity and Interracial Sex in the Law of Colonial and Antebellum Virginia," *Geo. L J.* 77 (1989): 1977.

38. *Id.*

39. Higginbotham, *Shades of Freedom,* 38; see also Higginbotham and Kopytoff, "Racial Purity," 1977.

40. Higginbotham, *Shades of Freedom,* 36.

41. *Id.* at 38.

42. *Id.*

43. *Id.*

44. *Id.*

45. *Id.*

46. Higginbotham and Kopytoff, "Racial Purity," 1976-78.

47. Dwight L. Smith, *Afro-American History: A Bibliography,* vol 2. (ABC-CLIO, 1981), 64.

48. *Id.*

49. *Id.*

50. Jeffrey R. Brackett, *The Negro in Maryland: A Study of Slavery* (North Stratford, NH: Ayer, 1989) (1889), 101, 201.

51. *Negro History Bulletin* 10 (1946): 19.

52. John Hope Franklin, *From Slavery to Freedom: A History of African Americans*, 6th ed. (New York: Random House, 1988), 141.

53. *Id.* at 140.

54. *Id.*

55. *Id.*

56. *Id.*

57. Oscar Reiss, *Blacks in Colonial America* (Jefferson, NC: McFarland, 1997), 105.

58. *Id.*

59. *See* Daniel J. Sharfstein, "Crossing the Color Line: Racial Migration and the One-Drop Rule, 1600-1860," *Minn. L. Rev.* 91 (2007): 592.

60. *Id.*

61. *Hudgins v. Wright,* 11 Va. 134 (1806).

62. *Id.*

63. *Id.*

64. *Id.*

65. *Id.* at 140.

66. Higginbotham and Kopytoff, "Racial Purity," 1975-83.

67. Va. Const. Art. 1, § 1.

68. 11 Va. 134, 140 (1806).

69. 1795 Va. Acts 16.

70. Higginbotham and Higginbotham, "Yearning to Breathe Free," 1213.

71. *Id.*

72. *Id.*

73. *Id.*

74. *See Peter v. Hargrave,* 46 Va. 12 (1848).

75. *Id.*

76. *Id.*

77. *Id.*

78. *Id.*

79. *Id.*

80. *Id.*

81. *Id.*

82. Higginbotham and Higginbotham, "Yearning to Breathe Free," 1213.

83. *Id.*

84. 11 Va. 134 (1806).

85. *State v. Cantey,* 20 S.C.L. 614, 616 (1835). Discussion of *Hudgins* substantially

relies on the research and analysis in Higginbotham and Higginbotham, "Yearning to Breathe Free."

86. 41 U.S. 539 (1842).

87. 11 Va. 134 (1806).

88. 41 U.S. 539 (1842).

89. *Id.*

90. *Id.*

91. *Id.*

92. *Id.*

93. *Id.*

94. *Id.*

95. Solomon Northup and David Wilson, *Twelve Years a Slave: Narrative of Solomon Northup, a Citizen of New York, Kidnapped in Washington City in 1841, and Rescued in 1853, from a Cotton Plantation Near the Red River, in Louisiana* (Auburn, NY: Miller, Orton & Mulligan, 1855).

96. *Id.*

97. *Id.*

98. *Id.*

99. *Id.*

100. *Id.*

101. *Id.*

102. *Id.*

103. *Id.*

104. *Id.*

105. *Id.*

106. *Id.*

107. F. Michael Higginbotham, *Race Law: Cases, Commentary, and Questions* (Durham, NC: Carolina Academic Press, 2005), 141. *See also* A. Leon Higginbotham Jr., *In The Matter of Color*, 193-99.

108. *Id.*

109. Melton Alonza McLaurin, *Celia, a Slave* (New York: Avon Books, 1993).

110. *Id.*

111. *Id.*

112. *Id.*

113. *Id.*

114. *Id.*

115. Harriet C. Frazier, *Runaway and Freed Missouri Slaves and Those Who Helped Them, 1763-1865* (Jefferson, NC: McFarland, 2004), 35.

116. *See State v. Mann*, 13 N.C. 263 (1829).

117. Stewart E. Tolnay, *The Bottom Rung: African American Family Life on Southern Farms* (Urbana: University of Illinois Press, 1999), 5.

118. *Id.*

119. *Id.*

120. Winthrop D. Jordan, *White over Black: American Attitudes toward the Negro, 1550-1812* (Chapel Hill: University of North Carolina Press, 1968).

121. *Id.*

122. Carter G. Woodson, *The Mis-Education of the Negro* (Washington, DC: Associated Publishers, 1933), 3.

123. *Id.*

124. *Id.*

125. Francis Fredric, *Slave Life in Virginia and Kentucky; or, Fifty Years of Slavery, in the Southern States of America* (Farmington Hills, MI: Gale, 2012) (1863).

126. Robert Pierce Forbes, *The Missouri Compromise and Its Aftermath: Slavery and the Meaning of America* (Chapel Hill: University of North Carolina Press, 2007), 5.

127. *Id.*

128. *See generally* Eric Foner, *Reconstruction: America's Unfinished Revolution, 1863-1877* (New York: HarperCollins, 1988).

129. *Id.*

130. John Hope Franklin and Alfred A. Moss Jr., *From Slavery to Freedom: A History of Negro Americans,* 5th ed. (New York: Knopf, 1980), 157, 173-74.

131. *Id.* at 158-76.

132. *See generally* G. Frederickson, *The Black Image in the White Mind* (New York: Harper & Row, 1971).

133. 60 U.S. 393 (1856).

134. *Id.*

135. *Id.*

136. *Id.*

137. *Id.*

138. *Id.*

139. *Id.*

140. *Id.*

141. *Id.*

142. *Id.* at 407.

143. *Id.*

144. *Id.*

145. *Id.*

146. *Id.*

147. *Id.* at 408.

148. *Id.*

149. *Id.*

150. *Id.* at 396-97.

151. *Id.* at 403.

152. Higginbotham, *Shades of Freedom,* 65.

153. 60 U.S. 393, 426 (1856).

154. *Id.* at 405.

155. *Id.* at 409.

156. *See* Don Fehrenbacher, *The Dred Scott Case: Its Significance in American Law and Politics* (New York: Oxford University Press, 1978), 136.

157. *Id.*

158. Allen C. Guelzo, *Lincoln's Emancipation Proclamation: The End of Slavery in America* (New York: Simon & Schuster, 2004).

159. Emancipation Proclamation.

160. Bernard C. Nalty, *Strength for the Fight: A History of Black Americans in the Military* (New York: Free Press, 1986), 43.

161. *Id.*

162. *Id.*

163. *Id.*

164. *Id.* at 46.

165. Abraham Lincoln, Stephen Arnold Douglas, and Harold Holzer, *The Lincoln-Douglas Debates: The First Complete, Unexpurgated Text* (New York: HarperCollins, 1993), 245. These words are from a speech given by Abraham Lincoln on September 18, 1958, during a debate with Stephen A. Douglas.

166. Higginbotham, *Race Law,* 141.

167. Emancipation Proclamation.

168. Leslie M. Harris, *In the Shadow of Slavery: African Americans in New York City, 1626-1863* (Chicago: University of Chicago Press, 2004).

169. *Id.*

170. "The Riots at New York: The Rioters Burning and Sacking the Colored Orphan Asylum," *Harper's Weekly Reports on Black America, 1857-1874,* Aug. 1, 1863, 493, http://blackhistory.harpweek.com/7illustrations/CivilWar/ColoredOrphanAsylum.htm.

Chapter 2

1. Qtd. in A. Leon Higginbotham Jr., *Shades of Freedom: Racial Politics and Presumptions of the American Legal Process* (New York: Oxford University Press, 1996), 95.

2. 13 N.C. 263 (1829).

3. 11 Va. 134 (1806).

4. Helen Tunnicliff Catterall, *Judicial Cases concerning American Slavery and the Negro.* 5 vols. (New York: Octagon Books, 1968).

5. *See generally* Theodore B. Wilson, *The Black Codes of the South* (Tuscaloosa: University of Alabama Press, 1965).

6. *Id.*

7. *Id.*

8. *Id.*

9. Fourteenth Amendment.

10. Fifteenth Amendment.

11. *See* Civil Rights Acts of 1866, 1870, and 1875.

12. *Id. See also* Thirteenth, Fourteenth, and Fifteenth Amendments.

13. James D. Anderson, *The Education of Blacks in the South, 1860-1935* (Chapel Hill: University of North Carolina Press, 1988), 9.

14. *Id.*

15. *Id.*

16. *Id.* at 11-15.

17. *Id.*

18. *Id.* at 5-6.

19. *Id.* at 67-68.

20. *Id.* at 24-32.

21. *Id.*

22. *Id.*

23. *Id.* at 37.

24. Michael O'Brien, *Conjectures of Order: Intellectual Life and the American South, 1810-1860*, vols. 1 and 2 (Chapel Hill: University of North Carolina Press, 2004).

25. *Id.*

26. King James Bible, Acts 17:26.

27. John Hope Franklin and Alfred A. Moss Jr., *From Slavery to Freedom: A History of Negro Americans,* 5th ed. (New York: Knopf, 1980), 239.

28. *Id.*

29. *Id.*

30. *Id.* at 210.

31. Gene Smith, "Pathfinders," *American Legacy,* Spring 1999, 12.

32. *Id.*

33. *Id.*

34. Anderson, *The Education of Blacks in the South,* 4.

35. *See id.*

36. *Id.* at 18-19.

37. *Id.*

38. *Id.* at 19.

39. *Id.*

40. *Id.*

41. Franklin and Moss, *From Slavery to Freedom,* 239.

42. *Id.*

43. *Id.*

44. *Id.*

45. *Id.*

46. *Id.*

47. Charles Lane, *The Day Freedom Died: The Colfax Massacre, the Supreme Court, and the Betrayal of Reconstruction* (New York: Henry Holt, 2008), 3.

48. *See generally id.*

49. Eric Foner, *Reconstruction: America's Unfinished Revolution, 1863-1877* (New York: HarperCollins, 1988), 425-26.

50. *Id.*

51. *Id.*

52. *Id.*

53. Robert J. Kaczorowski, *The Politics of Judicial Interpretation: The Federal Courts, Department of Justice, and Civil Rights, 1866-1876* (Bronx, NY: Fordham University Press, 2005), 40-42.

54. *Id.* Also, originally enacted in Section I of the Civil Rights Act 1866.

55. Ku Klux Klan Act (1871).

56. *Id.*

57. *Id.*

58. *See generally,* Lane, *The Day Freedom Died.*

59. *Id.*

60. *Id.*

61. *Id.*

62. *Id.*

63. *Id.*

64. *Id.*

65. *Id.*

66. *Id.*

67. *Id.*

68. *Id.*

69. *Id.* at 22.

70. *United States v. Cruikshank,* 92 U.S. 542 (1875).

71. *Id.*

72. *Id.*

73. 83 U.S. 36 (1872).

74. *Id.*

75. *Id.*

76. 92 U.S. 542 (1875).

77. 83 U.S. 36 (1872).

78. 109 U.S. 3 (1883).

79. 92 U.S. 542 (1875).

80. F. Michael Higginbotham, *Race Law: Cases, Commentary, and Questions* (Durham, NC: Carolina Academic Press, 2005), 267-69.

81. *Id.*

82. 92 U.S. 542, 544-47 (1875).

83. F. Michael Higginbotham, *Race Law*, 268.

84. 60 U.S. (19 How.) 393, 414 (1856).

85. 60 U.S. 393 (1856).

86. 41 U.S. 539 (1842).

87. 92 U.S. 542 (1875).

88. Franklin and Moss, *From Slavery to Freedom*, 226.

89. A. Leon Higginbotham Jr., *Shades of Freedom*, 92-93.

90. *Id.*

91. *Id.*

92. Eric Foner, *Reconstruction*, 581 (quoting the Kansas Republican State Committee chairman); Lowell Hayes Harrison and James C. Klotter, *A New History of Kentucky* (Lexington: University Press of Kentucky, 1997), 247.

93. *Strauder v. West Virginia*, 100 U.S. 303, 306 (1879).

94. *Id.*

95. *Id.*

96. *Batson v. Kentucky*, 476 U.S. 79 (1986).

97. Kim Taylor Thompson, "Empty Votes in Jury Deliberations," *Harv. L. Rev.* 113 (2000): 1279-83.

98. *See* Alexander Keyssar, *The Right to Vote: The Contested History of Democracy in the United States* (New York: Basic Books, 2000), 111. Experiments with these legal strategies had occurred in the 1870s and 1880s, but it was between 1890 and 1905 that they became the primary mechanism for imposing discrimination.

99. 92 U.S. 214 (1876).

100. Adam Fairclough, *Better Day Coming: Blacks and Equality, 1890-2000* (New York: Penguin, 2001), 197.

101. Edward L. Ayers, *The Promise of the New South: Life after Reconstruction* (New York: Oxford University Press, 1993), 309.

102. *Id.*

103. *Id.*

104. *Id.*

105. Virginia E. Hench, "The Death of Voting Rights: The Legal Disenfranchisement of Minority Voters," *Case W. Res. L. Rev.* 48 (1998): 735 n. 25.

106. *See* J. Morgan Kousser, *The Shaping of Southern Politics: Suffrage Restriction and the Establishment of the One-Party South, 1880-1910* (New Haven, CT: Yale University Press, 1974), 63.

107. Frederic D. Ogden, *The Poll Tax in the South* (Tuscaloosa: University of Alabama Press, 1958), 51 (quoting Ala. Con. Con. *Proceedings* (1901), vol. 3, p. 3374).

108. Kousser, *The Shaping of Southern Politics*, 63-72.

109. One researcher's statistics indicated that the bottom 76% of the population in 1880 and 1890 averaged only $55 to $64 per person per year. Cash income was extremely limited for agriculturalists in particular. Three-fourths of black farmers

were sharecroppers or tenants by 1900 and saw very little cash at all during the year. *See id.* at 64-65.

110. *Id.*

111. *Id.* at 65.

112. *Id.*

113. *Id.*

114. *Id.*

115. Lane, *The Day Freedom Died,* 5.

116. Kousser, *The Shaping of Southern Politics,* 57-58.

117. *See State of S.C. v. Katzenbach,* 383 U.S. 301, 311 (1966) (citing *Brown v. Bd. of Educ.,* 347 U.S. 483, 489-90 n. 4).

118. Kousser, *The Shaping of Southern Politics,* 58.

119. Benno C. Schmidt Jr., "Principle and Prejudice: The Supreme Court and Race in the Progressive Era. Part 3: Black Disenfranchisement from the KKK to the Grandfather Clause," *Colum. L. Rev.* 82 (1982): 845.

120. *Id.*

121. Kousser, *The Shaping of Southern Politics,* 58.

122. *Id.*

123. H. R. McIlwaine, ed., *Minutes of the Council and General Court of Colonial Virginia* (Richmond: Virginia State Library, 1924) (July 1640), 466.

124. *See* Ayers, *The Promise of the New* South, 149.

125. Kousser, *The Shaping of Southern Politics,* 59 n. 31.

126. *See Williams v. Mississippi,* 170 U.S. 213 (1898).

127. *Id.* at 225.

128. *Id.* at 222.

129. *Id.*

130. 109 U.S. 3 (1883).

131. *Id.*

132. *Id.*

133. *Id.*

134. *See* Fairclough, *Better Day Coming,* 6.

135. *See* Keyssar, *The Right to Vote,* 111-12.

136. *Id.*

137. *See* Hench, "The Death of Voting Rights," 743.

138. Okon Edet Uya, *From Slavery to Public Service: Robert Smalls, 1839-1915* (New York: Oxford University Press, 1971), 2-3.

139. Edward A. Miller Jr., *Gullah Statesman: Robert Smalls from Slavery to Congress, 1839-1915* (Columbia: University of South Carolina Press, 1995), 9.

140. *Id.* In 1861, Smalls was actually the pilot of the steamer, but it was against southern custom to call a black man a pilot.

141. *Id.* at 1.

142. Uya, *From Slavery to Public Service,* 15-16.

143. *Id.* at 12.

144. *Id.* at 20.

145. *Id.* at 20-21.

146. *Id.* at 20.

147. Miller, *Gullah Statesman*, 51.

148. *Id.*

149. *Id.* at 78-79.

150. *Id.* at 114.

151. *Id.* at 115.

152. *Id.*

153. *Id.*

154. James D. Anderson, *The Education of Blacks in the South*, 23.

155. *Id.*

156. *Id.*

157. "Second Lieutenant Henry O. Flipper," Fort Davis National Historic Site, http://www.buffalosoldier.net/HenryO.Flipper2.htm.

158. *Id.*

159. *Id.*

160. *Id.*

161. *Id.*

162. *Id.*

163. *Id.*

164. *Id.*

165. *Id.*

166. *Id.*

167. *Id.*

168. *Id.*

169. *Id.*

170. *Id.*

171. *Id.*

172. *Id.*

173. *Id.*

174. *Id.*

175. *Id.*

176. *Id.*

177. *Id.*

178. 100 U.S. 303 (1879).

179. 92 U.S. 542 (1875).

180. 83 U.S. 36 (1872).

181. PBS Online, "People & Events: Daniel Decatur Emmett, 1815-1904," *American Experience: Stephen Foster,* http://www.pbs.org/wgbh/amex/foster/peopleevents/p_emmett.html.

Chapter 3

1. Qtd. in A. Leon Higginbotham Jr., Gregory A. Clarick, and Marcella David, "*Shaw v. Reno:* A Mirage of Good Intentions with Devastating Racial Consequences," *Fordham L. Rev.* 62 (1994): 1610.

2. Jerrold M. Packard, *American Nightmare: The History of Jim Crow* (New York: St. Martin's, 2002), 42-49.

3. Marianne L. Engelman Lado, "A Question of Justice: African-American Legal Perspectives on the 1883 *Civil Rights Cases,*" *Chi.-Kent L. Rev.* 70 (1995): 1123.

4. Packard, *American Nightmare,* 42-49.

5. *Id.*

6. *Id.*

7. *Id.* at 66.

8. Leon Litwack, *Trouble in Mind: Black Southerners in the Age of Jim Crow* (New York: Knopf, 1998), xiv. *See also* Robert C. Toll, "Behind the Blackface: Minstrel Man and Minstrel Myths," *American Heritage Magazine,* April/May 1978, 93-105, http://www.americanheritage.com/content/behind-blackface; PBS Online, "People & Events: Daniel Decatur Emmett, 1815-1904," *American Experience: Stephen Foster,* http://www.pbs.org/wgbh/amex/foster/peopleevents/p_emmett.html.

9. Toll, "Behind the Blackface."

10. Jim Crow lyrics by Thomas Rice, ca. 1832. *See also* John Strausbaugh, *Black Like You: Blackface, Whiteface, Insult, and Imitation in American Popular Culture* (New York: Penguin, 2006), 59; American RadioWorks, "Behind the Veil: Remembering Jim Crow," October 2001, http://americanradioworks.publicradio.org/features/remembering/transcript.html and http://www.neh.gov/projects/transcripts/behindtheveiltranscript.html.

11. The lyrics are as follows:

> Come listen all you gals and boys
> I's jist from Tuckyhoe,
> I'm goin to sing a little song,
> My name is Jim Crow[.]
> Chorus: Weel about and turn about, and do jis so,
> Eb'ry time I weel about and jump Jim Crow.

For a more complete version with more offensive lyrics, *see* W. T. Lhamon Jr., *Jump Jim Crow: Lost Plays, Lyrics, and Street Prose of the First Atlantic Popular Culture* (Cambridge, MA: Harvard University Press, 2003), 95-102.

12. Alexander Saxton, "Blackface Minstrelsy and Jacksonian Ideology," *Am. Q.* 27, no. 1 (Mar. 1975): 3, 7.

13. Robert B. Winans, "The Folk, the Stage, and the Five-String Banjo in the Nineteenth Century," *Journal of American Folklore* 89, no. 354 (Oct.–Dec. 1976): 407-37.

14. Strausbaugh, *Black Like You*, 144.

15. *Id.* at 61.

16. Saxton, "Blackface Minstrelsy and Jacksonian Ideology," 29.

17. Toll, "Behind the Blackface," 102.

18. *Id.*

19. Jennifer Ritterhouse, "Reading, Intimacy, and the Role of Uncle Remus in White Southern Social Memory," *J. Southern His.* 69, no. 3 (Aug. 2003): 585.

20. Lee Sandlin, *Wicked River: The Mississippi When It Last Ran Wild* (New York: Pantheon, 2010), 176.

21. Stephen Railton, "Blackface Minstrelsy," University of Virginia, http://etext.virginia.edu/railton/huckfinn/minstrl.html.

22. *Id.*

23. Saxton, "Blackface Minstrelsy and Jacksonian Ideology," 17. "For the Jacksonian party the three basic principles of its period ascendancy were: expansion (nationalism), antimonopoly (egalitarianism), and white supremacy." Democrats were founding members of several minstrel companies.

24. Packard, *American Nightmare*, 14.

25. *Id.*

26. *Id.* at 14-15.

27. *Id.*

28. *Id.*

29. *See generally* Douglas A. Blackmon, *Slavery by Another Name: The Re-Enslavement of Black Americans from the Civil War to World War II* (New York: Doubleday, 2008).

30. Packard, *American Nightmare*, 73.

31. 163 U.S. 537 (1896).

32. *Id.*

33. *Id.*

34. Packard, *American Nightmare*, 73.

35. 163 U.S. 537, 538 (1896).

36. *Id.*

37. *Id.*

38. Packard, *American Nightmare*, 74.

39. *Id.*

40. *Id.*

41. *Id.* at 74-75.

42. *Id.* at 75.

43. *Id.*

44. 163 U.S. 537, 550 (1896).

45. David W. Bishop, "*Plessy v. Ferguson:* A Reinterpretation," *Journal of Negro History* 62, no. 2 (Apr. 1977): 125.

46. 163 U.S. 537, 551 (1896).

47. Harry E. Groves, "Separate but Equal: The Doctrine of *Plessy v. Ferguson,*" *Phylon* 12, no. 1 (1st qtr. 1951): 66, 69.

48. *Plessy v. Ferguson,* 163 U.S. 537, 556-57 (dissenting opinion).

49. Groves, "Separate but Equal," 69.

50. *Id.*

51. Lado, "Question of Justice," 1123.

52. Valeria W. Weaver, "The Failure of Civil Rights, 1875-1883, and Its Repercussions," *Journal of Negro History* 54, no. 4 (Oct. 1969): 368.

53. Bishop, "*Plessy v. Ferguson,*" 127.

54. *Id.*

55. *Id.*

56. Groves, "Separate but Equal," 69.

57. *Plessy v. Ferguson,* 163 U.S. 537, 559 (dissenting opinion).

58. Packard, *American Nightmare,* 81.

59. A. Leon Higginbotham Jr., *Shades of Freedom: Racial Politics and Presumptions of the American Legal Process* (New York: Oxford University Press, 1996), 176 (citing William A. Sinclair, *The Aftermath of Slavery: A Study of the Condition and Environment of the American Negro* [University Press, 1905], 187-96).

60. Genna Rae McNeil, *Groundwork: Charles Hamilton Houston and the Struggle for Civil Rights* (Philadelphia: University of Pennsylvania Press, 1985), xvi.

61. Higginbotham, *Shades of Freedom,* 176.

62. Edward L. Ayers, *The Promise of the New South: Life after Reconstruction* (New York: Oxford University Press, 1993), 301-4.

63. *Id.*

64. *Id.*

65. 1898 Wilmington Race Riot Commission, "Wilmington Race Riot: 1898," http://www.ah.dcr.state.nc.us/1898-wrrc/powerpoint/powerpoint.htm.

66. Charles E. Cobb Jr., *On the Road to Freedom: A Guided Tour of the Civil Rights Trail* (Chapel Hill, NC: Algonquin, 2008), 92-93.

67. *Id.*

68. *Id.*

69. *Id.*

70. *Id.*

71. Timothy B. Tyson, "The Ghosts of 1898: Wilmington's Race Riot and the Rise of White Supremacy," (Raleigh, NC) *News & Observer,* Nov. 17, 2006.

72. John J. Dinan, *The Virginia State Constitution: A Reference Guide* (Westport, CT: Praeger, 2006), 29 n. 99.

73. F. Michael Higginbotham, "Hard-Won Victory Must Be Secured," *Baltimore Sun,* Aug. 7, 2005, C5.

74. J. Morgan Kousser, *The Shaping of Southern Politics: Suffrage Restriction and the Establishment of the One-Party South, 1880-1910* (New Haven, CT: Yale University Press, 1974), 58-62; Barret Kaubisch, "The Grandfather Clause," Blackpast.org, http://www.blackpast.com/?q=aah/grandfather-clause-1898-1915.

75. Kousser, *The Shaping of Southern Politics*, 58-62.

76. *Id.*

77. *Id.*

78. *See* Rayford W. Logan, *The Betrayal of the Negro: From Rutherford B. Hayes to Woodrow Wilson* (Cambridge, MA: Da Capo Press, 1997) (1965).

79. George Sinkler, *The Racial Attitudes of American Presidents: From Abraham Lincoln to Theodore Roosevelt* (New York: Doubleday, 1971), 227.

80. *Id.*

81. R. Logan, *The Betrayal of the Negro*, 360.

82. *Id.*

83. *Id.* at 361 (quoting A. Walters, *My Life and Work* [1917], 257).

84. *Id.*

85. *Id.*

86. William Barlow, *Voice Over: The Making of Black Radio* (Philadelphia: Temple University Press, 1999), 3.

87. *See generally* Christopher Silver, "The Racial Origins of Zoning in American Cities." In *Urban Planning and the African American Community: In the Shadows,* June Manning Thomas and Marsha Ritzdorf, eds. (Thousand Oaks, CA: Sage, 1997). http://www.asu.edu/courses/aph294/total-readings/silver%20—%20oracialoriginsofzoning.pdf.

88. *Id.*

89. *Id.*

90. Franklin Johnson, *The Development of State Legislation concerning the Free Negro* (New York: Arbor Press, 1918), 199.

91. *See* Thomas L. Philpott, *The Slum and the Ghetto: Neighborhood Deterioration and Middle-Class Reform, Chicago 1880-1930* (New York: Oxford University Press, 1978), 146-47.

92. Prior to 1910, San Francisco had passed a residential segregation ordinance that required all Chinese inhabitants to move from whatever area they lived in to a designated section of the city. However, the ordinance was invalidated on what appeared to be both equal protection and due process grounds. *See In re Lee Sing,* 43 F. 359 (N.D. Cal. 1890).

93. Baltimore, Md., Ordinance 692 (May 25, 1911). Two prior ordinances, Ordinance 610 of December 19, 1910, and Ordinance 654 of April 7, 1911, had been nominally revised. *See* Garrett Power, "Apartheid Baltimore Style: The Residential Segregation Ordinances of 1910-1913," *Md. L.Rev.* 42 (1983): 300-305.

94. *See generally,* Power, "Apartheid Baltimore Style." *See also* Petition to the Mayor and City Council, Baltimore City Archives, Mahool Files, File 406 (July 5, 1910).

95. *See* W. Ashbie Hawkins, "A Year of Segregation in Baltimore," *Crisis* 3 (1911): 28; Power, "Apartheid Baltimore Style," 298-300.

96. *Id.*

97. Hawkins, "A Year of Segregation in Baltimore," 28.

98. *Id. See also* Petition to the Mayor and City Council.

99. *See* Baltimore, Md., Ordinance 610 (Dec. 19, 1910), in Power, "Apartheid Baltimore Style."

100. *See* Power, "Apartheid Baltimore Style," 305.

101. *Id. See also* Baltimore, Md., Ordinance 692 (May 15, 1911), in Power, "Apartheid Baltimore Style."

102. *Id.*

103. *See generally* Michael Jones-Correa, "The Origins and Diffusion of Racial Restrictive Covenants," *Political Science Quarterly* 115, no. 4 (Winter 2000-2001): 541-68.

104. *American Heritage Dictionary*, 3rd ed., s.v. "ghetto." "Ghetto" means "[a] section of a city [or larger area] occupied by a minority group who live there especially because of social, economic, or legal pressure." Consequently, the connotation is not necessarily a reference to an area of substandard housing or to a "slum."

105. Stewart E. Tolnay, Robert M. Adelman, Kyle D. Crowder, "Race, Regional Origin, and Residence in Northern Cities at the Beginning of the Great Migration," *Am. Soc. Rev.* 67, no. 3 (June 2002): 456.

106. George Lipsitz, "The Possessive Investment in Whiteness: Racialized Social Democracy and the 'White' Problem in American Studies," *Am. Q.* 47, no. 3 (Sept. 1995): 369-87.

107. Tolnay, Adelman, and Crowder, "Race, Regional Origin, and Residence in Northern Cities at the Beginning of the Great Migration," 456.

108. *Id.* at 457.

109. Lipsitz, "The Possessive Investment in Whiteness," 373.

110. Michael Jones-Correa, "The Origins and Diffusion of Racial Restrictive Covenants," 561-63.

111. Kenneth T. Jackson, *The Ku Klux Klan in the City: 1915-1930* (New York: Oxford University Press, 1967).

112. Susan Olzak and Suzanne Shanahan, "Racial Policy and Racial Conflict in the Urban United States, 1869-1924," *Soc. Forces* 82, no. 2 (Dec. 2003): 481-571.

113. Michael Jones-Correa, "The Origins and Diffusion of Racial Restrictive Covenants," 541. A "racial restrictive covenant" is a "private agreement[] barring non-Caucasians from occupying or owning property."

114. *Id.* at 548.

115. *See generally* Michael Jones-Correa, "The Origins and Diffusion of Racial Restrictive Covenants."

116. Jeanine Bell, "The Fair Housing Act and Extralegal Terror," *Indiana Law Review* 41, no. 3 (2008): 537-53.

117. James W. Loewen, *Sundown Towns: A Hidden Dimension of American Racism* (New York: New Press, 2005), 3.

118. *Id.* at 173.

119. *Id.* at 95.

120. John Hope Franklin, *From Slavery to Freedom: A History of Negro Americans*, 6th ed. (New York: Random House, 1988), 207-11.

121. *Id.*

122. *Id.*

123. *Id.*

124. Michelle Connolly, "Human Capital and Growth in the Postbellum South: A Separate but Unequal Story," *Journal of Economic History* 64, no. 2 (June 2004): 363.

125. Louis R. Harlan, *Separate and Unequal: Public School Campaigns and Racism in the Southern Seaboard States, 1901-1915* (Chapel Hill: University of North Carolina Press, 1958), 13.

126. Brett Gadsden, "'He Said He Wouldn't Help Me Get a Jim Crow Bus': The Shifting Terms of the Challenge to Segregated Public Education, 1950-1954," *Journal of African American History* 90, no. 1/2 (Winter 2005): 9-28; V. P. Franklin, "*Brown v. Board of Education:* Fifty Years of Educational Change in the United States, 1954-2004," *Journal of African American History* 90, no. 1/2 (Winter 2005): 1-8.

127. *Id.*

128. *Id.* at 13.

129. *Id.*

130. *Id.* at 14-15.

131. *Id.* at 15.

132. James D. Anderson, *The Education of Blacks in the South, 1860-1935* (Chapel Hill: University of North Carolina Press, 1988), 192.

133. Pamela Barnhouse Walters, David R. James, Holly J. McCammon, "Citizenship and Public Schools: Accounting for Racial Inequality in Education in the Pre- and Post-Disfranchisement South," *Am. Soc. Rev.* 62, no. 1 (Feb. 1997): 34.

134. Anderson, *The Education of Blacks in the* South, 193.

135. Stephan Thernstrom and Abigail Thernstrom, *America in Black and White: One Nation, Indivisible* (New York: Touchstone, 1997), 39.

136. *Id.*

137. *See Cumming v. County Board of Education,* 175 U.S. 528 (1899); *Gong Lum v. Rice,* 275 U.S. 78 (1927); *Gaines v. Canada,* 305 U.S. 337 (1938).

138. *See Milliken v. Bradley,* 418 U.S. 717 (1974).

139. *Id.*

140. Janell Byrd-Chichester, "The Federal Courts and Claims of Racial

Discrimination in Higher Education," *Journal of Negro Education* 69, no. 1/2 (Winter/Spring 2000): 12-26; Walter R. Allen, Robert Teranishi, Gniesha Dinwiddie, and Gloria Gonzalez, "Knocking at Freedom's Door: Race, Equity, and Affirmative Action in U.S. Higher Education," *Journal of Public Health Policy* 23, no. 4 (2002): 440-52.

141. Aldon Morris, Walter Allen, David Maurrasse, and Derrick Gilbert, "White Supremacy and Higher Education: The Alabama Higher Education Desegregation Case," 14 *Nat'l Black L.J.* 14 (Fall 1995): 74.

142. *Id.*

143. Bill Weaver and Oscar C. Page, "The Black Press and the Drive for Integrated Graduate and Professional Schools," *Phylon* 43, no. 1 (1982).

144. Janell Byrd-Chichester, "The Federal Courts and Claims of Racial Discrimination in Higher Education," 12.

145. Faustine Childress Jones-Wilson, et al., eds., *Encyclopedia of African-American Education* (Westport, CT: Greenwood, 1996), 492.

146. *Id.*

147. Rufus E. Clement, "Racial Integration in the Field of Sports," *Journal of Negro Education* 23, no. 3 (Summer 1954): 222.

148. "Benjamin O. Davis," *Air and Space Power Journal*, http://www.airpower. maxwell.af.mil/airchronicles/cc/davis.html. *See also* Kennedy Hickman, "World War II: General Benjamin O. Davis, Jr.," about.com, http://militaryhistory.about. com/od/WorldWarIIAces/p/World-War-Ii-General-Benjamin-O-Davis-Jr.htm.

149. *Id.*

150. *Id.*

151. Benjamin O. Davis Jr., *Benjamin O. Davis, Jr., American: An Autobiography* (New York: Plume, 1992), 27.

152. Frank E. G. Weil, "The Negro in the Armed Forces," *Soc. Forces* 26 (1947-1948): 95.

153. *Id.*

154. "Benjamin O. Davis."

155. *Id.*

156. *See* Vance O. Mitchell, *Air Force Officers: Personnel Policy Development, 1944-1974* (Washington, DC: U.S. Government Printing Office, 1996), 323.

157. *See* Mitchell, *Air Force Officers*, 324; Kenneth L. Karst, "The Pursuit of Manhood and Desegregation of the Armed Forces," *UCLA L. Rev.* 38 (1991): 512, 518.

158. Mitchell, *Air Force Officers*, 324.

159. Richard Dalfiume, *Desegregation of the U.S. Armed Forces: Fighting on Two Fronts, 1939-1953* (Columbia: University of Missouri Press, 1969), 44.

160. *Id.*

161. *Id.*

162. *Id.* at 44-47.

163. Mitchell, *Air Force Officers*, 320-23.

164. *Id.*

165. *See* Dalfiume, *Desegregation of the U.S. Armed Forces*, 71. The army never came near its own policy of enlisting enough black men to meet its own self-imposed 10% guideline. *See id* at 46. In fact, the draft boards began to turn away black volunteers because there were not enough segregated facilities or divisions for minorities. *See id.* at 71.

166. Dalfiume, *Desegregation of the U.S. Armed Forces*, 97.

167. *See* Mary Frances Berry and John W. Blassingame, *Long Memory: The Black Experience in America* (New York: Oxford University Press, 1982), 324. For example, the Air Corps had planned to institute a policy similar to that of the army, whereby it would assign the few black officers in its ranks to posts in Africa. Generally, these posts were not involved in combat. Accordingly, the Air Corps was to assign the all-black 99th Fighter Squadron to patrol missions on the west coast of Africa. These plans were abandoned, however, when the invasion of North Africa in November 1942 created a sudden demand for more fighters. *See* Mitchell, *Air Force Officers*, 326.

168. *See* Mitchell, *Air Force Officers*, 326.

169. "Eugene Jacques Bullard," National Museum of the U.S. Air Force, http://www.nationalmuseum.af.mil/factsheets/factsheet.asp?id=705.

170. Jamie H. Cockfield, "All Blood Runs Red," *Legacy: A Supplement to American Heritage*, February/March 1995, 7-15.

171. *Id.* at 12.

172. *Id.*

173. William I. Chivalette, "Corporal Eugene Jacques Bullard: First Black American Fighter Pilot," *Air and Space Power Journal*, http://www.airpower.maxwell.af.mil/apjinternational/apj-s/2005/3tri05/chivaletteeng.html.

174. *Id.*

175. *Id.*

176. *Id.*

177. Jamie H. Cockfield, *All Blood Runs Red*, 12.

178. Craig Lloyd, *Eugene Bullard: Black Expatriate in Jazz-Age Paris* (Athens: University of Georgia Press 2000), 60-61.

179. John Hope Franklin and Evelyn Brooks Higginbotham, *From Slavery to Freedom: A History of African Americans* (New York: McGraw Hill, 2010), 307.

180. Blackmon, *Slavery by Another Name*, introduction.

181. *Id.*

182. Franklin and Higginbotham, *From Slavery to Freedom*, 307.

183. *Id.*

184. Lado, "A Question of Justice," 1124.

185. *See generally* Stewart E. Tolnay, "The African American Great Migration and Beyond," *Annual Review of Sociology* 29 (2003): 209-32.

186. *Id.*

187. *Id.*

188. *Id.*

189. *Id.* at 214-15.

190. *See generally* Stewart E. Tolnay, "The African American Great Migration and Beyond," 209.

191. *Id.*

192. *Id.*

193. *Id.*

194. *Id.*

195. *Id.*

196. *Id.*

197. *Id.*

198. John Hope Franklin, *From Slavery to Freedom* (6th ed.), 305.

199. *Id.*

200. *Id.* at 307.

201. *Id.*

202. *Id.* at 306.

203. *Id.* at 307.

204. *Id.* at 279.

205. *Id.* at 305.

206. *Id.* at 305-7.

207. *Id.* at 256, 260-61.

208. *Id.* at 256.

209. *Id.* at 257.

210. *Id.* at 419-20.

211. *Id.* at 351.

212. *Id.* 351-59.

213. *Id.* at 342, 352.

214. *Id.*

215. *Id.*

216. Paul Robeson Jr., *The Undiscovered Paul Robeson: An Artist's Journey, 1898-1939* (Hoboken, NJ: Wiley, 2001), 111; *see also* H.B.R., "In Memoriam: Paul Robeson (April 9, 1898-January 23, 1976)," *Phylon* 37, no. 1 (1976): v-vi.

217. H.B.R., "In Memoriam: Paul Robeson."

218. Robeson, *The Undiscovered Paul Robeson*, 71-72.

219. *Id.*

220. Charles M. Christian, *Black Saga: The African American Experience; A Chronology* (New York: Houghton Mifflin, 1995), 320.

221. Michael J. Klarman, *From Jim Crow to Civil Rights: The Supreme Court and the Struggle for Racial Equality* (New York: Oxford University Press, 2004), 109.

222. John Hope Franklin, *From Slavery to Freedom* (6th ed.), 352.

223. David Levering Lewis, *W. E. B. Du Bois: The Fight for Equality and the American Century, 1919-1963* (New York: Henry Holt, 2000), 326.

224. *Id.*

225. United States Census Bureau, Census of Housing, http://www.census.gov/hhes/www/housing/census/historic/values.html.

226. Ira Katznelson, *When Affirmative Action Was White: An Untold History of Racial Inequality in Twentieth-Century America* (New York: Norton, 2005).

227. *See generally* Edward Humes, "How the GI Bill Shunted Blacks into Vocational Training," *J. Blacks in Higher Educ.*, no. 53 (Autumn 2006).

228. *Id.*

229. *Id.*

230. *Id.*; *See also* Hilary Herbold, "Never a Level Playing Field: Blacks and the GI Bill," *J. Blacks in Higher Educ.*, no. 6 (Winter 1994-1995): 104.

231. Meizhu Lui, Bárbara Robles, Betsy Leondar-Wright, Rose Brewer, and Rebecca Abramson, with United for a Fair Economy, *The Color of Wealth: The Story behind the U.S. Racial Divide* (New York: New Press, 2006), 92.

232. *Id.* at 22.

233. Harold D. Woodman, "Sequel to Slavery: The New History Views the Postbellum South," *J. Southern His.* 43, no. 4 (Nov. 1977): 523.

234. Leon Litwack, *Trouble in Mind: Black Southerners in the Age of Jim Crow* (New York: Knopf, 1998), 122.

235. *Id.*

236. *Id.*

237. *Id.*

238. *Id.*

239. Woodman, "Sequel to Slavery," 530.

240. Lui, Robles, Leondar-Wright, Brewer, and Abramson, *The Color of Wealth*, 8.

241. *Id.*

242. Kenneth L. Shropshire, *In Black and White: Race and Sports in America* (New York: New York University Press, 1996), 27.

243. *Id.*

244. Dexter Rogers, "Kentucky Derby Aftermath: How African-American Dominance Was Derailed by Race," *African-American Sports Examiner*, May 4, 2010, http://www.examiner.com/x-17321-AfricanAmerican-Sports-Examiner~y2010m5d4-Kentucky-Derby-Aftermath-How-AfricanAmerican-dominance-was-derailed-by-race.

245. *Id.*

246. The Jockey Club was the governing body of professional horse racing. It mandated that all jockeys be licensed.

247. *Id.* at 28.

248. *Id.*

249. Johnson was the first black to win the heavyweight boxing championship of the world. He held that title from 1910 to 1915.

250. One of the finest heavyweights in history, James J. Jeffries was the heavyweight champion of the world from 1899 until his retirement in 1905. He retired undefeated but six years later was coaxed into an ill-fated comeback fight with Jack Johnson. He was dubbed the "Great White Hope" by sportswriters. *See* "James J. Jeffries," International Boxing Hall of Fame, http://www.ibhof.com/jeffries.htm.

251. Shropshire, *In Black and White: Race and Sports in America*, 28.

252. *See e.g.*, Tex. Penal Code art. 614 § 11(f) (1933), which prohibited "boxing, sparring or wrestling contest or exhibition between any person of the Caucasian or 'White' race and one of the African or 'Negro' race."

253. *See generally* Clement, "Racial Integration in the Field of Sports," 222.

254. Al-Tony Gilmore, "Jack Johnson and White Women: The National Impact," *Journal of Negro History* 58, no. 1 (Jan. 1973).

255. *Id.*

256. *Id.*

257. *Id.*

258. *Id.*

259. *Id.*

260. *Id.*

261. *Id.*

262. Ken Burns, *Unforgivable Blackness: The Rise and Fall of Jack Johnson* (PBS 2005).

263. B. Lauderdale, "Allensworth Comes Back," *American Legacy*, Fall 1996, 18-21.

264. *Id.*

265. *Id.*

266. Franklin and Higginbotham, *From Slavery to Freedom*, 309.

267. *Id.*

268. Nathan Aaseng, *Black Inventors* (Facts on File, 1997), 87-99.

269. Edward S. Jenkins, "Impact of Social Conditions: A Study of the Works of American Black Scientists and Inventors," *Journal of Black Studies* 14, no. 4 (June 1984): 477.

270. *Id.*

271. *Id.*

272. *Id.*

273. *Id.*

274. *Id.*

275. *Id.*

276. *Id.*

277. *Id.*

278. *Id.*

279. *Id.*

280. *Id.*

281. *Id.*

282. *Id.*

283. *Id.*

284. *Id.*

285. Karen Hudson and Paul R. Williams, *Architect: A Legacy of Style* (New York: Rizzoli International, 2000).

286. *Id.*

287. *Id.*

288. *Id.*

289. *Id.*

290. *Id.*

291. *See generally* Mary Ann Ayd, "Almost a Miracle," *Dome* 54 (Feb. 2003). *See also* Katie McCabe, "Like Something the Lord Made," *Washingtonian,* August 1989, 108-11, 226-33, http://pdf.washingtonian.com/pdf/mccabe.pdf.

292. *Id.*

293. *Id.*

294. *Id.*

295. *Id.*

296. *Id.*

297. *Id.*

298. *Id.*

299. *Id.*

300. *Id.*

301. *Id.*

302. *Id.*

303. *Id.*

304. Daniel S. Davis, *Mr. Black Labor: The Story of A. Philip Randolph, Father of the Civil Rights Movement* (New York: Dutton, 1972), 70-71.

305. *Id.*

306. *Id.*

307. *Id.*

308. *Id.*

309. *Id.*

310. Interview with Troy Brown, Senator, Maryland State Senate, Special Collections Dept., University of Baltimore Library (July 2, 1986), 5.

311. Michael F. Blevins, "Restorative Justice, Slavery, and the American Soul: A Policy-Oriented Intercultural Human Rights Approach to the Question of Reparations," 31 *T. Marshall L. Rev.* 31 (2006): 269.

312. Jerome H. Skolnick, "American Interrogation: From Torture to Trickery."

In *Torture: A Collection*, Sanford Levinson, ed. (New York: Oxford University Press, 2004), 105.

313. David M. Oshinsky, *"Worse Than Slavery": Parchman Farm and the Ordeal of Jim Crow Justice* (New York: Free Press, 1996), 21.

314. *Id.* at 69.

315. *Id.* at 74.

316. *Id.* at 60.

317. *Id.*

318. *Id.*

319. *Id.*

320. *Id.*

321. *Id.* at 60.

322. *Id.* at 137.

323. *Id.*

324. *Id.*

325. *Id.* at 143-45.

326. *Id.*

327. *Id.* at 148.

328. *See generally id.* at 179-204.

329. *Id.* at 190.

330. *See generally id.* at 179-204.

331. *Id.*

332. *Id.*

333. *Id.*

334. Loren Miller, *The Petitioners: The Story of the Supreme Court of the United States and the Negro* (New York: Pantheon, 1966), 333. *See generally* José F. Anderson, *Genius for Justice: Charles Hamilton Houston and the Reform of American Law* (Durham, NC: Carolina Academic Press, 2013).

335. Miller, *The Petitioners*, 333.

336. Genna Rae McNeil, *Groundwork: Charles Hamilton Houston and the Struggle for Civil Rights* (Philadelphia: University of Pennsylvania Press, 1983), 143.

337. *Id.*

338. *Id.*

339. *Id.*

340. *Id.*

341. *Id.* at 150.

342. *Id.*

343. *Gaines*, 305 U.S. at 353 (1938).

344. *Id.*

345. *Id.* at 352.

346. *See generally* Weaver and Page, "The Black Press," 15.

347. Sherrilyn A. Ifill, *On the Courthouse Lawn: Confronting the Legacy of Lynching in the Twenty-First Century* (Boston: Beacon, 2007), 16.

348. *Id.*

349. *Id.*

350. *Id.*

351. *Id.*

352. *Id.*

353. The facts of this event are taken from James Cameron, *A Time of Terror: A Survivor's Story* (Baltimore, MD: Black Classic Press, 1982), and also reported in James Madison, *A Lynching in the Heartland: Race and Memory in America* (New York: Palgrave MacMillan, 2001), and Alan D. Wright, *The God Moment Principle* (Colorado Spring, CO: Multnomah Publishers, 1999). Cameron turned his energies toward education and social justice. Over several decades of work, in the 1940s and 1950s, he opened four NAACP chapters in Indiana. In 1988, he founded the Black Holocaust Museum in Milwaukee to document slavery and lynching in America.

354. *See generally* Cameron, *A Time of Terror.*

355. *Id.*

356. *Id.*

357. *Id.*

358. *Id.*

359. *Id.*

360. *Id.*

361. *Id.*

362. *Id.*

363. *Id.*

364. *Id.*

365. *Id.*

366. *Id.*

367. *Id.*

368. *Id.*

369. *Id.*

370. *Id.*

371. *Id.*

372. *Id.*

373. *Id.*

374. *Id.*

375. *Id.*

376. *Id.*

377. *Id.*

378. Ben Green, *Before His Time: The Untold Story of Harry T. Moore, America's First Civil Rights Martyr* (New York: Free Press, 1999), 3-11.

379. *Id.* at 12.

380. *Id.*

381. *Id.* at 127.

382. *Id.* at 137.

383. *Id.*

384. *Id.* at 141-44.

385. *Id.*

386. *Id.* at 195.

387. 163 U.S. 537 (1896).

388. *See* Warren B. Hunting, "The Constitutionality of Race Distinctions and the Baltimore Negro Segregation Ordinance," *Colum. L. Rev.* 11 (1911): 24; Garrett Power, "Apartheid Baltimore Style: The Residential Segregation Ordinances of 1910-1913," *Md. L. Rev.* 42 (1983): 310.

389. Jenkins, "Impact of Social Conditions: A Study of the Works of American Black Scientists and Inventors," 477.

390. Mary Ann Ayd, "Almost a Miracle," *Dome* 54, no. 1 (Feb. 2003).

391. *Gaines,* 305 U.S. 337 (1938).

Chapter 4

1. Qtd. in Keith Reeves, *Voting Hopes or Fears? White Voters, Black Candidates, and Racial Politics in America* (New York: Oxford University Press, 1997).

2. 347 U.S. 483 (1954).

3. Bernard Schwartz, *Super Chief: Earl Warren and His Supreme Court; A Judicial Biography* (New York: New York University Press, 1984), 112-13.

4. *Id.* at 655 n. 60.

5. *See* James T. Patterson, *Brown v. Board of Education: A Civil Rights Milestone and Its Troubled Legacy* (New York: Oxford University Press, 2001), 81.

6. *See Briggs v. Elliott,* 342 U.S. 350 (1952).

7. 347 U.S. 483 (1954).

8. *Id.*

9. *Brown v. Board of Education of Topeka,* 349 U.S. 294 (1955).

10. *Id.* at 493.

11. 163 U.S. 537 (1896).

12. 347 U.S. 483, 495 (1954).

13. *Id.* at 494.

14. 349 U.S. 294 (1955).

15. *Id.* at 301.

16. Remarks of Chief Justice Earl Warren at the United States Supreme Court Conference (Dec. 12, 1953). In *The Supreme Court in Conference, 1940-1985: The Private Discussions behind Nearly 300 Supreme Court Decisions,* Del Dickson, ed. (New York: Oxford University Press, 2001), 649.

17. *Id.* at 654.

18. *Id.* at 653.

19. 347 U.S. 483, 494 (1896).

20. *Id.* at 495.

21. *Id.* at 493.

22. *See* Mark Whitman, *Removing a Badge of Slavery: The Record of Brown v. Board of Education* (Princeton, NJ: Markus Wiener, 1993), 280-83.

23. Jack M. Balkin, *What Brown v. Board of Education Should Have Said: The Nation's Top Legal Experts Rewrite America's Landmark Civil Rights Decision* (New York: New York University Press, 2001), 52.

24. *Mayor of Baltimore v. Dawson*, 350 U.S. 877 (1955) (public beaches); *Holmes v. Atlanta*, 350 U.S. 879 (1955) (golf courses); *Gayle v. Browder*, 352 U.S. 903 (1956) (buses). *See* Balkin, *What Brown v. Board of Education Should Have Said,* 9.

25. *See, e.g., Plummer v. Casey*, 148 F. Supp. 326 (S.D. Tex., 1955), aff'd, 240 F.2d 922 (5th Cir., 1956), cert. denied, 353 U.S. 924 (1957); *Dawley v. Norfolk*, 159 F. Supp. 642 (E.D. Va.), aff'd, 260 F.2d 647 (4th Cir., 1958), cert. denied, 359 U.S. 935 (1959).

26. Whitman. *Removing a Badge of Slavery*, 10-14.

27. *See* Kevin Brown, "The Road Not Taken in *Brown*: Recognizing the Dual Harm of Segregation," *Va. L. Rev.* 90 (2004): 1582.

28. 347 U.S. 483, 494 n. 11 (1954). *See also* K. B. Clark, *Effect of Prejudice and Discrimination on Personality Development*, Fact Finding Report, Mid-century White House Conference on Children and Youth, Children's Bureau, Federal Security Agency, 1950 (parenthetical facts may be useful here to better explain the "doll" reference).

29. 349 U.S. 294 (1955).

30. *See McLaurin v. Oklahoma State Regents for Higher Education*, 339 U.S. 637 (1950); *Sweatt v. Painter*, 339 U.S. 629 (1950); and *Brown v. Board of Education*, 347 U.S. 483 (1954).

31. 349 U.S. 294, 301 (1955).

32. *Id.* at 682.

33. *See Borders v. Rippy*, 188 F. Supp. 231, 232 (N.D. Tex. 1960).

34. 349 U.S. 294, 301 (1955).

35. *Id.* at 300.

36. *Id.*

37. *See* James E. Pfander, "*Brown II*: Ordinary Remedies for Extraordinary Wrongs," *Law & Ineq.* 24 (2006): 49-52 (citing institutional limitations amid predictable opposition from the South among reasons why the Court adopted the "all deliberate speed" standard).

38. Richard Kluger, *Simple Justice: The History of Brown v. Board of Education and Black America's Struggle for Equality* (New York: Vintage Books, 1977), 698.

39. J. W. Peltason, *Fifty-Eight Lonely Men: Southern Federal Judges and School Desegregation* (Champaign: University of Illinois Press, 1971), 55.

40. Lisa Aldred, *Thurgood Marshall* (Langhorne, Pa: Chelsea House, 2004); and Heather Lehr Wagner, *Thurgood Marshall: Supreme Court Justice* (Philadelphia: Chelsea House, 2005), 77.

41. Derrick Bell, *Race, Racism, and American Law*, 4th ed. (New York: Aspen, 2000), 169; Kluger, 132, 155-58, 734-36, 751.

42. *Id.*

43. *See* Bell, *Race, Racism, and American Law*, 169; *Kelly v. Bd. of Educ. of City of Nashville, Davidson County, Tenn.*, 270 F.2d 209 (6th Cir. 1959), cert. denied, 361 U.S. 924 (1959).

44. *Id.*

45. *See* Reynolds Farley and Alma F. Taeuber, "Racial Segregation in the Public Schools," *Am. J. Sociol.* 79, no. 4 (Jan. 1974): 888-905. *The Supreme Court in Conference, 1940-1985: The Private Discussions behind Nearly 300 Supreme Court Decisions*, Del Dickson, ed. (New York: Oxford University Press, 2001), 649.

46. *See* Dickson, ed., *The Supreme Court in Conference*, 665, n. 5; Kathleen A. Bergin, "Authenticating American Democracy," *Pace L. Rev.* 26 (2006): 424.

47. *See* Dickson, *The Supreme Court in Conference*, 649, 652-53.

48. *Id.* at 655.

49. *See* John D. Fassett, *New Deal Justice: The Life of Stanley Reed of Kentucky* (New York: Vantage, 1994), 567.

50. *See* Kluger at 598.

51. *Id.* at 618.

52. *Id.* at 693.

53. *See, e.g., Youngstown Sheet & Tube Co. v. Sawyer*, 343 U.S. 579, 668-69 (1952) (Vinson, C. J., and Reed, Minton, J. J., dissenting).

54. 163 U.S. 537 (1896).

55. *See* Sherrilyn A. Ifill, *On the Courthouse Lawn: Confronting the Legacy of Lynching in the Twenty-First Century* (Boston: Beacon, 2007), ix-xi.

56. Michael J. Klarman, *From Jim Crow to Civil Rights: The Supreme Court and the Struggle for Racial Equality* (New York: Oxford University Press, 2004), 412.

57. *See* Peter H. Irons, *Jim Crow's Children: The Broken Promise of the Brown Decision* (New York: Viking Adult, 2002).

58. Irons, 178-79.

59. *See* Taylor Branch, *Parting the Waters: America in the King Years 1954–1963* (New York: Simon & Schuster, 1988), 380.

60. *See* 102 Cong. Rec. 4515-16 (1956).

61. James O. Eastland, Senator, Address at Senatobia, Mississippi, *Look Magazine*, Apr. 3, 1956, 24.

62. *See generally* John J. Ansbro, *Martin Luther King Jr.: Nonviolent Strategies and Tactics for Social Change* (Madison Books, 2000).

63. Stephan Thernstrom and Abigail Thernstrom, *America in Black and White: One Nation, Indivisible* (New York: Simon & Schuster, 1997).

64. *See* Steven F. Lawson and Charles Payne, *Debating the Civil Rights Movement, 1945-1968*, 2nd ed. (Lanham, MD: Rowman & Littlefield, 2006) (1999).

65. *See* David Bradley and Shelley Fisher Fishkin, *The Encyclopedia of Civil Rights in America* (Armonk, NY: Sharpe Reference, 1998), 411.

66. *See* Clayborne Carson, *In Struggle: SNCC and the Black Awakening of the 1960s* (Cambridge, MA: Harvard University Press, 1981), 1.

67. *Id.* at 31.

68. David Niven, Preface, *The Politics of Injustice: The Kennedys, the Freedom Rides, and the Electoral Consequences of a Moral Compromise* (Knoxville: University of Tennessee Press, 2003), xv.

69. *See* Lawson and Payne, *Debating the Civil Rights Movement*; Roger S. Powers et al., *Protest, Power, and Change: An Encyclopedia of Nonviolent Action from ACT-UP to Women's Suffrage* (New York: Taylor & Francis, 1997), 92.

70. *See* Mary L. Dudziak, *Cold War Civil Rights: Race and the Image of American Democracy* (Princeton, NJ: Princeton University Press, 2000), 158-59.

71. *See* Thomas F. Jackson, *From Civil Rights to Human Rights: Martin Luther King, Jr., and the Struggle for Economic Justice* (Philadelphia: University of Pennsylvania Press, 2007), 18.

72. Robert H. Mayer, *When the Children Marched: The Birmingham Civil Rights Movement* (Berkeley Heights, NJ: Enslow, 2008), 67.

73. *See* Kwame Anthony Appiah and Henry Louis Gates, *Africana: Civil Rights; An A-to-Z Reference of the Movement That Changed America* (Philadelphia: Running Press, 2005), 238.

74. Taylor Branch, *Pillar of Fire: America in the King Years, 1963-1965* (New York: Simon & Schuster, 1999), part 2, pp. 137-39.

75. *See generally* Patrik Henry Bass, *Like a Mighty Stream: The March on Washington, August 28, 1963* (Philadelphia: Running Press, 2003).

76. Rev. Martin Luther King Jr., March on Washington: "I Have a Dream" (Aug. 28, 1963), reprinted in Bass, *Like a Mighty Stream*, 131-35.

77. E. W. Kensworthy, "200,000 March for Civil Rights in Orderly Washington Rally: President Sees Gain for Negro," *New York Times,* Aug. 28, 1963, http://www.nytimes.com/learning/general/onthisday/big/0828.html.

78. *See* David B. Oppenheimer, "Kennedy, King, Shuttlesworth, and Walker: The Events Leading to the Introduction of the Civil Rights Act of 1964," *U.S.F. L. Rev.* 29 (1995): 645.

79. Klarman, *From Jim Crow to Civil Rights*, 389.

80. Another statute stripped any value from mixed-race schools by withholding public funding from desegregated schools, repealing state certification for mixed-race schools, and prohibiting state-run colleges or universities from accepting

graduate certificates from mixed-race high schools. *Orleans Parish Sch. Bd. v. Bush,* 242 F.2d 156 (5th Cir. 1957).

81. *Adkins v. School Bd. of City of Newport News,* 148 F. Supp. 430, 436 (E.D. Va. 1957).

82. *See James v. Almond,* 170 F. Supp. 331 (E.D. Va. 1959).

83. *See* Werner Sollors, *Neither Black nor White Yet Both: Thematic Explorations of Interracial Literature* 21 (Cambridge, MA: Harvard University Press, 1999) (referring to Garth Williams, *The Rabbits' Wedding* [New York: HarperCollins, 1958]).

84. *See, e.g., Brown v. Bd. of Educ. of Topeka, Kan.,* 139 F. Supp. 468, 468-69 (1955). For instance, the district court in Topeka approved of a desegregation plan that required school children to attend neighborhood schools. Even though the schools were inhabited entirely by black students, there was no violation because they were not forced to go to school on the basis of race.

85. *See* Jeffrey A. Raffel, *Historical Dictionary of School Segregation and Desegregation: The American Experience* (Westport, CT: Greenwood, 1998), 203-4.

86. *Carson v. Warlick,* 238 F.2d 724, 728 (4th Cir. 1956), cert. denied, 353 U.S. 910 (1957).

87. By the mid-1950s, at least ten southern states adopted pupil placement laws. Raffel, *Historical Dictionary of School Segregation and Desegregation,* 203.

88. Civil Rights Act of 1964, Pub. L. No. 88-352, 78 Stat. 241 (1964).

89. *Id.*

90. Civil Rights Act of 1964, Pub. L. No. 88-352, 78 Stat. 241 (1964).

91. *See* United States, Revised Statement of Policies for School Desegregation Plans under Title VI of the Civil Rights Act of 1964, December 1966, as Amended for the School Year 1967-68 (Department of Education, 1966).

92. Elementary and Secondary Education Act, Pub. L. 89-10, 79 Stat. 27, 20 U.S.C. ch.70 (1965).

93. The Voting Rights Act of 1965 worked in tandem with education-based legislation to encourage school improvements as well as desegregation by wresting local political control in the South away from white segregationists. The act prohibited racial discrimination in voting, authorized the attorney general to initiate voting rights claims, and required southern states to obtain the approval of the attorney general or a federal district court before implementing any change in a voting requirement or procedure that could be used to disenfranchise black voters. As a result, a record number of blacks were elected to public office, including school boards that made desegregation a priority.

94. *See Green v. New Kent County,* 391 U.S. 430.

95. *See* Lawson and Payne, *Debating the Civil Rights Movement,* 92.

96. Voting Rights Act of 1965, 42 U.S.C. § 1973-1973 aa-6 (2010).

97. *See* Tomiko Brown-Nagin, "Toward a Pragmatic Understanding of Status-Consciousness: The Case of Deregulated Education," 50 *Duke L. J.* 50 (2000): 844-45.

98. *See* Thomas Baldino and Kyle Krieder, *Of the People, by the People, for the People: A Documentary Record of Voting Rights and Electoral Reform* (ABC-CLIO, 2010), 303; Kai Wright, *The African American Experience: Black History and Culture through Original Speeches, Letters, Editorials, Poems, Songs, and Stories* (London: Black Dog, 2009), 554.

99. *Id.*

100. Reeves, *Voting Hopes or Fears,* 5.

101. *See* Albert K. Karnig and Susan Welch, *Black Representation and Urban Policy* (Chicago: University of Chicago Press, 1980), 7. The total number of registered black voters in Alabama, Georgia, Louisiana, Mississippi, South Carolina, and Virginia increased from 918,500 in 1964 to 1,617,000 in 1968. *Id.* at 5 tbl.4.

102. *Shuttlesworth v. Birmingham Bd. of Educ. of Jefferson County, Ala.,* 162 F. Supp. 372, 374 (N.D. Ala. 1958). In Charlotte, North Carolina, three blacks were placed in white schools in 1957, four in 1958, and only one in 1959. In Alabama, only one black student was placed in a white school until he decided to transfer amid threats and intimidation. It was not until the 1960s that federal courts began to respond forcefully to pupil placement laws that produced only token levels of mixed-race student assignments. *See Green v. Sch. Bd. of City of Roanoke, Va.,* 304 F.2d 118 (4th Cir. 1962).

103. *See* J. Harvie Wilkinson, *From Brown to Bakke: The Supreme Court and School Integration, 1954-1978* (New York: Oxford University Press, 1979), 95.

104. *See* Klarman, *From Jim Crow to Civil Rights,* 359.

105. *See Goss v. Board of Edu. of Knoxville,* 83 S.Ct 1405 (1963), where the Supreme Court found that a Knoxville desegregation plan allowing such "minority-to-majority" transfers violated the constitutional requirement of a nondiscriminatory public school system mandated by *Brown.*

106. Michael J. Klarman, *Brown v. Board of Education and the Civil Rights Movement* (New York: Oxford University Press, 2007), 118. Because of the threat of violence, "in Texas, only 1 black student out of 1,229 who were eligible attended a desegregated school in Amarillo; 6 out of 2,111 in Lubbock; and 31 out of 1,100 in Austin. . . . In 1957, every black parent in Nashville who registered a child in a white school received a threatening call from the Klan." *Id.*

107. *See Kelley v. Bd. of Educ. of City of Nashville, Davidson County, Tenn.,* 361 U.S. 924 (1959), denying cert. to 270 F.2d 209 (6th Cir. 1959).

108. 347 U.S. 483, 494 (1954).

109. *See* Schwartz, *Super Chief,* 51-53. Step plans were adopted in Texas, Tennessee, Arkansas, Louisiana, Kentucky, Georgia, Virginia, and Maryland.

110. *See* Bell, *Race, Racism, and American Law,* 169.

111. 270 F.2d 209, 225 (6th Cir. 1959).

112. *Griffin v. County School Board of Prince Edward County,* 377 U.S. 218 (1964).

113. *Id.* at 223.

114. *Bradley v. Sch. Bd., City of Richmond, Va.,* 382 U.S. 103, 105 (1965).

115. 377 U.S. 218, 234 (1964).

116. *Id.* at 222. Virginia, like any other state, had no obligation to provide a system of free public education. State and local governments routinely withheld local services rather than comply with forced integration, and the public schools would be no exception. *See, e.g., Hampton v. City of Jacksonville, Fla.,* 304 F.2d 319 (5th Cir. 1962) (declining to hold defendants in contempt for willfully violating injunction precluding racially segregated municipal swimming pools); *Willie v. Harris County, Tex.,* 202 F. Supp. 549 (E.D. Tex. 1962) (stating plaintiffs deserved declaratory and injunctive relief for defendants' operation of segregated public recreational facilities). *See* Patterson, *Brown v. Board of Education: A Civil Rights Milestone,* 142.

117. 391 U.S. 430 (1968).

118. *Green v. County School Board of New Kent County, Va.,* 391 U.S. 430, 433 (1968).

119. *Id.* at 440.

120. *Id.* at 437-38.

121. *Id.* at 439.

122. "Judge Accepts Plan to End Chicago Desegregation Case He Calls Outdated," *New York Times,* Mar. 3, 2004, http://www.nytimes.com/2004/03/03/nyregion/judge-accepts-plan-to-end-chicago-desegregation-case-he-calls-outdated.html.

123. *See Swann v. Charlotte-Mecklenburg Bd. of Educ.,* 402 U.S. 1 (1971).

124. 379 F. Supp. 410 (D. Mass. 1974).

125. *Id.* at 482.

126. *Morgan v. Kerrigan,* 509 F.2d 580, 588 (1974).

127. *See* Charles V. Willie, "Racial Balance or Quality Education?" *Sch. Rev.* 84 (May 1976): 313.

128. Thomas Adams Upchurch, *Race Relations in the United States, 1960-1980* (Westport, CT: Greenwood, 2008), 127.

129. David Frum, *How We Got Here: The 70s, the Decade That Brought You Modern Life (for Better or Worse)* (New York: Basic Books, 2000), 258.

130. Charles J. Ogletree, *All Deliberate Speed: Reflections on the First Half-Century of Brown v. Board of Education* (New York: Norton, 2004), 67-68.

131. J. Anthony Lukas, *Common Ground: A Turbulent Decade in the Lives of Three American Families* (New York: Knopf, 1985), 244.

132. *See* Jack Tager, *Boston Riots: Three Centuries of Social Violence* (Lebanon, NH: University Press of New England, 2001), 207-8, 215.

133. *Id.*

134. Ogletree, *All Deliberate Speed,* 69.

135. *See* Jeremy D. Mayer, *Running on Race: Racial Politics in Presidential Campaigns, 1960-2000* (New York: Random House, 2002), 124.

136. Henry Hampton, Steve Fayer, and Sarah Flynn, *Voices of Freedom: An Oral*

History of the Civil Rights Movement from the 1950s through the 1980s (New York: Bantam Books, 1990), 602.

137. Frum, *How We Got Here*, 258.

138. *Id.* at 259.

139. *Id.*

140. *Id.*

141. *Id.*

142. U.S. Census, 2006-2008 American Community Survey 3-Year Estimates: Boston, Massachusetts, http://factfinder.census.gov. Twenty-three percent of Boston residents are black; 16% are Hispanic.

143. Boston Public Schools at a Glance 2009-2010, No. 17, Feb. 2010, http://www.bostonpublicschools.org/files/BPS%20at%20a%20Glance%2010-0225.pdf. About 25% of Boston's school-age children do not attend public schools. Of Boston's 18,850 total private school students, 37% are white. This is almost three times the percentage of Boston public school attendees who are white (13%) out of 55,560 public school students.

144. 402 U.S. 1 (1971).

145. *United States v. Yonkers Bd. of Educ.*, 624 F. Supp. 1276 (S.D.N.Y. 1985).

146. 624 F. Supp. 1276 (S.D.N.Y. 1985); *see also* "Segregation: Yonkers, New York, Battles Segregation," Law Library, http://law.jrank.org/pages/10116/Segregation-Yonkers-New-York-Battles-Segregation.html [hereinafter "Yonkers Battles Segregation"].

147. 624 F. Supp. 1276 (S.D.N.Y. 1985).

148. *Id.* at 1375, 1428-29.

149. *Yonkers Bd. of Educ. v. United States*, 837 F.2d 1181 (2d Cir. 1987), aff'd 624 F. Supp. 1276 (S.D.N.Y. 1985).

150. Lawrence H. Fuchs, *The American Kaleidoscope: Race, Ethnicity, and the Civic Culture* (Hanover, NH: Wesleyan University Press, 1990), 421.

151. *Id.*

152. Kathleen McGowan with Sasha Abramsky, "Yonkers Race Trap," *City Limits*, Sept. 1, 1998, http://www.citylimits.org/content/articles/viewarticle.cfm?article_id=2459.

153. "Yonkers Battles Segregation."

154. *Id.*

155. *United States v. Yonkers Bd. of Educ.*, 96 F.3d 600 (2d Cir. 1996), vacating 880 F. Supp. 212 (S.D.N.Y. 1995) and 888 F. Supp. 591 (S.D.N.Y. 1995).

156. *United States v. Yonkers Bd. of Educ.*, 984 F. Supp. 687, 694 (S.D.N.Y. 1997).

157. "Yonkers Battles Segregation." *See also* Edward Glenn Goetz, *Clearing the Way: Deconcentrating the Poor in Urban America* (Washington, DC: Urban Institute, 2003), 64-65.

158. Fernanda Sants, "After 27 Years, Yonkers Housing Desegregation Battle

Ends Quietly in Manhattan Court," *New York Times*, May 2, 2007, http://www.nytimes.com/2007/05/02/nyregion/02yonkers.html.

159. United States Department of Justice, Yonkers Settlement Agreement (1997), http://www.justice.gov/crt/edo/documents/yonkersagmt.pdf.

160. *Id.*

161. Sants, "After 27 Years."

162. *See* Ogletree, *All Deliberate Speed*, 263.

163. *See generally* Eric Avila, *Popular Culture in the Age of White Flight: Fear and Fantasy in Suburban Los Angeles* (Berkeley: University of California Press, 2006).

164. 347 U.S. 483 (1954).

165. *See generally* Charles T. Clotfelter, *After Brown: The Rise and Retreat of School Desegregation* (Princeton, NJ: Princeton University Press, 2004).

166. "White Flight," NationMaster.com Encyclopedia, http://www.statemaster.com/encyclopedia/White-flight.

167. *See* James A. Kushner, *Apartheid in America: An Historical and Legal Analysis of Contemporary Racial Segregation in the United States, How. L. J.* 22 (1979): 559.

168. *Id.*

169. *See generally* Gregory D. Squires, *Insurance Redlining: Disinvestment, Reinvestment, and the Evolving Role of Financial Institutions* (Washington, DC: Urban Institute, 1997).

170. Baltimore City Public Schools, "From the Old Order to the New Order: Reasons and Results, 1957-1997," http://lemmel.baltimorecityschools.org/About/History/From_the_Oldorder1.asp.

171. Baltimore City Public Schools, "From the Old Order to the New Order."

172. *See generally* Erica Frankenberg and Chungmei Lee, "Race in American Public Schools: Rapidly Resegregating School Districts," Civil Rights Project, August 2002, http://www.civilrightsproject.ucla.edu/research/deseg/Race_in_American_Public_Schools1.pdf.

173. *Milliken v. Bradley*, 418 U.S. 717 (1974).

174. *Bradley v. Milliken*, 345 F.Supp. 914 (E.D. Mich. 1972).

175. 418 U.S. 717 (1974) (*Milliken I*). (The district court held that the Detroit public school system was racially segregated because of official state action. It further found that a Detroit-only plan was not sufficient to eliminate the dual school system and therefore the decree involved a remedy that went beyond the Detroit school zone limits. The district court stated, "school district lines are simply matters of political convenience and may not be used to deny constitutional rights." The court of appeals approved the metropolitan desegregation plan, which included fifty-three outlying districts, as the only solution to eliminate the dual school system.)

176. *Id.* at 719.

177. *Id.* at 718.

178. *Id.* at 801.

179. *Bradley v. Milliken*, 484 F.2d 215, 249 (6th Cir. 1973).

180. *See Milliken*, 418 U.S. at 746-47.

181. *See* G. Orfield and J. T. Yun, "Resegregation in American Schools," The Civil Rights Project, 1999, http://civilrightsproject.ucla.edu/research/k-12-education/integration-and-diversity/resegregation-in-american-schools.

182. *See* Stephen L. Wasby, *American Government and Politics* (New York: Scribners, 1973), 334.

183. Fair Housing Act (Title VIII of the Civil Rights Act of 1968), Pub. L. No. 90-284, 82 Stat. 73 (1968) (codified as amended at 42 U.S.C. §§ 3601-19 (2010)). *See* Robert G. Schwemm, "Private Enforcement and the Fair Housing Act," *Yale L. & Pol'y Rev.* 6 (1988): 375.

184. The federal Fair Housing Act of 1968 initially exempted privately owned, single-family housing. William Collins, "Fair Housing Laws," EH.Net Encyclopedia (Robert Whaples ed.), Nov. 26, 2004, http://eh.net/encyclopedia/article/collins.fair.housing.

185. As Professor Phyliss Craig-Taylor explains, the Court in *Wards Cove Packaging Co. v. Antonio* decided that employees alleging discriminatory hiring and promoting practices have the burden of proving that the employer's practices had a statistically "disparate impact" on them. 490 U.S. 642, 656 (1989). Phyliss Craig-Taylor, "To Be Free: Liberty, Citizenship, Property, and Race," 14 *Harv. BlackLetter L. J.* 14 (1998): 74-75.

186. *See* Jonathan Kozol, *Savage Inequalities: Children in America's Schools* (New York: Harper Perennial, 1992) (1991), 3; Betsy Levin and Willis D. Hawley, *The Courts, Social Science, and School Desegregation* (Piscataway, NJ: Transaction, 1977), 95-97. The "tipping point" theory is related to that of white flight. Observers have noted that when the black population within a community reaches the point of comprising between 6% and 50% of the total, white flight is more likely to be triggered. The exact percentage differs depending on the intensity of prejudice within the community, among other factors.

187. *See* Matthew D. Lassiter and Joseph Crespino, *The Myth of Southern Exceptionalism* (New York: Oxford University Press, 2009), 29.

188. *See* Mwangi S. Kimenyi, *Economics of Poverty, Discrimination, and Public Policy* (Cincinnati, OH: South-Western College Publishing, 1995), 255.

189. Kenneth B. Clark, *Dark Ghetto: Dilemmas of Social Power* (New York: Harper & Row, 1965), 21-62.

190. *See* Niki Dickerson, "Occupational and Residential Segregation: The Confluence of Two Systems of Inequality," *Labor Studies Journal* 33, no. 4 (December 2008): 393-411.

191. *See, e.g., Griffin*, 77 U.S. 218; *see also, Green*, 391 U.S. 430.

192. *See* Wilkinson, *From Brown to Bakke*, 95.

Chapter 5

1. Justice Ruth Ginsburg dissenting in *Adarand Constructors, Inc. v. Peña,* 515 U.S. 200 (1995).

2. *See generally,* Howard Shuman, *Racial Attitudes in America: Trends and Interpretations* (Cambridge, MA: Harvard University Press, 1997).

3. *See, e.g.,* K. R. Athey, et al., "Two Experiments Showing the Effect of the Interviewer's Racial Background on Responses to Questionnaires concerning Racial Issues," *J. Applied Psych.* 44, no. 4 (Aug. 1960): 244-46.

4. Associated Press, "Boater Rescued from Sea/Sharks," *St. Petersburg Times* (online), Nov. 12, 2005.

5. *Id.*

6. *Id.*

7. *Id.*

8. *Id.*

9. *Id.*

10. Karen Aaiza, "Pool Boots Kids Who Might 'Change the Complexion,'" NBC Philadelphia, July 8, 2009, http://www.nbcphiladelphia.com/news/local-beat/Pool-Boots-Kids-Who-Might-Change-the-Complexion.html?corder=&pg=1.

11. *Id.*

12. *Id.*

13. *Id.*

14. *Id.*

15. *Id.*

16. *Id.*

17. *Id.*

18. *Id.*

19. Mary Rinzel, "Man Posts 'No Negros Allowed' Sign on Future Business," WEAU 13 News, Dec. 6, 2010, http://www.weau.com/news/headlines/Man_posts_No_Negros_Allowed_sign.html.

20. *Id.*

21. Jason B. Johnson, "Black CEOs Gaining in Corporate America," *San Francisco Chronicle,* Feb. 10, 2005.

22. Aaiza, "Pool Kids Who Might 'Change the Complexion.'"

23. 347 U.S. 483 (1954).

24. *See* Civil Rights Act of 1964, Pub. L. No. 88-352, 78 Stat. 241 (1964).

25. U.S. Commission on Civil Rights, *Understanding Fair Housing* (Clearinghouse Publication 42, 1973), 6.

26. *Id.*

27. Richard Carlson, "The Small Firm Exemption and the Single Employer Doctrine in Employment Discrimination Law," *St. John's L. Rev.* 80 (2006): 1197. The U.S. Equal Employment Opportunity Commission, "Federal Laws

Prohibiting Job Discrimination Questions and Answers," http://www.eeoc.gov/facts/qanda.html.

28. Carlson, "The Small Firm Exemption," 1199.

29. John Kimble, "Insuring Inequality: The Role of the Federal Housing Administration in the Urban Ghettoization of African Americans," *Law & Soc. Inquiry* 32 (2007): 422-23.

30. DeWayne Wickham, "Are There Still Two Americas?" *Ebony*, Aug. 2008.

31. *Id.* at 132.

32. *Id.*

33. *Id.*

34. Jerome M. Culp Jr., "To the Bone: Race and White Privilege," *Minn. L. Rev.* 83 (1998): 1637-97.

35. Marc D. Allan, "Bigotry Still Big," *Nuvo*, Feb. 27, 2008.

36. *Id.*

37. President Bill Clinton, "Remarks by the President to the Legal Profession on a New Call to Action," July 20, 1999, http://www.adversity.net/legalnews_clinton072099.htm.

38. Pew Research Center, "Blacks See Growing Values Gap between Poor and Middle Class," Nov. 13, 2007, http://pewsocialtrends.org/assets/pdf/Race.pdf.

39. On February 4, 2007, Tony Dungy became the first African American head coach to win a Super Bowl when he led the Indianapolis Colts to a 29-17 victory over the Chicago Bears. *See* Richard Lapchick, "2010 Racial and Gender Report Card: National Football League," released September 29, 2010, by the Institute for Diversity and Ethics in Sport.

40. Bill Wisdom, "Skepticism and Credulity: Finding the Balance between Type I and Type II Errors," *The Skeptic Encyclopedia of Pseudoscience*, vol. 1 (ABC-CLIO, 2002). 455.

41. *Id.*

42. *Id.*

43. *Id.*

44. Mary Bruce, "Students Improving but Black-White Education Gap Persists," ABC News.com, July 14, 2009.

45. *See generally*, Linda K. Fuller, *The Cosby Show: Audiences, Impact, and Implications* (Westport, CT: Greenwood, 1992).

46. *See* Leda Cosmides, John Tooby, and Robert Kurzban, "Perceptions of Race," *Trends in Cognitive Sci.* 7, no. 4 (April 2003): 173-79; *see also* Beth Roy, *Bitters in the Honey* (Fayetteville: University of Arkansas Press, 1999).

47. *See* Jody Armour, "'Black Tax': The Tithe That Binds," *Los Angeles Times*, Nov. 20, 2005; Jody Armour, *Negrophobia and Reasonable Racism: The Hidden Costs of Being Black in America* (New York: New York University Press, 1997).

48. Richard Wormser, *The Rise and Fall of Jim Crow* (New York: St. Martin's, 2003), 105.

49. L. Scott Miller, *Promoting Sustained Growth in the Representation of African Americans, Latinos, and Native Americas among Top Students in the United States at All Levels of the Education System* (Storrs, CT: National Research Center on the Gifted and Talented, 2004), 5-6.

50. *Id.*

51. "Once Again a Decline in Doctoral Degree Awards to African Americans," *J. Blacks Higher Educ.*, 2010, http://www.jbhe.com.

52. *Id.*

53. Kenneth E. Reid, Data Sources: Aspirations to Graduate School, Council of Graduate Schools, http://www.cgnet.org.

54. *See* Angelia Dickens, "Revisiting *Brown v. Board of Education*: How Tracking Has Resegregated America's Public Schools," *Colum. J. L. & Soc. Probs.* 29 (Summer 1996): 469.

55. *See* John Charles Boger and Gary Orfield, *School Resegregation: Must the South Turn Back?* (Chapel Hill: University of North Carolina Press, 2005).

56. *See id.*

57. Roslyn Arlin Mickelson, "Achieving Equality of Educational Opportunity in the Wake of Judicial Retreat from Race-Sensitive Remedies: Lessons from North Carolina," *Am U. L. Rev.* 52 (2003): 1490.

58. Stanford News Service, "School Tracking Harms Millions, Sociologist Finds," Mar. 2, 1994 (study by Sanford Dornbusch), http://news.stanford.edu/pr/94/940302Arc43.

59. *See* Boger and Orfield, *School Resegregation: Must the South Turn Back?*

60. *See* Charles T. Clotfelter, *After Brown: The Rise and Retreat of School Desegregation* (Princeton, NJ: Princeton University Press, 2004).

61. *Id.* at 472.

62. Advanced Placement Report to the Nation, College Board, 2006, http://www.ecs.org/html/offsite.asp?document=http%3A%2F%2Fwww.collegeboard.com%2Fprod_downloads%2Fabout%2Fnews_info%2Fap%2F2006%2F2006_ap-report-nation.pdf.

63. *See* Graham C. Kinloch, "White Perspectives on Black Americans: A Study of Journal Articles in Professional Sociology," *Phylon* 46 (1985): 319-22.

64. *Id.* at 474.

65. *See* Eric Quinones, "Tracking Political Impact of Racial Disparity in Schools," Princeton University, Apr. 30, 2009, http://www.princeton.edu/main/news/archive/S24/10/99A40/index.xml?section+featured.

66. 539 U.S. 306 (2003).

67. *Id.*

68. *Id.*

69. *Id. See also Comfort v. Lynn School District*, 418 F.3d 1 (1st Cir. 2005) (en banc).

70. 539 U.S. 306, 330 (2003).

71. *Id.*

72. 551 U.S. 701 (2007).

73. *Id.* at 709-10, 720-21. De facto segregation refers to those conditions caused by "housing patterns or generalized societal discrimination." *Id.* at 806 (Breyer, J., dissenting).

74. *Id.* at 710 (plurality opinion).

75. *Id.* at 726.

76. *Id.*

77. *Id.* at 705.

78. *See generally,* Ann LaGrelius Siqueland, *Without a Court Order: The Desegregation of Seattle's Schools* (Seattle: Madrona, 1981).

79. 551 U.S. 701, 868 (2007).

80. *Id.*

81. 551 U.S. 701 (2007).

82. *Id.* at 841-42.

83. *See* Kimberley S. Johnson, *Reforming Jim Crow: Southern Politics and State in the Age before Brown* (New York: Oxford University Press, 2010).

84. Gaston Alonso, *Our Schools Suck: Students Talk Back to a Segregated Nation on the Failures of Urban Education* (New York: New York University Press, 2009), 3.

85. Studies reveal that 34% of black children are in the lowest rung of the socioeconomic ladder, compared to only 9% of white children. Valerie E. Lee and David T. Burkam, *Inequality at the Starting Gate* (Washington, DC: Economic Policy Institute, 2002).

86. *See* Patrick R. Colabella, *The Effect of Public School Districts' Property Values on State Educational Funds* (Ph.D. dissertation, School of Education, St. John's University, 2008).

87. John Rogers, et al., *Free Fall: Educational Opportunities in 2011* (Los Angeles: UCLA IDEA, UC/ACCORD, 2011).

88. Kim Rueben and Sheila Murray, "Racial Disparities in Education Finance: Going beyond Equal Revenues," Tax Policy Center, Nov. 2008, http://www.taxpolicycenter.org/UploadedPDF/411785_EQUAL_REVENUES.pdf.

89. *Id.*

90. *Id.*

91. Julian Betts, Kim S. Rueben, and Anne Danenberg, "Equal Resources, Equal Outcomes? The Distribution of School Resources and Student Achievement in California" (Sacramento: Public Policy Institute of California, 2000).

92. Allyson Dickman, "Maryland Qualified Teacher Gap Is Nation's Largest," Southern Maryland Online, Sept. 14, 2008, http://somd.com/news/headlines/2008/8288.html. A "highly qualified teacher" is considered one who has a bachelor's degree in the subject he or she teaches, a state teacher's certification, and demonstrated knowledge of the subject.

93. *Id.*

94. *See* Hanna Avalon et al., "Diversification and Inequality in Higher Education: A Comparison of Israel and the United States," *Soc. Educ.* 81 (2008): 224.

95. Sam Dillon, "'No Child' Law Is Not Closing a Racial Gap," *New York Times*, Apr. 28, 2009.

96. Ellison S. Ward, "Toward Constitutional Minority Recruitment and Retention Programs: A Narrowly Tailored Approach," *N.Y.U. L. Rev.* 84 (2009): 609.

97. S. Aud, et al. *The Condition of Education 2011* (NCES 2011-033). U.S. Department of Education, National Center for Education Statistics (Washington, DC: U.S. Government Printing Office, 2011), table A-26-2.

98. Gary Orfield and Chungmei Lee, "Racial Transformation and the Changing Nature of Segregation," Civil Rights Project, Jan. 2006, http://www.civilrightsproject.ucla.edu/research/deseg/RacialTransformation.pdf.

99. *Id.*

100. *Milliken v. Bradley*, 418 U.S. 717 (1974).

101. Orfield and Lee, "Racial Transformation."

102. Derrick Bell, *Race, Racism, and American Law*, 3rd ed. (New York: Wolters Kluwer Law & Business, 1995), 659.

103. *Id.* (citing G. Orfield and F. Monfort, *Are American Schools Resegregating in the Reagan Era? A Statistical Analysis of Segregation Levels from 1980 to 1984* [National School Desegregation Project of the University of Chicago Working Papers, Paper No. 14], 7, 10).

104. Gary Orfield, *Brown at 50: King's Dream or Plessy's Nightmare?* (Cambridge, MA: Harvard Civil Rights Project, 2004), 2.

105. Jonathan Kozol, "Still Separate, Still Unequal: America's Educational Apartheid," *Harper's Magazine*, Sept. 1, 2005.

106. *See* Andrew Hacker, *Two Nations: Black and White, Separate, Hostile, Unequal* (New York: Scribners, 1992), 19, 163.

107. Barack Obama, Foreword. In *The State of Black America 2007: Portrait of the Black Male*, Stephanie J. Jones, ed. (New York: National Urban League, 2007), 9-12.

108. *Id.* at 9.

109. *Id.*

110. *Id.* at 10.

111. Thomas M. Shapiro, Tatjana Meschede, and Laura Sullivan, "The Racial Wealth Gap Increases Fourfold," Institute on Assets and Social Policy, May 2010, http://iasp.brandeis.edu/pdfs/Racial-Wealth-Gap-Brief.pdf.

112. Renee Hanson, Mark McArdle, and Valerie Rawlston Wilson, "Invisible Men: The Urgent Problems of Low-Income African-American Males." In *The State of Black America 2007: Portrait of the Black Male*, Stephanie J. Jones, ed. (New York: National Urban League, 2007), 210.

113. *Id.*

114. *Id.*

115. *Id.*

116. "Employment Crisis Worsens for Black Women during the Recovery," National Women's Law Center, Aug. 3, 2011, http://www.nwlc.org/resource/employment-crisis-worsens-black-women-during-recovery.

117. *Id.*

118. U.S. Census Bureau, Current Population Survey, 2010 Annual Social and Economic Supplement, Table POV-07: Families with Related Children under 18 by Number of Working Family Members and Family Structure: 2009, http://www.census.gov/hhes/www/cpstables/032010/pov/toc.htm.

119. Algernon Austin, "Reversal of Fortune: Economic Gains of 1990s Overturned for African Americans from 2000-07," Economic Policy Institute (Briefing Paper), Sept. 18, 2008, 1, http://www.epi.org/publication/bp220.

120. *Id.* at 2, 7.

121. *Id.* at 7-8.

122. *Id.* at 8.

123. *Id.* at 9.

124. For an historical comparison, *see* Lori G. Kletzer, "Job Displacement, 1979-86: How Blacks Fared Relative to Whites," *Monthly Lab. Rev.* 114 (1991): 17.

125. U.S. Dep't of Labor, Bureau of Labor Statistics, "Economic News Release: Table A-2, Employment Status of the Civilian Population by Race, Sex, and Age," 2009, http://www.bls.gov/news.release/empsit.to2.htm.

126. *Id.*

127. Patrick McGeehan and Mathew R. Warren, "Job Losses Show Wider Racial Gap in New York," *New York Times*, July 12, 2009.

128. *Id.*

129. *Id.*

130. *Id.*

131. M. C. Black et al., *The National Intimate Partner and Sexual Violence Survey (NISVS): 2010 Summary Report* (Atlanta, GA: National Center for Injury Prevention and Control, Centers for Disease Control and Prevention, 2011).

132. Bureau of Justice Statistics, "Homicide Trends in the U.S.: Trends in Intimate Homicides." Source: FBI, Supplementary Homicide Reports, 1976-2005., http://bjs.ojp.usdoj.gov/content/homicide/race.cfm.

133. Ansley Hamid, *Drugs in America: Sociology, Economics, and Politics* (Gaithersburg, MD: Aspen, 1998), 216.

134. "Races: America's Rising Black Middle Class," *Time*, June 17, 1974, http://www.time.com/time/magazine/article/0,9171,879319,00.html.

135. "The African American Middle Class," Black Demographics, http://www.blackdemographics.com/middle_class.html.

136. Martin Marger, *Race and Ethnic Relations: American and Global Perspectives* (Belmont, CA: Wadsworth Cengage Learning, 2009), 184.

137. *See* "1945-1950s: Economic Boom, Discrimination," MSNBC, May 27, 2008, http://www.msnbc.msn.com/id/24714312.

138. Ira Katznelson, *When Affirmative Action Was White* (New York: Norton, 2005).

139. F. Michael Higginbotham, "Soldiers for Justice," *Wm & Mary Bill Rts. J.* 8 (2000): 279.

140. *See* "1945-1950s: Economic Boom, Discrimination."

141. William Branigin, "Debt Commission Produces Plan, Schedules Vote for Friday," *Washington Post,* Nov. 30, 2010, http://www.washingtonpost.com/wp-dyn/content/article/2010/11/30/AR2010113004652.html.

142. Brian Faler, "Bennett under Fire for Remark on Crime and Black Abortions," *Wash. Post,* Sept. 30, 2005.

143. Robert M. Entman, et al., *Mass Media and Reconciliation: A Report to the Advisory Board and Staff, the President's Race Initiative* (Washington, DC: 1998), 49.

144. *Id.*

145. *See* Michael J. Klarman, "Is the Supreme Court Sometimes Irrelevant? Race and the Southern Criminal Justice System in the 1940s," *J. Am. His.* 89, no. 1 (June 2002): 119-53.

146. *See* David Harris, "The Stories, the Statistics, and the Law: Why 'Driving While Black' Matters," *Min. L. Rev.* 84 (2000): 265-326.

147. *See* Katheryn Russell-Brown, *The Color of Crime: Racial Hoaxes, White Fear, Black Protectionism, Police Harassment, and Other Macroaggressions,* 2nd ed. (New York: New York University Press, 2008).

148. *See* Jon Meyer and Paul Jesilow, "Research on Bias in Judicial Sentencing," *N.M. L. Rev.* 26 (1996): 107.

149. Associated Press, "Study Shows Racial Disparities in Prison," *USA Today,* July 17, 2007.

150. T. G. Chiricos and W. D. Bales, "Unemployment and Punishment: An Empirical Assessment," *Criminology* 29 (1991): 701–24.

151. Kate Randall, "Voting Rights Denied to 3.9 Million Americans Due to Criminal Convictions," World Socialist Web Site (see wsws.org) Nov. 8, 2000.

152. Garima Malhorta, "Maryland Ends Prison-Based Gerrymandering," Brennan Center for Justice, New York University School of Law, May 4, 2010, http://www.brennancenter.org/blog/archives/maryland_ends_prison-based_gerrymandering.

153. *See id.*

154. Bryan Stevenson Testimony on Criminal Justice and Race, United Nations Special Rapporteur on Racism, May 2008, http://www.eji.org/eji/files/ot.28.08%20UntestimonyonRace.pdf.

155. David Cole, *No Equal Justice: How the Criminal Justice System Uses Inequality* (New York: New Press, 2000).

156. Lynn Hulsey, "Cincinnati Tops List of Police Killings of Blacks," *Dayton Daily News*, Apr. 28, 2001.

157. Heather MacDonald, "The *New York Times* Peddles More 'Driving While Black' Malarkey," *National Review*, Sept. 26, 2005, http://www.manhattan-institute.org/html/_national_rev-reporting.htm.

158. Bryan Stevenson Testimony on Criminal Justice and Race.

159. *Id.*

160. Anti-Drug Abuse Act of 1986, Pub.L. 99-570, 100 Stat. 3207, enacted Oct. 27, 1986.

161. *See* Dan Weikel, "War on Crack Targets Minorities over Whites," *Los Angeles Times*, May 21, 1995, A1, A26.

162. *See* U.S. Sentencing Comm., *Special Report to Congress: Cocaine and Federal Sentencing Policy* (2002), 63.

163. Mandatory Minimum Sentencing Laws: Hearing before the Subcommittee on Crime, Terrorism, and Homeland Security of the Committee on the Judiciary, House of Representatives, 110th Cong., 1st sess., June 26, 2007, 170, http://judiciary.house.gov/hearings/printers/110th/36343.PDF.

164. *See* The Sentencing Project at 3-5, http://www.sentencingproject.org/template/index.cfm.

165. *Id.* at 3.

166. *Id.*

167. Brett Joseph, "Prosecutors Have Too Much Power," *Washington Examiner*, Jan. 22, 2010; Angela J. Davis, *Arbitrary Justice: The Power of the American Prosecutor* (New York: Oxford University Press, 2007).

168. Eric Lotke, "Racial Disparity in the Justice System: More Than the Sum of Its Parts," *Focus*, May–June 2004.

169. *Id.*

170. *Id.*

171. *Id.*

172. *Id.*

173. *Id.*

174. Adrian Walker, "Stuart Case Still Felt," *Boston Globe*, Oct. 21, 2009, http://www.boston.com/news/local/massachusetts/articles/2009/10/23/stuart_case_still_felt.

175. "This Day in History: Susan Smith Reports a False Carjacking to Cover Her Murder," History.com, http://www.history.com/this-day-in-history/susan-smith-reports-a-false-carjacking-to-cover-her-murder.

176. Christopher J. Wilmot, "Another White Criminal Falsely Blames an African American Man," Rochester, NY, *Smugtown Beacon*, May 29, 2009, http://www.smugtownbeacon.com/news.php?viewstory=287.

177. *See* Russell-Brown, *The Color of Crime*.

178. "Police: Washington Woman Admits Acid Attack Was a Hoax," CNN, Sept. 16, 2010.

179. 481 U.S. 279 (1978).

180. *Id.* at 279.

181. David C. Baldus, et al., "Comparative Review of Death Sentences: An Empirical Study of the Georgia Experience," *J. Crim. L. & Crim.* (1983): 661-753.

182. *Id.*

183. 481 U.S. 279.

184. *Id.* at 290.

185. *See id.* at 297.

186. *Id.*

187. American Civil Liberties Union, "The Persistent Problem of Racial Disparities in the Federal Death Penalty," June 2007, http://www.aclu.org/capital/general/30237pub20070625.html.

188. Bryan Stevenson Testimony on Criminal Justice and Race.

189. Anti-Drug Abuse Act of 1986, Pub.L. 99-570.

190. American Civil Liberties Union, "Cracks in the System: Twenty Years of the Unjust Federal Crack Cocaine Law," 2006, http://www.aclu.org/drugpolicy/sentencing/27181pub20061026.html.

191. *Id.*

192. United States Drug Enforcement Administration, "Federal Trafficking Penalties," http://www.justice.gov/dea/agency/penalties.htm.

193. *See id.*

194. *Id.*

195. *Id.*

196. "Crack and Powder: They're Equally Criminal, So Equalizing Sentencing Is Fair," *Daily Press*, Aug. 25, 2008.

197. Elizabeth Merrill, "Gaps in the Road," ESPN, http://sports/espn.go.com/espn/eticket/story?page-090715/aikens.

198. *Id.*

199. Jade Hindmon, "South Carolina Native Released from Federal Prison: Native's Case Helped Overturn Sentencing Guidelines," *Fox News*, June 5, 2008.

200. *Id.*

201. *Id.*

202. *U.S. v. Johnson,* 43 F.3d 1484 (1994).

203. Mary Mitchell, "Did Civil Rights Movement Pass Louisiana By?" *Chicago Sun Times*, Aug. 30, 2007.

204. Gretel C. Kovach and Arian Campo-Flores, "A Town in Turmoil," *Newsweek*, Aug. 20, 2007.

205. Darryl Fears, "La. Town Fells 'White Tree,' but Tension Runs Deep," *Wash. Post*, Aug. 4, 2007.

206. *Id.*

207. *See id.*

208. Doug Simpson, "Jena 6 Teen Released on $45,000 Bail," Associated Press, Sept. 27, 2007.

209. "'Jena Six' Story Gained Momentum Online," *NPR News*, Sept. 24, 2007, http://www.npr.org/templates/story/story.php?storyId=14658077.

210. Howard Witt, "Charges Reduced in 'Jena 6' Case," *Chicago Tribune*, June 26, 2007.

211. Clarence Waldron and Kevin Chappell, "Blacks Cry for Justice in Louisiana Town Rocked by High School Racial Violence," *Jet*, Aug. 20, 2007.

212. *Id.*

213. "5 Defendants Plead No Contest in 'Jena Six' Case," CNN, June 26, 2009.

214. Michael Eric Dyson, "It's Not Only 'The Jena 6,'" *Ebony*, Dec. 2007.

215. *Id.*

216. *See* Ashley Nellis and Ryan S. King, "No Exit: The Expanding Use of Life Sentences in America," Sentencing Project, July 2009.

217. Elizabeth Cauffman, "A Statewide Screening of Mental Health Symptoms among Juvenile Offenders in Detention," *J. Am. Acad. Child Adolesc. Psychiatry* 43, no. 4 (2004): 430–39.

218. "Record Number of Prison Inmates Receive Life Sentences: Report," July 23, 2009, http://www.google.com/hostednews/afp/article/ALeqM5jEKwi19n6s HlApOxfUdY05Pcuojw.

219. Christopher Hartney and Linh Vuong, *Created Equal: Racial and Ethnic Disparities in the U.S. Criminal Justice System*, National Council on Crime and Delinquency, 2009.

220. *Id.*

221. Radley Balko, "Railroaded onto Death Row?" *Fox News*, Feb. 15, 2006.

222. *Id.*

223. *Id.*

224. *Id.*

225. *Id.*

226. *Id.*

227. *Id.*

228. *Id.*

229. *Id.*

230. Miss. Code Ann. 97-3-19 (1972).

231. Balko, "Railroaded Onto Death Row?"

232. *Id.*

233. "Covington Secures Retrial for Former Death Row Inmate," Covington & Burling, LLP, Nov. 19, 2009, http://www.cov.com/news/detail.aspx? news=1474.

234. *Id.*

235. *Maye v. State*, 49 So.3d 1124 (Miss. 2010).

236. Radley Balko, "Cory Maye to Be Released from Prison," *Huffington Post*, July 1, 2011.

237. *Id.*

238. Patty Davis, "Wrongful Convicted Take Center Stage at Death Penalty Forum," Fight the Death Penalty, Nov. 15, 1998, http://www.fdp.dk/uk/released.htm; "Stories of Wrongful Convictions from California," Death Penalty Focus, http://www.deathpenalty.org/article.php?id=407.

239. David M. Rafky, "Racial Discrimination in Urban Police Departments," *Crime & Delinquency* 21, no. 3 (July 1975), http://cad.sagepub.com/content/21/3/233.abstract.

240. American Civil Liberties Union, "The Persistent Problem of Racial Disparities in the Federal Death Penalty," June 25, 2007, http://www.aclu.org/capital/general/30237pub2007.

241. Adam Liptak, "Death Penalty Found More Likely If Victim Is White," *New York Times*, Jan. 8, 2003.

242. Fair Housing Act (Title VIII of the Civil Rights Act of 1968), Pub. L. No. 90-284, 82 Stat. 73 (1968) (codified as amended at 42 U.S.C. §§ 3601-19 (2010)).

243. Http://www.minhousing.gov/idc/secure/documents/admin/mhfa_010263.pdf.

244. *Id.*

245. *Id.*

246. *See* Manning Marable and Kristen Clarke, *Seeking Higher Ground: The Hurricane Katrina Crisis, Race, and Public Policy* (New York: Macmillan, 2008), 273.

247. *Id.* at 273.

248. *Id.* at 275.

249. *Id.* at 265.

250. Thomas Korosec, "Survey Finds Bias in Evacuee Housing," *Houston Chronicle*, Dec. 27, 2005, A1.

251. *Id.*

252. *Id.*

253. *See* Campbell Robertson, "Battle over Low-Income Housing Reveals Post-Katrina Anxiety," *New York Times*, Oct. 4, 2009, A15.

254. *See* Gary Gately, "Man Pleads Guilty to Arson Spree in Maryland," *New York Times*, Apr. 29, 2005.

255. Gately, "Man Pleads Guilty," A22.

256. *United States v. Parady*, Nos. 05cr1 RWT, 06cv2656 RWT, 2007 WL 2475946 (D. Md. Aug. 27, 2007).

257. Amaad Rivera, et al., *The Silent Depression: State of the Dream 2009* (United for a Fair Economy, 2009), 38, heep://www.community-wealth.org/_pdfs/news/recent-articles/04-09/report-rivera-et-al.pdf.

258. Marianne Bertrand and Sendhil Mullainathan, "Are Emily and Greg More Employable Than Lakisha and Jamal? A Field Experiment on Labor Market

Discrimination," June 20, 2004, http://scholar.harvard.edu/mullainathan/files/emilygreg.pdf; "Case Profile: *Cherry v. Amoco Oil Co.*," Civil Rights Litigation Clearinghouse, http://www.clearinghouse.net/detail.php?id=10099.

259. Wilhelmina A. Leigh and Danielle Huff, "African-Americans and Home Ownership: The Subprime Lending Experience, 1995 to 2007," Joint Center for Political and Economic Studies (Brief 2), Nov. 2007, 1.

260. *Id.*

261. *See* Monique W. Morris, "Discrimination and Mortgage Lending in America: A Summary of the Disparate Impact of Subprime Mortgage Lending on African Americans," NAACP, 2009, 2, http://www.naacp.org/about/resources/reports/Lending_Discrimination_Campaign_Document_Edited_FINAL.pdf.

262. U.S. Dep't of Housing and Urban Dev., Office of Policy Dev. and Research, "Unequal Burden in Baltimore: Income and Racial Disparities in Subprime Lending," 2000, 1, http://www.huduser.org/Publications/pdf/unequal_full.pdf.

263. *Id.* at 1, 3.

264. *Id.*

265. *Id.*

266. *Id.* at 3.

267. *Id.* at 4.

268. *Id.*

269. *See id.*

270. *Id.* at 2.

271. Morris, "Discrimination and Mortgage Lending," 3.

272. Leigh and Huff define redlining as "'the illegal practice of refusing to make residential loans or imposing more onerous terms on any loans made because of the predominant race, national origin, etc., of the residents of the neighborhood in which the property is located.'" Leigh and Huff, "African Americans and Home Ownership," 2 n. 8 (quoting U.S. Department of Housing and Urban Development, Office of the Assistant Secretary for Housing—Federal Housing Commissioner. Mortgagee Letter 94-22 (May 1994): "Fair Lending Practices and Policy Statement on Discrimination," http://www.fha.gov/reference/ml1994).

273. Leigh and Huff, "African Americans and Home Ownership," 1, 2.

274. *Id.* at 8.

275. *Id.*

276. Morris, "Discrimination and Mortgage Lending," 2.

277. Press Release, NAACP, "NAACP Files Landmark Lawsuit Today against Wells Fargo and HSBC," March 13, 2009, http://www.naacp.org/news/press/2009-03-13/index.htm.

278. Morris, "Discrimination and Mortgage Lending," 3.

279. Michael Powell, "Bank Accused of Pushing Mortgage Deals on Blacks," *New York Times*, June 7, 2009.

280. *Id.*

281. *Id.*

282. Morris, "Discrimination and Mortgage Lending," 3-6.

283. *Id.* at 6.

284. *Id.*

285. *Id.*

286. *Id.*

287. *See* Michael Powell and Janet Roberts, "Minorities Affected Most as New York Foreclosures Rise," *New York Times,* May 15, 2009.

288. U.S. Conference of Mayors, "Hunger and Homelessness Survey," Dec. 2008, http://usmayors.org/pressreleases/documents/hungerhomelessnessreport_121208.pdf.

289. *Id.* at 19.

290. *Id.*

291. U.S. Census Bureau, "USA QuickFacts," http://quickfacts.census.gov/qfd/states/00000.html.

292. U.S. Conference of Mayors, "Hunger and Homelessness Survey," Dec. 2007, 15, http://usmayors.org/HHSurvey2007/hhsurvey07.pdf.

293. U.S. Census Bureau.

294. U.S. Conference of Mayors, "Hunger and Homeless Survey," Dec. 2007, 15.

295. Hanson, McArdle, and Wilson, "Invisible Men," 212-13.

296. *Id.* at 210-13.

297. *Id.* at 213-14.

298. *Id.*

299. Marian Wright Edelman, "Losing Our Children in America's Cradle to Prison Pipeline." In *The State of Black America 2007: Portrait of the Black Male,* Stephanie J. Jones, ed. (New York: National Urban League, 2007), 219.

300. Monique W. Morris, "Year One: Toward Safe Communities, Good Schools, and a Fair Chance for All Americans, NAACP, 2009, 5, http://www.naacp.org/about/resources/reports/NAACP.white.paper.pdf (internal citations omitted).

301. Edelman, "Losing Our Children," 220.

302. 42 U.S.C. § 1973.

303. "The right of citizens of the United States to vote shall not be denied or abridged by the United States or by any State on account of race, color, or previous condition of servitude." U.S. Const. amend. XV, §1.

304. President Lyndon Johnson, "Remarks in the Capitol Rotunda at the Signing of the Voting Rights Act," Aug. 6, 1965, http://www.lbjlib.utexas.edu/johnson/archives.hom/speeches.hom/650806.asp.

305. A. Leon Higginbotham Jr., *Shades of Freedom: Racial Politics and Presumptions of the American Legal Process* (New York: Oxford University Press, 1996), 169-82.

306. *Id.*

307. Ferraro told one newspaper, "If Obama was a white man, he would not be in this position. . . . He happens to be very lucky to be who he is. And the country is caught up in the concept." Katharine Q. Seelye, "Ferraro's Obama Remarks Become Talk of Campaign," *New York Times*, March 12, 2008.

308. "Elections 2006: Governor / New York," CNN, http://www.cnn.com/ELECTION/2006/pages/results/states/NY/G/00.

309. "Paterson Sworn in as New York Governor, Spitzer Resignation Final," Associated Press, March 17, 2008.

310. *See* "Illinois Governor Says Burris Should Resign," MSNBC, Feb. 20, 2009, http://www.msnbc.msn.com/id/29302412.

311. "Harold Ford's Rising Star Heads toward the Senate," Democratic Party, August 2006.

312. Jack E. White, "Harold Ford Jr. Reaches for the Stars," *Time*, Dec. 10, 2002, http://www.time.com/time/nation/article/0,8599,397281,00.html.

313. *Id.*

314. *See* www.fordfortennessee.com.

315. *See* advertisement: http://www.youtube.com/watch?v=kkiz1_d1GsA.

316. *Id.*

317. The Corker campaign called the spot "tacky" and asked for it to be removed (Robin Toner, "Ad Seen as Playing to Racial Fears," *New York Times*, Oct. 26, 2006, http://www.nytimes.com/2006/10/26/us/politics/26tennessee.html?pagewanted=1&_r=1).

318. Laura Holson, "The Politician's Wife Claims No Baggage," *New York Times*, Feb. 10, 2010.

319. Erik Schelzig, "Republican Corker Wins Tenn. Senate Seat," Associated Press, Nov. 8, 2006, http://www.washingtonpost.com/wpdyn/content/article/2006/11/08/AR2006110800038.html.

320. *Meet the Press* (NBC television broadcast, Oct. 19, 2008).

321. *Can I Just Tell You?* (NPR radio broadcast, Oct. 20, 2008).

322. *See* David Brooks, "The Obama-Clinton Issue," *New York Times*, Dec. 18, 2007, http://www.nytimes.com/2007/12/18/opinion/18brooks.html?_r=1&hp&oref=slogin.

323. *See* Brent Staples, Editorial, "The Ape in American Bigotry, from Thomas Jefferson to 2009," *New York Times*, Feb. 28, 2009, A22.

324. *See* Brendan Bigelow, "Limbaugh Compares Obama's New Healthcare Logo to Nazi Swastika," *Los Angeles Times*, Aug. 6, 2009.

325. David A. Lieb, "Tea Party Leaders Anxious about Extremists," April 15, 2010, http://today.msnbc.msn.com/id/36555655/ns/today-today_news/t/tea-party-leaders-anxious-about-extremists/#.UBd2-qBIobA.

326. "The Challenge," The Birthers, http://birthers.org/challenge/challenge.html.

327. *See* Carl Hulse, "House Votes to Rebuke Lawmaker Who Shouted 'You Lie' at the President," *International Herald Tribune*, Sept. 17, 2009, 4.

328. 163 U.S. 537 (1896).

329. Foon Rhee, "Advocacy Ad Takes Aim at Obama Hype," *Boston Globe*, July 22, 2008, http://www.boston.com/news/politics/politicalintelligence/2008/07/advocacy_aid_ta.html.

330. Jason Carroll, "Rove, Critics Try to Pin 'Arrogant' Label on Obama," CNN Politics, June 26, 2008, http://www.cnn.com/2008/POLITICS/06/26/obama.rove.

331. John Ridley, "When Rove Calls Obama Arrogant, He Means 'Uppity,'" *Huffington Post*, June 27, 2008, http://www.huffingtonpost.com/john-ridley/when-rove-calls-obama-arr_b_109639.html.

332. *Id.*

333. *Id.*

334. *Id.*

335. Philip Rucker, "Gingrich Promises to Slash Taxes, Calls Obama 'Food Stamp President,'" *Washington Post*, May 13, 2011.

336. Beth Fouhy, "Trump: Obama a 'Terrible Student' Not Good Enough for Harvard," NBC New York, Apr. 26, 2011.

337. Becky Brittain, "U.S. Representative Apologizes for 'Tar Baby' Comment," CNN Politics, Aug. 2, 2011.

338. Lois Romano, "Not His Father's Campaign," *Washington Post*, Sept. 26, 1999.

339. Fouhy, "Trump: Obama a 'Terrible Student.'"

340. Jonathan Weisman, "Obama Rebuffs Challenges on His Israel Stance," *Washington Post*, Feb. 28, 2008.

341. *See* "Some Say Obama's Hawaii Roots Not American Enough," KITV (see kitv.com), Aug. 12, 2008.

342. William Skordelis, "Rush Limbaugh Considers Health Care Reform Income Redistribution," *Examiner*, Feb. 25, 2010.

343. *Id.*

344. Glenn Beck, "What's Driving President Obama's Agenda?" *Fox News*, July 23, 2009.

345. Eric Knowles, Brian Lowery, and Rebecca Schaumberg, "Racial Prejudice Predicts Opposition to Obama and His Health Care Reform Plan," *J. Experimental Soc. Psychol.* 46 (2010): 420-23.

346. "Carter Again Cites Racism as Factor in Obama's Treatment," CNN Politics, Sept. 15, 2009, http://articles.cnn.com/2009-09-15/politics/carter.obama_1_president-jimmy-carter-president-obama-health-care-plan?_s=pm.politics.

347. Thurgood Marshall and J. Clay Smith, *Supreme Justice: Speeches and Writings; Thurgood Marshall* (Philadelphia: University of Pennsylvania, 2003).

348. Michael Falcone, "Does President Obama Love America? Rick Perry: You Need to Ask Him," *ABC News*, Aug. 16, 2011.

349. Fox Butterfield, "First Black Elected to Head Harvard's Law Review," *New York Times*, Feb. 6, 1990.

350. *See* "Text of Obama's Speech: A More Perfect Union," *Wall Street Journal*, March 18, 2008.

351. Roland G. Fryer, "Acting White," Education Next 6, no. 1 (Winter 2006), http://www.economics.harvard.edu/faculty/fryer/files/aw_ednext.pdf.

352. *Id.*

353. *Id.*

354. *See id.*

355. *See id.*

356. "Racial Shocker: Jesse Rips Obama for 'Acting White,'" *New York Post*, Sept. 20, 2007, 13.

357. Transcript of "Bill Cosby's Speech to NAACP," delivered on May 17, 2004, in Washington, DC, available online.

358. Eugene Kane, "Cosby identifies Lack of Black Fathers, Out of Wedlock Births as the Problem," *Journal Sentinel*, Oct. 15, 2007.

359. Transcript of "Bill Cosby's Speech to NAACP."

360. Myron Magnet, "The Great African-American Awakening," *City Journal*, Summer 2008, http://www.city-journal org/2008/18_3_African_american_awakening.html.

361. *Id.*

362. *Id.*

363. *Id.*

364. George E. Curry and Cornel West, *The Affirmative Action Debate* (Reading, MA: Addison-Wesley, 1996).

365. Senator Barack Obama, "Father's Day Speech," June 15, 2008, http://www.cnn.com/2008/POLITICS/06/27/obama.fathers.ay.

366. *Id.*

367. *Id.*

Chapter 6

1. Qtd. in Beverly Daniel Tatum, *"Why Are All The Black Kids Sitting Together in the Cafeteria?": A Psychologist Explains the Development of Racial Identity* (New York: Basic Books, 1997), xix.

2. Debra Dickerson, *The End of Blackness* (New York: Anchor Books, 2004), 128.

3. Transcript of "Bill Cosby's Speech to NAACP," delivered on May 17, 2004, in Washington, DC, available online.

4. Adam Hochberg, "Longtime Sen. Jesse Helms Was Conservative Purist," National Public Radio, *All Things Considered*, July 4, 2008, http://www.npr.org/templates/story/story.php?storyId=92241325.

5. "The most infamous Helms attack ad of the campaign was dubbed 'White Hands.' It showed the hands of a white male crumpling a job rejection letter, and claimed Gantt supported 'racial quotas.' On election day, Helms defeated Gantt by a 53-47% margin." Erik Ose, "How Jesse Helms Ruled North Carolina," *Huffington Post*, June 14, 2010, http://www.huffingtonpost.com/erik-ose/how-jesse-helms-ruled-nor_b_111305.html.

6. Charles R. Lawrence III and Mari J. Matsuda, *We Won't Go Back: Making the Case for Affirmative Action* (New York: Houghton Mifflin, 1997).

7. Indicated in PEW's most recent survey on racial attitudes.

8. *See generally*, Ken Timmerman, *Shakedown: Exposing the Real Jesse Jackson* (Washington, DC: Regnery Publishing, 2003).

9. *Paula Zahn Now*, CNN television broadcast, April 17, 2006, http://transcripts.cnn.com/TRANSCRIPTS/0604/17/pzn.01.html.

10. *See generally* Shelby Steele, *The Content of Our Character: A New Vision of Race in America* (New York: Harper Perennial, 1991); John McWhorter, *Losing the Race: Self-Sabotage in Black America* (New York: Free Press, 2000).

11. Steele, *Content of Our Character*, 26.

12. *Id.* at 24.

13. *Id.* at 25.

14. *Id.* at 26.

15. *Id.* at 30.

16. *Id.* at 33.

17. *Id.*

18. *Id.*

19. *Id.*

20. *Id.*

21. *Id.* at 5.

22. McWhorter, *Losing the Race,* 32-33.

23. *Id.* at 8.

24. *Id.*

25. *Id.* at 9.

26. Richard Kahlenberg, "White Flight in Higher Education," June 3, 2010, http://chronicle.com/blogs/innovations/white-flight-in-higher-education/24498.

27. Kara Miles Turner, "'Getting It Straight': Southern Black School Patrons and the Struggle for Equal Education in the Pre– and Post–Civil Rights Eras," *J. Negro Educ.* 72, no. 2 (2003): 217-29. "Many remedies to the daunting problems surrounding the education of Black youth today have been suggested, including better teacher training, school vouchers, and Afro- centric curricula." *Id.* at 218.

28. *Id.*

29. Steven F. Cohn, "The Effects of Funding Changes upon the Rate of Knowledge Growth in Algebraic and Differential Topology, 1955-75," *Soc. Stud. Sci.* 16, no. 1 (1986): 23-59.

30. Richard D. Kahlenberg, "Turnaround Schools That Work," The Century Foundation, http://tcf.org/events/pdfs/ev264/turnaround.pdf.

31. President Franklin Delano Roosevelt drafted a set of economic and social amendments called the "Second Bill of Rights." The set of rights included a good education. In regard to his position on these rights, Roosevelt stated, "rights spell security." Cass R. Sunstein and Randy E. Barnett, "Constitutive Commitments and Roosevelt's Second Bill of Rights: A Dialogue," 53 *Drake L. Rev.* (2004-2005): 208.

32. *Rodriguez*, 411 U.S. 1, at 36 (1973) (exercise of the right to vote); *Griswold v. Connecticut*, 381 U.S. 479 (1965) (first amendment); *Board of Education v. Pico*, 457 U.S. 853 (1982) (first amendment); *Meyer v. Nebraska*, 262 U.S. 390 (1923) (liberty); *Pierce v. Society of Sisters*, 268 U.S. 510 (1925) (liberty); *Donnell C. v. Illinois State Board of Education*, 829 F. Supp. 1016 (N.D. Ill. 1993) (substantive due process)).

33. *See generally* George Lackoff, *Don't Think of an Elephant! Know Your Values and Frame the Debate* (White River Junction, VT: Chelsea Green, 2004), 15-16 (noting that conservatives have "started magazines and think tanks, and invested billions of dollars. . . . People associated with them have written more books than people on the left. The conservatives support their intellectuals. They create media opportunities. . . . Eighty % of the talking heads on television are from the conservative think tanks.").

34. *See* Harlem Children's Zone 2011 Biennial Report, http://www.hcz.org/books/HCZ%202011%20Biennial/index.html.

35. "Black unemployment rose again from 15.5 to 15.8 % overall and from 39.6 to 42.1 among African-American teens." Associated Press, "Unemployment Rises for Blacks as It Falls for Everyone Else," News One, Jan. 6, 2012, http://newsone.com/nation/associatedpress6/unemployment-falls-but-rises-for-blacks.

36. The most recent study by the Pew Research Center provided figures from 2009 and calculated black wealth to be $5,677 in comparison to white wealth at $113,149. Paul Taylor, et al., "Twenty-to-One: Wealth Gaps Rise to Record Highs between Whites, Blacks, and Hispanics," Pew Research Center, July 26, 2011.

37. The New Deal established many programs for Americans; however, for some reason, minorities, including African Americans, Jewish Americans, foreign-born white Americans (Italian, Polish Americans) were left out as recipients. Jon C. Dubin, "From Junkyards to Gentrification: Explicating a Right to Protective Zoning in Low-Income Communities of Color," *Minn. L. Rev.* 77 (1993): 739.

38. Carlos Garriga, William T. Gavin, and Don Schlagenhauf, "Recent Trends in Homeownership," Federal Reserve Bank of St. Louis Review, September/October 2006, http://research.stlouisfed.org/publications/review/06/09/Garriga.pdf.

39. *Id.*

40. Kerwin Kofi Charles and Erik Hurst, "The Transition to Home Ownership and the Black-White Wealth Gap," *Rev. Econ. & Stat.* 84, no. 2 (2002): 281-97.

41. Greg Graber, "Thanks to Rooney Rule, Doors Opened," ESPN.com, 2007, http://sports.espn.go.com/nfl/playoffs06/news/story?id=2750645.

42. *Id. See also* Douglas C. Proxmire, *Coaching Diversity: The Rooney Rule, Its Application, and Ideas for Expansion,* American Constitution Society for Law and Policy, December 2008, http://www.acslaw.org/sites/default/files/Proxmire_Issue_Brief.pdf.

43. 2006 Hearing to Examine the Impact and Effectiveness of the Voting Rights Act, Before the Subcommittee on the Constitution of the Committee on the Judiciary, House of the Representatives, One Hundred Ninth Congress, First Session, Oct. 18, 2005, http://commdocs.house.gov/committees/judiciary/hju24033.000/hju24033_of.htm.

44. Grant Hayden, *Majority-Minority Voting Districts and Their Role in Politics: Their Advantages, Their Drawbacks, and the Current Law,* Findlaw.com, Oct. 7, 2004, http://writ.news.findlaw.com/commentary/20041007_hayden.html.

45. "Majority-Minority District," Wikipedia, http://en.wikipedia.org/wiki/Majority-minority_district.

46. David Becker, "Reviving Jim Crow," *Washington Post,* Aug. 22, 2005, A17.

47. "Voter ID," Brennan Center for Justice, www.brennancenter.org/content/section/category/voter_id.

48. Tom Curry, "Do Absentee Ballots Facilitate Fraud?" MSNBC.com, Oct. 16, 2008.

49. Becker, "Reviving Jim Crow."

50. *See* Shannon McCaffrey, "Department of Justice Rejects Georgia's Citizenship Checks for Those Registering to Vote," *Gaea Times,* June 2, 2009, http://news.gaeatimes.com/department-of-justice-rejects-georgias-citizenship-checks-for-those-registering-to-vote-69262.

51. *Id.*

52. Deborah Barfield Berry, "Debate Heats Up over Voter ID Laws," *USA Today,* Nov. 10, 2011, http://www.usatoday.com/news/washington/story/2011-11-10/voter-identification-laws/51159106/1.

53. The Sentencing Project, "Felony Disenfranchisement Law in the United States," 2012, http://www.sentencingproject.org/doc/publications/fd_bs_fdlawsinus_Jun2012.pdf.

54. "Criminal Disenfranchisement Laws across The United States," Brennan Center for Justice, 2011, 1, http://www.brennancenter.org/page/-/download_file_48642.pdf.

55. The Sentencing Project, "Felony Disenfranchisement Law," 3.

56. *See id.*

57. *Id.* at 1.

58. *See id.*

59. *Id.*

60. *Id.*

61. "Criminal Disenfranchisement Laws," 3.

62. *See* The Sentencing Project, "Felony Disenfranchisement Law," 3; "Criminal Disenfranchisement Laws," 3.

63. Michelle Alexander, *The New Jim Crow* (New York: New Press, 2010), 159.

64. *Id.* at 8.

65. *Id.*

66. *Id.* at 9. If a person has an ability to walk into a voting booth, there would be no question as to his or her voting eligibility.

67. Jeff Manza and Christopher Uggen, *Locked Out: Felon Disenfranchisement and American Democracy* (New York: Oxford University Press, 2006), 95.

68. Bailey Figler, Note, "A Vote for Democracy: Confronting the Racial Aspects of Felon Disenfranchisement," *N.Y.U. Ann. Surv. Am. L.* 62 (2006): 748.

69. *Id.*

70. A "voting death penalty" often refers to former felons being restricted from voting for life, as they are in Iowa, Florida, Kentucky, and Virginia. The Sentencing Project, "Felony Disenfranchisement Law," 3.

71. *See, e.g.,* "Developments in the Law: The Law of Prisons: VI. One Person, No Vote: The Laws of Felon Disenfranchisements," *Harv. L. Rev.* 115 (2002): 1942.

72. The Sentencing Project, "Felony Disenfranchisement Law," 2.

73. *Id.*

74. *Id.*

75. *Id.*

76. Decennial Census, U.S. Census Bureau, http://www.census.gov/history/www/programs/demographic/decennial_census.html.

77. "Redistricting and Reapportionment," Redistricting in Colorado, http://www.colorado.gov/cs/Satellite/CGA-ReDistrict/CBON/1251581558103.

78. John Gibeaut, "As Other States Watch, Florida's Redistricting Fracas May Set the Lines for the Future," *ABA Journal*, June 1, 2011, http://www.abajournal.com/magazine/article/adjustable_seating.

79. *Id.*

80. *Id.*

81. *Id.*

82. *See* F. Michael Higginbotham, *Race Law: Cases, Commentary, Questions*, 3rd ed. (Durham, NC: Carolina Academic Press, 2010), 610.

83. *Id.*

84. *Id.*

85. *Id.*

86. *Id.*

87. *Id.*

88. Eric McGhee, "Redistricting and Legislative Partisanship," Public Policy Institute of California, web.ppic.org/content/pubs/report/R_908EMR.pdf.

89. Ilene K. Grossman, "Drawing the Lines: Midwestern Lawmakers Turn

Their Attention to Redistricting," Firstline Midwest, February/March 2010, http://www.csgmidwest.org/policyresearch/febmarch10flmwredistricting.aspx.

90. *Id.*

91. *Id.*

92. *Id.*

93. *Id.*

94. *Id.*

95. *Id.*

96. *Id.*

97. "Blacks currently make up about 13% of the US population, but have historically been underrepresented in Congress. In the 111th Congress, 42 members (9.5%) of the House were black." "Members of the 111th United States Congress," Wikipedia, http://en.wikipedia.org/wiki/Members_of_the_111th_United_States _Congress.

98. *Id. See also* Office of History and Preservation, Office of the Clerk, *Black Americans in Congress, 1870–2007* (Washington, DC: U.S. Government Printing Office, 2008), http://baic.house.gov/historical-essays/essay.html?intSectionID=47.

99. *Id.*

100. Michael D. Minta, *Representing Black and Latino Interests in the U.S. Senate*, Washington University in St. Louis, 2009, http://missouri.academia.edu/ MichaelMinta/Papers/104759/Representing_Black_and_Latino_Interests_ in_the_U.S._Senate.

101. Blacks represented 38% of Mississippi's population in 2009. "Black (African-American) History Month: February 2011," Facts for Features, U.S. Census Bureau, Dec.2, 2010, http://www.census.gov/newsroom/releases/archives/facts_ for_features_special_editions/cb11ff_01.html.

102. Adam H. Kurland, "Partisan Rhetoric, Constitutional Reality, and Political Responsibility: The Troubling Constitutional Consequences of Achieving D.C. Statehood by Simple Legislation," *Geo. Wash. L. Rev.* 60 (1992): 475.

103. Article Four, Section 3 of the U.S. Constitution.Some aspects of the D.C. statehood agenda were achieved with the District of Columbia Home Rule Act, passed in 1973. Still more were encompassed in the District of Columbia Voting Rights Amendment, which passed Congress in 1978 but failed to be ratified by a sufficient number of states to become an amendment to the U.S. Constitution. The deadline for ratification of the D.C. Voting Rights Amendment passed on August 22, 1985. Since that time, legislation to enact this proposed state constitution has routinely been introduced in Congress, but has never been passed. The last serious debate on the issue in Congress took place in November 1993, when D.C. statehood was defeated in the House of Representatives by a vote of 277 to 153.

104. U.S. Electoral College Frequently Asked Questions (Office of the Federal Register), http://www.archives.gov/federal-register/electoral-college/faq.html.

105. Adam H. Kurland, "Partisan Rhetoric, Constitutional Reality, and Political Responsibility," 475.

106. "Twenty-Third Amendment (1961)," Annenberg Classroom, Leonore Annenberg Institute for Civics, http://www.annenbergclassroom.org/Files/Documents/Books/Our%20Constitution/Twentythird%20Amendment_Our%20Constitution.pdf.

107. *Id.*

108. "The Local Struggle for Democracy: Arguments for and against Full Congressional Voting Representation for the District of Columbia," DCVote, http://www.dcvote.org/trellis/struggle/argumentsforandagainst.cfm.

109. Noble V, "Life Saving Triage: Education and Crime in Poor Black Communities," Hub Pages, http://noblev.hubpages.com/hub/Life-Saving-Triage-Education-Crime-and-Poor-Black-communities.

110. Todd A. Smith, "Black Men, You're Headed for Self-Destruction," *Regal Magazine,* Jan. 8, 2009, http://www.regalmag.com/report-shows-rise-blackon-black-crime-a-315.html.

111. Cathy T. Maston, "Criminal Victimization in the United States, 2007: Statistical Tables," U.S Department of Justice, Bureau of Justice Statistics, March 2, 2010, http://bjs.ojp.usdoj.gov/index.cfm?ty=pbdetail&iid=1743.

112. A. Leon Higginbotham Jr., *In the Matter of Color: Race and the American Legal Process* (New York: Oxford University Press, 1978), 252-59.

113. The punishment for a slave who committed a crime against another slave was unusually low. This was an attempt to mitigate losses by the owner of the slaves. If a master had already lost the services of one of his slaves at the hands of another slave, it hardly served the master's interest to afford justice to the victim by incarcerating or punishing the offender for any length of time (or otherwise incapacitating the offender). Orlando Patterson, *Slavery and Social Death: A Comparative Study* (Cambridge, MA: Harvard University Press, 1982), 196.

114. *See generally* Dorothy E. Roberts, "Crime, Race, and Reproduction," *Tul. L. Rev. 67* (June 1993): 1945.

115. For example, here is an excerpt from the *Slave Codes of the State of Georgia, 1848:*

> *Punishment for teaching slaves or free persons of color to read.*—If any slave, Negro, or free person of color, or any white person, shall teach any other slave, Negro, or free person of color, to read or write either written or printed characters, the said free person of color or slave shall be punished by fine and whipping, or fine or whipping, at the discretion of the court.

Slave Codes of the State of Georgia, 184. Sec. II. 11, http://academic.udayton.edu/race/02rights/slavelaw.htm#11.

116. Peter Irons, *Jim Crow's Children: The Broken Promise of the Brown Decision* (New York: Penguin, 2002), 13.

117. Gregory Parks and Matthew Hughey, eds., *The Obamas and a (Post) Racial America?* (New York: Oxford University Press, 2011); Bill Cosby and Alvin Poussaint, *Come On People: On the Path from Victims to Victors* (Nashville, TN: Thomas Nelson, 2007).

118. *Id.*

119. Shaun Harper, *Black Male Student Success in Higher Education: A Report from the National Black Male College Achievement Study* (Philadelphia: University of Pennsylvania , Center for the Study of Race and Equity in Education, 2012).

Chapter 7

1. Justice Brennan dissenting in *McCleskey v. Kemp,* 481 U.S. 279, 344 (1987).

2. F. Michael Higginbotham, Editorial, "Hard-Won Victory Must Be Secured," *Baltimore Sun,* Aug. 7, 2005, C5.

3. *See generally,* Ellis Cose, *The End of Anger: A New Generation's Take on Race and Rage* (New York: Ecco Press, 2011).

4. *Id.*

5. *Id.*

6. Mike Brunker, "Wealth in America: Whites-Minorities Gap Is Now a Chasm," MSNBC, July 26, 2011, http://www.msnbc.msn.com/id/43887485/ns/business_ eye_on_the_economy/t/wealth-gap-widens-betweem-whites-minorities/from/ toolbar.

7. "Increase in cross-race integration and friendships resulting from desegregation will improve confidence in interracial interaction, reduce stereotypes and in the long run, contribute to a more integrated and equal society." Lincoln Quillian and Mary E. Campbell, "Beyond Black and White: The Present and Future of Multiracial Friendship Segregation," *Am. Soc. Rev.* 68, no. 4 (Aug. 2003): 540-66.

8. Erika Frankenberg, *Voluntary Integration after Parents Involved: What Does Research Tell Us about Available Options?* (Inst. for Race & Just., Working Paper, 2007), 5 [hereinafter Race & Justice] (explaining that interacting with students from diverse backgrounds increases critical thinking skills).

9. *Id.* at 4.

10. The term "majority minority" is used to explain that whites will no longer be the majority in terms of population as compared with all other minority groups combined. Conner Dougherty, "U.S. Nears Racial Milestone," *Wall Street Journal,* June 11, 2010, http://online.wsj.com/article/SB10001424052748704312104575298512006681060.html.

11. Race & Justice at 5.

12. Sabrina Zirkel, "What Will You Think of Me?" Racial Integration, Peer Relationships and Achievement among White Students and Students of Color," *J. Soc. Issues* 60 (2004): 59.

13. *See* Race & Justice at 5 (citing research that finds higher levels of civic

engagement from students attending diverse schools as opposed to segregated schools).

14. Janet Ward Schofield and Leslie R. M. Hausmann, "The Conundrum of School Desegregation: Positive Student Outcomes and Waning Support," U. Pitt. L. Rev. 66 (2004): 89.

15. Id.

16. "Race to the Top Program Executive Summary," U.S. Department of Education, November 2009, http://www2.ed.gov/programs/racetothetop/executive-summary.pdf.

17. National Coalition on School Diversity, "Reaffirming the Role of School Integration in K-12 Education" (2009), 2, http://prrac.org/pdf/DiversityIssueBrief-Stmt.pdf [hereinafter School Diversity].

18. See generally Adai Tefera, Genevieve Siegel-Hawley, and Erica Frankenberg, "School Integration Efforts Three Years after Parents Involved," June 28, 2010, http://civilrightsproject.ucla.edu/legal-developments/court-decisions/school-integration-efforts-three-years-after-parents-involved/teferea-school-integration-three-years-after.pdf.

19. Id.

20. Mary Ann Zehr, "Backers of Magnet Schools Question Charter Push," Education Week, http://www.edweek.org/ew/articles/2010/02/24/22magnets_ep.h29.html.

21. School Diversity at 2.

22. Id.

23. Xavier de Souza Briggs, "More Pluribus, Less Unum? The Changing Geography of Race and Opportunity." In Neighborhood Renewal and Housing Markets: Community Engagement in the U.S. and U.K., Harris Beider, ed. (Oxford, U.K.: Blackwell, 2008), http://www.eslarp.uiuc.edu/courses/FAA391_Spring11/Briggs.pdf.

24. "Major Provisions of the Fair Housing Amendments Act of 1988," Mountain State Centers for Independent Living, http://www.mtstcil.org/skills/housing-2.html.

25. Id.

26. Id.

27. Id. at 5.

28. Id.

29. Id.

30. John Relman, Fred Rivera, Meera Trehan, and Shilpa Satoskar, Chapter 7: "Designing Federal Legislation That Works: Legal Remedies for Predatory Lending." In Why the Poor Pay More: How to Stop Predatory Lending, Gregory Squires, ed. (Westport, CT: Praeger Publishers, 2004), 168.

31. Id.

32. "Fair Housing in a Changing Nation," National Fair Housing Alliance 2012

Fair Housing Trends Report, April 30, 2012, p. 33, http://www.national fairhousing. org/portals/33/Fair%20Housing%20Trends%20Report%202012%20with%20 date.pdf.

33. Dwight M. Jaffee and John M. Quigley, "Housing Subsidies and Homeowners: What Role for Government-Sponsored Enterprises?" *Brookings-Wharton Papers on Urban Affairs* no. 8 (2007): 103-30, http://urbanpolicy.berkeley.edu/pdf/ Jaffee-Quigley%20Brookings%20Final%20020107.pdf .

34. Todd Sinai and Joel Waldfogel, "Do Low-Income Housing Subsidies Increase Housing Consumption?" December 4, 2001, http://realestate.wharton. upenn.edu/research/papers/full/394.pdf.

35. Jaffe and Quigley, "Housing Subsidies."

36. Elizabeth Julian and Michael M. Daniel, "HUD-Assisted Low-Income Housing: Is It Working and for Whom?" *Poverty & Race*, July/August 2009.

37. New Jersey and Baltimore, Maryland, have been involved in the Live Where You Work program. "Live Where You Work (LWYW)," State of New Jersey Housing Mortgage Finance Agency, http://www.state.nj.us/dca/hmfa/consu/buyers/ close/live.html; "Baltimore City Live Near Your Work Program," Baltimore Housing, http://www.baltimorehousing.org/homeownership_livenear. Washington, DC, started a pilot program in August 2011. "OP Releases Request for Applications for a Live Near Your Work Pilot Program," District of Columbia Office of Planning, April 29, 2011, http://planning.dc.gov/DC/Planning/About+Planning/ News+Room/Press+Releases/OP+Releases+Request+for+Applications+for+a+ Live+Near+Your+Work+Pilot+Program.

38. *Civil Rights Cases*, 109 U.S. 3 (1883).

39. 539 U.S. 306 (2003).

40. U.S. Equal Employment Opportunity Commission, "Charge Statistics FY 1997 through FY 2010," http://eeoc.gov/eeoc/statistics/enforcement/charges. cfm.

41. *Id.*

42. Nicola Persico, "Racial Profiling, Fairness, and Effectiveness of Policing," *Am. Econ. Rev.* 92, no. 5 (2002): 1472-97.

43. Shea Connelly, "Banks Talks to Law Students about Current Issues in Racial Profiling," *UVA Lawyer*, Fall 2007, http://www.law.virginia.edu/html/alumni/ uvalawyer/f07/racialprofiling.htm.

44. John Knowles, Nicola Persico, and Petra Todd, "Racial Bias in Motor Vehicle Searches: Theory and Evidence," *J. Pol. Econ.* 109, no. 1 (2001): 203-29.

45. Reginald T. Shuford, "Civil Rights in the Next Millenium: Any Way You Slice It; Why Racial Profiling Is Wrong," *St. Louis U. Pub. L. Rev.* 18 (1999): 374.

46. David A. Harris, "The Stories, the Statistics, and the Law: Why 'Driving While Black' Matters," *Minn. L. Rev.* 84 (Dec. 1999): 273-74.

47. *Id.*

48. *Id.*

49. *Frank Ricci et al. v. John Destefano et al.*,129 S.Ct. 2658 (2009).

50. *See* Beverly Moran and Stephanie Wildman, "Race and Wealth Disparity: The Role of Law and the Legal System," *Fordham Urb. L.J.* 34, no. 4 (May 2007): 1219-38.

51. The laws created classes of people on the basis of national origin.

The creation of two classes of people with significantly different statuses based on their personal or ancestral origin— "race"—broke up burgeoning class solidarity that threatened to unite Euro- and African-American bond laborers against the ownership class in the late 1600s and early 1700s by attaching "Whites" of that class to the economic elite (all of whom were Euro-American) on the basis of common ancestry and carefully selected shared privileges. (Palma J. Strand, "Inheriting Inequality: Wealth, Race, and the Laws of Succession," *Or. L. Rev.* 89 (2010): 474).

52. Press Release, American Civil Liberties Union, "President Obama Signs Bill Reducing Cocaine Sentencing Disparity," Aug. 3, 2010 (on file with ACLU), http://www.aclu.org/drug-law-reform/president-obama-signs-bill-reducing-cocaine-sentencing-disparity.

53. *Id.*

54. "Under the measure, approved by a voice vote, the ratio would be reduced to 18-1." Jim Abrahms, "Durbin Cocaine Bill Passes Senate: Would Reduce Disparity in Crack and Powder Sentences," *Huffington Post,* March 17, 2010, http://www.huffingtonpost.com/2010/04/05/durbin-cocaine-bill-passe_n_525625.html. *See also* "Judiciary Committee Reports Durbin's Fair Sentencing Act," March 11, 2010, Dick Durbin Press Release, http://durbin.senate.gov/public/index.cfm/pressreleases?ID=c70fe72b-3b06-48af-81ab-c7dcb9fbb388.

55. Theo Emory, "Will Crack-Cocaine Sentencing Reform Help Current Cons?" *Time,* Aug. 7, 2009, http://www.time.com/time/nation/article/0,8599,1915131,00.html.

56. Rosemary C. Hunter and Elaine W. Shoben, "Disparate Impact Discrimination: American Oddity or Internationally Accepted Concept?" *Berkeley. J. Emp. & Lab. L.* 19 (1998): 109-112.

57. *Id.*

58. *Griggs v. Duke Power Co.,* 401 U.S. 424, 430 (1971).

59. *Id.* at 432.

60. Hunter and Shoben, "Disparate Impact Discrimination," 152.

61. *Id.* at 114.

62. *See generally* 426 U.S. 229 (1976).

63. Charles R. Lawrence III, "The Id, the Ego, and Equal Protection: Reckoning with Unconscious Racism," *Stan. L. Rev.* 39 (1987): 369.

64. *Id.*

65. Hunter and Shoben, "Disparate Impact Discrimination," 125.

66. Daniel J. Losen, "Silent Segregation in our Nation's Schools," *Harv. C.L.L. Rev.* 30 (1997): 528.

67. 426 U.S. 229 (1976).

68. Sheryll D. Cashin, "Respondent: The Civil Rights Act of 1964 and Coalition Politics," *St. Louis L.J.* 49 (2005): 1029.

69. 539 U.S. 306 (2003).

70. *Id.*

71. *See* Sami M. Abassi and Kenneth W. Hollman, "Managing Cultural Diversity: The Challenge of the '90s Management," *Records Mgt. Q.* 25 (1991): 24.

72. 539 U.S. 306 (2003).

73. William G. Bowen, "Grutter: Where Do We Go from Here? The Impact of the Supreme Court Decisions in the University of Michigan Affirmative Action Cases," *J. Blacks Higher Educ.*, no. 44 (2004): 76-81.

74. *See Wygant*, 476 U.S. 267 (Marshall, J. dissenting).

75. *See Ford Motor Co. v. Huffman*, 345 U.S. 330, 345 (1953).

76. *See Aeronautical Industrial District Lodge 727 v. Campbell*, 337 U.S. 521, 528-29 (1949).

77. Derrick Bell, *Silent Covenants: Brown v. Board of Education and the Unfulfilled Hopes for Racial Reform* (New York: Oxford University Press, 2004), 134, 137.

78. *See* John Larow, "Who's the Real Affirmative Action Profiteer?" *Washington Monthly*, June 1991, 10. For more than forty years, one-fifth of Harvard's students received admissions preferences because their parents attended the school.

79. Cal. Const. art. I, § 31. This provision was added by initiative measure, Proposition 209. 1996 Cal. Legis. Serv. Prop. 209.

80. Ethan Bronner, "Study of Doctors Sees Little Effect of Affirmative Action on Careers," *New York Times*, Oct. 8, 1997, A1.

81. *Id.*

82. *Id.*

83. 539 U.S. 306 (2003).

84. *Id.*

85. *Id.*

86. Cynthia Gordy, "An Apology Comes Late, but with Feeling," *The Root*, May 13, 2011, http://npr.org/2011/05/13/136270171/the-root-an-apology-comes-late-but-with-feeling.

87. Jo Becker, "Bias Victims Get Empathy, No Funds," *Washington Post*, Feb. 26, 2004, B01.

88. *Id.*

89. *Id.*

90. *Id.*

91. *Id.*

92. *Id.*

93. Gordy, "An Apology Comes Late."

94. *Id.*

95. Alfred L. Brophy, "Reparations Talk: Reparations for Slavery and the Tort Law Analogy," *B.C. Third World L. J.* 24 (2004): 81.

96. *Id.*

97. "Slave Auctions in Richmond, Virginia," *Illustrated London News*, Feb. 16, 1861, 138-40, http://beck.library.emory.edu/iln/browse.php?id=iln38.1075.038.

98. "Lawsuit Chases Companies Tied to Slavery," *Fox News*, Mar. 27, 2002, http://www.foxnews.com/story/0,2933,48781,00.html.

99. Keith W. Stokes, "A Short History of African Slavery in Rhode Island," NAACP Providence Branch, http://www.naacpprov.org/articleDetails.cfm?articleid=46.

100. H.R. Res. 194, 115th Cong. 2008.

101. "House Apologizes for Slavery, 'Jim Crow' Injustices" CNN Money, July 29, 2008, http://articles.cnn.com/2008-07-29/politics/house.slavery_1_african-american-slavery-white-lawmaker?_s=PM:POLITICS.

Table of Cases

Index

abolition, 58, 60, 69, 120; abolitionist organizations, 65; abolitionists, 53, 55, 69; American Missionary Society, 65

affirmative action, 14, 20, 34, 170, 173, 181-182, 203, 216-218, 221

Ali, Muhammad: Nation of Islam Church, 3; Vietnam War, 3, 224n13

alternative dispute resolution, 209-210

ancestry, mixed race, 36, 41, 49, 88, 297n51; slave, 51

antidiscrimination laws, 12, 17-18, 30, 34, 66-67, 126, 138, 143-144, 188-189, 207-210, 215; authority of Congress to enact legislation under the Commerce Clause, 209; Civil Rights Act, 11, 67, 127, 167, 209, 214-215; Enforcement Act, 66, 68, 70; Fifteenth Amendment, 36, 64, 66-67, 74, 79, 170; Fourteenth Amendment, 36, 64, 66, 71, 73-74, 78-79, 88, 149, 207, 211, 214, 231n12; Ku Klux Klan Act, 67-68; Reconstruction Act, 66, 178; Reconstruction Amendments, 30, 41, 64, 71, 73, 78, 83; Thirteenth Amendment, 36, 63-64, 66, 215. *See also* civil rights movement

Beverly Hills, California, 1, 4-6, 10, 23, 224n15; Beverly Hills High School, 8, 12, 224-225n19; Beverly Hills Hotel, 108

Black Codes, 63-64, 83, 159, 174

black excellence, 30, 85, 105, 107-108, 112, 114

black infantry: during the Civil War, 60; during World War II, 98

black inferiority, 17-18, 22, 28-30, 33, 35, 39-41, 50, 62, 66, 72, 75-76, 79, 81-83, 87, 97, 108, 115, 138-139, 143-144, 156, 158-159, 172-173, 175, 177-178, 181, 183, 196, 199, 202-203, 205, 211, 226n34; Judge St. George Tucker's opinion in *Hudgins v. Wright*, 51-53

black separation, 83, 85, 87-88, 94, 97, 100, 104, 108-109, 112, 114-115, 119, 121-123, 131, 134-138, 141, 143, 146-150, 158, 165, 177, 202-203, 205-207, 211, 215-216

black victimization, 63, 67, 83, 114-116, 138, 141, 150, 158, 160-161, 176-178, 183-185, 196, 202-203, 207, 211, 215

Blalock, Dr. Alfred, heart surgery at Johns Hopkins, 108-109, 115. *See also* Thomas, Vivien

Bradley, Justice Joseph, 78-79

Brennan, Justice William, 201, 211

Breyer, Justice Stephen, 150

Brown University, 9-11

Bullard, Eugene, 98-99; volunteered for the Eagle Squadron in the French Air Force, 98

Cambridge University, 1, 12, 23; Cambridge University Basketball Club, 12

Cameron, James, 112-114

citizenship, 45, 55, 58, 64, 67, 85, 172

About the Author

F. MICHAEL HIGGINBOTHAM is the Wilson H. Elkins Professor of Law at University of Baltimore School of Law and the former interim dean. A renowned law professor, author, and international political consultant, he is an expert in the areas of civil rights, human rights, and constitutional law. Higginbotham has appeared in media worldwide. His Race Law books are used in law schools across the United States and abroad. Higginbotham has published in leading law reviews, newspapers, and magazines.